Glencoe
Keyboarding
with Computer Applications

Lessons 1–150

Jack E. Johnson, Ph.D.
Director of Business Education
Department of Management
    and Business Systems
State University of West Georgia
Carrollton, Georgia

Judith Chiri-Mulkey
Adjunct Teacher
Department of Computer
    Information Systems
Pikes Peak Community College
Colorado Springs, Colorado

Delores Sykes Cotton
Supervisor, Business Education
Detroit Public Schools
Detroit, Michigan

Carole G. Stanley, M.Ed.
Keyboarding and Computer
    Literacy Teacher, Retired
Rains Junior High School
Emory, Texas

 **Glencoe**

New York, New York
Columbus, Ohio
Chicago, Illinois
Peoria, Illinois
Woodland Hills, California

Glencoe Keyboarding with Computer Applications, Lessons 1-150

Printed in the United States of America.

Send all inquiries to:
Glencoe/McGraw-Hill
21600 Oxnard Street, Suite 500
Woodland Hills, CA 91367

ISBN 0-07-860256-4

3 4 5 6 7 8 9 027 07 06 05 04

REVIEWERS

Judy Senden
West High School
Anchorage, AK

Betty Gross Malone
Jackson-Olin High School
Birmingham, AL

Debra Scott
Arkansas High School
Texarkana, AR

Donna Green
Mingus Union High School
Cottonwood, AZ

Sue Julian
El Molino High School
Forestville, CA

Dr. Rita Schnittgrund
Denver West High School
Denver, CO

Janyce Wininger
Stafford High School
Stafford Spring, CT

Marjorie Stewart
Caesar Rodney High School
Camden Wyoming, DE

Patricia McCollough
Fort Walton Beach High School
Fort Walton Beach, FL

Barbara Williams-Mims
Columbus High School
Columbus, GA

Patricia Pierce
Linn-Marr High School
Marion, IA

Dan Petersen
State Division of Vocational
Education
Business and Office Technology
Education
Boise, ID

Gerrie L. Trossman
Good Counsel High School
Chicago, IL

Barbara Coleman
Salina High School South
Salina, KS

N. Jean Andrada
Pleasure Ridge High School
Louisville, KY

Terry Smith
Alcee Fortier High School
New Orleans, LA

Betsy Nilsen
Cape Elizabeth High School
Cape Elizabeth, ME

Kathy Jensen
Mankato West High School
Mankato, MN

Judy Cox
J. H. Rose High School
Greenville, NC

Nancy Stevens
Manteo High School
Manteo, NC

Mike Opdahl
Larimore High School
Larimore, ND

Betty Sup
Creighton Preparatory School
Omaha, NE

Maria Alvarez
Farmington High School
Farmington, NH

Sandra M. Richardson
Life Center Academy
Burlington, NJ

Bernadine Elmore
New Mexico Military Institution
Roswell, NM

Leesa Lyman
Roy Martin School
Las Vegas, NV

Lorraine Harrison
HS for Arts and Business
Corona, NY

Michael Prandy
John Marshall High School
Oklahoma City, OK

Sherri Sollars
Westview High School
Portland, OR

Susan Howe
Chariho Regional High School
Wood River Junction, RI

Patricia B. Hook
Airport High School
West Columbia, SC

Jane Bradfield
O'Gorman High School
Sioux Falls, SD

Edna Earle Bond
Central High School
Memphis, TN

Susan Shirey
Grand Prairie High School
Grand Prairie, TX

Patricia Kay Fordham
Central High School
Salt Lake City, UT

Patricia Smith
Kennewick High School
Kennewick, WA

Gail Springsteen
Waupaca High School
Waupaca, WI

Nancy Byrd
Morgantown High School
Morgantown, WV

TABLE OF CONTENTS

About Your Book   x
Reference Section   R1

UNIT 1 KEYBOARDING

Lesson		Page
1	New Keys: A S D F J K L ; Space Bar Enter	2
2	New Keys: H E O	7
3	New Keys: M R I	10
4	Review	13
5	New Keys: T N C	16
6	New Keys: V Right Shift Period (.)	19
7	New Keys: W Comma (,) G	23
8	Review	27
9	New Keys: B U Left Shift	30
10	New Keys: Q /	33
11	New Keys: ' "	36
12	Review	39
13	New Keys: P X	41
14	New Keys: Y Tab	44
15	New Keys: Z Colon (:)	47
16	Review	50
17	New Keys: ? Caps Lock	53
18	New Keys: - _	56
19	Skillbuilding	59
20	Skillbuilding	62

UNIT 2 KEYBOARDING

Lesson		Page
21	New Keys: 4 $ 7 &	68
22	New Keys: 3 # 8 *	72
23	New Keys: 2 @ 9 (	76
24	Review	79
25	New Keys: 1 ! 0)	82
26	New Keys: 5 % 6 ^	85
27	Special Symbols	89
28	Numeric Keypad: 4 5 6 Enter	94
29	Numeric Keypad: 7 8 9	98
30	Review	102
31	Numeric Keypad: 1 2 3	106
32	Numeric Keypad: 0 .	110
33	Review	114
34	Skillbuilding	117
35	Skillbuilding	120
36	Orientation to Word Processing	123
37	Orientation to Word Processing	125
38	Orientation to Word Processing	128
39	Orientation to Word Processing	131
40	Orientation to Word Processing	134

UNIT 3 WORD PROCESSING

Lesson		Page	Reports	Correspondence	Tables
41	One-Page Academic Reports	138	1–2		
42	One-Page Business Reports	143	3–4		
43	Lists, Outlines, and Agendas	147	5–6		
44	Reports With Headings	151	7–8		
45	Minutes of Meetings	154	9–10		
46	Multipage Reports	158	11		
47	Review	162	12–14		
48	Personal-Business Letters	167		Letters 1–2	
49	Reinforcement	172		Letters 3–4	

TABLE OF CONTENTS *(continued)*

Lesson		Page	Reports	Correspondence	Tables
50	Envelopes	175		Env. 1–4; Letter 5	
51	Business Letters	180		Letters 6–7; Env. 5	
52	Business Letters	184		Letters 8–11; Env. 6–7	
53	Review	187		Letters 12–13	
54	Modified-Block Letters	190		Letters 14–15	
55	Letters With Indented Paragraphs	193		Letters 16–17	
56	Letters With Enclosures and Attachments	197		Letters 18–19	
57	Letter Reinforcement	200		Letters 20–22	
58	Resumes	204	15–16		
59	Application Letters	208		Letters 23–24	
60	Review	213		Letters 25–26	

UNIT 4 WORD PROCESSING

Lesson		Page	Reports	Correspondence	Tables
61	Letters With Copy and Delivery Notations	218		Letters 27–29	
62	Letters With Postscripts	222		Letters 30–32	
63	Reinforcement: Letters	226		Letters 33–35	
64	Letter Review	230		Letters 36–38	
65	Tables: Creating	234			1–2
66	Tables: Column Size and Position	237			3–5
67	Tables: Column Headings	240			6–8
68	Tables: Number Columns	244			9–11
69	Tables: Reinforcement	247			12–14
70	Tables: Titles, Subtitles, and Braced Column Headings	250			15–16
71	Tables: Review	253			17–19
72	Reports With Parenthetical References and Quotes	257	17		
73	Reports With Works Cited Page	261	18		
74	Reports Review	265	19–20		
75	Footnotes and Endnotes in Reports	268	21		
76	Reports: Multipage, Left Bound	273	22		
77	Reports: Multipage, Left Bound	276	23		
78	Reports: Title Page, Contents, Bibliography	281	24–26		
79	Review	284	27–30		
80	Simulation	288	31	Letter 39	20–21

TABLE OF CONTENTS *(continued)*

UNIT 5 WORD PROCESSING

Lesson	Page	Reports	Correspondence	Tables	Spreadsheets	Databases
81 Skillbuilding	294					
82 Skillbuilding	297					
83 Two-Page Letters	299		Letter 40			
84 Letters With Attention and Subject Lines	303		Letters 41–43			
85 Merge: Form Letters	308		Letters 44–45			
86 Merge: Form Letters	311		Letters 46–49			
87 Review	314		Letters 50–53			
88 Letters With Numbered Lists	318		Letters 54–55			
89 Memo Templates	322		Memos 1–2			
90 Review	325		Letters 56–57; Memos 3–4			
91 Tables: Reversing Lines	329			22–24		
92 Tables: Borders/Fill	333			25–27		
93 Tables: Reinforcement	336			28–30		
94 Tables: Page Orientation	340			31–32		
95 Tables: Add/Delete Columns and Rows	344			33–35		
96 Totals in Table	347			36–38		
97 Review	350			39–41		
98 Letters With International Addresses	353		Letters 58–60			
99 Memo With Copy Notations and Attachments	358		Memos 5–7			
100 Formatting Review	362		Letters 61–62; Memo 8	42		

UNIT 6 DESKTOP PUBLISHING

Lesson	Page	Reports	Correspondence	Tables	Spreadsheets	Databases
101 Desktop Publishing: Special Characters	368	32–34				
102 Font Colors and Features	372	35				
103 Borders and Fill	376	36–39				
104 Graphic Lines/Rules	380	40–42				
105 Drawing	383	43–44				
106 Boxes: Text and Graphics Boxes	386	45–46				
107 Boxes: Fill, Borders	388	47–49				
108 Boxes: Wrapping Text	392	50–51				

TABLE OF CONTENTS *(continued)*

Lesson	Page	Reports	Correspondence	Tables	Spreadsheets	Databases
109 Personal Notepads	395	52–53				
110 Personal Stationery	399	54–55				
111 Text/Word Art	402	56–57				
112 Desktop Publishing Review	406	58				
113 Desktop Publishing Designs: Flyers	408	59–60				
114 Designing a Certificate	411	61				
115 Designing an Invitation	414	62–63				
116 Columns	417	64–65				
117 Desktop Publishing: Newsletters	420	66–67				
118 Newsletters	423	68				
119 Newsletters	427	69				
120 Desktop Publishing Review	431	70–71				

UNIT 7 SPREADSHEETS

Lesson	Page	Reports	Correspondence	Tables	Spreadsheets	Databases
121 Spreadsheets: Orientation	436					
122 Spreadsheets: Navigating	439				Act. 1, SS1 Act. 2, SS1 Act. 3, SS1	
123 Spreadsheets: Entering Data	442				Act. 4, SS1	
124 Spreadsheets: Create, Align Columns	445				Act. 5, SS2 Act. 6, SS3 Act. 7, SS4	
125 Spreadsheets: Copying Data, Changing Column Widths	448				Act. 8, SS5 Act. 9, SS6	
126 Spreadsheets: Moving Data, Changing Row Height	453				Act. 10, SS7 Act. 11, SS8 Act. 12, SS9	
127 Spreadsheets: Formatting Values	457				Act. 13, SS10 Act. 14, SS11 Act. 15, SS12	
128 Spreadsheets: Printing	461				Act. 16, SS5 Act. 17, SS3 Act. 18, SS6 Act. 19, SS7	

TABLE OF CONTENTS *(continued)*

Lesson	Page	Reports	Correspondence	Tables	Spreadsheets	Databases
129 Spreadsheets: Entering Formulas	464				Act. 20, SS13 Act. 21, SS14 Act. 22, SS15 Act. 23, SS16	
130 Spreadsheets: Entering Formulas	469				Act. 24, SS17 Act. 25, SS18	
131 Spreadsheets: SUM Function, Center Data	472				Act. 26, SS19 Act. 27, SS20 Act. 28, SS21	
132 Spreadsheets: AVERAGE Function	476				Act. 29, SS22 Act. 30, SS23 Act. 31, SS24	
133 Spreadsheets: Inserting Rows/Sorting Data	480				Act. 32, SS25 Act. 33, SS26 Act. 34, SS27 Act. 35, SS28	
134 Spreadsheets: Inserting Columns, Borders, and Shading	484				Act. 36, SS29 Act. 37, SS30 Act 38, SS31	
135 Spreadsheets: Clear Cells, Delete Rows and Columns	488				Act. 39, SS32 Act. 40, SS33	
136 Spreadsheets: Fill Right/ Fill Down Commands	492				Act. 41, SS34 Act. 42, SS35 Act. 43, SS36	
137 Spreadsheets: Creating Bar Charts	496				Act. 44, SS37 Act. 45, SS38	
138 Spreadsheets: Creating Pie Charts	502				Act. 46, SS39 Act. 47, SS40 Act. 48, SS41 Act. 49, SS42	
139 Spreadsheets: Review	506				Act. 50, SS43 Act. 51, SS44	
140 Spreadsheets: Review	510				Act. 52, SS45 Act. 53, SS46 Act. 54, SS47 Act. 55, SS48	

TABLE OF CONTENTS *(continued)*

UNIT 8 DATABASES

Lesson	Page	Reports	Correspondence	Tables	Spreadsheets	Databases
141 Databases: Database Orientation	516					
142 Databases: Create Database Tables	519					Act. 1, DBT1 Act. 2, DBT2
143 Databases: Revise and Add Records	522					Act. 3, DBT1 Act. 4, DBT3 Act. 5, DBT2
144 Databases: Rename, Add, and Position Fields	526					Act. 6, DBT2 Act. 7, DBT3
145 Databases: Monetary and Numeric Fields	530					Act. 8, DBT4 Act. 9, DBT5 Act. 10, DBT5
146 Databases: Review	534					Act. 11, DBT3
147 Databases: Sort and Query	539					Act. 12, DBT3 Act. 13, DBT3 Act. 14, DBT3 Act. 15, DBT3 Act. 16, DBT3 Act. 17, DBT3, Q1 Act. 18, DBT3, Q2 Act. 19, DBT3, Q3 Act. 20, DBT3, Q4 Act. 21, DBT3, Q5 Act. 22, DBT3, Q6 Act. 23, DBT3, Q7 Act. 24, DBT3, Q8 Act. 25, DBT3, Q9 Act. 26, DCT3, Q10
148 Databases: Reports	544					Act. 27, DBT4, R1 Act. 28, DBT2, R2
149 Databases: Formulas	547					Act. 29, DBT5 Act. 30, DBT5, R3
150 Databases: Simulation	550					Act. 31, SS49 Act. 32, DBT6 Act. 33, R72

Skillbuilding	SB1
Glossary	G1
Index	IN1

ABOUT YOUR BOOK

STRUCTURE

Your book is divided into 8 units. **Note:** If you are using the book with Lessons 1–80, your book will have just 4 units. Each unit except the last one is further divided into 20 lessons. Unit 8, because of its complexity, contains only 10 lessons. Each unit opens with a two-page spread which provides a list of the unit objectives (what you will learn in the unit), *Words to Learn* (words that are introduced or used within the unit), and a *Career Bit* (a brief description of a career in which keyboarding skill is helpful).

UNITS

In Units 1 and 2 you will learn to operate the keyboard by touch with speed and accuracy—a skill you will be able to use throughout your education and career. In Unit 3, you will be introduced to the ten-key numeric keypad and some basic word processing features.

In Units 4 and 5 you will use your keyboarding skill to create documents and to format them correctly. In addition, you will continue to learn about more advanced word processing features as you progress.

Unit 6 includes desktop publishing lessons where you will continue to learn word processing features such as draw and text/word art and use them to create a variety of documents including some original designs. You will also learn about inserting, sizing, and positioning graphics.

In Unit 7, you will learn about spreadsheets: what they are, how to create them, how to use them for "what if" queries, and how to create pie and bar charts.

Finally, in Unit 8, you will learn about databases: what they are, how they can be used, how to create database tables, how to sort, and how to query databases.

ABOUT YOUR BOOK *(continued)*

LESSONS

Each lesson is divided into several sections. Every lesson (except the first) begins with a Warmup that you should begin typing as soon as you are settled at your keyboard. In the early lessons, *New-Key* sections introduce the new keys for that lesson and provide you with practice lines on these keys.

Every lesson contains a *Skillbuilding* section that is easy to identify because of its blue background. The skillbuilding sections contain a variety of different activities including Technique Timings, Diagnostic Practice, Paced Practice, and 1-, 3-, and 5-minute timings.

Many skillbuilding sections include a *Pretest, Practice, Posttest* routine. This routine is designed to help you improve either speed or accuracy through step-by-step procedures. The Pretest helps you identify your speed or accuracy needs. The Practice activities contain a variety of intensive improvement drills. Finally, the Posttest measures your improvement.

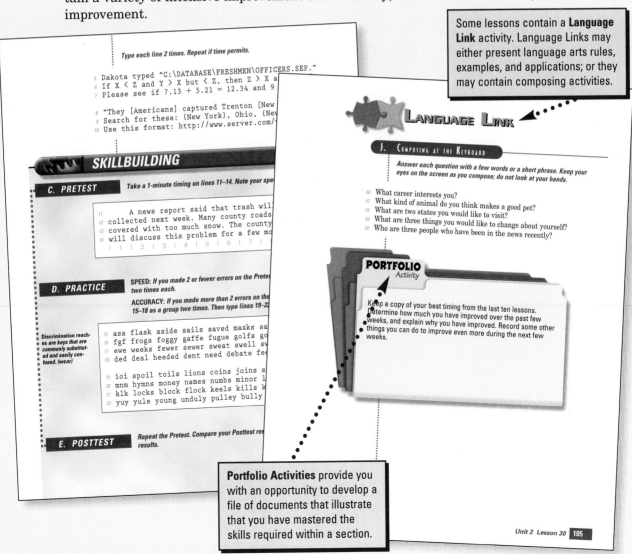

Some lessons contain a **Language Link** activity. Language Links may either present language arts rules, examples, and applications; or they may contain composing activities.

Type each line 2 times. Repeat if time permits.

```
 5  Dakota typed "C:\DATABASE\FRESHMEN\OFFICERS.SEP."
 6  If X < Z and Y > X but < Z, then Z > X a
 7  Please see if 7.13 + 5.21 = 12.34 and 9

 8  "They [Americans] captured Trenton [New
 9  Search for these: {New York}, Ohio, {Nev
10  Use this format: http://www.server.com/1
```

SKILLBUILDING

C. PRETEST   Take a 1-minute timing on lines 11–14. Note your spe

```
11      A news report said that trash wil
12  collected next week. Many county roads
13  covered with too much snow. The county
14  will discuss this problem for a few mc
    | 1 | 2 | 3 | 4 | 5 | 6 | 7 |
```

D. PRACTICE

SPEED: If you made 2 or fewer errors on the Pretes
two times each.

ACCURACY: If you made more than 2 errors on the
15–18 as a group two times. Then type lines 19–2

Discrimination reaches are keys that are commonly substituted and easily confused. (wear)

```
15  asa flask aside sails saved masks sa
16  fgf frogs foggy gaffe fugue golfs go
17  ewe weeks fewer sewer sweat swell sv
18  ded deal heeded dent need debate fee

19  ioi spoil toils lions coins joins s
20  mnm hymns money names numbs minor 1
21  klk locks block flock keels kills k
22  yuy yule young unduly pulley bully
```

E. POSTTEST   Repeat the Pretest. Compare your Posttest res
results.

LANGUAGE LINK

J. COMPOSING AT THE KEYBOARD

Answer each question with a few words or a short phrase. Keep your eyes on the screen as you compose; do not look at your hands.

```
46  What career interests you?
47  What kind of animal do you think makes a good pet?
48  What are two states you would like to visit?
49  What are three things you would like to change about yourself?
50  Who are three people who have been in the news recently?
```

PORTFOLIO *Activity*

Keep a copy of your best timing from the last ten lessons. Determine how much you have improved over the past few weeks, and explain why you have improved. Record some other things you can do to improve even more during the next few weeks.

Portfolio Activities provide you with an opportunity to develop a file of documents that illustrate that you have mastered the skills required within a section.

ABOUT YOUR BOOK *(continued)*

LESSONS

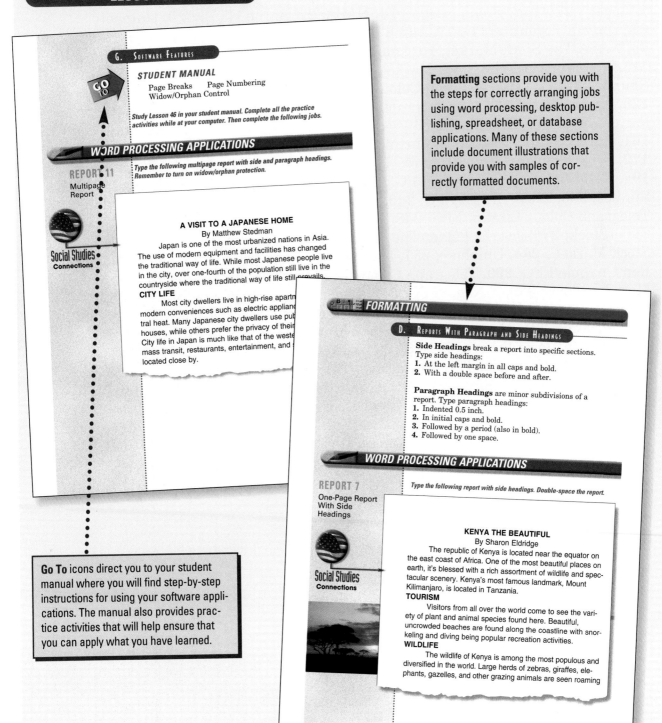

Formatting sections provide you with the steps for correctly arranging jobs using word processing, desktop publishing, spreadsheet, or database applications. Many of these sections include document illustrations that provide you with samples of correctly formatted documents.

Go To icons direct you to your student manual where you will find step-by-step instructions for using your software applications. The manual also provides practice activities that will help ensure that you can apply what you have learned.

About Your Book **xii**

Photo Credits

1, Roger Tully/Tony Stone Images; **17,** NASA; **22,** Aaron Haupt; **29,** Uniphoto; **67,** Yomafa Toyohiro/FPG; **71,** Aaron Haupt; **75,** Aaron Haupt; **88,** Aaron Haupt; **98,** NASA/The Stock Market; **101,** Aaron Haupt; **109,** Aaron Haupt; **110,** Fotosmith; **113,** Kennan Ward/The Stock Market; **116,** Richard Harrington/FPG; **117,** Gail Shumway/FPG; **119,** Telegraph Colour Library/FPG; **122,** Library of Congress; **128,** Aaron Haupt; **131,** Aaron Haupt; **137,** Michael Krasowitz/FPG; **139,** Al Satterwhite/FPG; **152,** Michele Burgess/The Stock Market; **153,** SuperStock; **161,** Aaron Haupt; **164,** Doug Martin; **166,** Gabe Palmer/The Stock Market; **172,** Syme Thayer/FPG; **179,** Aaron Haupt; **180,** Michael Keller/The Stock Market; **194,** Telegraph Colour Library/FPG; **217,** David Tejada/Tony Stone Images; **223,** KS Studios; **236,** TRAVELPIX/FPG; **240,** Frank P Rossotto/The Stock Market; **243,** Telegraph Colour Library/FPG; **248,** Art Wolfe/Tony Stone Images; **256,** SuperStock; **275,** Jose L. Pelaez/The Stock Market; **277,** Robert S Semeniuk/The Stock Market ; **284,** Uniphoto; **287,** Lawrence Sawyer/The Picture Cube, Inc.; **293,** Ron Chapple/FPG; **299,** Telegraph Colour Library/FPG; **302,** Aaron Haupt; **314,** Matt Meadows; **339,** E Nagel/FPG; **342,** Roger Tully/Tony Stone Images; **352,** Robert S Semeniuk/The Stock Market; **367,** Palmer Kane/The Stock Market; **382,** Aaron Haupt; **391,** Norbert Wu/The Stock Market; **398,** Palmer Kane/The Stock Market; **405,** Josef Polleross/The Stock Market; **426,** Ron Chapple/FPG; **435,** Borland; **468,** Uniphoto; **471,** Joe Cornish/Tony Stone Images; **483,** SuperStock; **487,** Jim Rorabaugh; **509,** Anthony Edgeworth/The Stock Market; **510,** Ian Murphy/Tony Stone Images; **515,** PhotoDisc/Nick Koudis; **517,** Thomas Brakefield/The Stock Market; **521,** Reuters/Mike Blake/Archive Photos; **526,** Glencoe File; **534,** Norbert Wu/The Stock Market; **548,** SuperStock; **COVER,** Aaron Haupt.

ABOUT YOUR BOOK *(continued)*

In addition to regular keyboarding lesson content, the lessons include a variety of special features. The following pages show samples of these features.

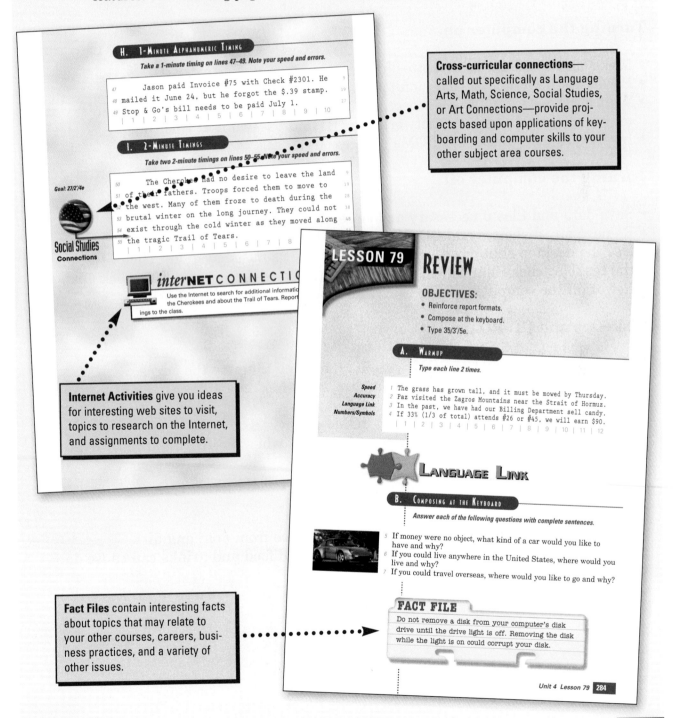

H. 1-Minute Alphanumeric Timing

Take a 1-minute timing on lines 47–49. Note your speed and errors.

```
47      Jason paid Invoice #75 with Check #2301. He      9
48 mailed it June 24, but he forgot the $.39 stamp.      19
49 Stop & Go's bill needs to be paid July 1.            27
   | 1 | 2 | 3 | 4 | 5 | 6 | 7 | 8 | 9 | 10
```

I. 2-Minute Timings

Take two 2-minute timings on lines 50–55. Note your speed and errors.

Goal: 27/2'/4e

```
50      The Cherokee had no desire to leave the land    9
51 of their fathers. Troops forced them to move to      19
52 the west. Many of them froze to death during the     28
53 brutal winter on the long journey. They could not    38
54 exist through the cold winter as they moved along     48
55 the tragic Trail of Tears.
   | 1 | 2 | 3 | 4 | 5 | 6 | 7 | 8
```

Social Studies Connections

interNET CONNECTION

Use the Internet to search for additional information the Cherokees and about the Trail of Tears. Report ings to the class.

Cross-curricular connections— called out specifically as Language Arts, Math, Science, Social Studies, or Art Connections—provide projects based upon applications of keyboarding and computer skills to your other subject area courses.

Internet Activities give you ideas for interesting web sites to visit, topics to research on the Internet, and assignments to complete.

LESSON 79 · REVIEW

OBJECTIVES:
* Reinforce report formats.
* Compose at the keyboard.
* Type 35/3'/5e.

A. Warmup

Type each line 2 times.

Speed
Accuracy
Language Link
Numbers/Symbols

```
1 The grass has grown tall, and it must be mowed by Thursday.
2 Paz visited the Zagros Mountains near the Strait of Hormuz.
3 In the past, we have had our Billing Department sell candy.
4 If 33% (1/3 of total) attends #26 or #45, we will earn $90.
  | 1 | 2 | 3 | 4 | 5 | 6 | 7 | 8 | 9 | 10 | 11 | 12
```

LANGUAGE LINK

B. Composing at the Keyboard

Answer each of the following questions with complete sentences.

5 If money were no object, what kind of a car would you like to have and why?
6 If you could live anywhere in the United States, where would you live and why?
7 If you could travel overseas, where would you like to go and why?

FACT FILE

Do not remove a disk from your computer's disk drive until the drive light is off. Removing the disk while the light is on could corrupt your disk.

Fact Files contain interesting facts about topics that may relate to your other courses, careers, business practices, and a variety of other issues.

Unit 4 Lesson 79 **284**

OPERATING YOUR COMPUTER

The following tips should be used to operate your computer correctly. Your teacher may provide you with additional instructions.

Turning the computer on

- Make sure there are no diskettes in the computer's diskette drive.
- Power on the computer and monitor.
- Wait for the start-up process (*booting*) to finish before starting any programs; you may be required to enter a network user ID and password at this time.
- Insert diskettes and/or CD-ROMs if necessary.

Turning the computer off

- Save data and files if necessary and close all windows.
- Remove any diskettes and CD-ROMs from the drives.
- Use the desktop shut-down procedure; in Windows-based systems, click Start on the taskbar, click Shut Down, choose the Shut down option, and then click OK.
- Power off the computer (if necessary) and monitor.

Diskettes and CD-ROMs

- Handle diskettes and CD-ROMs carefully, holding them by the edges.
- Protect diskettes and CD-ROMs from dirt, scratches, moisture, extremes in temperature, and magnetic fields.
- Insert and remove diskettes and CD-ROMs gently.
- Do not attempt to remove a diskette or CD-ROM when the drive indicator light is on.

Work area

- Keep the area around your computer neat and free from dust and dirt.
- Do not eat or drink near your computer, as spilled food and drinks can cause damage to the computer.

ABOUT YOUR BOOK *(continued)*

SPECIAL FEATURES

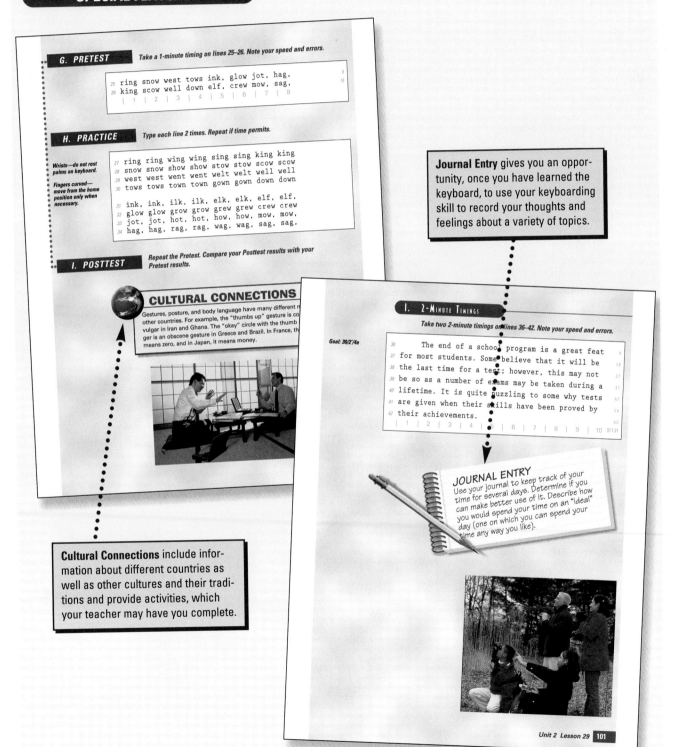

G. PRETEST Take a 1-minute timing on lines 25–26. Note your speed and errors.

```
25  ring snow west tows ink, glow jot, hag,          8
26  king scow well down elf, crew mow, sag,          16
   | 1 | 2 | 3 | 4 | 5 | 6 | 7 | 8 |
```

H. PRACTICE Type each line 2 times. Repeat if time permits.

Wrists—do not rest palms on keyboard.

Fingers curved— move from the home position only when necessary.

```
27  ring ring wing wing sing sing king king
28  snow snow show show stow stow scow scow
29  west west went went welt welt well well
30  tows tows town town gown gown down down

31  ink, ink, ilk, ilk, elk, elk, elf, elf,
32  glow glow grow grow grew grew crew crew
33  jot, jot, hot, hot, how, how, mow, mow,
34  hag, hag, rag, rag, wag, wag, sag, sag,
```

I. POSTTEST Repeat the Pretest. Compare your Posttest results with your Pretest results.

CULTURAL CONNECTIONS
Gestures, posture, and body language have many different m
other countries. For example, the "thumbs up" gesture is co
vulgar in Iran and Ghana. The "okay" circle with the thumb
ger is an obscene gesture in Greece and Brazil. In France, th
means zero, and in Japan, it means money.

Journal Entry gives you an opportunity, once you have learned the keyboard, to use your keyboarding skill to record your thoughts and feelings about a variety of topics.

I. 2-MINUTE TIMINGS

Take two 2-minute timings on lines 36–42. Note your speed and errors.

Goal: 30/2'/4e

```
36      The end of a school program is a great feat      9
37  for most students. Some believe that it will be      18
38  the last time for a test; however, this may not      27
39  be so as a number of exams may be taken during a     37
40  lifetime. It is quite puzzling to some why tests     47
41  are given when their skills have been proved by      56
42  their achievements.                                  60
   | 1 | 2 | 3 | 4 | 5 | 6 | 7 | 8 | 9 | 10 | SI 1.21
```

JOURNAL ENTRY
Use your journal to keep track of your time for several days. Determine if you can make better use of it. Describe how you would spend your time on an "ideal" day (one on which you can spend your time any way you like).

Cultural Connections include information about different countries as well as other cultures and their traditions and provide activities, which your teacher may have you complete.

Unit 2 Lesson 29 **101**

INDEX *(continued)*

V

Vertical centering, 170
Vertical page orientation, 341
Voice recognition, 278

W

Widow/orphan protection, 160
Word art, 402
Word processing features
  adjusting column width, 238
  alignment, 133
  backspacing, 127
  bold, 145
  borders and shading, 334
  bullets and numbering, 149
  center page, 170
  close file, 124
  correcting errors, 127
  cut, copy, paste, 145
  data file, 310
  date insert, 170
  dot leaders, 283
  endnotes, 270
  envelopes, 178
  find and replace, 185
  fonts, 130
  footnotes, 270
  form file, 313
  formulas, 348
  hanging indent, 259
  header/footer, 263
  help, 135
  italic, 145
  join cells, 252
  left indent, 259
  line spacing, 139
  line style, 381
  mail merge, 310
  margins, 139, 274
  moving, 127, 385
  new file, 124
  number columns, 245
  numbering and bullets, 149
  open file, 124
  orphan/widow control, 160
  page breaks, 160
  page numbering, 160
  page orientation, 341
  preview page, 130
  print, 130
  print preview, 130
  quit, 124
  reveal codes, 133
  right indent, 259
  ruler, 191
  saving files, 127
  select text, 133
  show/hide codes, 133
  spelling check, 127
  sizing, 385
  tab set, 191
  table lines, 331
  table position, 238
  tables, add columns and rows,
    345
  tables, create, 235
  tables, delete columns and
    rows, 345
  templates, 324
  underline, 139
  widow/orphan control, 160
Word wrap, 45
Works cited page, in reports,
  R3, 261, 262
Wrapping text, 392, 393
Writer's identification, 169

12-Second Sprints, 28, 38, 97, 112,
  118, 126, 138, 151, 181, 208, 230,
  241, 273, 303, 333, 368, 392, 403,
  431, 453, 476, 519, 548
30-Second Timings, 158, 188,
  218, 250, 277, 311, 380, 406,
  417, 461, 481, 502, 507,
30-Second OK Timings, 100, 132,
  148, 167, 175, 194, 227, 254, 281,
  323, 341, 386, 409, 443, 465, 492,
1-Minute Alphanumeric Timings,
  70, 75, 78, 81, 84, 87, 93, 116

1-Minute Timings

Page	Words
52	25
58	25
65	25

2-Minute Timings

Page	Words
75	27
78	27
81	27
84	27
88	27
93	27
97	30
101	30
104	30
109	30
113	30
116	30

3-Minute Timings

Page	Words
119	31
122	31
127	31
135	32
148	33
163	33
181	33
204	33
214	33
238	35
223	35
245	35
258	35
269	35
285	35

5-Minute Timings

Page	Words
300	37
315	37
330	37
337	37
354	37
373	38
389	38
400	38
415	38
424	38
437	39
449	39
458	39
473	39
489	39
498	39
518	40
527	40
536	40
545	40
551	40

SPECIAL FEATURES

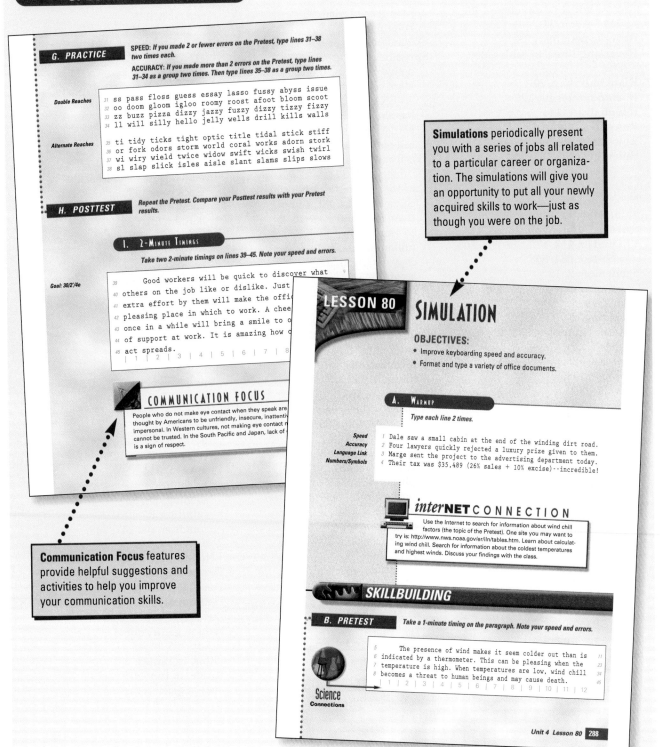

G. PRACTICE

SPEED: If you made 2 or fewer errors on the Pretest, type lines 31–38 two times each.

ACCURACY: If you made more than 2 errors on the Pretest, type lines 31–34 as a group two times. Then type lines 35–38 as a group two times.

Double Reaches

```
31 ss pass floss guess essay lasso fussy abyss issue
32 oo doom gloom igloo roomy roost afoot bloom scoot
33 zz buzz pizza dizzy jazzy fuzzy dizzy tizzy fizzy
34 ll will silly hello jelly wells drill kills walls
```

Alternate Reaches

```
35 ti tidy ticks tight optic title tidal stick stiff
36 or fork odors storm world coral works adorn stork
37 wi wiry wield twice widow swift wicks swish twirl
38 sl slap slick isles aisle slant slams slips slows
```

H. POSTTEST

Repeat the Pretest. Compare your Posttest results with your Pretest results.

I. 2-MINUTE TIMINGS

Take two 2-minute timings on lines 39–45. Note your speed and errors.

Goal: 30/2'/4e

```
39     Good workers will be quick to discover what     9
40 others on the job like or dislike. Just
41 extra effort by them will make the offic
42 pleasing place in which to work. A chee
43 once in a while will bring a smile to o
44 of support at work. It is amazing how o
45 act spreads.
   | 1 | 2 | 3 | 4 | 5 | 6 | 7 | 8 |
```

COMMUNICATION FOCUS

People who do not make eye contact when they speak are thought by Americans to be unfriendly, insecure, inattentiv impersonal. In Western cultures, not making eye contact m cannot be trusted. In the South Pacific and Japan, lack of is a sign of respect.

Simulations periodically present you with a series of jobs all related to a particular career or organization. The simulations will give you an opportunity to put all your newly acquired skills to work—just as though you were on the job.

Communication Focus features provide helpful suggestions and activities to help you improve your communication skills.

LESSON 80 — SIMULATION

OBJECTIVES:
- Improve keyboarding speed and accuracy.
- Format and type a variety of office documents.

A. WARMUP

Type each line 2 times.

Speed
Accuracy
Language Link
Numbers/Symbols

```
1 Dale saw a small cabin at the end of the winding dirt road.
2 Four lawyers quickly rejected a luxury prize given to them.
3 Marge sent the project to the advertising department today.
4 Their tax was $35,489 (26% sales + 10% excise)--incredible!
```

inter**NET** CONNECTION

Use the Internet to search for information about wind chill factors (the topic of the Pretest). One site you may want to try is: http://www.nws.noaa.gov/er/iln/tables.htm. Learn about calculating wind chill. Search for information about the coldest temperatures and highest winds. Discuss your findings with the class.

SKILLBUILDING

B. PRETEST

Take a 1-minute timing on the paragraph. Note your speed and errors.

Science Connections

```
5     The presence of wind makes it seem colder out than is     11
6 indicated by a thermometer. This can be pleasing when the     23
7 temperature is high. When temperatures are low, wind chill     34
8 becomes a threat to human beings and may cause death.        45
  | 1 | 2 | 3 | 4 | 5 | 6 | 7 | 8 | 9 | 10 | 11 | 12
```

Resumes, formatting, R4, 205, 374

Return address, envelopes, R6, 177

Reverse text, 396

Reversing lines, in tables, 329, 331

Right shift key, 20

Roman numerals, 125

Rough draft, 144

Rows in a table, 235

Rows, in tables, add/delete, 344

Rules, graphic, 380, 381

S

Salutation, in letters, 169

Science Connection, 26, 98, 113, 116, 119, 153, 172, 288 298, 300, 477, 489, 534, 553

Semicolon, 2, 13
between independent clauses, 213
spacing, 20, 51

Shading, in tables, 333, 334

Shapes
circles, 385
ellipses, 385
ovals, 385
rectangles, 385

Shift keys, 20, 31

Short quotations, in reports, 258, 259

Side headings, in reports, 151, 152

Signature, letters, 169

Skillbuilding (back-of-book exercises)
Diagnostic Practice: Alphabet, SB1–SB3
Diagnostic Practice: Numbers, SB4–SB6
Paced Practice, SB7–SB14
Supplementary Timings, SB15–SB31

Small envelope, R6, 177

Social Studies Connection, 17, 93, 122, 134, 135, 148, 152, 160, 163, 168, 176, 197, 280, 295, 323, 334, 437, 458, 469, 489, 497, 498, 518, 525, 526, 543

Space bar, 3

Spacing
after a period, 20
after a semicolon, 20
rules for, R9

Special characters, 368

Spreadsheet features
active cell, 438, 466
align columns, 445
AVERAGE function, 477
bar charts, 498, 499
borders and shading, 485
cell name/address, 438
cell ranges, 462
center data, 474
change column widths, 450
change row height, 454
clear cells, 490
column, 438
column heads, 462
copy data, 450
create, 445
delete rows/columns, 490
deselect cells, 440
enter formulas, 470
entry bar, 438, 466
enter data, 443
fill down, 493
fill right, 493
fill series, 493
format values, 459
formulas, 443, 465
gridlines, 462
insert columns, 485
insert rows, 481
labels, 443
mathematical operators, 465
move data, 454
orientation to, 438
pie charts, 503
print, 462
row heads, 462
select cells, 440
sort data, 481
SUM function, 474
values, 443

Subject line in letters, R5, 303, 304

Subtitle, 144

Subtitle in tables, R7, 251

Sum formula, in tables, 347, 348

Symbols
feet, 125
minutes and seconds, 125

multiply, 125
roman numerals, 125
subtract, 125

T

Tab key, 45, 60, 79

Table of contents, in reports, R1, 281, 282

Table position, 238

Tables, 235, 329, 333
add/delete columns, 344
add/delete rows, 344
adjust column widths, 238
block column headings, R7
body, 235
borders/fill, 333, 334
borders/shading, 334
boxed, R7, 235
braced column headings, R7, 251
column headings, R7, 242
column size, 237
column widths, 238
columns, 235
create, 235
formulas in, 348
join cells, 252
number columns, 244, 245
open, R7, 235
page orientation, 341
parts of, 235
position, R7, 237, 238
reversing lines, 329, 331
rows in, 344
ruled, R8
shading, R8, 334
subtitles, R7, 251
sum formula, 347, 348
titles, R7, 251
totals in, 347, 348

Technology Tip, 142, 146, 321

Templates, memos, 322–323

Text boxes, 393

Text/word art, 402, 404

Title page in reports, R1, 281, 282

Titles, in tables, 251

Totals, in tables, 347, 348

Two-page letters, R5, 299, 300

U

Unbound report, R1, R2, 143

REFERENCE SECTION *Table of Contents*

REPORTS

Report Outline... R1
Title Page R1
Table of Contents.. R1
Unbound Report, Page 1 (*With Side and Paragraph Headings*)............... R1
Unbound Report, Page 2 (*With Enumeration*).............................. R2
Bound Report (*With Footnotes*) R2
Bound Report, Page 1 (*With Endnotes*)................................... R2
Bound Report, Page 2 (*With Endnotes*) R2
Bibliography R3
MLA Report.. R3
Works Cited Page.. R3
Agenda.. R3
Minutes of a Meeting.. R4

EMPLOYMENT DOCUMENTS

Resume.. R4
Application Letter R4
Follow-Up Letter R4

CORRESPONDENCE

Block-Style Business Letter R5
Modified-Block Style Letter
    With Subject Line, Enclosure Notation, and Copy Notation............ R5
    With Open Punctuation and Table................................... R5
    With Enumeration, Attachment, Delivery Notation, Postscript.......... R5
Envelopes... R6
Folding Letters R6
Memo Template.. R7

TABLES

Open Table (*With Blocked Column Heads*)................................ R7
Boxed Table (*With Centered Column Heads*).............................. R7
Boxed Table (*With Multi-Line Heads and Footnote*)....................... R7
Boxed Table (*With Shading*) R8
Open Table R8

MISCELLANEOUS

Proofreaders' Marks... R8

LANGUAGE LINKS

Spacing Rules R9
Punctuation... R10–R11
Grammar.. R12–R14
Mechanics R14–R15

INDEX *(continued)*

inside address, 169
merge feature, 309
modified block, R5, 190, 191
personal business, R5, 167, 169
salutation, 169
signature, 169
subject line, R5, 304
two-page, R5, 299, 300
with attachments, R5, 197, 198
with attention line, R5, 303, 304
with copy notations, R5, 218
with delivery notations, R5, 219
with enclosures, R5, 197, 198
with indented paragraphs, 194
with international addresses, R5, 353, 355
with numbered lists, R5, 320
with postscripts, R5, 222, 224
with subject lines, R5, 303, 304
with tables, R5
writer's identification, 169
Lines in tables, 331
Lists, 147
Lists
bulleted, 149
numbered, 149
Long quotations in reports, 258, 259

M

Mailing address, envelopes, R6, 177
Masthead, in newsletters, 421
Math Connections, 264, 315, 465, 495, 504, 527, 531
Memos
templates, R7, 323
with attachment notations, R7, 358, 359
with copy notation, 358, 359
Merge feature, 309
Merge, form letters, 308, 309, 311
Military style date, 139
Minutes of a meeting, R4, 156
MLA style, R3, 139
Modified-block letters, R5, 190, 191
Multipage report, R2, 158, 159, 160, 273

N

Nameplate, in newsletter, 421
Newsletters, 420, 421, 422, 424, 425, 426, 427, 428, 429, 432
Notations in a letter, 219, 222
Number columns in tables, 244, 245
Numbered lists, 149, 318
Numbered lists, in letters, 318, 320
Numbers
as figures, 294
as words, 294
in dates, 420
in measurements, 420
mixed, 420
two or more related, 420
using, 295
Numeric keypad, 94, 98, 106, 110

O

Open table, 235
Outlines, 150, 286
Outlines, in reports, R1
Ovals (Ellipses), 385

P

Page
break, 160
design, 403
numbering, 160
Page orientation
horizontal, 341
in tables, 341
landscape, 341
portrait, 341
vertical, 341
Paragraph headings in reports, 151, 152
Parenthetical reference in reports, 257, 258
Parts of a table, 235
Period
for ellipsis, 125
spacing, 20, 51
Personal business letters, R5, 167, 169
Personal stationery, 395, 399
Portfolio Activity, 65, 105, 179, 195, 203, 207, 212, 221, 287, 343, 357, 361, 375, 394, 487, 513, 533, 546, 554

Portrait page orientation, 341
Postscripts, in letters, R5, 222, 224
Pretest/Practice/Posttest, 6, 9, 12, 15, 18, 22, 26, 29, 32, 35, 38, 40, 43, 46, 49, 51, 55, 58, 61, 64, 70, 73, 77, 80, 83, 87, 91, 100, 103, 108, 112, 115, 121, 124, 133, 168, 176, 230, 241, 254, 288, 295, 297, 298, 309, 312, 319, 345, 350, 377, 384, 396, 411, 428, 439, 454, 469, 477, 523, 535
Proofreaders' marks, R8, 144, 155
Punctuation marks, R10-R12
Punctuation spacing, R9, 20, 51

Q

Quotation mark
around titles, 383
for inches/seconds, 125
Quotes in reports, 258, 259

R

Rectangles, 385
Reference initials, R5, 182, 219
Reports
academic, 1-page, R3, 139
agendas and enumerations, R3, 147
bibliography, R3, 281, 283
business, 1-page, R1, 143, 144
contents page, R1, 281, 282
endnotes in, R2, 268, 270, 278
footnotes in, R2, 268, 270, 278
left-bound, 274
minutes of a meeting, 156
MLA, R3, 139
multi-page, 160, 273
multi-page, left bound, 273, 274, 276
outline in, R1, 149, 150, 286
table of contents, R1, 281, 282
title page, R1, 281, 282
with numbered list, 164
with paragraph and side headings, R1, 151
with parenthetical references, 257, 258
with quotations, 259
with Works Cited page, R3, 262

REPORT OUTLINE

↓6x

HOW TO MAKE DECISIONS ON THE JOB ↓2x

1) DETERMINE WHAT CHOICES YOU HAVE.
   a) Make use of all available reference materials.
      i) Check company policy manuals.
      ii) Go to the company library or files.
   b) Ask your co-workers and your supervisors questions.
   c) Be observant and pay close attention in meetings.
2) DO NOT MAKE DECISIONS HASTILY.
   a) Postpone any doubtful decisions.
   b) Decisions based on emotions are usually not the best ones.
      i) If you are angry, allow enough time to consider things calmly.
      ii) You will risk losing others' respect if you act impulsively.
3) EVALUATE YOUR DECISIONS OBJECTIVELY.
   a) Keep an open mind about the consequences of your decisions.
   b) Learn from past decisions you have made.
      i) Evaluate the results of each decision you make.
      ii) Learn something good from a poor decision.

TITLE PAGE

↓ center vertically

HOW TO MAKE DECISIONS ON THE JOB ↓12x

By Allen J. Springer ↓12x

Mr. Joseph Simka
Business Communications I
March 4, [year]

TABLE OF CONTENTS

↓6x

CONTENTS ↓2x

COMMUNICATION MANAGEMENT . . . . 3 ↓2x
MANAGERIAL ANALYSIS 15
INTERPERSONAL COMMUNICATIONS . . . . 18 ↓2x

    Interpersonal Motivation 21
    Interpersonal Perception 27

BARRIERS TO COMMUNICATIONS 30
GROUP COMMUNICATIONS 37

UNBOUND REPORT, PAGE 1

(with side and paragraph headings)

↓3x

THE INFORMATION EXPLOSION ↓1x
By Ann A. Minichiello
↓1x
Whether you work as an executive or an administrative assistant, in today's business world you will find yourself at the center of an information explosion. Today's offices are equipped with modems, fax machines, electronic mail, and voice mail—all designed to make the flow of communication faster and more effective. As a result, you must have excellent information skills to succeed in the business world. ↓1x

KNOW YOUR PRODUCT
↓1x
Every worker should know the product he or she is responsible for. If you work in an office, your product is information. Your primary responsibility will be to handle information—to receive it and store it for future use, to research information and share it with others, or to evaluate the information and report on your evaluation.

COMMUNICATION

The role of communication is receiving a great deal of attention. The need to write and speak effectively is critical to success. Equally important to communication is the individual's ability to plan and organize information.

Planning. It is important to plan and organize information. Every office worker must plan ahead to determine information needs. The first step in communicating is to anticipate needs.

INDEX *(continued)*

drop caps, 373
drop shadow, 378
figure boxes, 387
fill, 378
font colors, 373
graphic boxes, 387
graphic lines, 380, 381
inserting boxes, 386
line position, 381
line size, 381
line style, 381
orientation to, 369
page design, 403
reverse text, 396
rules, 380, 381
shapes, draw, insert, move,
    size, 385
special characters, 368
text boxes, 387
text/word art, 404
vertical text, 404
wrapping text, 393
Documents, columns, 418
Dot leaders, 282
Drawing, 383
Drop caps, 373
Drop shadow, documents, 378

E

Edit, 95
Ellipses (ovals), 385
Ellipsis, 125
Enclosure notation, R5, 198
Endnotes, in reports, R2, 268,
    270
End-of-class procedure, 6
Enter key, 4, 46, 49, 79
Enumerations, in reports, R2
Envelopes, R6, 177
Envelopes
    folding letters for, R6, 178
    formatting, R6, 177
    mailing address, R6, 177
    return address, R6, 177
    sizes, R6, 177

F

Fact File, 8, 22, 26, 35, 38, 71, 88,
    98, 110, 117, 139, 153, 163, 167,
    176, 222, 236, 242, 243, 248,
    256, 284, 285, 296, 307, 314,
    326, 328, 346, 368, 377, 387,

391, 395, 399, 405, 411, 416,
426, 439, 444, 447, 459, 471,
480, 482, 487, 493, 502, 507,
517, 520, 524, 525, 536, 537
Figuring speed, 21
Fill
    in documents, 378
    in tables, 333, 334
Find and replace, 185
Flyers, designing, 408
Folding letters, R6, 178
Fonts
    colors, 373
    features, 372
    special characters, 369
Footnotes in reports, R2, 268, 270
Form letters
    data file, 309
    data source, 309, 310
    form file, 312
    form letter, 309
    merge, 308, 309, 311
    merge: data source/file, 309
Formulas in tables, 348

G

Graphic boxes, 386
Graphic lines, 380, 381

H

Headlines in newsletter, 421
Home key position, 2
Home row keys, 2
Home-key position, keypad, 95
Horizontal page orientation,
    341
Hyphen, 56
    for subtraction, 125

I

Indent, 60
Indented paragraphs, 194
Insertion point, 4
Inside address, letters, R4, 169
International address, in
    letters, R5, 353, 355
Internet Activity, 11, 32, 48, 93,
    106, 127, 128, 174, 183, 237, 244,
    259, 280, 288, 303, 332, 336, 349,
    372, 380, 389, 401, 409, 423, 441,
    466, 476, 479, 483, 484, 501, 513,

521, 550, 554
Invitations, designing, 414
Italics, 383

J

Join/merge cells, tables, 252
Journal Entry, 15, 61, 101, 168,
    223, 228, 267, 382, 419, 433,
    450, 529

K

Keypad, home-key position, 95

L

Landscape, page orientation,
    341
Language Arts Connections,
    180, 239, 242, 308, 330
Language Link, R9, 52, 55, 81,
    95, 105, 109, 120, 129, 132,
    147, 154, 162, 180, 187, 193,
    213, 222, 226, 234, 240, 247,
    253, 261, 268, 276, 284, 294,
    308, 318, 322, 336, 340, 344,
    353, 362, 376, 383, 388, 395,
    402, 408, 414, 420, 427, 436,
    442, 448, 457, 464, 472, 480,
    488, 496, 506, 516, 522, 530,
    539, 547
Large envelope, R6, 177
Left-bound report, R2, 273, 274
Letterhead, 182
    designing, 400
Letters
    application, R4, 210
    attention line, R5, 304
    block style, R5, 182, 218
    body, 169
    business, R6, 180, 182, 299
    complimentary closing, 169
    copy notation, R5
    date line, 169
    enclosure notation, R5
    folding, 178
    follow up, R4
    form, 308–312

UNBOUND REPORT, PAGE 2

(with enumeration)

2

Organizing. Your ability to organize all notes, letters, memos, faxes, and other information will determine your success. No matter what your specific job title or duties may be, you will be surrounded with information. The key to handling that information overload effectively is to stay organized. To stay organized, follow these steps: ↓1x

1. Before leaving work each day, write your to-do list for the next day. ↓1x
2. Set aside some time each day for setting up files and filing documents that have accumulated on your desk.
3. Use a daily planner to keep track of appointments, deadlines, important telephone numbers, and the like so that they are all in one place and easily accessible.

Handling the flow of information to and from coworkers, clients, executives, and others can be done well if you analyze, plan, and prioritize.

BOUND REPORT

(with footnotes)

↓3x

HOW TO PREPARE A REPORT ↓1x
A Review of Some Basic Guidelines ↓1x

Prepared by Abby Leonard ↓1x

When you are preparing the final copy of a paper, you should be sure that it is of the highest quality and that your best efforts have been put into the project.[1] ↓1x

SELECTION OF SUPPLIES ↓1x

The following supplies are considered essential for an attractive report:

Paper. Only high-quality paper is appropriate for the final report. Also, most reports should be prepared on white paper. ↓1x

Many report writers believe that 20-pound paper should be used for reports; 15-pound paper would be the minimum quality. In addition, the minimum rag content used for reports should be no lower than 50 percent.[2] ↓1x

Printing. Always print your report using the best printer you have available. A laser printer or an ink-jet printer is a good choice. Be sure that once your report is printed that the pages are free of smudges and that the type looks crisp and clean.

Covers. Selecting a cover for your report is another very important decision to make. You want to be certain that your report is as attractive on the outside as you can make it so that it will enhance the overall appearance of the report. Choose a report cover that will not detract attention from the material contained within. You only have one chance to make a positive first impression.

[1] Samuel C. Jones, *Guidelines for Reports*, Walding Publishing Company, San Francisco, 1993, p. 138.
[2] Ibid.

BOUND REPORT, PAGE 1

(with endnotes)

↓3x

DESIGNING A COMPUTER SYSTEM ↓1x

Designing a computer system involves a variety of different operations such as word processing, data processing, communications, printing, and other office-related functions. These areas can be integrated into a very powerful computer system. ↓1x

DESIGNING THE SYSTEM ↓1x

One of the first steps is to determine what information is going to be computerized and what personnel will need these resources.[1] This decision should involve all departments in the planning stage of system design. If necessary, you may have to invite input from those departments which are going to be closely involved in computer use after the system has been designed.

There may also be a need to acquire the system design experience of outside experts—people whose careers consist primarily of planning and developing computer systems for management.[ii]

SELECTING HARDWARE AND SOFTWARE

Bailey believes that "the selection of software precedes any hardware choices. Too many people, however, select the hardware first and then try to match their software with the computer."[iii] After the software has been selected, a decision must be made as to whether hardware should be purchased or leased. Although many firms decide to purchase their own hardware, others have taken the route of time-sharing or

BOUND REPORT, PAGE 2

(with endnotes)

2

remote processing whereby the costs of processing data can be shared with other users

TRAINING OPERATORS

Many firms neglect this important phase of designing a computer system. It is not enough to offer a one-week training course in an applications package and then expect proficiency from a worker.[iv] Training must occur over time to help those who will be using computers every day on the job.

Finally, it should be recognized that training is an ongoing responsibility. As technology, software, hardware, and procedures change, training must occur regularly and on a continuing basis.

[1] Neal Swanson, *Information Management*, Glencoe/McGraw-Hill, Westerville, Ohio, 1992, p. 372.
[ii] Christine L. Seymour, "The Ins and Outs of Designing Computer Systems," *Information Processing Trends*, January 1991, p. 23.
[iii] Lee Bailey, *Computer Systems Management*, The University of New Mexico Press, Albuquerque, New Mexico, 1992, p. 413.
[iv] Paula Blair, *Administrative Management*, Southern Publishing Company, Atlanta, Georgia, 1992, p. 420.

INDEX

Individual Keys

A, 2
B, 30
C, 17
D, 2
E, 7
F, 2
G, 23
H, 7
I, 10
J, 2
K, 2
L, 2
M, 10
N, 16
O, 7
P, 41
Q, 33
R, 10
S, 2
T, 16
U, 30
V, 19
W, 23
X, 42
Y, 44
Z, 47

1, 82
2, 76
3, 72
4, 67
5, 85
6, 86
7, 67
8, 73
9, 77
0, 83

&, 69
', 36
*, 73
@, 76
:, 47
, 23
/, 33
$, 68
!, 82
-, 56
(, 76
%, 85
., 20
#, 72
?, 53
), 83
_, 56
;, 2
" ", 35
^, 86
<, 90
>, 90
\, 90
+, 90
=, 90
{, 90
}, 90
[, 90
], 90
~, 90

Shifts, 20, 30

A

Academic reports, R3, 138
Agendas, R3, 147, 149
All-capital letters, 54
Anchor keys, 3
Apostrophe, for feet/minutes, 125
Art connection, 398
Application letters, R4, 208, 210
Attachment notations
    in letters, R5, 198
    in memos, 358, 359
Attention line, in letters, R5, 303, 304

B

Bibliography, R3, 281, 283
Binding a report, 274
Blind copy notation, 219
Block-style letters, R5, 169, 182
Blocked column headings, R7
Borders
    boxes, 388
    documents, 378
    fill, 333
    tables, 333–334
Bound report
    with endnotes, R2
    with footnotes, R2
Boxed table, R7, 235
Boxes
    borders, 388
    fill, 388
    graphic, 386
    text, 386
    wrapping text, 392
Braced column headings, in tables, R7, 250–251
Bulleted list, 149
Business letters, formatting, 180, 182, 191
Business reports, 143
Byline, in reports, 144

C

Capitalization, 95, 120, 276, 277, 318
Caps lock key, 53, 54
Cell, in a table, 235
Center page, 170
Certificate, designing, 411
Circles, 385
Columns
    adding/deleting in tables, 344
    desktop publishing, 417
    headings in tables, 240, 242, 251
    in a table, 235
    in documents, 417, 418
    width in tables, 238
Communication Focus, 24, 104, 131, 209, 272, 273, 392, 456, 457, 478, 495, 519, 540,
Complimentary closing in letters, 169, 194
Composing, 52, 55, 81, 105, 109, 147, 180, 193, 222, 239, 261, 284, 308, 336, 353, 376, 395, 436, 457, 480, 530
Confusing words, 129, 132, 322, 340, 427
Contents page, in reports, R1, 281, 282
Copy notations
    in letters, 219
    in memos, 358, 359
Counting errors, 25
Cultural Connection, 14, 29, 42, 158, 161, 200, 214, 352, 356, 397, 412, 452, 490

D

Database features
    add fields, 527
    add records, 524
    create database table, 520
    database tables, 518
    date fields, 524
    formulas, 548
    insert database charts, 551
    insert database tables, 551
    monetary fields, 531
    navigating, 518
    numeric fields, 531
    position fields, 527
    query database tables, 540
    rename, 527
    reports windows, 518
    revise, 524
    selecting, 518
    sort database tables, 540
Date insert, 169
Date line in letters, 169
Dates, treatment of, 388
Default page orientation, 341
Delivery notation, in letters, R5, 219
Design, of a page, 404
Desktop publishing documents
    certificates, 411
    flyers, 408
    invitations, 414
    letterhead, 400
    newsletters, 420
    notepads, 395
Desktop publishing features
    borders, 378, 390
    columns, 418
    drawing tools, 404

BIBLIOGRAPHY FOR A BOUND REPORT

5

↓6x

BIBLIOGRAPHY ↓2x

Blanchard, Christie, *Experience a Successful Interview,* Beringson Printing, New York, 1998. ↓2x

Dolfeld, Kyle B., and Lisa R. Simmons, *Using an Interview to Get the Job,* Masterson Books, Aptos, California, 1999. ↓2x

Johnson, Karen C., "What to Do After the Interview," *Journal of Communications,* Vol. XVII, No. 6, May 1995, pp. 17-20.

Lymanski, James T., et al., "The Secrets to Interviewing: Style and Organization," *HRD Journal,* Vol. LXVII, No. 5, October 1999, pp. 58-61.

"Preparing for the Interview," *Sales Marketing Journal,* Vol. XXVII, No. 2, August 21, 1997, pp. 103-105.

Secretarial Association, *The Job Interview and Your Success,* Georgia College Press, Carrollton, Georgia, 1996.

MLA REPORT

↓1 inch   Finklestein 1

Cynthia Finklestein ↓1x

Professor Roberts ↓1x

Business Communication 300 ↓1x

2 February {year} ↓1x

Communication Skills Needed in International Business ↓1x

International business plays an increasingly important role in the U.S. economy, and U.S. companies recognize that to be competitive nationally, they must be competitive internationally. Reflecting this trend, direct investment by U.S. private enterprises in foreign countries increased from $409 billion in 1994 to $528 billion in 1999, an increase of 29 percent in four years (Connor 253). Today, more than 3,000 U.S. corporations have over 25,000 subsidiaries and affiliates in 125 foreign countries, and more than 25,000 American firms are engaged in international marketing (Newby 193, 205).

International business is highly dependent on communication. According to Arnold LePoole, chief executive officer of Amstrand Industries, an international supplier of automotive parts:

If a company cannot communicate with its foreign subsidiaries, customers, suppliers, and governments, it cannot achieve success. The sad fact is that most American managers are not equipped to communicate with their international counterparts. (143-144)

Because excellent business communication skills are one of the most important components for success in international business affairs, a survey instrument was designed to explore the importance of, level of competence in, and methods of developing four types of international business speaking skills. The survey was sent to over 5,000 international companies with staff members located around the world. Each company was asked to share the survey with

WORKS CITED PAGE

↓1 inch   Kyslowsky 17

Works Cited

Connor, Earl. "Exploring Body Language Cues." <u>Management Today</u> June 1994: 250-261, 273.

LePoole, Arnold. <u>What American Business Can (and Must) Learn From the Japanese</u>. New York: Management Press, 1990.

Newby, Corrine J. "Global Implications for American Business: the Numbers Don't Lie." <u>Marketing Research Quarterly</u> 50 (1994): 190-215.

Roncaro, Paul L., and Glenn D. Lance. "Losing Something in the Translation." <u>Winston-Salem Herald</u> 2 June 1992: 4A+.

"Tell It Like It Is: Making Yourself Understood in the New Russia." <u>International Times</u> 19 October 1999: 38.

AGENDA

↓6x

INTERNET, INC. EXECUTIVE COMMITTEE ↓2x

Meeting Agenda ↓2x

August 7, {year}, 2 p.m. ↓2x

1. Call to order
2. Approval of minutes of July 8 meeting
3. Progress report on building addition and parking lot restrictions (Satbir Bedi and Janelle Graham)
4. May 15 draft of Five-Year Plan
5. Review of National Computer Technology annual convention
6. Employee grievance filed by Letitia Burrows (Johann Lundstrom)
7. New expense-report form (John Constantino)
8. Announcements
9. Adjournment

U

Undo A software command that reverses the last action taken.

V

Vertical Text Text that is arranged vertically on a page.

W

Widow The last line of a paragraph that is carried forward to the top of the next page.

Word Wrap The automatic wrapping of text from the end of one line to the beginning of the next line.

Worksheet A spreadsheet form that enables you to input data and formulas.

X

X-Axis A horizontal bar-chart scale that displays a range of values.

Y

Y-Axis A vertical bar-chart scale that displays a range of values.

Z

Zoom A feature used to enlarge or reduce an image on the screen.

MINUTES OF A MEETING

↓6x

RESOURCE COMMITTEE ↓2x
Minutes of the Meeting ↓2x
March 13, {year} ↓2x

ATTENDANCE ↓2x
The Resource Committee met on March 13, {year}, at the Airport Sheraton in Portland,Oregon, in conjunction with the western regional meeting. Members present were Michael Davis, Cynthia Giovanni, Don Madsen, and Edna Pointer. Michael Davis, chairperson, called the meeting to order at 2:30 p.m. ↓2x

OLD BUSINESS ↓2x
The members of the committee reviewed the sales brochure on electronic copyboards. They agreed to purchase an electronic copyboard for the conference room. Cynthia Giovanni will secure quotations from at least two vendors.

NEW BUSINESS
The committee reviewed a request from the Purchasing Department for three new computers. After extensive discussion regarding the appropriate use of the computers in the Purchasing Department and software to be purchased, the committee approved the request.

ADJOURNMENT
The meeting was adjourned at 4:45 p.m. The next meeting has been scheduled for May 4, in the headquarters conference room. Members are asked to bring with them copies of the latest resource planning document. ↓2x

Respectfully submitted, ↓4x

D. S. Madsen, Secretary

RESUME

↓center vertically

Terry M. Martina
250 Maxwell Avenue, Apt. 8
Boulder, CO 80304
303-555-9331
tmm@netex.com ↓2x

OBJECTIVE ↓2x
To obtain a position as a resort manager in Colorado. ↓2x

EDUCATION ↓2x
Edgewood Community College, Boulder, Colorado 80304
Associate of Arts degree to be awarded May 2000
Major: Hotel Administration
Overall grade point average of 3.1 (on 4.0 scale).
Received Board of Regents' tuition scholarship.

Durango High School, Durango, Colorado 81301
Graduated: May 1998

EXPERIENCE

Burger King, 4404 Foxhound Road, Boulder, Colorado 80305
Position: Assistant Manager

July 1997 to present (full-time during summers, part-time during school year)
Developed work schedules for 19 part-time employees.
Supervised employees and handled daily receipts.

Ski Valley Haven, Aspen, Colorado 81612
Position: Assistant to the Night Manager of a 200-room ski resort

September-December 1998
Gained practical experience in operating First-Guest management system.
Produced daily occupancy reports.

PERSONAL

Secretary of Hospitality Services Association
Special Olympics volunteer—summer 1998

REFERENCES

References available upon request.

APPLICATION LETTER

(For an alternate style, see pages 210–211)

↓center page

March 2, [year] ↓4x

Ms. Lauren MacMillan, Director
Human Resources Department
Wilderness Lodge
P.O. Box 214
Denver, CO 80214 ↓2x

Dear Ms. MacMillan: ↓2x

Please consider me an applicant for the position of registration clerk for Wilderness Lodge as advertised in last Sunday's *Denver Times*. ↓2x

I will receive my A.A. degree in hotel administration from Edgewood Community College in May and will be available for full-time employment immediately. In addition to extensive coursework in hospitality services and business, I've had experience in working for a ski lodge in Aspen similar to Wilderness Lodge. As a lifelong resident of Colorado and an avid skier, I understand the needs of guests and how they should be treated. I would also be able to provide your guests with any information they request.

After you have reviewed my enclosed resume, I would appreciate having an opportunity to discuss with you in person why I believe I have the right qualifications and personality to serve as your registration clerk. I can be reached at 303-555-9311 after 4 p.m. daily. ↓2x

Sincerely, ↓4x

Chris L. Katroubis
250 Maxwell Avenue, Apt. 8
Boulder, CO 83035 ↓2x

Enclosure

FOLLOW-UP LETTER

↓center vertically

tab to centerpoint   May 10, {year} ↓4x

Mr. Herbert A. Juneau
Director of personnel
Apex Products Inc.
6532 Turtle Creek Boulevard
Dallas, TX 75205 ↓2x

Dear Mr. Juneau: ↓2x

Thank you for the time you spent telling me about the billing clerk position with Apex Products. The interview you gave me yesterday definitely reaffirmed my interest in working for your company.

I was especially impressed with the Payroll Department at Apex. The people and equipment in that department make this position very appealing to me.

The combination of my bookkeeping experience and the in-house training you provide for all new employees convinces me that this position is precisely the job that I have been seeking. When you have reached your decision, I will be most eager to hear from you. If you desire a second interview, I would be available after 12 noon any weekday. ↓2x

tab to centerpoint   Sincerely yours, ↓4x

Eleanor G. Corsi
672 Wesley Street
Greenville, TX 75401

Q

Query A database feature that enables you to locate records that meet certain criteria.

R

Range A group of spreadsheet cells.

Record A group of fields that contain the data that makes up a file.

Reveal Codes A software feature available in some programs that enables you to display formatting codes on screen.

Reverse Printing A method of printing type in white or another light color on a black or dark background.

Right Justification A software feature used to align copy at the right.

Right Tab A tab stop that aligns text at the right.

Row Height The distance between the top and bottom borders of a cell.

Ruler A graphic display that can show margin settings and tab stops.

S

Scrolling The activity of moving text up and down or left and right to reveal additional copy on your screen.

Search A software feature that enables you to to look for text or formats within a document.

Search and Replace A software feature that enables you to look for text or formats and replace them with other text or formats.

Shading A software feature used to add fill to cells or boxes to add visual interest.

Soft Page Break A page break that is automatically created by the software when text is too long to fit on a page.

Sort A software feature that enables you to rearrange data in a particular order.

Special Characters Unusual characters that are not available on the regular keyboard.

Spell Check A software feature that checks the spelling of words in a document.

Spreadsheet A software program that enables you to perform various calculations on the data.

Standard Punctuation Punctuation that consists of a colon after the salutation and a comma after the complimentary close.

Status Line A line displayed at the bottom of the screen that provides the page number, section number, vertical position in inches, and line number of a document as well as the horizontal position of the insertion point.

Subscript A character that is positioned a half line below the writing line.

SUM Function A built-in spreadsheet formula that adds a range of cells.

Superscript A character that is positioned a half line above the writing line.

T

Tab Stop A set position that enables you to quickly move the insertion point to that position.

Table A grid of rows and columns that intersect to form cells into which information can be typed.

Template A predefined document format.

Text Box A created box that can contain text or art.

Text/Word Art A word processing feature used to create special effects with text.

Thesaurus A software feature that you can use to find words that are similar to words you want to replace.

BLOCK-STYLE PERSONAL LETTER

(For an alternate style, see pages 169–170)

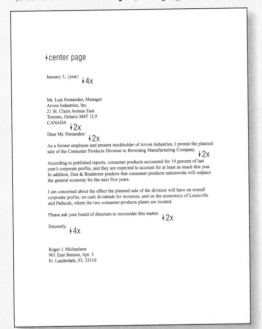

MODIFIED-BLOCK STYLE LETTER

(with subject line, enclosure notation, and copy notation)

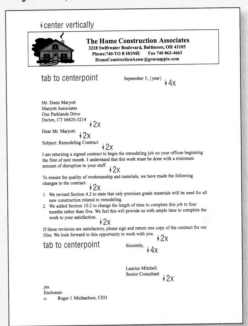

MODIFIED-BLOCK STYLE LETTER

(with open punctuation, table)

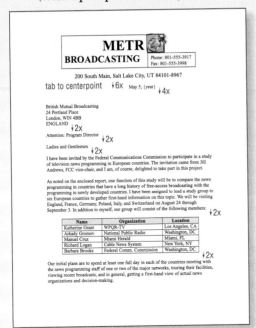

MODIFIED-BLOCK STYLE LETTER

(with enumeration, attachment, delivery notation, postscript)

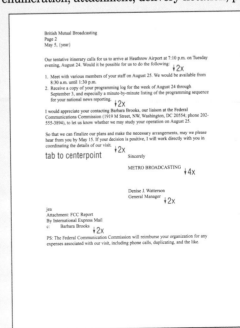

GLOSSARY *(continued)*

Insertion Point A vertical blinking bar on the computer screen that indicates where an action will begin.

Italic A special font attribute used to highlight text.

L

Landscape Page orientation in which data prints across the wider portion of the page.

Leaders A row of characters that leads the reader's eye across a page.

Left Justification A feature that aligns text at the left margin.

Left Tab A tab setting that moves the insertion point to the left when the tab key is pressed.

Letterhead Stationery that has information such as the company name, address, and telephone number printed at the top.

Line Draw A software feature that enables you to draw a variety of lines in a document.

Line Spacing A software command that enables you to set the amount of space between lines of type.

M

Mail Merge A process of combining information from two documents to produce personalized documents.

Margins The blank space at the top, bottom, left, and right sides of a document.

Military Style Date A date typed in the following sequence: day, month, and year (12 March {year}).

Modem A device that enables computers to "talk" to one another.

N

Nonprinting Character A character or symbol that appears on the screen but does not print.

O

OCR Format A format for an envelope address in which all lines are typed in all capital letters with no punctuation.

Open A software command that enables you to retrieve a file that was previously created and saved.

Open Punctuation A punctuation style for letters in which there is no colon after the salutation and no comma after the complimentary close.

Orphan A single line of a paragraph that appears at the bottom of a page.

P

Page Numbering A software command that automatically numbers the pages of a document.

Page Orientation The direction in which you can print on a page.

Password A word or series of characters that are used to limit access to files or computer systems.

Pie Chart A graphic illustration of spreadsheet data that compares the sizes of pieces to a whole.

Point Size A reference to the size of type; 72 points equal one inch.

Portrait Page orientation in which the data prints across the narrower portion of a page.

Print Preview A software feature that enables you to view an entire document before it is printed.

FORMATTING ENVELOPES

A standard large (No. 10) envelope is 9½ by 4⅛ inches. A standard small (No. 6¾) envelope is 6½ by 3⅝ inches. Although either address format shown below is acceptable, the format shown for the large envelope (all capital letters and no punctuation) is recommended by the U.S. Postal Service for mail that will be sorted by an electronic scanning device.

George Ellis
1553 Oak Lane
Muncie, IN 47302

Ms. Louise Tye
P.O. Box 770
Shreveport, LA 71101

Cape Cod Resorts
1408 Oceanside
Sandwich, MA 02563

DR MIA JENNINGS
9019 LAYTON AVENUE
LUBBOCK TX 79041-9019

FOLDING LETTERS

To fold a letter for a small envelope:

1. Place the letter *face up* and fold up the bottom half to 0.5 inch from the top edge of the paper.

2. Fold the right third over to the left.

3. Fold the left third over to 0.5 inch from the right edge of the paper.

4. Insert the last crease into the envelope first, with the flap facing up.

To fold a letter for a large envelope:

1. Place the letter *face up* and fold up the bottom third.

2. Fold the top third down to 0.5 inch from the bottom edge of the paper.

3. Insert the last crease into the envelope first, with the flap facing up.

GLOSSARY *(continued)*

F

Field A category of information in a database.

Field Name A name used to identify the contents of a field.

File A document or a collection of related records.

File Name A unique name given to a document so that it can be saved and retrieved.

Fill Shading or patterns used to fill an area. In a spreadsheet, to enter common or repetitive values into a group of cells.

Fill Handle The small box in the lower right corner of an active spreadsheet cell that can be dragged to create the desired fill.

Filtering The process of finding and selecting information from a database.

Find and Replace A software command that enables you to search for and replace specific text, formatting commands, or special attributes.

Flush Right Alignment of text at the right margin.

Font A set of type characters of a particular design and size.

Footers Repetitive information or text that is repeated at the bottom of a page throughout a section or a document.

Footnote Feature A software feature that automatically positions reference notations at the bottom of the page on which the footnote number appears.

Form File The main document or form letter to which variable information must be added.

Formula A mathematical expression that solves a problem (for example, adding, subtracting, multiplying, dividing, or averaging).

Full Justification An alignment feature that aligns text at the left and right margins by adding space between characters.

Function Keys Special keys located at the top of the keyboard (F1, F2, F3, etc.) that are used alone or with the Ctrl, Alt, and Shift keys to execute software commands.

G

Graphics Pictures, clip art, bar graphs, pie charts, or other images available on or created on a computer.

Gridlines The lines appearing around the cells in a table.

H

Hanging Indent A temporary left margin that indents all lines but the first line of the text.

Hard Page Break A manually inserted page break that does not change regardless of the changes made within the document.

Hard Return A code entered into a document by pressing the ENTER key that indicates the end of a paragraph or section.

Header Repetitive information or text that is repeated at the top of each page of a section or a document.

Help On-screen information about how to use a program and its features.

I

Indent A temporary left margin that is used to align text at a set position to the right of the margin.

Insert A software command that enables you to add text, page and column breaks, graphics, tables, charts, cells, rows, columns, formulas, dates, time, fields, and so on, to a document.

Insertion Mode An input mode in which the existing text moves to the right as new text is added.

MEMO (TEMPLATE)

Memorandum

To: Elizabeth Barnett
From: Catherine Argetes
Date: Current
Re: Flexible Scheduling

Several of our employees who have certain family obligations have asked us to explore the possibility of flexible scheduling. These staff members feel that a flexible schedule will help to increase morale and productivity and reduce absenteeism and turnover.

We are now considering several options, which include flextime, job sharing, and compressed workweeks.

Flextime is the most popular option. Employees would work a set number of hours per day with flexible start and finish times. However, employees would be required to be on the job during particular hours of the day.

Job sharing involves two employees sharing the same job. The employees might have divided job responsibilities, or they might have totally unrelated responsibilities. The two employees involved in sharing a job would need to work out the hours that each would work so that we have full coverage of the position at all times.

Compressed workweeks are those in which employees work the same number of total hours, but they do so over a shorter number of days. Using a compressed workweek would enable us to extend our business hours and provide employees with an opportunity to handle their personal obligations during the week.

I have attached more complete descriptions for your review and will schedule a meeting before the end of the month to discuss all of these options with you.

urs
Attachment

CONFIDENTIAL

1

OPEN TABLE

(with blocked column heads)

↓center page

SALES ANALYSIS
Borden Manufacturing Company
June 30, (year) ↓1X

Salesperson	Units	Gross Sales ($)
Brazinski, Robert	10	427.70
Dawkins, Carol	18	769.86
Greene, Janice	20	855.40
Herrera, Jose	17	727.09
Kessler, Diane	15	641.55
Yeung, Joe	19	812.63

BOXED TABLE

(with centered column heads)

↓center page

SALES ANALYSIS				
Borden Manufacturing Company				
June 30, (year) ↓1X				
	1st Quarter		2nd Quarter	
Salesperson	Units	Gross Sales ($)	Units	Gross Sales ($)
Brazinski, Robert	10	427.70	29	1,240.33
Dawkins, Carol	18	769.86	17	727.09
Greene, Janice	20	855.40	28	1,197.56
Herrera, Jose	17	727.09	24	1,026.48
Kessler, Diane	15	641.55	25	1,069.25
Yeung, Joe	19	812.63	32	1,368.64
TOTAL	99	4,234.23	155	6,629.35

BOXED TABLE

(with multi-line heads, footnote)

↓center page

RETIREMENT CALCULATION*				
↓1X Age	↓1X Annual Salary	1-Percent of Earnings ($)	↓1X Year	Annual Benefit Times Years
35-39	$15,000	$150	5	$750.00
40-49	$20,000	$200	10	$2,000.00
50-59	$30,000	$300	10	$3,000.00
60-64	$50,000	$500	5	$2,500.00
Annual Retirement Payment				$8,250.00
*Based on joining the plan at age 35.				

GLOSSARY

A

Alignment The horizontal positioning (such as left, right, or center) of text.

Anchor A home-key position that helps bring each finger back to its home-key position. Also indicates what a text box is attached (anchored) to.

Ascending Sort A sort of data in alphabetical (A-Z) order or numerical (0-9) order.

AVERAGE A built-in spreadsheet formula that adds and divides numbers.

B

Bar Chart A graphic illustration of spreadsheet data.

Bibliography An alphabetical listing of all the books and articles consulted by the author of a report.

Bold A print enhancement used to make characters appear darker than other text to add emphasis.

Bullets and Numbering A word processing feature used to arrange items in a list with each item beginning with a bullet or a number.

Byline The name of the author of a report typed a double space below the title.

C

Cell The box formed at the intersection of a row and a column.

Center Justification An alignment feature that centers text between margins.

Center Page A software command that automatically centers copy vertically on a page.

Center Tab A type of tab used to horizontally center text at a particular position on a line.

Clip Art Graphic images that can be inserted into documents.

Close File A software command that enables you to exit the current document without exiting from the program.

Columns Information arranged vertically.

Constants Unchanging values that are used in formulas.

Cut/Copy/Paste A feature that enables you to move or copy text from one place to another.

D

Data File or Data Source The document that contains the variable information, such as name and address, used to personalize a form document.

Database A software program used to organize, find, and display information.

Date Insert A software feature that enables you to insert the current date into a document.

Decimal Tab A tab setting used to align a column of numbers at the decimal point.

Default Settings Settings that are preset by the software and that remain in effect until the user changes them.

Descending Sort A sort of data in descending alphabetical (Z-A) or numerical (9-0) order.

Desktop Publishing Special software or software features that enable you to design and create documents such as newsletters, flyers, and brochures.

Dot Leader Tab A tab setting that inserts leaders (a line of dots or other characters) between one column and another.

Drop Cap A large first letter that drops below the regular text.

BOXED TABLE

(with shading)

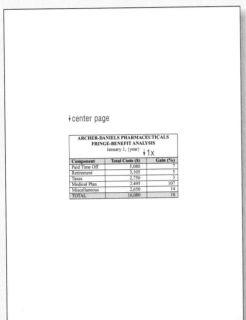

RULED TABLE

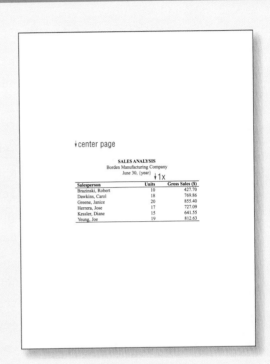

PROOFREADERS' MARKS

Proofreaders' Marks	Draft	Final Copy
⌒ Omit space	data base	database
∨ or ∧ Insert	if he's not going,	if he's not going,
≡ Capitalize	Maple street	Maple Street
⋏ Delete	a final draft	a draft
# Insert space	allready to	all ready to
when Change word	and if you	and when you
/ Use lowercase letter	our President	our president
¶ Paragraph	¶ Most of the	Most of the
⋯ Don't delete	a true story	a true story
○ Spell out	the only ①	the only one
∽ Transpose	they all see	they see all

Proofreaders' Marks	Draft	Final Copy
SS Single-space	first line / second line	first line / second line
ds Double-space	first line / second line	first line / second line
Move right	Please send	Please send
Move left	May I	May I
∿ Bold	Column Heading	**Column Heading**
ital Italic	*Time* magazine	*Time* magazine
u/l Underline	Time magazine	Time magazine readers
☌ Move as shown	readers will see	will see

1	Some specialists who work in memory training tell us	11
2	to think of memory as something we can control through the	23
3	use of strategies and organization. If you are trying to	34
4	remember a new name, spend a few seconds creating a mental	46
5	image to go along with the name. For example, to remember	57
6	the name Morehouse, you could make a mental image of a	68
7	person standing by a growing house. If you often misplace	80
8	your keys or your glasses, you could keep these objects in	92
9	one specific location. Then, make a conscious effort to	103
10	return them to the same spot each time you have finished	114
11	using them.	117
12	Anxiety is the number one cause of slips of memory.	127
13	There are several strategies that can help with recall.	139
14	You can reduce anxiety block by not drawing attention to	150
15	it. For example, if a word is at the tip of your tongue,	161
16	keep talking while the brain keeps searching for it. A	172
17	helpful way to remember numbers is by connecting them to	184
18	a phrase, such as the old adage about Columbus sailing	195
19	the ocean blue in fourteen hundred and ninety-two. You	206
20	can also try to remember numbers by connecting them with a	218
21	birthday or by making number patterns. Another approach to	229
22	improve memory could be aerobic exercising, which speeds	241
23	blood to the brain and sharpens memory performance.	251

| 1 | 2 | 3 | 4 | 5 | 6 | 7 | 8 | 9 | 10 | 11 | 12 |

REFERENCE SECTION *(continued)*

LANGUAGE LINKS

ALWAYS SPACE ONCE...

- After a comma.
  We ordered two printers, one computer, and three monitors.

- After a semicolon.
  They flew to Dallas, Texas; Reno, Nevada; and Rome, New York.

- After a period following someone's initials.
  Mr. A. Henson, Ms. C. Hovey, and Mrs. M. Syzmanski will attend the meeting.

- After a period following the abbreviation of a single word.
  We will send the package by 7 p.m. next week. [Note: space once after the final period in the "p.m." abbreviation, but do not space after the first period between the two letters.]

- Before a ZIP code.
  Send the package to 892 Maple Street, Grand Forks, ND 58201.

- Before and after an ampersand.
  We were represented by the law firm of Argue & Johnson; they were represented by the law firm of Crandall & Humphries.

- After a period at the end of a sentence.
  Don't forget to vote. Vote for the candidate of your choice.

- After a question mark.
  When will you vote? Did you vote last year?

- After an exclamation point.
  Wow! What a performance! It was fantastic!

- After a colon.
  We will attend on the following days: Monday, Wednesday, and Friday.

1 Do you live beyond your means? Are your expenses more 11
2 than your income? Do you borrow money to pay off debts? 22
3 If you do, you are in the best of company. Our government 34
4 consistently operates on a deficit. In fact, it runs two 45
5 different deficits: one with its citizens, and the other 57
6 with the rest of the world. Some economists feel these 68
7 two deficits are related because if one of them were not 79
8 so large, the other would not be as large either. 89

9 Is all debt bad? No, deficit spending, within reason, 100
10 is healthy. It fuels the economy. When you buy a new car 111
11 on credit, you support the autoworkers. A problem arises 123
12 when the government has to borrow money to spend beyond its 135
13 means. It borrows from its citizens—you and me. It also 146
14 borrows from foreigners. Foreign countries purchase our 157
15 treasury debt. These investors want to be properly 168
16 compensated for assuming the debt. The almost daily 178
17 borrowing that the government has to do often overwhelms 189
18 credit markets. This keeps interest rates high, which 200
19 creates an appealing investment. 207

20 Government debt is a bit like individual debt. The 217
21 difference is that the government debt is much larger. 228
22 The moral of this story is that a little debt is okay, 239
23 but a lot of debt can get you into big trouble. 249

| 1 | 2 | 3 | 4 | 5 | 6 | 7 | 8 | 9 | 10 | 11 | 12 |

COMMAS:

1. Use a comma between independent clauses joined by a conjunction. (An independent clause is one that can stand alone as a complete sentence.)
We requested Brown Industries to change the date, and they did so within five days.

2. Use a comma after an introductory expression (unless it is a short prepositional phrase).
Before we can make a decision, we must have all the facts.
In 1992 our nation elected a president.

3. Use a comma before and after the year in a complete date.
We will arrive at the plant on June 2, 2003, for the conference.

4. Use a comma before and after a state or country that follows a city (but not before a ZIP Code).
Joan moved to Vancouver, British Columbia, in September.
Send the package to Douglasville, GA 30135, by express mail.

5. Use a comma between each item in a series of three or more.
We need to order paper, toner, and font cartridges.

6. Use a comma before and after a transitional expression (such as *therefore* and *however*).
It is critical, therefore, that we finish the project on time.

7. Use a comma before and after a direct quotation.
When we left, James said, "Let us return to the same location next year."

8. Use a comma before and after a nonessential expression. (A nonessential expression is a word or group of words that may be omitted without changing the basic meaning of the sentence.)
Let me say, to begin with, that the report has already been finalized.

9. Use a comma between two adjacent adjectives that modify the same noun.
We need an intelligent, enthusiastic individual for this job.

SEMICOLONS:

1. Use a semicolon to join two closely related independent clauses that are not connected by a conjunction (such as *and, but,* or *nor*).
Management favored the vote; stockholders did not.

2. Use a semicolon to separate three or more items in a series if any of the items already contain commas.
Region 1 sent their reports in March, April, and May; and Region 2 sent their reports in September, October, and November.

1 Taking tests can be an ordeal. Even for students   10
2 who are fully prepared and aware of the teacher's goals,   21
3 testing can be stressful. They can become victim to test   33
4 anxiety. It is perfectly natural for people to feel some   44
5 anxiety when confronted with a test. Anxiety can work as   56
6 a positive motivational factor at times. It can improve   67
7 your concentration, encourage you to do well, and sharpen   78
8 your performance. However, if it does cause stress, try   90
9 to rid yourself of sweaty palms, the fear of failure, and 101
10 the knot in your stomach.   106

11 It might help to realize that most teachers want   116
12 their students to do well on tests. They might discuss a   128
13 test ahead of time. Pay attention to these discussions.   139
14 There are strategies you can use to help reduce anxiety   150
15 in a test situation. You might use relaxation techniques   162
16 before and during a test when you feel yourself becoming   173
17 anxious. You could visualize yourself as being successful 185
18 and keep a confident attitude during the test. You could   196
19 remind yourself that the test is not a life-threatening   207
20 situation and you can survive it. You need to recognize   218
21 that the test is important, but you might ask yourself   229
22 just how much of an effect it will have on your life five 241
23 years from now.   244

| 1 | 2 | 3 | 4 | 5 | 6 | 7 | 8 | 9 | 10 | 11 | 12 |

HYPHENS:

1. Hyphenate compound adjectives that come before a noun (unless the first word is an adverb ending in *-ly*).

We reviewed an up-to-date report on Wednesday.

We attended a highly rated session on multimedia software.

2. Hyphenate compound numbers (between twenty-one and ninety-nine) and fractions that are expressed as words.

We observed twenty-nine infractions during the investigation.

Bancroft Industries reduced their sales force by one-third.

3. Hyphenate words that are divided at the end of a line. Do not divide one-syllable words, contractions, or abbreviations; divide other words only between syllables.

To appreciate the full significance of our actions, you must review the entire document that was sent to you.

APOSTROPHES:

1. Use *'s* to form the possessive of singular nouns.

The hurricane caused major damage to Georgia's coastline.

2. Use only an apostrophe to form the possessive of plural nouns that end in *s*.

The investors' goals were outlined in the annual report.

3. Use *'s* to form the possessive of indefinite pronouns (such as *someone's* or *anybody's*); do not use an apostrophe with personal pronouns (such as *hers, his, its, ours, theirs,* and *yours*).

She was instructed to select anybody's paper for a sample.

Each computer comes carefully packed in its own container.

COLONS:

Use a colon to introduce explanatory material that follows an independent clause. (An independent clause is one that can stand alone as a complete sentence.)

The computer satisfies three criteria: speed, cost, and power.

DASHES:

Use a dash instead of a comma, semicolon, colon, or parenthesis when you want to convey a more forceful separation of words within a sentence. (If your keyboard has a special dash character, use it. Otherwise, form a dash by typing two hyphens, with no space before, between, or after.)

At this year's meeting, the speakers—and topics—were superb.

PERIODS:

Use a period to end a sentence that is a polite request. (Consider a sentence a polite request if you expect the reader to respond by doing as you ask rather than by giving a yes-or-no answer.)

Will you please call me if I can be of further assistance.

TIMING 16

1	Although heavy campaigning for a number of months	10
2	now leads up to a national convention for both parties,	21
3	this was not practiced in the early days of elections in	33
4	our country. Originally, candidates were selected by the	44
5	members of their party congress. Selecting candidates in	56
6	this manner is called the caucus method. Caucusing was	67
7	later dropped, and nominations were made informally at	78
8	meetings by state officials.	83
9	When the national convention process started, it	93
10	brought more national participation into the selection	104
11	process. When the first television camera was used, the	116
12	exposure increased even more. More citizens began to get	127
13	actively involved in politics. The use of the camera made	139
14	it seem as though they were at the convention. It has been	150
15	judged that over seventy million people watched during	161
16	the early years when conventions were televised. Today,	173
17	most Americans have watched at least one convention.	183
18	The expense of a national convention is quite high.	194
19	Citizens who are delegates feel that their participation	205
20	is worth whatever it costs to go. The parties do not pay	217
21	for television time. Sponsors pay for the commercials, and	228
22	any difference is paid for by the media itself.	238

| 1 | 2 | 3 | 4 | 5 | 6 | 7 | 8 | 9 | 10 | 11 | 12 |

QUOTATION MARKS:

1. Use quotation marks around the titles of newspaper articles, magazine articles, chapters in a book, reports, conferences, and similar items.
The best article I found in my research was entitled "Multimedia for Everyone."

2. Use quotation marks around a direct quotation.
Harrison responded by saying, "This decision will not affect our merger."

ITALIC (OR UNDERLINE):

Italicize (or underline) the titles of books, magazines, newspapers, and other complete published works.
I read The Pelican Brief *last month. I read* <u>The Pelican Brief</u> *last month.*

GRAMMAR

AGREEMENT:

1. Use singular verbs and pronouns with singular subjects and plural verbs and pronouns with plural subjects.
I was pleased with the performance of our team.
Reno and Phoenix were selected as the sites for our next two meetings.

2. Some pronouns (*anybody, each, either, everybody, everyone, much, neither, no one, nobody,* and *one*) are always singular and take a singular verb. Other pronouns (*all, any, more, most, none,* and *some*) may be singular or plural, depending on the noun to which they refer.
Each employee is responsible for summarizing the day's activities.
Most of the workers are going to get a substantial pay raise.

3. Disregard any intervening words that come between the subject and verb when establishing agreement.
The box containing the books and pencils has not been found.

4. If two subjects are joined by *or, either/or, nor, neither/nor,* or *not only/but also,* the verb should agree with the subject nearer to the verb.
Neither the players nor the coach is in favor of the decision.

5. The subject *a number* takes a plural verb; *the number* takes a singular verb.
The number of new students has increased to six.
We know that a number of students are in sports.

6. Subjects joined by *and* take a plural verb unless the compound subject is preceded by *each, every,* or *many a (an).*
Every man, woman, and child is included in our survey.

7. Verbs that refer to conditions that are impossible or improbable (that is, verbs in the *subjunctive* mood) require the plural form.
If the total eclipse were to occur tomorrow, it would be the second one this year.

TIMING 15

1	Before the middle of the twentieth century, workers	11
2	were treated as just another element of the production	22
3	process. Men and women worked under dismal conditions.	33
4	Most of the time, they were required to work twelve to	44
5	sixteen hours a day and the work week was six days long.	55
6	Wages were low. Health and safety hazards were ignored by	67
7	employers. If the employer provided any fringe benefits,	78
8	they were meager. Even though workers were exploited, they	90
9	were grateful to have a job. Over time, working conditions	102
10	and the treatment of workers have improved.	110
12	Effective management is a focus in today's work world.	122
12	A scientific approach in the management of employees may	133
13	be used. The scientific management tool allows managers	144
14	to motivate workers by offering a pay incentive to improve	156
15	both the quality and quantity of the product workers	167
16	produced. For example, if a project generally took an	177
17	employee ten minutes to do, a wage incentive plan would	189
18	pay a bonus for work completed in less than ten minutes.	200
19	Management has learned that workers produce more and better	212
20	products when their working conditions are improved, and	223
21	wage incentives are provided.	229

| 1 | 2 | 3 | 4 | 5 | 6 | 7 | 8 | 9 | 10 | 11 | 12 |

REFERENCE SECTION *(continued)*

PRONOUNS:

1. Use nominative pronouns (such as *I, he, she, we,* and *they*) as subjects of a sentence or clause.
They traveled to Minnesota last week but will not return until next month.

2. Use objective pronouns (such as *me, him, her, us,* and *them*) as objects in a sentence or clause.
The package has been sent to her.

ADJECTIVES AND ADVERBS:

1. Use comparative adjectives and adverbs (*-er, more,* and *less*) when referring to two nouns; use superlative adjectives and adverbs (*-est, most,* and *least*) when referring to more than two.
Of the two movies you have selected, the shorter one is the more interesting.
The highest of the three mountains is Mt. Everest.

WORD USAGE:

1. Do not confuse the following pairs of words:

- *Accept* means "to agree to"; *except* means "to leave out."
*We **accept** your offer for developing the new product.*
*Everyone **except** Sam and Lisa attended the meeting.*

- *Affect* is most often used as a verb meaning "to influence"; *effect* is most often used as a noun meaning "result."
*Mr. Smith's decision will not **affect** our programming plans.*
*It will be weeks before we can assess the **effect** of this action.*

- *Farther* refers to distance; *further* refers to extent or degree.
*Did we travel **farther** today than yesterday?*
*We need to discuss our plans **further**.*

- *Personal* means "private"; *personnel* means "employees."
*The letters were very **personal** and should not have been read.*
*We hope that all **personnel** will comply with the new regulations.*

- *Principal* means "primary"; *principle* means "rule."
*The **principal** means of research were interviewing and surveying.*
*They must not violate the **principles** under which our company was established.*

- *Passed* means "went by"; *past* means "before now."
*We **passed** another car from our home state.*
*In the **past**, we always took the same route.*

- *Advice* means "to provide guidance"; *advise* means "help."
*The **advice** I gave her was simple.*
*I **advise** you to finish your project.*

- *Council* is a group; *counsel* is a person who provides advice.
*The student **council** met to discuss graduation.*
*The court asked that **counsel** be present at the hearing.*

SKILLBUILDING (continued)

1   The Hawaiian Islands have much to offer the tourist.   11
2   One attraction is the beautiful parks. The flora, fauna,   22
3   and buildings are protected by federal law. Hawaii's state   34
4   bird, the nene, is endangered. When visitors feed these   45
5   birds, they attract them to parking lots and roadsides.   56
6   This places the birds in danger from auto traffic that   67
7   might injure or kill them. Visitors should avoid feeding   79
8   the birds or animals found in state parks.   87

9   The volcanoes of the Hawaiian Islands add mystery   97
10 and exotic scenery. A wonderful way to observe the raw   108
11 power of a volcano is by taking a helicopter tour. The   119
12 helicopter is well-suited for the air maneuvers needed   130
13 to get a close view. The pilot usually flies over areas   142
14 with the most volcanic activity. They often dip low over   153
15 lava pools, skim still-glowing flows, and circle towering   165
16 steam clouds rising from where the lava enters the sea.   176
17 You might like to spend a full day at Kilauea enjoying   187
18 the sights. Atop Kilauea, you can quietly appreciate the   198
19 beauty of this impressive volcano. It is four thousand   209
20 feet above sea level and about ten degrees cooler than   220
21 the coast.   222

| 1 | 2 | 3 | 4 | 5 | 6 | 7 | 8 | 9 | 10 | 11 | 12 |

- *Then* means "at that time"; *than* is used for comparisons.
  *He read for a while; **then** he turned out the light.*
  *She reads more books **than** I do.*

- *Its* is the possessive form of it; *it's* is a contraction for it is.
  *We researched the country and **its** people.*
  ***It's** not too late to finish the project.*

- *Two* means "one more than one"; *too* means "also"; *to* means "in a direction."
  *There were **two** people in the boat.*
  *We wished we were on board, **too**.*
  *The boat headed out **to** sea.*

- *Stationery* means "paper"; *stationary* means "fixed position."
  *Please buy some **stationery** so that I can write letters.*
  *The **stationary** bike at the health club provides a good workout.*

MECHANICS

CAPITALIZATION:

1. Capitalize the first word of a sentence.
Please prepare a summary of your activities for our next meeting.

2. Capitalize proper nouns and adjectives derived from proper nouns. (A proper noun is the official name of a particular person, place, or thing.)
Judy Hendrix drove to Albuquerque in her new automobile, a Pontiac.

3. Capitalize the names of the days of the week, months, holidays, and religious days (but do not capitalize the names of the seasons).
On Thursday, November 25, we will celebrate Thanksgiving, the most popular fall holiday.

4. Capitalize nouns followed by a number or letter (except for the nouns *line, note, page, paragraph,* and *size*).
Please read Chapter 5, but not page 94.

5. Capitalize compass points (such as *north, south,* or *northeast*) only when they designate definite regions.
The Crenshaws will vacation in the Northeast this summer.
We will have to drive north to reach the closest Canadian border.

6. Capitalize common organizational terms (such as *advertising department* and *finance committee*) when they are the actual names of the units in the writer's own organization and when they are preceded by the word *the*.
The quarterly report from the Advertising Department will be presented today.

7. Capitalize the names of specific course titles but not the names of subjects or areas of study.
I have enrolled in Accounting 201 and will also take a marketing course.

SKILLBUILDING *(continued)*

1   It is quite possible that Ellis Island is part of   10
2 your family history. For many years, Ellis Island was an   22
3 immigration station. In the early part of the twentieth   33
4 century, it served as the main gateway to our country.   44
5 Twelve million foreigners had passed through its doors by   55
6 the middle of the twentieth century, when it closed. Ships   67
7 unloaded their passengers at the docks in New York. Then,   79
8 passengers quickly transferred to boats and barges for the   91
9 the trip to Ellis Island in New York Harbor. It was the   102
10 first place many of our forebears saw when they arrived   113
11 in America.   115
12   This country is made up of immigrants, along with   126
13 native American Indians. An immigrant is someone who moves   137
14 from one country to another. The immigrant usually plans   149
15 to make the new country home. Millions of Americans can   160
16 trace their family history to one or more ancestors who   171
17 first arrived in the United States through Ellis Island.   183
18 Today, it is a museum. Millions of dollars were raised to   194
19 fix up the neglected building. The museum is located only   206
20 one mile from New York City and a few hundred yards from   217
21 the docks of New Jersey.   222

| 1 | 2 | 3 | 4 | 5 | 6 | 7 | 8 | 9 | 10 | 11 | 12 |

NUMBER EXPRESSION:

1. In general, spell out numbers 1 through 10, and use figures for numbers above 10.

We have rented two movies for tonight.

The decision was reached after 27 precincts had sent in their results.

2. Use figures for:
- Dates (use *st, d,* or *th* only if the day precedes the month).

  We will drive to the camp on the 23d of May.

  The tax report is due on April 15.

- All numbers if two or more related numbers both above and below ten are used in the same sentence.

  Mr. Carter sent in 7 receipts; Ms. Cantrell sent in 22 receipts.

- Measurements (time, money, distance, weight, and percentage).

  At 10 a.m. we delivered the $500 coin bank in a 17-pound container.

- Mixed numbers.

  Our sales are up 9½ percent over last year.

3. Spell out:
- Numbers used as the first word in a sentence.

  Seventy people attended the conference in San Diego last week.

- The smaller of two adjacent numbers.

  We have ordered two 5-pound packages for the meeting.

- The words *millions* and *billions* in even amounts (do not use decimals with even amounts).

  The lottery is worth 28 million this month.

- Fractions.

  About one-half of the audience responded to the questionnaire.

ABBREVIATIONS:

1. In nontechnical writing, do not abbreviate common nouns (such as *dept.* or *pkg.*), compass points, units of measure, or the names of months, days of the week, cities, or states (except in addresses).

The Sales Department will meet on Tuesday, March 7, in Tempe, Arizona.

2. In lowercase abbreviations made up of single initials, use a period after each initial but no internal spaces.

We will be including several states (e.g., Maine, New Hampshire, Vermont, Massachusetts, and Connecticut).

3. In all-capital abbreviations made up of single initials, do not use periods or internal spaces. (Exception: Keep the periods in most academic degrees and in abbreviations of geographic names other than two-letter state abbreviations.)

You need to call the EEO office for clarification on that issue.

1   Productivity measurement techniques are often used   10
2 in word processing installations today to evaluate the   21
3 output that is produced. This technique allows management   33
4 to compare workloads in order to improve scheduling and   44
5 work dispersal.   47

6   Productivity measurement also can help a company   57
7 by recording, calculating, and tracking employee production   69
8 over a period of time. Supervisors are then able to create   81
9 performance standards designed for their organization.   92
10 This method of measurement can be used to assist managers   104
11 in making reliable decisions regarding salary increases   115
12 and promotion of word processing personnel.   124

13   A measure of production might also assist those   134
14 who are more capable in a variety of ways. For example,   145
15 when compared to their peers, their abilities and skills   156
16 will be highlighted. Using this particular technique, all   168
17 the employees can be evaluated on a parallel basis. Very   179
18 talented workers can be rewarded. Lastly, this measurement   191
19 technique can assist in removing the subjectivity that is   203
20 found in company measurement systems that are used for   214
21 employee evaluations.   218

| 1 | 2 | 3 | 4 | 5 | 6 | 7 | 8 | 9 | 10 | 11 | 12 |

UNIT 1

LESSONS 1–20

KEYBOARDING

OBJECTIVES

- Demonstrate which fingers control each key on the keyboard.

- Use home key anchors to assist in developing location security.

- Develop and practice correct keyboarding techniques.

- Type at a speed of 25 words a minute for 1 minute with 2 or fewer errors.

- Use proper spacing after common marks of punctuation.

- Compose single word responses at the keyboard.

1	If you love mystery, you will be intrigued by the	10
2	speculation over how plants and animals first arrived in	22
3	Hawaii. Most people's ideas of a Hawaiian paradise include	33
4	swaying palms, dense jungles, and luscious fruit ready to	45
5	be picked. For millions of years, the chain of Hawaiian	56
6	Islands were raw and barren places where there were no	67
7	plants or birds. These lush Pacific Ocean islands are a	78
8	geological mystery. They formed spontaneously more than	90
9	two thousand miles from any continental land. They were	101
10	isolated from the normal spread of plants and animals.	112
11	The flora and fauna that did reach them found a foreign	123
12	ecosystem. They had to adapt or perish. Many of the birds	135
13	and plants became so specialized that they were not only	146
14	limited to specific islands but also to single isolated	157
15	island valleys. It was fortunate that the soil was rich.	169
16	There were no other plants or animals with which to	179
17	compete. The climate was variable and nearly perfect for	190
18	most growing things. The evolution of the plants and	201
19	animals on these isolated islands appears to have evolved	213
20	very quickly.	215

| 1 | 2 | 3 | 4 | 5 | 6 | 7 | 8 | 9 | 10 | 11 | 12 |

WORDS TO LEARN

cursor   insertion point   word scale   word wrap
default   technique   word count

CAREER BIT

NURSING   Many modern hospitals use computers to store medical records of their patients. Information from each patient's medical chart is entered into a computer file. Nurses update this file every time they give medications or check the patient's blood pressure, pulse rate, temperature, and overall progress.

When nurses change shifts, they need only to have a quick briefing because the essential information about the patient's care is already on the computer.

SKILLBUILDING (continued)

1 If you are not a classical music fan and do not   10
2 often go to the theater, you probably think, as do most 21
3 concert goers, that music before Bach is a mystery. Many 32
4 music fans think of classical music as intensely lyrical, 44
5 with madrigals and dances that are accompanied by various 56
6 horns, bells, drums, violins, and other instruments. But, 67
7 music and opera have been performed and listened to for 78
8 almost five centuries. One way to approach this music is 90
9 to just relax and enjoy its strangeness. While you are   101
10 listening, make a mental note of what sounds are pleasing 112
11 to your ear and what sounds seem like irradiating noise. 124
12 You can train your ear to pick up the music of the violin, 136
13 cello, trumpet, clarinet, harp, piano, piccolo, xylophone, 147
14 tuba, and even the flute. Melodies played as intended by 159
15 the composer may sound quite odd to the untrained ears   170
16 of today's listeners. One reason for this might be that 181
17 the tuning of instruments has changed. Also, the listeners 193
18 of the fifteenth century most likely had their own ideas 204
19 of what constituted harmony and enjoyable music.   214

| 1 | 2 | 3 | 4 | 5 | 6 | 7 | 8 | 9 | 10 | 11 | 12 |

LESSON 1

NEW KEYS: A S D F J K L ; SPACE BAR ENTER

OBJECTIVE:

- Learn the home keys, the space bar, and the ENTER key.

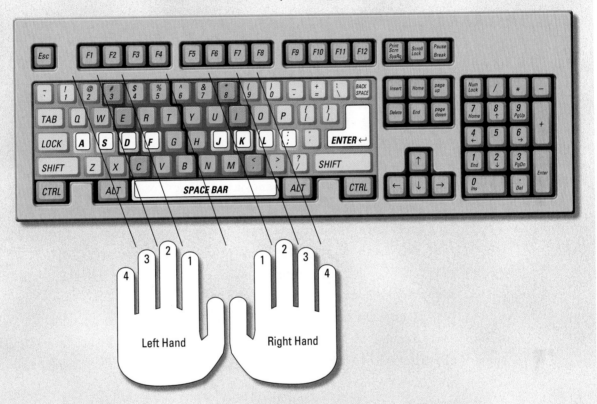

NEW KEYS

A. HOME-KEY POSITION

The A S D F J K L ; keys are called the home keys. Each finger controls a specific key and is named for its home key: A finger, S finger, D finger, and so on, ending with the Sem finger on the ; (semicolon) key.

1. Place the fingers of your left hand on A S D and F. Use the illustration as a guide.
2. Place the fingers of your right hand on J K L ;. Again, use the illustration as a guide.

1	One of the many unique features of a democracy is	10
2	that everyone of legal age has the right to vote. Voting	22
3	should be taken seriously because it is a responsibility.	33
4	It is obvious that a government will not be representative	45
5	if citizens do not take an active part in choosing the	56
6	people to represent them. It is easy to be critical of our	68
7	leaders, but some of the blame rests with those who do not	80
8	care enough about our country to vote.	87
9	Citizens can vote for many levels of government.	97
10	Federal, state, county, and city elections must be planned	109
11	for every year in which the terms of officials have ended.	121
12	Primaries are held to narrow the number of candidates. The	133
13	year in which a president is chosen can create a lot of	144
14	excitement, but citizens should be interested in and vote	156
15	for their choice in each election.	163
16	A good voter should pay careful attention to the	173
17	main issues and the candidates. Newspapers, public debates,	185
18	and interviews are good sources of information. Choose the	196
19	officials who share your views and are qualified to do	207
20	the job.	209

| 1 | 2 | 3 | 4 | 5 | 6 | 7 | 8 | 9 | 10 | 11 | 12 |

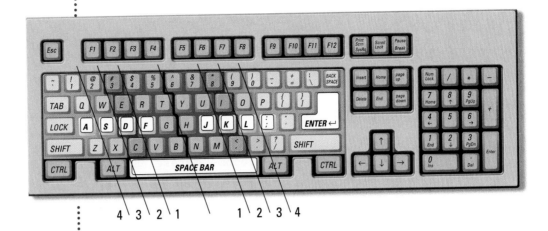

You will feel a raised marker on the F and J keys. These markers will help you keep your fingers on the home keys.

3. Curve your fingers.
4. Using the correct fingers, type each letter as you say it to yourself: a s d f j k l ;.
5. Remove your fingers from the keyboard and replace them on the home keys.
6. Type each letter again as you say it:
   a s d f j k l ;.

B. USING ANCHORS

An anchor is a home key that helps you return each finger to its home-key position after reaching for another key. Try to hold the anchors listed, but be sure to hold the first one, which is most important.

C. SPACE BAR

The space bar, located at the bottom of the keyboard, is used to insert spaces between letters and words, and after punctuation. Use the thumb of your writing hand (left or right) to press the space bar.

1. With your fingers on the home keys, type the letters a s d f. Then press the space bar once.
2. Type j k l ;. Press the space bar once.
3. Type a s d f. Press the space bar once; then type j k l ;.
4. Repeat Steps 1-3.

1 Genealogy has become a fascinating science to some 10
2 people. You do not need to be a scientist to get involved 22
3 in genealogy. You do not even need a college degree to 33
4 trace your roots. There was a time when you might have 44
5 wanted to trace your family tree to prove that one or more 56
6 of your ancestors came over from Europe on the Mayflower. 67
7 But, today we trace our roots as expressions of personal 79
8 and cultural pride and identity, no matter how humble a 90
9 person's origins might be. 95

10 There are genealogical societies throughout the 105
11 country. It seems we all want to know where we came from 117
12 and how we arrived here. Genealogy can be a complex field. 128
13 It can encompass religion, demographics, geography, legal 140
14 history, ethnic and women's studies, photographic imaging 152
15 and library research. But, getting started at tracing your 163
16 roots does not have to be complicated. You simply start 175
17 with what you know and then move toward the unknown. The 186
18 library at your school or in your city can help you get 197
19 started with your research. 203

| 1 | 2 | 3 | 4 | 5 | 6 | 7 | 8 | 9 | 10 | 11 | 12 |

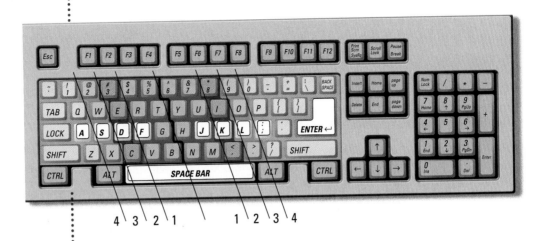

4   3   2   1   1   2   3   4

D.   ENTER KEY

The ENTER key moves the insertion point to the beginning of a new line. Reach to the ENTER key with the Sem finger. Lightly press the ENTER key. Return the Sem finger to home position.

Practice using the ENTER key. Type each line 1 time, pressing the space bar where you see a space and pressing the ENTER key at the end of a line.

```
asdf jkl; asdf jkl; asdf jkl;↵
asdf jkl; asdf jkl; asdf jkl;↵
asdf jkl; asdf jkl; asdf jkl;↵
asdf jkl; asdf jkl; asdf jkl;↵
```

E.    KEYS

Type each line 1 time.

Use F and J fingers.
```
1 fff jjj fff jjj fff jjj ff jj ff jj f j↵
2 fff jjj fff jjj fff jjj ff jj ff jj f j↵
```

F.    KEYS

Type each line 1 time.

Use D and K fingers.
```
3 ddd kkk ddd kkk ddd kkk dd kk dd kk d k↵
4 ddd kkk ddd kkk ddd kkk dd kk dd kk d k↵
```

1	Did you ever look up at the sky during the night and	11
2	see a shooting star? Most likely what you saw was a meteor	23
3	racing across the sky. Sometimes meteor showers are visible	35
4	to the naked eye. At such times you do not need special	46
5	glasses or binoculars to view these space voyagers. Between	58
6	midnight and dawn is the best time to look for them. If you	70
7	are outdoors you will get a much better view.	79
8	Every year meteor showers are caused by the extra	89
9	scrap matter of comets. When the comets are quite close	100
10	to the sun, more debris accumulates and there are likely	112
11	to be more meteors. Each summer, from around the middle of	124
12	July through the middle of August, a meteor show may light	135
13	up the night sky. At peak times, you may be able to see as	147
14	many as a hundred meteors in a night. In the city, the	158
15	bright meteor show has to compete with the bright city	169
16	lights. From the ground, the meteors may look as though	180
17	they are coming from the constellation Perseus.	190

| 1 | 2 | 3 | 4 | 5 | 6 | 7 | 8 | 9 | 10 | 11 | 12 |

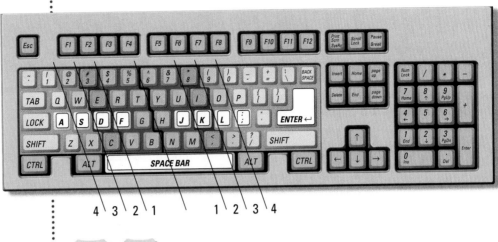

G. **S** **L** **K**EYS

Type each line 1 time.

Use S and L fingers.
   5 sss lll sss lll sss lll ss ll ss ll s l↵
   6 sss lll sss lll sss lll ss ll ss ll s l↵

H. **A** **;** **K**EYS

Type each line 1 time.

Use A and Sem fingers.
   7 aaa ;;; aaa ;;; aaa ;;; aa ;; aa ;; a ;↵
   8 aaa ;;; aaa ;;; aaa ;;; aa ;; aa ;; a ;↵

SKILLBUILDING

I. TECHNIQUE CHECKPOINT

Technique Checkpoints enable you to practice new keys. They also give you and your teacher a chance to evaluate your keyboarding techniques. Focus on the techniques listed in the margin, such as:

- Use correct fingers.
- Keep eyes on copy.
- Press ENTER without pausing.
- Maintain correct posture.
- Maintain correct arm, hand, and finger position.

SKILLBUILDING (continued)

TIMING 6

1   Many people have wondered what might possibly be   10
2 the greatest structure on earth. The tallest buildings,   21
3 the longest bridges, and the mightiest dams might all be   33
4 examined in order to find the answer to this difficult   44
5 question. In the minds of many people, one of the greatest   55
6 structures ever built was the Great Wall of China. It is a   67
7 well-known fact that its features are so impressive that   79
8 astronauts can view the wall from their spaceships.   89
9   The structure was built primarily by mixing earth   99
10 and bricks. It is wide enough at the top to permit several   111
11 people to walk abreast on it. It winds for miles through a   123
12 large section of the country, over mountains and across   134
13 valleys. It was constructed to keep out unwelcome tribes.   146
14 It is believed that building the wall required the labor   157
15 of many thousands of persons for dozens of decades. The   168
16 first sections of the Great Wall were built in the Age of   180
17 Warring States.   183

| 1 | 2 | 3 | 4 | 5 | 6 | 7 | 8 | 9 | 10 | 11 | 12 |

Type lines 9 and 10 one time.

Focus on these techniques:
- Keep eyes on copy.
- Keep fingers on home keys.

```
 9 ff jj dd kk ss ll aa ;; f j d k s l a ;↵
10 ff jj dd kk ss ll aa ;; f j d k s l a ;↵
```

J. PRETEST

Type lines 11–12 for 1 minute. Repeat if time permits. Keep your eyes on the copy.

Hold Anchor Keys

```
11 sad sad fad fad ask ask lad lad dad dad↵
12 as; as; fall fall alas alas flask flask↵
```

K. PRACTICE

Type lines 13–24 one time. Repeat if time permits.

Leave a blank line after each set of lines (13–14, 15–16, and so on) by pressing ENTER 2 times.

```
13 aaa ddd sad sad aaa sss lll lll all all↵
14 aaa ddd sad sad aaa sss lll lll all all↵↵

15 aaa sss kkk ask ask fff aaa ddd fad fad↵
16 aaa sss kkk ask ask fff aaa ddd fad fad↵↵

17 aaa ddd ddd add add lll aaa ddd lad lad↵
18 aaa ddd ddd add add lll aaa ddd lad lad↵↵

19 aaa sss ;;; as; as; ddd aaa ddd dad dad↵
20 aaa sss ;;; as; as; ddd aaa ddd dad dad↵↵

21 f fl fla flas flask; l la las lass lass↵
22 f fl fla flas flask; l la las lass lass↵↵

23 f fa fal fall falls; a al ala alas alas↵
24 f fa fal fall falls; a al ala alas alas↵↵
```

L. POSTTEST

Type lines 11–12 for 1 minute. Repeat if time permits. Keep your eyes on the copy. Compare your Posttest results with your Pretest results.

M. END-OF-CLASS PROCEDURE

To keep hardware and software in good working order, treat them carefully. Your teacher will tell you what should be done at the end of each class period and at the end of the day. You can also refer to the tips on p. IN6 regarding the proper operation and care of your computer.

1	Have you ever felt rundown, tired, and fatigued?	10
2	The symptoms listed above are common to many of us today.	22
3	They affect our job performance; they limit the fun we	33
4	have with our family and friends; and they can even affect	44
5	our good health. Here are a few of the ways by which we	56
6	can quickly minimize the problem and become more active in	67
7	all the things we do daily.	73
8	It is essential that we get plenty of sleep so that	84
9	we are rested when we get up each morning. We must eat a	95
10	good breakfast so that we can build up energy for the day	107
11	that follows. Physical exercise is a necessity, and it	118
12	might be the one most important ingredient in building up	129
13	our energy reserves. We must engage in vigorous exercise	141
14	to make our hearts beat faster and cause our breathing	152
15	rate to appreciably increase. These are things that can	163
16	help us increase our energy and make us healthier people.	174

| 1 | 2 | 3 | 4 | 5 | 6 | 7 | 8 | 9 | 10 | 11 | 12 |

LESSON 2

NEW KEYS: H E O

OBJECTIVE:

- Learn the H, E, and O keys.

Hold Anchor Keys
For **H** anchor ; **L K**
For **E** anchor **A**
For **O** anchor **J** or ;

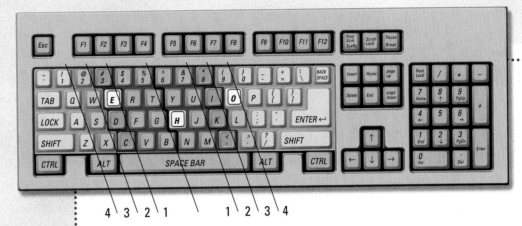

4 3 2 1   1 2 3 4

A. WARMUP

Type each line 2 times. Leave 1 blank line after each set of lines.

```
1 ff jj dd kk ss ll aa ;; f j d k s l a ;
2 adds adds fads fads asks asks lads lads
```

NEW KEYS

B. H KEY

Type each line 2 times. Repeat if time permits.

Use J finger.
For H anchor ; L K.

```
3 jjj jhj jhj hjh jhj jjj jhj jhj hjh jhj
4 jhj ash ash jhj has has jhj had had jhj
5 jhj a lass has; adds a half; a lad had;
6 has a slash; half a sash dad shall dash
```

SKILLBUILDING (continued)

TIMING 3

1	Businesses and individuals can write letters to	10
2	officials in Washington. There are several persons to whom	22
3	you might send such a letter. These include the President,	33
4	senators, or representatives. The people who are elected	45
5	to go to Washington take along a staff who answers most	56
6	of the mail from their constituents. Using the mail is one	68
7	way legislators continually keep in touch with what is	79
8	going on in their individual congressional districts.	89
9	People send inquiries on many topics. They may want	100
10	to express a positive feeling or they may want to complain	112
11	about taxes, pollution, or foreign policy. Some letters do	124
12	influence how lawmakers make their decisions.	133

| 1 | 2 | 3 | 4 | 5 | 6 | 7 | 8 | 9 | 10 | 11 | 12 |

TIMING 4

1	Autumn in the "northlands" is very exciting. You	10
2	jump up in the early morning; walk out under a clear, blue	22
3	sky; and feel the strong chill in the air. The leaves have	34
4	lost their brilliant green. It appears that they have been	45
5	tinted by someone passing by. The truth is that during	56
6	the night hours, a frost has painted the green to hues of	68
7	brown, yellow, orange, and scarlet. It is a breathtaking	79
8	panorama in Technicolor. The leaves seem not to move in	91
9	the quiet breeze. Then, suddenly, a brisk puff lifts them	102
10	from the limbs and carries them gently like feathers to	113
11	the ground below. You watch as legions of leaves jump free	125
12	and float to the earth, covering it like a quilted blanket	137
13	that looks much like moss. When you walk on top of the	148
14	blanket, it cushions each step you take as though you were	160
15	walking on air.	163

| 1 | 2 | 3 | 4 | 5 | 6 | 7 | 8 | 9 | 10 | 11 | 12 |

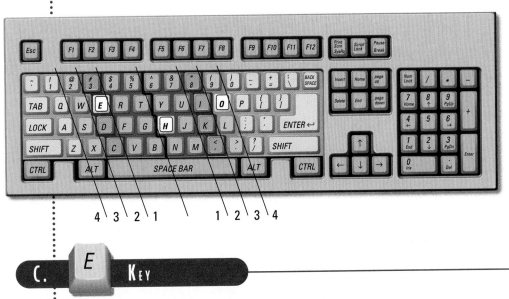

4 3 2 1   1 2 3 4

C. E KEY

Type each line 2 times. Repeat if time permits.

Use D finger.
For D anchor A S.

7 ddd ded ded ede ded ddd ded ded ede ded
8 ded led led ded she she ded he; ded he;
9 ded he led; she fell; he slashes sales;
10 he sees sheds ahead; she sealed a lease

D. O KEY

Type each line 2 times. Repeat if time permits.

Use L finger.
For L anchor J K.

11 lll lol lol olo lol lll lol lol olo lol
12 lol odd odd lol hoe hoe lol foe foe lol
13 load sod; hold a foe; old oak hoes; lol
14 she sold odd hooks; he folded old hoses

FACT FILE

Many word processing programs now include special fonts for other languages. Some of the more commonly found fonts are Greek, Arabic, and Hebrew. If you know any of those languages, you can now type documents using the correct characters rather than writing them by hand.

SKILLBUILDING *(continued)*

SUPPLEMENTARY TIMINGS

TIMING 1

```
1    Raising dogs can be a combination of both fun and hard   11
2  work. Before you even start, you have to decide just which   23
3  breed can best adapt to your lifestyle. If you need a dog   35
4  to protect your house, a poodle will not give you enough   46
5  protection. If you are in your own apartment, a collie may   58
6  be too large. When you have chosen the dog for you, expect   70
7  to have to train it. This can be done quickly with a new   81
8  puppy that is willing to learn.   87
```

| 1 | 2 | 3 | 4 | 5 | 6 | 7 | 8 | 9 | 10 | 11 | 12 |

TIMING 2

```
1     For students who can speak a foreign language, there    11
2  is an amazing job market today. Many major companies in    22
3  other countries have been buying control of or investing    33
4  in American firms. Their demand for workers with foreign    45
5  language skills can be seen in the large number of help    56
6  wanted ads for experts with language skills.    65
7     The fact that so many Americans cannot speak, read,    76
8  or write another language is tragic because the countries    87
9  of the world today are closely linked. International trade    99
10 is now vital to business and government, and young people   111
11 cannot afford to be unequipped to meet the changes and   122
12 challenges of the future.   127
```

| 1 | 2 | 3 | 4 | 5 | 6 | 7 | 8 | 9 | 10 | 11 | 12 |

SKILLBUILDING

E. TECHNIQUE CHECKPOINT

Type each line 2 times. Repeat if time permits. Focus on the technique at the left.

Focus on this technique:
Press and release each key quickly.

```
15 ddd ded ded ede ded ddd ded ded ede ded
16 lll lol lol olo lol lll lol lol olo lol
17 jjj jhj jhj hjh jhj jjj jhj jhj hjh jhj
18 she has old jokes; he has half a salad;
```

F. PRETEST

Type lines 19–20 for 1 minute. Repeat if time permits. Keep your eyes on the copy.

Hold anchor keys.

```
19 heed jade hoof elf; hash folk head hole
20 seed lake look jell sash hold dead half
```

G. PRACTICE

Type each line 2 times. Repeat if time permits.

When you repeat a line:
* *Speed up as you type the line.*
* *Type it more smoothly.*
* *Leave a blank line after the second line (press ENTER 2 times).*

```
21 heed heed feed feed deed deed seed seed
22 jade jade fade fade fake fake lake lake
23 hoof hoof hood hood hook hook look look
24 elf; elf; self self sell sell jell jell

25 hash hash lash lash dash dash sash sash
26 folk folk fold fold sold sold hold hold
27 head head heal heal deal deal dead dead
28 hole hole hale hale hall hall half half
```

H. POSTTEST

Type lines 19–20 for 1 minute. Repeat if time permits. Keep your eyes on the copy. Compare your Posttest results with your Pretest results.

60 wam

Many standard dictionaries give brief essays on topics such as the history of English, what is good usage, and the different dialects of English. Usage refers to how words are used in speaking and writing. A regional way of pronouncing a word is considered dialect. Quite frequently, a dictionary will give instructions on how to use the word. The most obvious information appears first. It is correct syllable division and spelling. When you type a paper, you need to be razor sharp on the correct way to hyphenate a word. Do not be lax in your writing. Use a dictionary to help check every report.

LESSON 3

NEW KEYS: M R I

OBJECTIVE:

- Learn the M, R, and I keys.

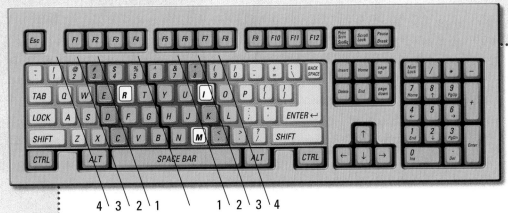

4 3 2 1   1 2 3 4

A. WARMUP

Type each line 2 times. Leave 1 blank line after each set of lines.

1 asdf jkl; heo; asdf jkl; heo; asdf jkl;
2 jade jade fake fake held held lose lose

NEW KEYS

B. M KEY

Type each line 2 times. Repeat if time permits.

Use J finger.
For M anchor ; L K.

3 jjj jmj jmj mjm jmj jjj jmj jmj mjm jmj
4 jmj mom mom jmj mad mad jmj ham ham jmj
5 jmj make a jam; fold a hem; less flame;
6 messes make some moms mad; half a dome;

56 wam

Each June, July, or August, some firms put a closed sign at the front door. They let their employees have the entire month off. All of them like to zip out of town for a nice relaxing vacation. During this month, everyone can enjoy a little time in the sun, or in a boat. Some head for the mountains for a camping or hiking trip. In the summer, most of us usually do less indoors and spend quite a lot of time outside. Many winter resorts have summer activities. Their activities can be enjoyable and quite varied. They do a lot of business during the summer.

58 wam

It has been more than a hundred years since the phone first touched our lives. It has modified the way all of us around the world converse. There are more ways than just a phone to help us quickly stay in touch with others. A computer connected to a modem or fax machine or a pager can be used to carry messages from place to place. The use of these carriers can be quicker and more cost-efficient than the use of the telephone. Today, using more than one of these communication devices is a common practice. We can choose to stay in touch by phone, fax, e-mail, page, or letter.

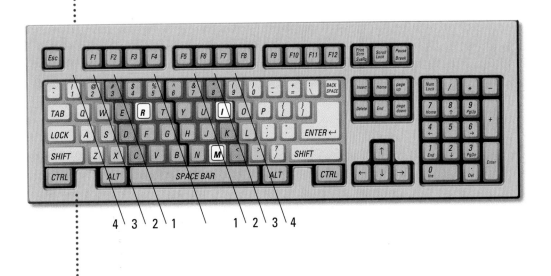

4 3 2 1   1 2 3 4

C. **R** KEY

Type each line 2 times. Repeat if time permits.

Use F finger.
For R anchor A S D.

```
7  fff frf frf rfr frf fff frf frf rfr frf
8  frf far far frf for for frf err err frf
9  frf more rooms; for her marks; from me;
10 he reads ahead; more doors are far ajar
```

D. **I** KEY

Type each line 2 times. Repeat if time permits.

Use K finger.
For I anchor ;.

```
11 kkk kik kik iki kik kkk kik kik iki kik
12 kik dim dim kik lid lid kik rim rim kik
13 kik if she did; for his risk; old mill;
14 more mirrors; his middle silo is filled
```

*inter*NET CONNECTION

Whatis.com is an easy-to-use, searchable technology dictionary that alphabetically lists hundreds of terms. The site also has resources for computer novices.

50 wam

The Inca Indians lived hundreds of years ago near what is now called Peru. They were a great nation known for their many unique buildings. These buildings, in fact, are still visible in ruins deep in the jungle. The temples that remain can be scrutinized for clues about their religion, beliefs, culture, and way of life. Some knowledge already exists, for we have learned that they were a people of numerous skills. Perhaps in time we can uncover the answer to the secret of why the Incas vanished.

52 wam

The brain controls conscious behavior like walking and thinking. It also controls involuntary behavior like the heartbeat and breathing. In humans, it is known to be the site of emotions, memory, and thought. It functions by receiving information through nerve cells from every part of the body. When the brain receives an influx of data, it needs to evaluate the data and then zip off commands to an area of the body like a muscle. Or, the brain might simply store the data. Neurons can process a large amount of data.

54 wam

Working in a place where everyone gets along would be great. However, we all know that the chance of finding a job in a place like that really seldom happens. Each of us has a different personality. When we mix together all of those personalities, the results are quite varied. There will be those who get along with everyone and find no fault with anything. But, by and large, each of us can and will have a difference of opinion with someone at some point. We need to bring qualities like zeal and a good attitude to every job situation.

SKILLBUILDING

E. TECHNIQUE CHECKPOINT

Type each line 2 times. Repeat if time permits. Focus on the techniques at the left.

Focus on these techniques:
- Fingertips touching home keys.
- Wrists up, off keyboard.

```
15  jjj jmj jmj mjm jmj jjj jmj jmj mjm jmj
16  fff frf frf rfr frf fff frf frf rfr frf
17  kkk kik kik iki kik kkk kik kik iki kik
18  he did; his firm red desk lid is a joke
```

F. PRETEST

Type lines 19–20 for 1 minute. Repeat if time permits. Keep your eyes on the copy.

```
19  joke ride sale same roam aims sire more
20  jars aide dark lame foal elms hire mare
```

G. PRACTICE

Type each line 2 times. Repeat if time permits.

Keep eyes on copy. It will be easier to keep your eyes on the copy if you:
- Review the charts for key positions and anchors.
- Maintain an even pace.
- Resist looking up from your copy.

```
21  joke joke jade jade jams jams jars jars
22  ride ride hide hide side side aide aide
23  sale sale dale dale dare dare dark dark
24  same same fame fame dame dame lame lame

25  roam roam loam loam foam foam foal foal
26  aims aims arms arms alms alms elms elms
27  sire sire dire dire fire fire hire hire
28  more more mire mire mere mere mare mare
```

H. POSTTEST

Type lines 19–20 for 1 minute. Repeat if time permits. Keep your eyes on the copy. Compare your Posttest results with your Pretest results.

44 wam

Most successful newspapers are large businesses with an extensive staff and several readers. Now, though, there is a growing number of smaller papers. Their aim is to focus on a community or one subject. A small paper that is well produced will concentrate on and promote a local public. In addition, for those who are in the business, operating it is challenging and rewarding. Moreover, papers provide everyone a vehicle for free speech.

46 wam

Results of a citizenship test taken by a selected group of high school students were surprising. The test was conducted to determine how much knowledge young people have about our system of government. Also, it questioned whether they know how to split their ballot when they vote. Only one-third of the students participating in the program knew that a voter could divide his or her party choice. The majority was ignorant of the political system altogether.

48 wam

Veterinarians are doctors who are trained to treat and to prevent disease in animals. Although they attend different medical schools than doctors trained to treat people, their program of study and training are similar. Vets can limit their practice to one kind of animal. If they choose to specialize in horses, they can be highly paid because the patients might be priceless race horses. Some vets, on the other hand, would rather work with or conduct research on wild animals.

LESSON 4

REVIEW

OBJECTIVE:

- Improve keyboarding skill.

4 3 2 1   1 2 3 4

A. WARMUP

Type each line 2 times. Leave 1 blank line after each set of lines.

1 joke fade home jade mom lads lose less;
2 jell sods from jars adds half ash lead;

SKILLBUILDING

B. ENTER KEY

Type each line 1 time. Repeat if time permits.

Press ENTER after each semicolon and continue to type smoothly.

3 dad adds a home;↵ a sad lass sees ahead;↵
4 he led her here;↵ she folded old flames;↵
5 some lasses are moms;↵ he had less jade;↵
6 he sold old hooks;↵ she had jade flakes;↵

36 wam

An interesting and exciting hobby for you could be working with plants. You have missed a joy if you have never waited with expectation for a tiny sprig to sprout into a plant. Actually, plants make wonderful pets for apartment dwellers. They neither bark nor meow, and the neighbors don't grumble about being kept awake or about being annoyed by a noisy pet.

38 wam

Have you ever been on a fairly long trip by car only to find yourself bored because you didn't have much to do? You, the passenger, can engross yourself in a great book. This answer to the boredom can make time appear to pass more rapidly. You could purchase several paperbacks at a local bookstore; and as you read, you can capture numerous hours of entertainment and enjoyment.

40 wam

Today, a quick way to get from one destination to another is by plane. For your flight, you can choose from among many airlines. In addition, airlines throughout the nation offer daily service to many cities here and abroad. Passengers on domestic and international flights should allow enough time before departure to secure seats on board the plane and to check in baggage at the airport terminal.

42 wam

Every year when winter approaches, you might look up at the sky and see hundreds and maybe even thousands of birds flying toward warmer weather. Quite simply, they migrate south just to escape the severe days that come so soon. Some experts hypothesize that birds migrate because they physically cannot last in the harsh winters of the frigid north. Other experts think that birds migrate to locate better food sources.

C. SPACE BAR

Type each line 1 time. Repeat if time permits.

Space between words without pausing.

```
 7 as a sad lass; ask a lad; as a sad dad;
 8 he had old sod; she made me mad; a door
 9 mom hems; dad marked rare oak; mash ash
10 see her; make me; a sad lad; ash doors;
```

D. CONCENTRATION

Fill in the missing vowels shown at the left as you type each line 1 time.

Keep eyes on copy.

E
A
O
I

```
11 h- s--s s-al-d l-as-s; sh- h-ars a r--d
12 al-s - s-d l-d h-d - lo-d of f-ke smoke
13 ask her f-r a l-ad -f s-me -ld -ak m-ld
14 she sa-d d-m m-rrors make h-m look sl-m
```

E. TECHNIQUE CHECKPOINT

Type each line 2 times. Repeat if time permits. Focus on the techniques at the left.

Focus on:
- *Fingertips touching home keys.*
- *Wrists up.*

```
15 his dark oak desk lid is a joke; he did
16 make a firm door from some rare red ash
17 a lad made a shed; he slashed odd sales
18 foals roam a farm; she sees a small elm
```

CULTURAL CONNECTIONS

Education is very different in European countries. For example, in Great Britain, education is divided into three stages. Primary education is for pupils ranging in age from 5 through 11. Secondary is for pupils from ages 11 or 12 through 16 (the age at which compulsory education ends) or older. Some students continue on to what is known as sixth form to gain additional education that will enable them to attend universities or other schools of higher education.

28 wam

When shopping in this country, we generally accept the price tag on merchandise for the final price the store will consider. If we really want an item, we pay the amount asked. In other nations, prices might vary each moment, depending on the ability of the purchaser to bargain.

30 wam

National parks are owned by the people of America, and they are preserves for wildlife and timber. The parks are cared for by the government to be sure they remain protected and guarded resources. The rangers help prevent forest fires, analyze weather conditions, and keep watch on the wild animals.

32 wam

You simply do not go rafting down the quick river flowing through the Grand Canyon without plenty of skill and help. The hazards can be just too severe. The beautiful canyon is rocky, thorny, and hot during summer months. At times, it is so windy that sand sprays may hit you in the face with a brisk and stinging jolt.

34 wam

A batik is a dyed cloth that has hot wax placed on it to form a design. First the artist melts wax, tints it various colors, paints a design, and then dyes the cloth. Some artists prefer to paint the cloth with a clear wax. Then the batik is dyed again and again with many colors. Only the portion not covered with the wax becomes colored.

F. PRETEST

Type lines 19–20 for 1 minute. Repeat if time permits. Keep your eyes on the copy.

```
19  more sire aims roam same sale ride joke
20  mare hire elms foal lame dark aide jars
```

G. PRACTICE

Type each line 2 times. Repeat if time permits. Keep your eyes on the copy.

Keep eyes on copy. It will be easier to keep your eyes on the copy if you:
- Review the charts for key positions and anchors.
- Maintain an even pace.
- Resist looking up from the copy.

```
21  more more mire mire mere mere mare mare
22  sire sire dire dire fire fire hire hire
23  aims aims arms arms alms alms elms elms
24  roam roam loam loam foam foam foal foal

25  same same fame fame dame dame lame lame
26  sale sale dale dale dare dare dark dark
27  ride ride hide hide side side aide aide
28  jade jade made made mode mode mole mole
```

H. POSTTEST

Type lines 19–20 for 1 minute. Repeat if time permits. Keep your eyes on the copy. Compare your Posttest results with your Pretest results.

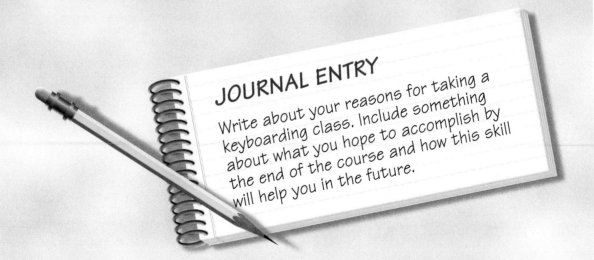

JOURNAL ENTRY

Write about your reasons for taking a keyboarding class. Include something about what you hope to accomplish by the end of the course and how this skill will help you in the future.

18 wam

Each year, many Americans suffer a stroke. It can cause serious problems. For some, it can become difficult to walk or to use an arm. For others, a stroke can affect their speech.

20 wam

Many people think angora is the wool of sheep but it comes from goats. The goats are sheared two times a year. The wool is washed through a special process. It can then be dyed and spun into strands.

20 wam

The old woman who walks in the park always has a huge smile on her face. She talks to the people who cross her path. When she makes new friends, she offers assistance in her quiet way and is excited.

22 wam

There is no substitute for the taste of ice cream on hot, humid days. Choices of all types are out to engage the eye, and the sharp clerks will fix just the mix and size to suit you best. A cup or a cone would be great.

24 wam

To see the artists' pain is a joy. To watch the zeal with which they work to have the exact color show up on the pad is exciting. As they glide the new brush quickly across the pad, the radiant hues take form and bring smiles to our faces.

26 wam

When you work with people every day, you get to know what it is that they like best. You also find out quickly what does make them frown. A bit of extra kind effort in a dozen little ways will make your office a pleasant place in which to complete all duties.

LESSON 5

NEW KEYS: T N C

OBJECTIVE:

- Learn the T, N, and C keys.

4 3 2 1   1 2 3 4

A. WARMUP

Type each line 2 times. Leave 1 blank line after each set of lines.

```
1 asdf jkl; heo; mri; asdf jkl; heo; mri;
2 herd herd mild mild safe safe joke joke
```

NEW KEYS

B. T KEY

Type each line 2 times. Repeat if time permits.

Use F finger.
Anchor A S D.

```
3 fff ftf ftf tft ftf fff ftf ftf tft ftf
4 ftf kit kit ftf toe toe ftf ate ate ftf
5 ftf it is the; to them; for the; at it;
6 that hat is flat; it ate at least three
```

PACED PRACTICE

The Paced Practice routine builds speed and accuracy in short, easy steps, using individualized goals and immediate feedback. You can use this routine any time after completing Lesson 18.

This section contains a series of 2-minute timings for speeds ranging from 14 wam to 60 wam. The first time you use these timings, take a 1-minute entry timing. Then, select a passage that is 2 wam higher than your current keyboarding speed. Use a two-stage practice pattern to achieve each speed goal—first concentrate on speed, and then work on accuracy.

SPEED GOAL: Take three 2-minute timings on the same passage until you can complete it in 2 minutes (do not worry about the number of errors).

When you have achieved your speed goal, work on accuracy.

ACCURACY GOAL: To type accurately, you need to slow down—just a little bit. To reach your accuracy goal, drop back 2 wam to the previous passage. Take three 2-minute timings on this passage until you can complete it in 2 minutes with no more than 2 errors.

For example, if you achieved a speed goal of 30 wam, you should work on an accuracy goal of 28 wam. When you have achieved the 28 wam goal for accuracy, you would then move up 4 wam (for example, to the 32 wam passage) and work for speed again.

ENTRY TIMING

If your mailbox is full of mail that you do not want,   11
your name is on a mailing list. Firms buy mailing lists so   23
that they can send you their ads. Unless you write and ask   34
each company to take your name off its list, you will keep   46
getting junk mail.   50

14 wam

Tourists like to meander through the Boston Gardens during the summer. They stroll the shady paths and then stop to ride on the swan boats.

16 wam

Pleasure boats and large tankers pass through the Cape Cod canal every day. The canal is spanned by two high bridges for auto traffic and by a railroad bridge.

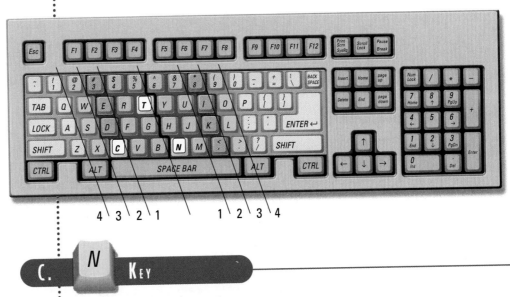

4 3 2 1   1 2 3 4

C. **N** Key

Type each line 2 times. Repeat if time permits.

Use J finger.
Anchor ; L K.

7 jjj jnj jnj njn jnj jjj jnj jnj njn jnj
8 jnj ten ten jnj not not jnj and and jnj
9 jnj nine tones; none inside; on and on;
10 nine kind lines; ten done in an instant

D. **C** Key

Type each line 2 times. Repeat if time permits.

Use D finger.
Anchor A.

11 ddd dcd dcd cdc dcd ddd dcd dcd cdc dcd
12 dcd ace ace dcd can can dcd arc arc dcd
13 dcd on a deck; in each car; cannot act;
14 act at once; call to cancel the tickets

SOCIAL STUDIES CONNECTION

Apollo flights (named after Apollo, the Greek god of learning) had the goal of landing a human on the moon. Apollo 11 achieved the first lunar landing by humans on July 20, 1969, when Neil Armstrong set foot on the moon.

INDIVIDUAL REACHES

8 kik ki8k k8k 888 k8k 8/88 k8k 88.8 k8k ki8k 88.8 88,888 k8k
8 kegs, 88 kits, 888 kilns, 878 kickers, 876 knocks, or 8.8
The 8 keys fit 887 kits; Kim found 8,876 knots in the kits.
The 8 kind ladies got 882 kimonos for 188 kids in the play.

9 lol lo91 191 999 191 9/99 191 99.9 191 lo91 99.9 99,999 191
9 laps, 99 lots, 999 loops, 989 lilies, 987 lifters, or 9.9
Lillian said 9 times to leave 99 lilies for the 989 ladies.
My 9 lawyers had 19 leaky pens, 89 legal pads, and 9 limos.

10 ;p; ;p0; ;0; 000 ;0; 0/00 ;0; 00.0 ;0; ;p0; 00.0 00,000 ;0;
10 pots, 20 pins, 300 parts, 400 plants, 500 parades or 0.0
The 10 party stores put 100 pots and 200 pans to pick from.
The 10 books had 23,000 pages in each; Paul read 500 pages.

All numbers ala s2s d3d f4f f5f j6j j7j k8k 191 ;0; Add 6 and 8 and 29.
That 534-page script called for 10 actors and 17 actresses.
After 1,374 miles in the car, she must then drive 185 more.
The 141 professors asked 4,690 sportscasters 230 questions.

All numbers ala s2s d3d f4f f5f j6j j7j k8k 191 ;0; Add 3 and 4 and 70.
They built 1,200 houses on 345 acres in just under 3 years.
Six boys arrived on May 26, 1994, and left on May 30, 1998.
Marlee bought 15 new books, 62 used books, and 47 new pens.

All numbers ala s2s d3d f4f f5f j6j j7j k8k 191 ;0; Add 5 and 7 and 68.
The 4 stores are open from 9:30 a.m. until 6:00 p.m. daily.
I gave away 2 pans, 4 plates, 8 glasses, and 25 containers.
She moved to 705 Garfield Street, not 507, on June 4, 2000.

SKILLBUILDING

E. TECHNIQUE CHECKPOINT

Type each line 2 times. Repeat if time permits. Focus on the techniques at the left.

Hold anchor keys. Eyes on copy.

```
15  fff ftf ftf tft ftf fff ftf ftf tft ftf
16  jjj jnj jnj njn jnj jjj jnj jnj njn jnj
17  ddd dcd dcd cdc dcd ddd dcd dcd cdc dcd
18  the carton of jam is here on this dock;
```

F. PRETEST

Type lines 19–20 for 1 minute. Repeat if time permits. Keep your eyes on the copy.

```
19  sail farm jets kick this none care ink;
20  rain hand jots tick then tone came sink
```

G. PRACTICE

Type each line 2 times. Repeat if time permits.

To increase skill:
- **Keep eyes on copy.**
- **Maintain good posture.**
- **Speed up on the second typing.**

```
21  sail sail said said raid raid rain rain
22  farm farm harm harm hard hard hand hand
23  jets jets lets lets lots lots jots jots
24  kick kick sick sick lick lick tick tick

25  this this thin thin than than then then
26  none none lone lone done done tone tone
27  care care cake cake cane cane came came
28  ink; ink; link link rink rink sink sink
```

H. POSTTEST

Type lines 19–20 for 1 minute. Repeat if time permits. Compare your Posttest results with your Pretest results.

1 aqa aqla ala 111 ala 1/11 ala 11.1 ala aqla 11.1 11,111 ala
1 ant, 11 arms, 111 aunts, 101 apples, 131 animals, or 1.11
Henry read 111 pages in 1 hour and ate 1 apple in 1 minute.
Crystal wrote 1 story that was 1,111 pages long on 1 topic.

2 sws sw2s s2s 222 s2s 2/22 s2s 22.2 s2s sw2s 22.2 22,222 s2s
2 sips, 22 sets, 222 sites, 212 socks, 231 soldiers, or 2.2
She moved to Room 221 with 2,223 students for about 2 days.
Today 202 computer students were solving 322 math problems.

3 ded de3d d3d 333 d3d 3/33 d3d 33.3 d3d de3d 33.3 33,333 d3d
3 dots, 33 dogs, 333 drops, 323 dimes, 321 daisies, or 3.33
The 3 doctors and 3 nurses did the 3 surgeries in 33 hours.
Your 3 cats and 23 dogs liked to romp on the 330-acre farm.

4 frf fr4f f4f 444 f4f 4/44 f4f 44.4 f4f fr4f 44.4 44,444 f4f
4 figs, 44 fans, 444 farms, 434 finals, 431 friends, or 4.4
Meredith flew 444 miles to see 4 friends at 434 Oak Street.
Florence sold 41 fish dinners to the 44 customers at 4 p.m.

5 ftf ft5f f5f 555 f5f 5/55 f5f 55.5 f5f ft5f 55.5 55,555 f5f
5 foes, 55 facts, 555 foals, 545 fowls, 543 flights, or 5.5
Fred found 55 facts in 545 flights from 514 foreign places.
Theo found that flight 5253 leaves at 5 a.m. from gate 545.

6 jyj jy6j j6j 666 j6j 6/66 j6j 66.6 j6j jy6j 66.6 66,666 j6j
6 jaws, 66 jets, 666 jeeps, 656 jokes, 654 journals, or 6.6
She had 6 jobs to do in 66 hours. Julia worked 664 minutes.
Her 6 math tests had 165 problems to be done in 60 minutes.

7 juj ju7j j7j 777 j7j 7/77 j7j 77.7 j7j ju7j 77.7 77,777 j7j
7 jugs, 77 jars, 777 jumps, 767 joggers, 765 jewels, or 7.7
Joe saw 7 joggers run 177 miles across 7,777 acres of land.
The 7 suits were shipped to 7167 East 7th Avenue on July 7.

LESSON 6

NEW KEYS: V RIGHT SHIFT PERIOD (.)

OBJECTIVES:

- Learn the V, right shift, and period keys.
- Learn spacing with the period.
- Figure speed (typing rate in words a minute).

4 3 2 1   1 2 3 4

A. WARMUP

Type each line 2 times.

```
1 asdf jkl; jh de lo jm fr ki ft jn dc ;;
2 cash free dine jolt milk iron trim star
```

NEW KEYS

B. V KEY

Type each line 2 times. Repeat if time permits.

Use F finger.
Anchor A S D.

```
3 fff fvf fvf vfv fvf fff fvf fvf vfv fvf
4 fvf vie vie fvf eve eve fvf via via fvf
5 fvf vie for love; move over; via a van;
6 vote to move; even vitamins have flavor
```

DIAGNOSTIC PRACTICE: NUMBERS

The Diagnostic Practice: Numbers routine is designed to diagnose and then correct your keystroking errors. You may use this program at any time throughout the course after you complete Lesson 26.

DIRECTIONS:

1. Type one set of the Pretest/Posttest lines 1 time. Identify your errors.
2. Note your results—the number of errors you made on each key and your total number of errors. For example, if you typed *24* for *25*, that would count as 1 error on the number *5*.
3. For any number on which you made 2 or more errors, select the corresponding drill lines, on p. SB5 and p. SB6, and type them 2 times. If you made only 1 error, type the drill 1 time. If you made no errors on the Pretest/Posttest lines, type the drills that contain all numbers on page SB6 and type each line 1 time.
4. Finally, retype the Pretest/Posttest, and compare your performance with your Pretest.

PRETEST/POSTTEST

Set 1
ripe 4803, ire 843, wee 233, ore 943, pier 0834, wire 2843,
Silvio marked the chalkboard at 25, 30, and 45 centimeters.
Alice put markers at 10 km, 29 km, 38 km, 47 km, and 56 km.
Bob lost checks Nos. 234, 457, and 568. Mandy lost No. 901.
Please clean Rooms 340 and 380. Kerbey will clean Room 443.
Those five passengers are 25, 39, 42, 45, and 50 years old.

Set 2
wee 233, tie 583, toe 593, pure 0743, pour 0974, rout 4975,
Iva put 428 in group 1, 570 in group 2, and 396 in group 3.
The party governed during 1910, 1929, 1938, 1947, and 1956.
The total of 198, 384, 275, 470, and 672 is easy to figure.
They had 92 or 83. He has 10 or 74. We have 56 or maybe 57.
Check lockers 290, 471, 356, and 580 before school Tuesday.

Set 3
pie 083, rye 463, your 6974, tier 5834, eye 363, pipe 0803,
Read pages 100, 129, and 138; summarize Chapters 47 and 56.
By May 1, ship 29 seats, 38 stoves, 47 tents, and 56 coats.
The 29 females lived 180 days at 4387 South Parkview Court.
Janet read pages 105 through 120 and pages 387 through 469.
Marvin easily won the bulletins numbered 12,345 and 67,890.

4 3 2 1   1 2 3 4

C. RIGHT SHIFT KEY

Type each line 2 times. Repeat if time permits.

Use Sem finger.
Anchor J.

```
7   ;;; T;; T;; ;;; C;; C;; ;;; S;; S;; ;;;
8   ;;; Ted Ted ;;; Cal Cal ;;; Sam Sam ;;;
9   ;;; Ed likes Flint; Rick ran; save Tom;
10  Vera loved Florida; Aaron and Sam moved
```

D. . KEY

Type each line 2 times. Repeat if time permits.

Use L finger.
Anchor ; or J.

```
11  111 1.1 1.1 .1. 1.1 111 1.1 1.1 .1. 111
12  1.1 Fr. Fr. 1.1 Sr. Sr. 1.1 Dr. Dr. 1.1
13  1.1 std. ctn. div. Ave. Rd. St. Co. vs.
14  Calif. Conn. Tenn. Colo. Fla. Del. Ark.
```

SKILLBUILDING

E. SPACING AFTER PUNCTUATION

Type each line 2 times. Repeat if time permits.

Space once after:
- **A period at the end of a sentence.**
- **A period used with an abbreviation.**
- **A semicolon.**

```
15  The draft is too cold. Close this door.
16  Ask Vera to start a fire. Find a match.
17  Dr. T. Vincent sees me; he made a cast.
18  Ash Rd. is ahead; East Ave. veers left.
```

SKILLBUILDING (continued)

TROUBLESOME PAIRS

A/S	Sal said he asked Sara Ash for a sample of the raisins.
B/V	Vera very bravely was verbose with a bevy of beverages.
C/D	Candie decided the December calendar decal could decay.
E/W	Weni knew in weekday weather weak weeds grew elsewhere.
F/G	Goeff goofed by finding the gulf for the grateful frog.
H/J	Judith wore jodhpurs; she joshed with John and Johanna.
I/O	Iona totally foiled Olin's spoiled oily ointment plans.
K/L	Karl liked to walk seven kilometers quickly with Kelly.
M/N	Many have names of maidens among the main mason manors.
O/P	Opal and Polly phoned three opera pollsters in Phoenix.
Q/A	Quin quickly qualified this quality quart quartz quota.
R/T	Robert tried trading rations to three terrific skaters.
U/Y	If you are busy, buy your supply of yucca Yule in July.
X/C	Cal expected the excitement to exceed all expectations.
Z/A	The five sizable, lazy zebras zigzagged as Eliza gazed.

Type each line 2 times. Focus on the technique at the left.

Hold anchor keys.
Eyes on copy.

```
19  fff fvf fvf vfv fvf fff fvf fvf vfv fvf
20  ;;; T;; T;; ;;; C;; C;; ;;; S;; S;; ;;;
21  111 1.1 1.1 .1. 1.1 111 1.1 1.1 .1. 111
22  Dee voted for vivid vases on her visit.
```

G. FIGURING SPEED

Typing speed is measured in words a minute (wam). To determine your typing speed:

- Type for 1 minute.
- Determine the number of words you typed. Every 5 strokes (characters and spaces) count as 1 word. Therefore, a 40-stroke line equals 8 words. Two 40-stroke lines equal 16 words.
- Use the cumulative word count at the end of lines to determine the number of words in a complete line.

To determine the number of words in an incomplete line:

- Use the word scale below the last line (below line 24 on this page).
- The number over which you stopped typing is the number of words for that line. For example, if you typed line 23 and completed up to the word *vice* in line 24, you have typed 14 words a minute (8 + 6 = 14).

```
23  fold hide fast came hold ride mast fame        8
24  hone rice mask fade none vice task jade        16
    | 1 | 2 | 3 | 4 | 5 | 6 | 7 | 8
```

SKILLBUILDING (continued)

INDIVIDUAL REACHES

A	Ada and Anna had an allowance and always had adequate cash.
B	Barbara grabbed back the brown bag Bob bought at a bargain.
C	Charles can accept and cash any checks the church collects.
D	David drove down and deducted the dividends he had divided.
E	Everyone here exerted extra effort each week we were there.

F	Fred Ford offered to find fresh food for five fine fellows.
G	Guy suggested getting eight guys to bring George's luggage.
H	Hank hoped that she had withheld the cash they had to have.
I	Iris insists their idea is simply idiotic in this instance.
J	Jack and Jerry joined Joe just to enjoy a journey to Japan.

K	Kathy asked Ken to take a blank checkbook back to her bank.
L	Larry helped several little fellows learn to play baseball.
M	Mr. Ammon made many mistakes in estimating minimum markets.
N	Nan never knew when any businessman wanted an announcement.
O	One or two of those older tool orders ought to go out soon.

P	Please provide proper paper supplies for plenty of persons.
Q	Quentin quietly inquired what sequences required questions.
R	Run over for another order from the firm across the street.
S	She says she sold us some shiny scissors sometime Saturday.
T	Try to get the truth when they talk about better attitudes.

U	Unless you pour out your mixture, you could hurt our stuff.
V	Vivian raved over violets and even saved several varieties.
W	William will work well whenever we know where we will work.
X	X-rays exceed examinations except for external exploration.
Y	Yes, any day they say you may be ready, you may try to fly.
Z	Zenith Franz realizes that he idealized the zigzag friezes.

H. PRETEST

Type lines 23–24 for 1 minute. Repeat if time permits. Note your speed. Keep your eyes on the copy.

```
23  fold hide fast came hold ride mast fame        8
24  hone rice mask fade none vice task jade        16
    | 1 | 2 | 3 | 4 | 5 | 6 | 7 | 8
```

I. PRACTICE

Type each line 2 times. Repeat if time permits.

Build speed on repeated word patterns.

```
25  fold fold hold hold sold sold told told
26  hide hide ride ride rice rice vice vice
27  fast fast mast mast mask mask task task
28  came came fame fame fade fade jade jade

29  last last vast vast cast cast case case
30  mats mats mars mars cars cars jars jars
31  fell fell jell jell sell sell seal seal
32  dive dive five five live live love love
```

J. POSTTEST

Repeat the Pretest. Compare your Posttest results with your Pretest results.

FACT FILE

The modern computer is a descendant of the abacus—one of the world's first calculators. The abacus used units of ones, tens, hundreds, and thousands. Today, we still use the base ten, or decimal, number system.

SKILLBUILDING

DIAGNOSTIC PRACTICE: ALPHABET

The Diagnostic Practice: Alphabet routine is designed to diagnose and then correct your keystroking errors. You may use this program at any time throughout the course after you complete Lesson 18.

DIRECTIONS:

1. Type one set of the Pretest/Posttest lines 1 time. Identify your errors.
2. Note your results—the number of errors you made on each key and your total number of errors. For example, if you typed *rht* for *the,* that would count as 1 error on the letter *t.*

3. For any letter on which you made 2 or more errors, select the corresponding drill lines, on p. SB2, and type them 2 times. If you made only 1 error, type the drill 1 time.
4. If you made no errors on the Pretest/Posttest lines, turn to the practice on Troublesome Pairs on page SB3 and type each line 1 time. This section provides intensive practice on those pairs of keys commonly confused.
5. Finally, retype the same set of Pretest/Posttest lines, and compare your performance with your Pretest.

PRETEST/POSTTEST

Set 1
Buzz quickly designed five new projects for the wax museum.
John's wacky quip amazed but also vexed his new girlfriend.
Zed quickly jumped five huge barrels to warn Max and Teddy.
Orville quickly objected to Wes dumping five toxic hazards.
From the tower Dave saw six big jet planes quickly zoom by.
Beverly, has John kept that liquid oxygen frozen with care?

Set 2
Did Robert move that psychology quiz to next week for John?
Stanley, cover this oozy liquid wax before Jack mops again.
The six heavy guys jumped for eighty waltzing quarterbacks.
Skip was quite vexed by the seventeen jazzmen from Cologne.
The eight taxi drivers quickly zip by the jumble of wagons.
While having Joel wait, Ben quickly fixed the many zippers.

Set 3
Last week Jed McVey was quite busy fixing the frozen pipes.
Vic quickly mixed frozen strawberries into the grape juice.
Five big jet planes zoomed quickly by the six steel towers.
Jeff amazed the audience by quickly giving six new reports.
Sixty equals only five dozen, but we promised Jackie eight.
Joel quietly picked sixteen razors from the blue woven bag.

LESSON 7

NEW KEYS: W COMMA (,) G

OBJECTIVES:

- Learn the W, comma, and G keys.
- Learn the spacing with a comma.

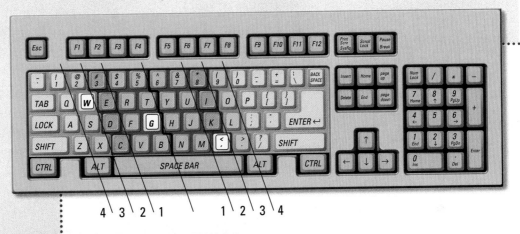

4 3 2 1   1 2 3 4

A. WARMUP

Type each line 2 times.

1 fail not; jest mist chin Rev. card sake
2 Rick did not join; Val loves that fame.

NEW KEYS

B.  KEY

Type each line 2 times. Repeat if time permits.

**Use S finger.
Anchor F.**

3 sss sws sws wsw sws sss sws sws wsw sws
4 sws was was sws own own sws saw saw sws
5 sws white swans swim; sow winter wheat;
6 We watched some whales while we walked.

alphabet used at that time—Able, Baker, Charlie, etc. Beginning in 1953, female names were assigned to hurricanes; but since 1979 male and female names have been alternated.

Separate sets of hurricane names are used in the central Pacific, the eastern Pacific, and the Atlantic Basin. The first hurricane of the year in the Atlantic Basin and the eastern Pacific receives a name beginning with the letter A. The name of the central Pacific's first storm of the year continues from the list of names from the previous year.

The following table is a random list of hurricanes and the damage they left behind. In general, the table illustrates the decrease in the number of fatalities in recent decades.

*inter*NET C O N N E C T I O N

Connect to the Internet. Learn more about weather and hurricane names by searching using the key words: hurricane names.

PORTFOLIO
Activity

Make a list of the names of the most destructive hurricanes that have hit the U.S. in the last twenty years. Illustrate the information in a table or chart that you feel shows your information in a format that is easy to understand. Then, print a copy of your chart and a copy of the report in this lesson and add them to your portfolio.

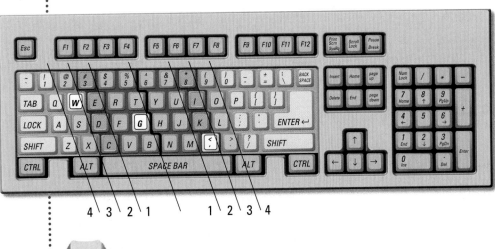

4 3 2 1   1 2 3 4

C. , KEY

Type each line 2 times. Repeat if time permits.

Use K finger.
Anchor ;.
Space once after a comma.

7 kkk k,k k,k ,k, k,k kkk k,k k,k ,k, k,k
8 k,k it, it, k,k or, or, k,k an, an, k,k
9 k,k if it is, two, or three, as soon as
10 Vic, his friend, lives in Rich, Alaska.

D. G KEY

Type each line 2 times. Repeat if time permits.

Use F finger.
Anchor A S D.

11 fff fgf fgf gfg fgf fff fgf fgf gfg fgf
12 fgf leg leg fgf egg egg fgf get get fgf
13 fgf give a dog, saw a log, sing a song,
14 Gen gets a large sagging gift of games.

COMMUNICATION FOCUS

An *emoticon* or *smiley* is a symbol used to compensate for the absence of nonverbal clues when communicating on the Internet. For example, <g> signifies a "grin," :) or :-) signifies a "smile" when inserted into the text of an e-mail message. These symbols alert the reader not to take the message seriously.

ACTIVITY 33

Report 72
2-Page Report

Science
Connections

Format the following 2-page report in MLA style. Follow these steps to complete the report:

1. Insert the spreadsheet chart that you created in Activity 31 after the first paragraph of the report.
2. Horizontally center the chart.
3. Insert the database table you created in Activity 32 at the end of the report.
4. Horizontally center the table.
5. Insert a row at the beginning of the table. Center, bold, and type in all caps the table title, Hurricane Damage.
6. Where possible, modify the appearance of the database table to resemble the format of a word processing table.
7. Size the chart as necessary to keep the report to two pages.
8. Save the report as R72.
9. Print the report.

Hurricanes

A hurricane is the most powerful type of storm. Hurricanes are large, swirling, low-pressure systems that form over oceans and have a minimum wind speed of 75 miles per hour. These storms kill people and animals and cause extensive damage. The deadliest hurricane ever recorded is the Great Hurricane of October 1780, which killed over 22,000 people in the Caribbean. The 1950s claimed the most hurricane fatalities in the United States, as illustrated in the following chart.

Because of improved forecasting and technological advances, the number of injuries and deaths from hurricanes has decreased. A hurricane watch is issued when there is a threat of hurricane conditions within 24–36 hours. A hurricane warning is issued when hurricane conditions are expected in 24 hours or less. Careful and strategic planning can also reduce the risk of injury or death. Hurricane preparations should include knowing the safest evacuation route, locating the nearest shelter, maintaining disaster supplies, developing an emergency communication plan, and making arrangements for pets.

Naming hurricanes began in 1951 to avoid confusion when more than one storm was being followed. For two years, the names were taken from the international phonetic

SKILLBUILDING

E. TECHNIQUE CHECKPOINT

Type each line 2 times. Repeat if time permits. Focus on the techniques at the left.

Hold anchor keys.
Keep elbows in.

```
15  sss sws sws wsw sws sss sws sws wsw sws
16  kkk k,k k,k ,k, k,k kkk k,k k,k ,k, k,k
17  fff fgf fgf gfg fgf fff fgf fgf gfg fgf
18  Wanda watched the team jog to the glen.
```

F. COUNTING ERRORS

Count 1 error for each word, even if it contains several errors. Count as an error:

1. A word with an incorrect character.
2. A word with incorrect spacing after it.
3. A word with incorrect punctuation after it.
4. Each mistake in following directions for spacing or indenting.
5. A word with a space.
6. An omitted word.
7. A repeated word.
8. Transposed (switched in order) words.

Compare these incorrect lines with the correct lines (19–21). Each error is highlighted in color.

```
Frank sold sold Dave old an washing mshcone .
      Carl joked with Al ice, Fran, Edith.
Wamda wore redsocks; Sadie wore  green,
```

Type each line 2 times. Proofread carefully and note your errors.

```
19  Frank sold Dave an old washing machine.
20  Carl joked with Alice, Fran, and Edith.
21  Wanda wore red socks; Sadie wore green.
```

DATABASE APPLICATIONS

ACTIVITY 31
Spreadsheet 49

Create a spreadsheet using the following data. Save the spreadsheet as SS49.

Decade	Number of Fatalities
1940s	216
1950s	877
1960s	587
1970s	217
1980s	118

1. Create a vertical bar chart.
2. Title the chart U.S. Hurricane Fatalities.
3. Title the x-axis Decade.
4. Title the y-axis Number of Fatalities.
5. Minimize the spreadsheet program.

ACTIVITY 32
Database Table 6

Follow these steps to create Database Table 6 and name it DT6:

1. Define the five fields as shown in the illustration. The only field that should be designated a number field is Fatalities.
2. Specify the size of each field as shown above the column.
3. Enter the records.
4. Close the table window.

13	6	20		40
Hurricane	**Year**	**$ Damage**	**Fatalities**	**Initial Hit**
Diane	1955	$4.2 billion	184	North Carolina
Betsy	1965	$6.5 billion	75	Bahamas and Florida
Camille	1969	$5.2 billion	259	Alabama, Mississippi, and Louisiana
Agnes	1972	$6.5 billion	129	Florida panhandle
Alicia	1983	$2.4 billion	18	Texas
Hugo	1989	$7.2 billion	56	South Carolina
Andrew	1992	$25.0 billion	26	South Florida

G. PRETEST

Take a 1-minute timing on lines 22–23. Note your speed and errors. Keep your eyes on the copy.

```
22  sag, mow, crew elf, down well scow king          8
23  hag, jot, glow ink, tows west snow ring          16
    | 1  | 2  | 3  | 4  | 5  | 6  | 7  | 8
```

H. PRACTICE

Type each line 2 times. Repeat if time permits.

Focus on:
- Wrists up; do not rest palms on keyboard.
- Fingers curved; move from home position only when necessary.

```
24  sag, sag, wag, wag, rag, rag, hag, hag,
25  mow, mow, how, how, hot, hot, jot, jot,
26  crew crew grew grew grow grow glow glow
27  elf, elf, elk, elk, ilk, ilk, ink, ink,

28  down down gown gown town town tows tows
29  well well welt welt went went west west
30  scow scow stow stow show show snow snow
31  king king sing sing wing wing ring ring
```

I. POSTTEST

Repeat the Pretest. Compare your Posttest results with your Pretest results.

Science
Connections

FACT FILE

Did you know that wood could turn to stone? For wood to become stone (petrified), it must be quickly covered by some material that prevents the wood from receiving any oxygen. This prevents the wood from decaying naturally. If conditions are right, the organic portion of the wood dissolves slowly and any organic matter is replaced by minerals. These minerals may be silica, calcite, pyrite, or marcasite.

C. 5-Minute Timings

Take two 5-minute timings on the paragraphs. Note your speed and errors.

Goal: 40/5'/5e

7 People with technical skills are in demand for many 11
8 kinds of jobs. Once on the job, however, you will need more 23
9 than technical skills to survive. You must be able to deal 34
10 with the unwritten company rules. 41

11 When you begin a new job, you will need to learn about 52
12 the rules of that particular workplace. Some rules will be 64
13 written, but others will not be. Observing these unwritten 76
14 rules can be vital to your success in business. 86

15 Every office has its own way of doing some things, yet 97
16 there are some basic rules of etiquette that are common in 109
17 all places of business. There are distinct behaviors that 120
18 seem to be required of each person who becomes an expert at 132
19 succeeding in business. For example, knowing the rules for 144
20 dressing appropriately and being well-groomed always helps. 156
21 In addition, if you are honest, courteous, well-mannered, 168
22 and punctual, you will probably be seen in a favorable way 179
23 by your peers. 182

24 Each employee should quickly become familiar with the 193
25 standard protocol of the company. 200

| 1 | 2 | 3 | 4 | 5 | 6 | 7 | 8 | 9 | 10 | 11 | 12 SI 1.48

FORMATTING

D. Software Features

STUDENT MANUAL

Inserting Database Tables and Charts

Study Lesson 150 in your student manual. Complete all the practice activities while at your computer. Then complete the jobs that follow.

LESSON 8

REVIEW

OBJECTIVES:

- Improve keyboarding skill.
- Improve speed and accuracy.
- Strengthen reaches to third, home, and bottom rows.

4 3 2 1   1 2 3 4

A. WARMUP

Type each line 2 times.

1 memo dock sink wave heed crag jolt jest
2 Tommi Ra has two free carnival tickets.

SKILLBUILDING

B. RIGHT SHIFT KEY

Type each line 2 times. Repeat if time permits.

Anchor right shift with J.
Keep your rhythm steady as you reach to the shift key and back to home position.

3 Wade Dana Alda Sami Cata Devo Wane Glen
4 Vera Edie Fran Seth Adam Cara Rene Dave
5 Gene Vick Rick Coel Fran Dave Carl Sadi
6 Anna Wade Gino Sali Vida Theo Dean Eric

LESSON 150

DATABASES: SIMULATION

OBJECTIVES:

- Improve keyboarding skill.
- Type 40/5'/5e.
- Insert database tables and charts.

A. WARMUP

Type each line 2 times.

Speed
Accuracy
Language Link
Numbers

1 Gloria has to read the pages of this book before she stops.
2 Paula rejoiced at the amazing reviews of six quality books.
3 As you can see the man will not be able to finish the exam.
4 I set tabs at 6, 15, 20, 35, 40, 60, 78, and 96 on the job.
| 1 | 2 | 3 | 4 | 5 | 6 | 7 | 8 | 9 | 10 | 11 | 12

interNET CONNECTION

Connect to the Internet. Search the Internet for rules governing e-mail and Internet communications. These rules are often called netiquette. Look up this word in an Internet dictionary and note its meaning in your journal.

SKILLBUILDING

B. PREVIEW PRACTICE

Type each line 2 times as a preview to the timings that follow.

Accuracy
Speed

5 honest business etiquette particular appropriate punctuality
6 common things demand doing learn about vital other seem rule

C. CONCENTRATION

Fill in the missing letters shown at the left as you type each line 1 time.

Keep eyes on copy.

O
E
R
H
M
I

7 S-me w-rk s- we make the w-rld cleaner.
8 W- hav- th-m saf-; V-ra l-ft to s-- it.
9 See, the -ive-s and st-eams a-e -ising.
10 A damaging c-emical mig-t -arm t-e men.
11 Their -o- -akes ja- and so-e sew ite-s.
12 W-ll-am -s -ll and w-ll l-ve -n Alaska.

D. TECHNIQUE CHECKPOINT

Type lines 13–16 twice. Remember to space once after a comma. Focus on the technique at the left.

*Right Shift Key
Keep your rhythm
steady as you reach to
the shift key and back
to home position.*

13 Deloris sold red, tan, and orchid ties.
14 Dana had dogs, cats, and a tan hamster.
15 Todd ate mangoes, kiwis, and an orange.
16 Alicia worked on math, French, and law.

E. TECHNIQUE TIMINGS

Take two 30-second timings on each line. Focus on the techniques at the left.

*Sit up straight and
keep both feet flat
on the floor.*

17 Edie Victor saw the Alo Reed dress too.
18 Tom Salt and Arti Wiggs saw Sam and Di.
19 Rick saw Chris at three Eastmoor games.
20 Donna wrote to Anna, Ellen, and Rachel.
   | 1 | 2 | 3 | 4 | 5 | 6 | 7 | 8

F. 12-SECOND SPRINTS

Take three 12-second timings on each line. Try to increase your speed on each timing.

*Each stroke in a 12-
second timing is
counted as 1 word. If
you complete a line,
your speed is 40
words a minute.*

21 Al had one good mark and told me later.
22 We want to go west to work in the rain.
23 The snow fell one dark night last fall.
24 Watch the river flow over the dark dam.
   | | | | 5 | | | | 10 | | | 15 | | | | 20 | | | | 25 | | | 30 | | | | 35 | | | | 40

Title	Wholesale Price
Out of the Dust	$9.57
View From Saturday	$2.70
The Midwife's Apprentice	$6.57
Walk Two Moons	$2.97
Sarah, Plain and Tall	$8.97
The Bridge to Terabithia	$2.97
Roll of Thunder, Hear My Cry	$9.57
Mrs. Frisby and the Rats of NIMH	$10.20
Summer of the Swans	$2.97
Sounder	$8.97
Island of the Blue Dolphins	$3.30
Johnny Tremain	$12.00

ACTIVITY 30
Database Table 5, Report 3

Create a report using Database Table 5 (DT5), and name it DR3. Complete the following steps to format the report and perform the calculations. (The exact sequence of steps will vary according to the software program you are using.)

1. Change the print orientation to landscape.
2. Include only the Code, Title, Quantity, Copies Available, Retail Price, Wholesale Price, Difference, and Inventory Value fields in the report.
3. Select a tabular format.
4. Select a format/style.
5. In the header, left-align the title Newbery Titles, and right-align your name.
6. Select a font size for the title and your name that is larger than the data text.
7. Enter a formula in the Difference field that will calculate the difference between the retail and wholesale prices of each book.
8. Enter a formula in the Inventory Value field that will calculate the total value of the inventory for each book.
9. Preview/run the report.
10. Print the report.
11. Close the report.

G. PRETEST

Take a 1-minute timing on lines 25–26. Note your speed and errors.

```
25 ring snow west tows ink, glow jot, hag,          8
26 king scow well down elf, crew mow, sag,          16
   | 1 | 2 | 3 | 4 | 5 | 6 | 7 | 8
```

H. PRACTICE

Type each line 2 times. Repeat if time permits.

Wrists—do not rest palms on keyboard.

Fingers curved—move from the home position only when necessary.

```
27 ring ring wing wing sing sing king king
28 snow snow show show stow stow scow scow
29 west west went went welt welt well well
30 tows tows town town gown gown down down

31 ink, ink, ilk, ilk, elk, elk, elf, elf,
32 glow glow grow grow grew grew crew crew
33 jot, jot, hot, hot, how, how, mow, mow,
34 hag, hag, rag, rag, wag, wag, sag, sag,
```

I. POSTTEST

Repeat the Pretest. Compare your Posttest results with your Pretest results.

CULTURAL CONNECTIONS

Gestures, posture, and body language have many different meanings in other countries. For example, the "thumbs up" gesture is considered offensive in Iran and Ghana. The "okay" circle with the thumb and forefinger is an insulting gesture in Greece and Brazil. In France, this gesture means zero, and in Japan, it means money.

SKILLBUILDING

C. 12-Second Sprints

Take three 12-second timings on each line. Try to increase your speed on each timing.

```
 9  Six men plan to take the boat trip to the side of the lake.
10  We must be ready when it is time for us to go to the shore.
11  This is what she said about it when she wanted to meet him.
12  Our real wish will come true many days from this very hour.
    | | | | 5 | | | | 10 | | | 15 | | | 20 | | | 25 | | | 30 | | | 35 | | | 40 | | | 45 | | | 50 | | | 55 | | | 60
```

FORMATTING

D. Software Features

GO TO

STUDENT MANUAL

Create Formulas in Database Reports

Study Lesson 149 in your student manual. Complete all the practice activities while at your computer. Then complete the jobs that follow.

DATABASE APPLICATIONS

ACTIVITY 29
Database Table 5

Open the file DT5 and make the following changes:

1. Add three new fields in this order at the end of the table: Wholesale Price, Difference, Inventory Value.
2. Enter the wholesale prices for the titles as shown in the illustration.
3. Close the table window.

LESSON 9

New Keys: B U Left Shift

OBJECTIVE:

- Learn the B, U, and left shift keys.

A. Warmup

Type each line 2 times.

1 dim logo wags jive foal corn them wags,
2 Wanda mailed the jewels that Carl made.

NEW KEYS

B. B Key

Type each line 2 times. Repeat if time permits.

*Use F finger.
Anchor A and S.*

3 fff fbf fbf bfb fbf fff fbf fbf bfb fbf
4 fbf rob rob fbf ebb ebb fbf bag bag fbf
5 fbf a bent bin, a back bend, a big bag,
6 That boat had been in a babbling brook.

LESSON 149

DATABASES: FORMULAS

OBJECTIVES:

- Improve keyboarding skill.
- Learn about hyphenating compound adjectives.
- Create and use formulas in database tables.

A. WARMUP

Type each line 2 times.

Speed
Accuracy
Language Link
Numbers/Symbols

1 We will try as hard as we can to start the car in the cold.
2 Two sax players in the jazz band gave a quick demo for Tom.
3 Al cut the grass, trimmed the bushes, and pulled the weeds.
4 Our guess was 15% off. Abe had #66; Vi had #77--nobody won.

| 1 | 2 | 3 | 4 | 5 | 6 | 7 | 8 | 9 | 10 | 11 | 12

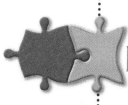

LANGUAGE LINK

B. HYPHENATED COMPOUND ADJECTIVES

Study the rule and examples below. Then edit lines 5–8 by inserting hyphens where needed.

Rule 48:

Hyphenate compound adjectives that come before a noun (unless the first word is an adverb ending in ly).

We reviewed an up-to-date report on Wednesday.

We attended a highly rated session on multimedia software.

5 As stated in the above mentioned letter, she went to court.
6 You can order our products by calling our toll free number.
7 Their new, easy to operate recorder goes on sale next week.
8 She drove behind a slow moving vehicle for seventeen miles.

4 3 2 1   1 2 3 4

C. U KEY

Type each line 2 times. Repeat if time permits.

Use J finger.
Anchor ; L and K.

7 jjj juj juj uju juj jjj juj juj uju juj
8 juj jug jug juj urn urn juj flu flu juj
9 juj jungle bugs, just a job, jumbo jets
10 Students show unusual business success.

D. LEFT SHIFT KEY

Type each line 2 times. Repeat if time permits.

Use A finger.
Anchor F.

11 aaa Kaa Kaa aaa Jaa Jaa aaa Laa Laa aaa
12 aaa Kim Kim aaa Lee Lee aaa Joe Joe aaa
13 aaa Jan left; Nora ran; Uncle Lee fell;
14 Mari and Ula went to Kansas in October.

SKILLBUILDING

E. TECHNIQUE CHECKPOINT

Type each line 2 times. Repeat if time permits. Focus on the technique at the left.

Keep F or J anchored
when shifting.

15 fff fbf fbf bfb fbf fff fbf fbf bfb fbf
16 jjj juj juj uju juj jjj juj juj uju juj
17 aaa Kaa Kaa aaa Jaa Jaa aaa Laa Laa aaa
18 Jo told Mike and Nel that she would go.

DATABASE APPLICATIONS

ACTIVITY 27
Database Table 4,
Report 1

Create a report using Database Table 4 and name it DR1. Complete the following steps to format the report. (The exact sequence of steps will vary according to the software program you are using.)

1. Select a column format for the report.
2. Select a format/style.
3. In the header, left-align the title *Salary Ranges*, and right-align your name.
4. Select a font size for the title and your name that is larger than the data text.
5. Preview/run the report.
6. Print the report.
7. Close the report.

ACTIVITY 28
Database Table 2,
Report 2

Create a report using Database Table 2 and name it DR2. Complete the following steps to format the report. (The exact sequence of steps will vary according to the software program you are using.)

1. Select a tabular format for the report.
2. Select a format/style.
3. In the header, left-align the title *Olympic Tryouts*, and right-align your name.
4. Select a font size for the title and your name that is larger than the data text.
5. Preview/run the report.
6. Print the report.
7. Close the report.

PORTFOLIO
Activity

Print one of the reports you just completed and place it in your portfolio. Then, write a short paragraph describing what you have learned about databases and what other uses you would have for setting up databases.

F. PRETEST

Take a 1-minute timing on lines 19–20. Note your speed and errors.

```
19  bran gist vast blot sun, bout just beef        8
20  craw just rest bran sum, dole hunk bear       16
     | 1 | 2 | 3 | 4 | 5 | 6 | 7 | 8
```

G. PRACTICE

Type each line 2 times. Repeat if time permits.

Place your feet:
- *In front of the chair.*
- *Firmly on the floor, square, flat.*
- *Apart, with 6 or 7 inches between the ankles.*
- *One foot a little ahead of the other.*

```
21  bran brad bred brew brow crow crew craw
22  gist list mist must gust dust rust just
23  vast vest jest lest best west nest rest
24  blot blob blow blew bled bred brad bran

25  sun, nun, run, bun, gun, gum, hum, sum,
26  bout boat boot blot bold boll doll dole
27  just dust dusk dunk bunk bulk hulk hunk
28  beef been bean bead beak beam beat bear
```

H. POSTTEST

Repeat the Pretest. Compare your Posttest results with your Pretest results.

inter**NET** C O N N E C T I O N

Did you know that one of the largest "bookstores" is available through the Internet? Locate *amazon.com* on the Internet, and search that site for a book you would like to read. Determine the price of the book and any shipping costs involved.

Take two 5-minute timings on the paragraphs. Note your speed and errors.

Goal: 40/5'/5e

Social Studies
Connections

11   All calendars begin with an epoch, a span of time   10
12 marked by a notable event. From the start, the method of   22
13 tracking time was based on one of three major cycles. The   33
14 cycles included the orbit of the sun, orbit of the moon, and   45
15 a combination of both of their paths.   53
16   Due to the errors and omissions of the calendars of   63
17 the sixteenth century, a French chronologist named Joseph   75
18 Scaliger, proposed a new plan. He sought a time prior to   86
19 any event written in history.   92
20   Scaliger based his work on three unique cycles. One of   104
21 these was the twenty-eight-year cycle, the time after which   116
22 weekdays and days of the month repeat in the exact same   127
23 order. Another cycle was the nineteen-year Metonic orbit,   138
24 the time after which moon phases repeat on the same day of   150
25 the year. The third cycle was the fifteen-year indication,   162
26 which is also the Roman business and tax cycle.   172
27   He used these cycles to calculate a start date earlier   183
28 than all written events. His epoch was named the Julian   194
29 period after his father, Julius.   200

| 1 | 2 | 3 | 4 | 5 | 6 | 7 | 8 | 9 | 10 | 11 | 12SI 1.46

FORMATTING

STUDENT MANUAL
Database Table Reports

Study Lesson 148 in your student manual. Complete all the practice activities while at your computer. Then complete the jobs that follow.

NEW KEYS: Q /

OBJECTIVE:

- Learn the Q and / (slash or diagonal) keys.

A. WARMUP

Type each line 2 times.

1 club face when silk mold brag java blue
2 Jana went biking, and Cila waved flags.

NEW KEYS

B. Q KEY

Type each line 2 times. Repeat if time permits.

Use A finger.
Anchor F.

3 aaa aqa aqa qaq aqa aaa aqa aqa qaq aqa
4 aqa quo quo aqa qui qui aqa que que aqa
5 aqa quail, quit quick quid, half quest,
6 The quints squabbled on a square quilt.

LESSON 148

DATABASES: REPORTS

OBJECTIVES:

- Improve keyboarding skill.
- Create reports based on database tables.
- Type 40/5'/5e.

A. WARMUP

Type each line 2 times.

Speed
Accuracy
Language Link
Numbers/Symbols

1 The paper might run low before we can finish that next job.
2 Judi's dog jumps over major hurdles to beat Max for prizes.
3 Lee attended a fast-paced meeting on January 23 at ten p.m.
4 On 10/14/98 Steven ran 38 laps; on 10/25/98 he ran 67 laps.
| 1 | 2 | 3 | 4 | 5 | 6 | 7 | 8 | 9 | 10 | 11 | 12

SKILLBUILDING

B. 30-SECOND OK TIMINGS

Take two 30-second OK (error-free) timings on lines 5–6. Then take two 30-second OK timings on lines 7–8. Goal: no errors.

5   Hazel hurt an elbow when she bumped into the chair as   11
6 she was quickly running through the room to avoid the fire. 23

7   The six jet-black vans zipped quietly through the wet   11
8 grass, but they could not finish the entire course in time. 23
| 1 | 2 | 3 | 4 | 5 | 6 | 7 | 8 | 9 | 10 | 11 | 12

C. PREVIEW PRACTICE

Type each line 2 times as a preview to the timings that follow.

Accuracy
Speed

9 events written calculate combination sixteenth chronologist
10 calendars tracking notable cycles errors unique epoch orbit

4 3 2 1   1 2 3 4

C. / KEY

Type each line 2 times. Repeat if time permits.

Use Sem finger.
Anchor J.
Do not space before
or after a slash
(diagonal).

7 ;;; ;/; ;/; /;/ ;/; ;;; ;/; ;/; /;/ ;/;
8 ;/; her/him ;/; us/them ;/; his/her ;/;
9 ;/; slow/fast, walk/ride, debit/credit,
10 The fall/winter catalog has new colors.

SKILLBUILDING

D. TECHNIQUE CHECKPOINT

*Type each line 2 times. Repeat if time permits. Focus on the technique
at the left.*

Keep fingers curved
and wrists level.

11 aaa aqa aqa qaq aqa aaa aqa aqa qaq aqa
12 ;;; ;/; ;/; /;/ ;/; ;;; ;/; ;/; /;/ ;/;
13 The quick squash squad requested quiet.
14 He/she said that we could do either/or.

E. TECHNIQUE TIMINGS

*Take two 30-second timings on each line. Focus on the technique at
the left.*

Keep your eyes on the
copy.

15 Louise will lead if she makes the team.
16 Their bands will march at the quadrant.
17 Brad just had time to finish his goals.
18 I was quiet as he glided over the wave.

| 1 | 2 | 3 | 4 | 5 | 6 | 7 | 8

ACTIVITY 23
Database Table 3,
Query 7

Create the following query on Database Table 3:

1. Select the *State* and *State Bird* fields, and sort the data on the *State Bird* field.
2. Print the results of the query table.
3. Close the query window(s).
4. Name the query Q7.

ACTIVITY 24
Database Table 3,
Query 8

Create the following query on Database Table 3:

1. Select the *State* and *State Bird* fields, and sort the data on the *State Bird* field.
2. In the *State Bird* field, specify selection of those states with the cardinal, mockingbird, or robin as the state bird.
3. Print the results of the query table.
4. Name the query Q8.

ACTIVITY 25
Database Table 3,
Query 9

Create the following query on Database Table 3:

1. Select the *State* and *State Bird* fields, and sort the data on the *State* field.
2. In the *State Bird* field, specify selection of those states with the cardinal, mockingbird, or robin as the state bird.
3. Print the results of the query table.
4. Close the query window(s).
5. Name the query Q9.

ACTIVITY 26
Database Table 3,
Query 10

Create the following query on Database Table 3:

1. Select the *State* and *Highest Point* fields, and sort the data on the *Highest Point* field.
2. In the *Highest Point* field, specify selection of those states with elevations of 10,000 feet or higher.
3. Print the results of the query table.
4. Close the query window(s).
5. Name the query Q10.

SOCIAL STUDIES CONNECTIONS

South Carolina was the first state to secede from the Union on December 20, 1860, so that it could become the first Confederate State. (It was readmitted to the Union on June 25, 1868.)

Take a 1-minute timing on lines 19–20. Note your speed and errors.

Hold those anchors.

| 19 | find/seek boat fate jail cube brad swat | 8 |
| 20 | walk shut quid mile vane aqua slot quit | 16 |

```
| 1 | 2 | 3 | 4 | 5 | 6 | 7 | 8
```

G. PRACTICE

Type each line 2 times. Repeat if time permits.

To build skill:
• Type each line two times.
• Speed up the second time you type the line.

21	find/lose cats/dogs hike/bike walk/ride
22	seek/hide soft/hard mice/rats shut/ajar
23	boat goat moat mode rode rude ruin quid
24	fate face race rice nice Nile vile mile
25	jail fail fall gall mall male vale vane
26	cube Cuba tuba tube lube luau quad aqua
27	brad brat brag quag flag flat slat slot
28	swat swam swim slim slid slit suit quit

H. POSTTEST

Repeat the Pretest. Compare your Posttest results with your Pretest results.

FACT FILE

The compact disc was first available for consumer purchase in 1983. In that year, only 100,000 CDs were sold. By 1988, sales of CDs topped sales of LPs. By 1992, CD sales exceeded cassette tape sales. Today, approximately two-thirds of all music sold is produced on CDs.

ACTIVITY 18
Database Table 3,
Query 2

Create the following query on Database Table 3:

1. Select the *State* and *Date of Statehood* fields, and sort the data on the *Date of Statehood* field.
2. In the *Date of Statehood* field, specify selection of those states that acquired statehood in the 1700s.
3. Print the results of the query table.
4. Close the query window(s).
5. Name the query Q2.

ACTIVITY 19
Database Table 3,
Query 3

Create the following query on Database Table 3:

1. Select the *State* and *Date of Statehood* fields, and sort the data on the *Date of Statehood* field.
2. In the *Date of Statehood* field, specify selection of those states that acquired statehood in the 1800s.
3. Print the results of the query table.
4. Close the query window(s).
5. Name the query Q3.

ACTIVITY 20
Database Table 3,
Query 4

Create the following query on Database Table 3:

1. Select the *State* and *Date of Statehood* fields, and sort the data on the *Date of Statehood* field.
2. In the *Date of Statehood* field, specify selection of those states that acquired statehood in the 1900s.
3. Print the results of the query table.
4. Close the query window(s).
5. Name the query Q4.

ACTIVITY 21
Database Table 3,
Query 5

Create the following query on Database Table 3:

1. Select the *State* and *Capital* fields, and sort the data on the *Capital* field.
2. Print the results of the query table.
3. Close the query window(s).
4. Name the query Q5.

ACTIVITY 22
Database Table 3,
Query 6

Create the following query on Database Table 3:

1. Select the *State* and *Capital* fields, and sort the data on the *Capital* field.
2. In the *Capital* field, specify selection of those states with capitals that begin with the letter *C*.
3. Print the results of the query table.
4. Close the query window(s).
5. Name the query Q6.

LESSON 11

NEW KEYS: ' "

OBJECTIVES:

- Learn the apostrophe (') and the quotation mark (") keys.
- Improve speed and accuracy.

A. WARMUP

Type each line 2 times.

1 quill wagon cabin valued helms, and/or;
2 Jake is quite good in math but not Val.

NEW KEYS

B. ' KEY

Type each line 2 times. Repeat if time permits.

**Use Sem finger.
Anchor J.
Do not space before
or after an apostrophe within a word.**

3 ;;; ;'; ;'; ';' ;'; ;;; ;'; ;'; ';' ;';
4 ;'; he's he's ;'; where's ;'; it's it's
5 ;'; ';' Kit's barn ;'; Ed's car ;'; ';'
6 Bill's car isn't running; it's at Li's.

DATABASE APPLICATIONS

ACTIVITY 12
Database Table 3

Open the file DT3 and follow these steps:

1. Sort the table on the *State Bird* field in ascending order.
2. Print the table.
3. Do not save your changes.

ACTIVITY 13
Database Table 3

Using Database Table 3, perform the following sort:

1. Sort the table on the *Date of Statehood* field in ascending order.
2. Print the table.

ACTIVITY 14
Database Table 3

Using Database Table 3, perform the following sort:

1. Sort the table on the *Highest Point* field in descending order.
2. Print the table.

ACTIVITY 15
Database Table 3

Continue using Database Table 3 and perform the following sort:

1. Sort the table on the *State Bird* field in ascending order, and then sort the *State* field in descending order. Be sure the *State Bird* field is listed first.
2. Print the table and compare your results with Activity 12 results.

ACTIVITY 16
Database Table 3

Perform the following sort to return Database Table 3 to its original format:

1. Sort the table on the *State* field in ascending order.
2. Close the table window.

ACTIVITY 17
Database Table 3,
Query 1

Create the following query on Database Table 3:

1. Select the *State* and *Date of Statehood* fields, and sort the data on the *Date of Statehood* field.
2. Print the results of the query table.
3. Close the query window(s).
4. Name the query Q1.

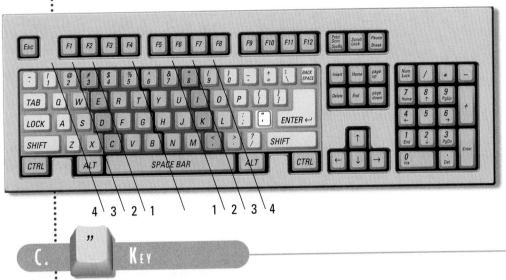

4 3 2 1   1 2 3 4

C. " KEY

Type each line 2 times. Repeat if time permits.

Shift of apostrophe.
Use Sem finger.
Anchor J.

7 ;;; ;"; ;"; ";" ;"; ;;; ;"; ;"; ";" ;";
8 ;"; "win" "win" ;"; "big" "big" ;"; ";"
9 ;"; "mew" "oink" "woof" "moo" "baa" ";"
10 "Green" means "go"; "red" means "wait."

SKILLBUILDING

D. TECHNIQUE CHECKPOINT

Type each line 2 times. Repeat if time permits. Focus on the technique at the left.

Keep your eyes on the copy.

11 ;;; ;'; ;'; ';' ;'; ;;; ;'; ;'; ';' ;';
12 ;;; ;"; ;"; ";" ;"; ;;; ;"; ;"; ";" ;";
13 He said "no thanks," but it was "lame."
14 Rita "forgot," but Milo added "favors."

E. TECHNIQUE TIMINGS

Take two 30-second timings on each line. Focus on the technique at the left.

Keep your eyes on the copy.

15 Robb's clothes and image don't "match."
16 Mr. Quill said, "Wait." Lee did not go.
17 Jane's visit was "quick"; she ran back.
18 I haven't enough time to "quibble" now.
   | 1 | 2 | 3 | 4 | 5 | 6 | 7 | 8

5 Two thirds of the membership must be present to enact a rule.
6 We observed twenty nine infractions during the investigation.
7 Bancroft Industries reduced their sales force by one fourth.
8 After we add all the numbers, we must increase it by fifty five.

SKILLBUILDING

C. 30-Second Timings

Take two 30-second timings on lines 9–10. Then take two 30-second timings on lines 11–12. Try to increase your speed on each timing.

9   Presentation software will enable you to create some   11
10 colorful, animated, and visually exciting presentations.   22

11   You can include photos, clip art, sound, animation,   11
12 and a variety of colors, which will make a great impact.   22
   | 1 | 2 | 3 | 4 | 5 | 6 | 7 | 8 | 9 | 10 | 11 | 12

COMMUNICATION FOCUS

Write a short paragraph or two about your opinions on graphic presentations. Ask a teacher how he or she uses graphical presentations such as transparencies and PowerPoint® slides.

FORMATTING

D. Software Features

STUDENT MANUAL

Sort Database Tables   Query Database Tables

Study Lesson 147 in your student manual. Complete all the practice activities while at your computer. Then complete the jobs that follow.

F. 12-Second Sprints

Take three 12-second timings on each line. Try to increase your speed on each timing.

19 Go to the cabin and get us the dog now.
20 Now is the time to call all men for me.
21 She made a face when she lost the race.
22 Ask them if the vase is safe with them.
| | | | 5 | | | | 10 | | | | 15 | | | 20 | | | | 25 | | | | 30 | | | | 35 | | | | 40

G. PRETEST

Take a 1-minute timing on lines 23–24. Note your speed and errors.

23 We can't "remember" how Bo got bruised.   8
24 Burt's dad "asked" Kurt to assist Ross.   16
| 1 | 2 | 3 | 4 | 5 | 6 | 7 | 8

H. PRACTICE

Type each line 2 times.

25 made fade face race lace lice nice mice
26 Burt Nora Will Mame Ross Kurt Olaf Elle
27 he's I've don't can't won't we've she's
28 Bo's dogs Lu's cows Mo's cats Di's rats

29 "mat" "bat" "west" "east" "gone" "tone"
30 He "quit"; she "tried." I hit a "wall."
31 sand/land vane/cane robe/lobe quit/suit
32 asks bask base vase case cast mast last

I. POSTTEST

Repeat the Pretest. Compare your Posttest results with your Pretest results.

FACT FILE

A computer *bug* is a programming error that causes a program or a computer system to malfunction, produce incorrect results, or crash.

LESSON 147

DATABASES: SORT AND QUERY

OBJECTIVES:

- Learn rules for hyphenating words.
- Improve keyboarding skill.
- Learn to sort database tables.
- Learn to query database tables.

A. WARMUP

Type each line 2 times.

Speed
Accuracy
Language Link
Numbers/Symbols

```
1 The dog and cat went to eat their food from the round dish.
2 Liza gave Max and Becky a quaint photo of a jar of flowers.
3 The 3 students tried to finish their project before Monday.
4 I concluded that 1/3 of $39 = $13, and that 20% of $10 = 2.
  | 1 | 2 | 3 | 4 | 5 | 6 | 7 | 8 | 9 | 10 | 11 | 12
```

LANGUAGE LINK

B. HYPHENATED WORDS

Study the rule and examples that follow. Then edit lines 5–8 by inserting hyphens where necessary.

Rule 47:

Hyphenate compound numbers (between *twenty-one* and *ninety-nine*) and fractions that are expressed in words.

> *Seventy-five of the members voted to repeal the law—this was nearly two-fifths of the membership.*

> *Thirty-five letters were sent to Mr. Alexander to thank him for his excellent service.*

LESSON 12 REVIEW

OBJECTIVE:

- Improve keyboarding skills.

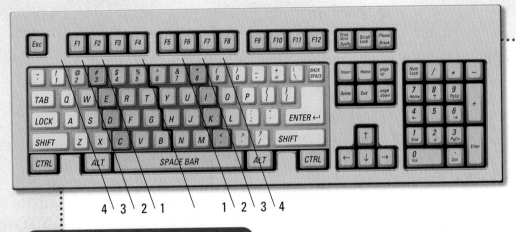

4 3 2 1   1 2 3 4

A. WARMUP

Type each line 2 times.

1 java blue club face when brag silk mold
2 Geof went sailing, but Lin was at home.

SKILLBUILDING

B. SHIFT KEYS

Type each line 2 times. Repeat if time permits.

Keep your rhythm steady as you reach to the shift keys. Anchor left shift with F. Anchor right shift with J.

3 Seth Kebo Otis Fran Iris Edie Jose Dave
4 Hans Cara Nita Rene Uris Vera Mark Adam
5 Theo Jean Saul Hugh Eric Noel Vida Ivan
6 Gino Leah Burt Olla Anna Kris Wade Mike

C. CONCENTRATION

Fill in the missing letters shown at the left as you type each line 1 time.

R
EO
H
ES

7 Ou- -ivers and oceans a-e being -uined.
8 W- must w-rk t- mak- -ur w-rld cl-an-r.
9 -armful c-emicals fill muc- of t-e air.
10 W- hav- lo-t u-ag- of -om- of our -oil.

State	Capital	Date of Statehood	State Bird	Highest Point
Kansas	Topeka	1/29/1861	Western meadowlark	4,039
Kentucky	Frankfort	6/1/1792	Cardinal	4,145
Louisiana	Baton Rouge	4/30/1812	Eastern brown pelican	535
Maine	Augusta	3/15/1820	Chickadee	5,268
Maryland	Annapolis	4/28/1788	Baltimore oriole	3,360
Massachusetts	Boston	2/6/1788	Chickadee	3,491
Michigan	Lansing	1/26/1837	Robin	1,980
Minnesota	St. Paul	5/11/1858	Common loon	2,301
Mississippi	Jackson	12/10/1817	Mockingbird	806
Missouri	Jefferson City	8/10/1821	Bluebird	1,772
Montana	Helena	11/8/1889	Western meadowlark	12,799
Nebraska	Lincoln	3/1/1867	Western meadowlark	5,424
Nevada	Carson City	10/31/1864	Mountain bluebird	13,143
New Hampshire	Concord	6/21/1788	Purple finch	6,288
New Jersey	Trenton	12/18/1787	Eastern goldfinch	1,803
New Mexico	Santa Fe	1/6/1912	Chaparral bird	13,161
New York	Albany	7/26/1788	Bluebird	5,344
North Carolina	Raleigh	11/21/1789	Cardinal	6,684
North Dakota	Bismarck	11/2/1889	Western meadowlark	3,506
Ohio	Columbus	3/1/1803	Cardinal	1,550
Oklahoma	Oklahoma City	11/16/1907	Scissor-tailed flycatcher	4,973
Oregon	Salem	2/14/1859	Western meadowlark	11,233
Pennsylvania	Harrisburg	12/12/1787	Ruffed grouse	3,213
Rhode Island	Providence	5/29/1790	Rhode Island red	812
South Carolina	Columbia	5/23/1788	Carolina wren	3,560
South Dakota	Pierre	11/2/1889	Red-necked pheasant	7,242
Tennessee	Nashville	6/1/1796	Mockingbird	6,643
Texas	Austin	12/29/1845	Mockingbird	8,749
Utah	Salt Lake City	1/4/1896	Sea gull	13,528
Vermont	Montpelier	3/4/1791	Hermit thrush	4,393
Virginia	Richmond	6/25/1788	Cardinal	5,729
Washington	Olympia	11/11/1889	Willow goldfinch	14,410
West Virginia	Charleston	6/20/1863	Cardinal	4,863
Wisconsin	Madison	5/29/1848	Robin	1,952
Wyoming	Cheyenne	7/10/1890	Western meadowlark	13,804

D. TECHNIQUE CHECKPOINT

Type each line 2 times. Repeat if time permits. Focus on the techniques at the left.

Sit up straight and keep your feet on the floor.

11 The cook went to work with cork boards.
12 Four foul jugs were left at the stream.
13 Toil in the weeds to get the seeds now.
14 Tell a joke, then gather other jesters.

E. TECHNIQUE TIMINGS

Take two 30-second timings on each line. Focus on the techniques at the left.

Keep your feet on the floor and sit up straight.

15 Ulan told Brian she would be glad to go.
16 In Boston one can see vast fish markets.
17 Bruce had this I/O switch changed again.
18 Treena saw quite a flock of "odd" birds.
| 1 | 2 | 3 | 4 | 5 | 6 | 7 | 8

F. PRETEST

Take a 1-minute timing on lines 19–20. Note your speed and errors.

19 Walter took a ride to the quiet street.   8
20 Quakes threw her around the trick door.   16
| 1 | 2 | 3 | 4 | 5 | 6 | 7 | 8

G. PRACTICE

SPEED: If you made 2 or fewer errors on the Pretest, type lines 21–28 two times each.
ACCURACY: If you made more than 2 errors on the Pretest, type lines 21–24 as a group two times; then type lines 25–28 as a group two times.

Third Row Keys
Check hands:
• *Curve fingers*
• *Hold home-key anchors.*

21 rook took cook cork work word ford fold
22 full fill file fire fore four foul fowl
23 jolt joke jets jerk jest just jugs jute
24 wire were went west jest quit quid quad

25 weed reed seed seat seal soil toil foil
26 dour sour sort tort tore wore sore lore
27 told hold sold sole hole role real teal
28 tire fire sire site suit quit whit with

H. POSTTEST

Repeat the Pretest. Compare your Posttest results with your Pretest results.

DATABASE APPLICATIONS

ACTIVITY 11
Database Table 3

Open the file DT3 and make the following changes:

1. Add a new field named *Highest Point;* specify it as a number field and format the field with commas.
2. Position the field *Highest Point* as the last field of the table.
3. Enter the elevations for the states as shown in the first illustration.
4. Add the records shown in the second illustration on the next page to Database Table 3.
5. Print the table.
6. Close the table window.

Alabama	2,407
Alaska	20,320
Arizona	12,633
Arkansas	2,753
California	14,494
Colorado	14,433
Connecticut	2,380
Delaware	442
Florida	345
Georgia	4,784
Hawaii	13,796
Idaho	12,662
Illinois	1,235
Indiana	1,257
Iowa	1,670

FACT FILE

The highest mountain in Africa is Mt. Kilimanjaro, which is 19,430 feet high.

LESSON 13

NEW KEYS: P X

OBJECTIVE:

- Learn the P and X keys.

A. WARMUP

Type each line 2 times.

1 fade cave what swim quad blot king jars
2 Black liquids vanish from the jug I saw.

NEW KEYS

B. P KEY

Type each line 2 times. Repeat if time permits.

Use Sem finger.
Anchor J and K.

3 ;;; ;p; ;p; p;p ;p; ;;; ;p; ;p; p;p ;p;
4 ;p; nap nap ;p; pen pen ;p; ape ape ;p;
5 ;p; perfect plot, a pale page, pen pal,
6 Pam pulled a pouting pup past a puddle.

Take two 5-minute timings on the paragraphs. Note your speed and errors.

Goal: 40/5'/5e

Science
Connections

19	Comets, which are composed of frozen particles of	10
20	water, can be many miles long. As they travel through our	22
21	solar system from space and become visible, they put on	33
22	quite a display.	36
23	The head of a comet is somewhat spherical, and it is	47
24	surrounded by a fuzzy halo called a coma. Comets also have	59
25	huge tails that are made up of gas and dust that fan out	70
26	behind the comet. Each comet can have as many as three	81
27	tails that extend miles from the head of the comet.	92
28	The white dust tail is the most visible. It is created	103
29	as heat from the sun causes frozen particles of the comet	115
30	to evaporate. As the particles evaporate, they create gas	126
31	molecules that stream off and carry dust with them.	137
32	A bluish tail is created as the energy from the sun	147
33	ionizes some of the gases of the comet. This tail streams	159
34	directly away from the sun.	164
35	The tail between the other two is formed at the head of	186
36	the comet by chemical reactions. It is made of hydrogen and	197
37	is not seen from Earth, since the atmosphere absorbs its	199
38	light.	200

| 1 | 2 | 3 | 4 | 5 | 6 | 7 | 8 | 9 | 10 | 11 | 12SI 1.42

FACT FILE

In 1994, comet Hyakutake, which was visible to the naked eye, passed the Earth at a distance of 9 million miles. Comet Hale-Bopp was sighted. The comet was named for a pair of astronomers who independently discovered it on the same night in July 1995. Hale-Bopp measured about 25 miles across and was the largest comet to pass Earth in at least four centuries. Hale-Bopp, also visible to the naked eye, passed Earth at a distance of 122 million miles, which is 30 million miles farther away than the sun.

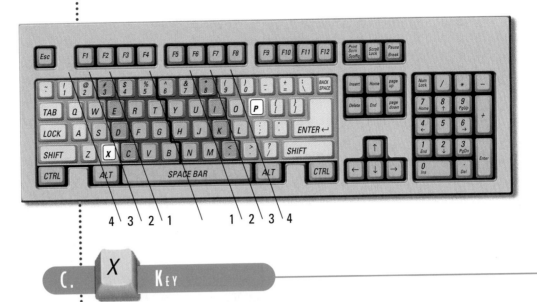

C. X KEY

Type each line 2 times. Repeat if time permits.

Use S finger.
Anchor A or F.

7 sss sxs sxs xsx sxs sss sxs sxs xsx sxs
8 sxs tax tax sxs mix mix sxs axe axe sxs
9 sxs lax taxes, vexed vixen, six Texans,
10 Fix the next six boxes on next weekend.

CULTURAL CONNECTIONS

Canada has two official languages—English and French. The majority of French-speaking Canadians live in the province of Quebec. Most of the rest of Canada is largely English-speaking.

SKILLBUILDING

D. TECHNIQUE CHECKPOINT

Type each line 2 times. Focus on the techniques at the left.

Remember to keep:
• **Wrists up.**
• **Fingers curved.**
• **Feet flat on the floor.**

11 ;;; ;p; ;p; p;p ;p; ;;; ;p; ;p; p;p ;p;
12 sss sxs sxs xsx sxs sss sxs sxs xsx sxs
13 Phil will fix ripped carpets alone now.
14 Go see that duplex before next weekend.

SKILLBUILDING

B. PRETEST

Take a 1-minute timing on the paragraph. Note your speed and errors.

5 The way the computer works is quite a mystery to some,	11
6 for it is able to execute its tasks at a speed difficult to	23
7 comprehend. To perceive how a computer operates is not that	35
8 complicated when you realize that it is like a light switch.	47

C. PRACTICE

In the following chart, find the number of errors you made on the Pretest. Then type each of the designated drill lines two times.

Pretest Errors	0–1	2	3	4+
Drill Lines	12–16	11–15	10–14	9–13

Accuracy

9 quite appears charged realize mystery electrical comprehend
10 some however capable millions complete character understand
11 able tedious special numbers execute processing electricity
12 switch current difficult computer's complicated five letter

Speed

13 appears turned moving speed works light data like when that
14 holding letter wanted store cells which used such with each
15 seconds symbol called tasks being would five need word only
16 matters stored memory works takes bytes take slow time work

D. POSTTEST

Repeat the Pretest. Compare your Posttest results with your Pretest results.

E. PREVIEW PRACTICE

Type each line 2 times as a preview to the timings that follow.

Accuracy
Speed

17 the year Romans season Ptolemy egyptian thousands calendars
18 centuries thirteen element ancient Julius Caesar Mayans and

Take two 30-second timings on each line. Press ENTER at the end of each sentence. Focus on the technique at the left.

Keep your rhythm steady as you reach to the ENTER key and back to home position.

```
15  Pull on the tabs.↵ The box will open.↵
16  Speed is good.↵ Errors are not good.↵
17  Glue the picture.↵ The book is done.↵
18  Get the clothes.↵ Bring me their caps.↵
    | 1 | 2 | 3 | 4 | 5 | 6 | 7 | 8
```

F. PRETEST

Take a 1-minute timing on lines 19–20. Note your speed and errors.

```
19  slag chop gate plop tops bows veal dart      8
20  apex slab gave quit fix, hoax text jell     16
    | 1 | 2 | 3 | 4 | 5 | 6 | 7 | 8
```

G. PRACTICE

Type each line 2 times.

To type faster:
• Read copy before typing.
• Type with smooth strokes.

```
21  slag flag flap flax flux flex Alex apex
22  chop clop clap clan claw slaw slap slab
23  gate gale pale page pave have cave gave
24  plop flop flip slip ship whip quip quit

25  tops tips sips sits sit, six, mix, fix,
26  bows bowl jowl howl cowl coal coax hoax
27  veal real seal meal meat neat next text
28  dart part park bark balk ball bell jell
```

H. POSTTEST

Repeat the Pretest. Compare your Posttest results with your Pretest results.

LESSON 146

DATABASE: REVIEW

OBJECTIVES:

- Improve keyboarding skill.
- Review database tables.
- Type 40/5'/5e.

A. WARMUP

Type each line 2 times.

Speed	1	These short, easy words help you when you build your speed.
Accuracy	2	Even Jacques may gaze up to find six crows in the blue sky.
Language Link	3	James and I grew up in Montana; we always go home in March.
Numbers	4	If we need 56 points, then 47, 29, 38, or 10 will not help.

| 1 | 2 | 3 | 4 | 5 | 6 | 7 | 8 | 9 | 10 | 11 | 12

SCIENCE CONNECTIONS

The hermit crab must use the empty shell of another animal for its home. Each time the hermit crab grows too large for its "borrowed" home, it moves out and finds a larger shell in which to live. During this time, the hermit crab is vulnerable to attack by predators. Most other crabs grow a new shell when they get too large for the current one.

LESSON 14

NEW KEYS: Y TAB

OBJECTIVE:

- Learn the Y and the tab keys.

4 3 2 1   1 2 3 4

A.   WARMUP

Type each line 2 times.

1 jibe wing more vase deft lack hex; quid
2 Max just put a pale slab over the gate.

NEW KEYS

B.    Y   KEY

Type each line 2 times. Repeat if time permits.

Use J finger.
Anchor ; L, and K.

3 jjj jyj jyj yjy jyj jjj jyj jyj yjy jyj
4 jyj yes yes jyj joy joy jyj aye aye jyj
5 jyj yard of yarn, July joy, yellow yam,
6 Shelley yearns to yodel but only yells.

ACTIVITY 10
Database Table 5

Open the file DT5 and make the following changes:

1. Add a new field named *Code;* specify 5 as the field size.
2. Position the field *Code* at the beginning of the table.
3. Add a new field named *Purchase Date,* and specify it as a date field; position it between the fields *Binding* and *Retail Price.*
4. Enter the codes and dates for the titles shown in the illustration.
5. Print the table.
6. Close the table window.

Code	Title	Purchase Date
H29	Out of the Dust	4/4/--
S15	View From Saturday	4/4/--
H25	The Midwife's Apprentice	4/4/--
S33	Walk Two Moons	4/4/--
H48	Sarah, Plain and Tall	4/11/--
S36	The Bridge to Terabithia	4/11/--
H59	Roll of Thunder, Hear My Cry	4/11/--
H16	Mrs. Frisby and the Rats of NIMH	4/11/--
S45	Summer of the Swans	4/18/--
H22	Sounder	4/18/--
S61	Island of the Blue Dolphins	4/18/--
H57	Johnny Tremain	4/18/--

PORTFOLIO
Activity

What would you do with the money if you won the big prize in a contest? Make a list in your portfolio of what would be the most important things you would purchase with the money. Create a database with the names and addresses of people with whom you would want to share your winnings.

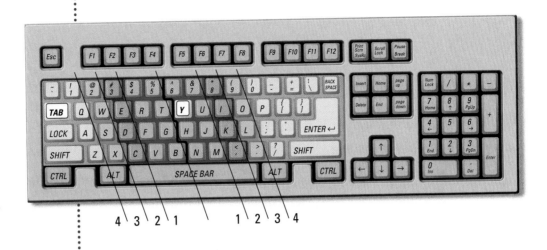

4 3 2 1   1 2 3 4

The tab key is used to indent paragraphs. The tab key is located to the left of the Q key. Reach to the tab key with the A finger. Keep your other fingers on home keys as you quickly press the tab key.

Pressing the tab key will move the cursor 0.5 inch (the default setting) to the right.

Type each paragraph 2 times. Press ENTER only at the end of a paragraph. Repeat if time permits.

Word wrap automatically moves a word that does not fit on one line down to the next line.

7   If you are happy, you will be able
8   to set goals. You will also smile more.
9   The jury was out and no one could
10 leave the room. We all had to stay put.

SKILLBUILDING

Type each line 2 times. Focus on the technique at the left. Repeat if time permits.

Keep your eyes on the copy.

11 jjj jyj jyj yjy jyj jjj jyj jyj yjy jyj
12 I saw yards of yellow fabric every day.
13 They happily played in the lonely yard.
14 Yes, the daily reports are ready today.

| 33 | 20 | | |
Position	Minimum Credentials	Low-End Salary	High-End Salary
Accountant	Bachelor's Degree	$23,300.00	$29,400.00
Administrative Services Manager	Associate Degree	$39,700.00	$53,300.00
Budget Analyst	Bachelor's Degree	$24,000.00	$65,000.00
Education Administrator	Master's Degree	$34,500.00	$200,200.00
Employment Interviewer	Bachelor's Degree	$20,000.00	$54,000.00
Human Resources Specialist	Bachelor's Degree	$25,000.00	$59,000.00
Food Services Manager	Bachelor's Degree	$21,000.00	$50,000.00

ACTIVITY 9
Database Table 5

Follow these steps to create Database Table 5 and name it DT5.

1. Define the five fields as shown in the illustration; identify the fourth field as a monetary field and the fifth field as a number field.
2. Specify the size of each text/alpha field as shown above the column.
3. Enter the records.
4. Print the table.
5. Close the table window.

| 34 | 22 | 11 | | |
Title	Author	Binding	Retail Price	Inventory
Out of the Dust	Karen Hesse	hardcover	$15.95	14
View From Saturday	E. L. Konigsburg	paperback	$4.50	20
The Midwife's Apprentice	Karen Cushman	hardcover	$10.95	25
Walk Two Moons	Sharon Creech	paperback	$4.95	18
Sarah, Plain and Tall	Patricia MacLachlan	hardcover	$14.95	17
The Bridge to Terabithia	Katherine Paterson	paperback	$4.95	22
Roll of Thunder, Hear My Cry	Mildred D. Taylor	hardcover	$15.99	30
Mrs. Frisby and the Rats of NIMH	Robert C. O'Brien	hardcover	$17.00	28
Summer of the Swans	Betsy Byars	paperback	$4.99	32
Sounder	William H. Armstrong	hardcover	$14.95	35
Island of the Blue Dolphins	Scott O'Dell	paperback	$5.50	15
Johnny Tremain	Esther Forbes	hardcover	$20.00	12

E. TECHNIQUE TIMINGS

Take two 30-second timings on each line. Focus on the technique at the left.

Keep your eyes on the copy as you take each timing.

15 Push your fingers to find the keys now.
16 You will see your typing speed improve.
17 Have a goal to type faster than before.
18 Try every day to achieve that new goal.
| 1 | 2 | 3 | 4 | 5 | 6 | 7 | 8

F. PRETEST

Take a 1-minute timing on lines 19–22. Note your speed and errors.

Remember: Press ENTER only at the end of the paragraph (line 22).

19   A jury will meet next January to   7
20 get a verdict. People stole costly fuel   15
21 from the boys. We found bags of cards   22
22 next to the mops in the broom closet.   30
| 1 | 2 | 3 | 4 | 5 | 6 | 7 | 8

G. PRACTICE

Type each line 2 times.

23 fuel duel duet suet suit quit quip quid
24 gape nape cape cave wave wage wags bags
25 mops pops maps hops tops toys joys boys
26 rope lope lops laps lips lids kids kiss

27 card cart curt hurt hurl furl fury jury
28 cost most lost lest best test text next
29 slab flab flap flaw flay slay clay play
30 pan, fan, tan, man, can, ran, Dan, Jan,

H. POSTTEST

Repeat the Pretest. Compare your Posttest results with your Pretest results.

SKILLBUILDING

C. DIAGNOSTIC PRACTICE: NUMBERS

Turn to the Diagnostic Practice: Numbers routine on page SB4. Type one of the Pretest/Posttest paragraphs and identify any errors made. Then type the corresponding drill lines 2 times for each number on which you made 2 or more errors and 1 time for each number on which you made only 1 error. Finally, repeat the same Pretest paragraph and compare your performance.

MATH CONNECTIONS

Assume that you won $10,000,000 dollars. Determine the amount you would actually receive after taxes.

FORMATTING

D. SOFTWARE FEATURES

STUDENT MANUAL

Monetary and Numeric Fields

Study Lesson 145 in your student manual. Complete all the practice activities while at your computer. Then complete the jobs that follow.

DATABASE APPLICATIONS

ACTIVITY 8
Database Table 4

Follow these steps to create Database Table 4 and name it DT4:

1. Define the four fields as shown in the illustration.
2. Identify the third and fourth fields as monetary fields.
3. Specify the size of each text/alpha field as shown above the column.
4. Enter the records.
5. Print the table.
6. Close the table window.

LESSON 15

NEW KEYS: Z COLON (:)

OBJECTIVE:

- Learn the Z and colon keys.

4 3 2 1   1 2 3 4

A. WARMUP

Type each line 2 times.

1 bake chin jogs wave quip dome onyx left
2 His soft big lynx quickly jumped waves.

NEW KEYS

B. Z KEY

Type each line 2 times. Repeat if time permits.

Use A finger.
Anchor F.

3 aaa aza aza zaz aza aaa aza aza zaz aza
4 aza zip zip aza zoo zoo aza zap zap aza
5 aza dozing zebu, he zags, dazed zebras,
6 Zachary ate frozen pizza in the gazebo.

LESSON 145

DATABASES: MONETARY AND NUMERIC FIELDS

OBJECTIVES:

- Compose at the keyboard.
- Increase keyboarding skill.
- Learn about monetary and numeric fields.

A. WARMUP

Type each line 2 times.

Speed
Accuracy
Language Link
Numbers/Symbols

1 Hard rain came down very fast, so I could not see the road.
2 Everybody expected Jack's golf technique to win him prizes.
3 We were told that it may be colder Friday than it is today.
4 Chris & David earned $7.75/hour loading 1,234# of #4 pines.

| 1 | 2 | 3 | 4 | 5 | 6 | 7 | 8 | 9 | 10 | 11 | 12

LANGUAGE LINK

B. COMPOSING AT THE KEYBOARD

Compose a one-page story to complete the following paragraph:

FACT FILE

Benjamin Franklin once proposed the turkey as the national bird of the United States instead of the eagle.

    I was watching the Super Bowl on television when the doorbell rang. Since I was the only one at home, I went to the door to see who would be interrupting my football game. Much to my surprise, I found the Prize Scout—complete with flowers and balloons. I could hardly believe my ears when he said, "Congratulations, you are the Publishing Giants $10 million winner!" Since that day, my life has changed, and now . . .

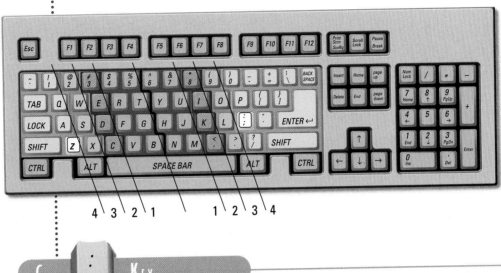

4 3 2 1   1 2 3 4

C. : KEY

Type each line 2 times. Repeat if time permits.

Shift of ;
Use left shift key.
Anchor J.
Space once after a
colon.

7 ;:; ::; ;:; :;: ;:; ;:; ;:; ;:; :;: ;:;
8 Dr. Webb: Mr. Que: Mrs. Downs: Ms. Lia:
9 Mr. Dode: Mrs. Chin: Ms. Finn: Dr. Mai:
10 To: From: Date: Subject: Attention: To:

*inter*NET C O N N E C T I O N

Many computer and Internet terms are not yet defined in dictionaries. Use your available search engine to locate a dictionary website. Search the dictionary for a definition of the following terms: *nanosecond, cupcake,* and *hyperlink.*

SKILLBUILDING

D. TECHNIQUE CHECKPOINT

Type each line 2 times. Repeat if time permits. Focus on the technique at the left.

Keep your elbows close to your body.

11 aaa aza aza zaz aza aaa aza aza zaz aza
12 ;:; ::; ;:; :;: ;:; ;:; ;:; ;:; :;: ;:;
13 Zach and zany Hazel visited local zoos.
14 They saw: lazy zebras, apes, and lions.

Alabama	Yellowhammer
Alaska	Willow ptarmigan
Arizona	Cactus wren
Arkansas	Mockingbird
California	California valley quail
Colorado	Lark bunting
Connecticut	Robin
Delaware	Blue hen chicken

State	Capital	Date of Statehood	State Bird
Florida	Tallahassee	3/3/1845	Mockingbird
Georgia	Atlanta	1/2/1788	Brown thrasher
Hawaii	Honolulu	8/21/1959	Nene
Idaho	Boise	7/3/1890	Mountain bluebird
Illinois	Springfield	12/3/1818	Cardinal
Indiana	Indianapolis	12/11/1816	Cardinal
Iowa	Des Moines	12/28/1846	Eastern goldfinch

JOURNAL ENTRY

What is your state bird? Why do states choose a particular bird to represent them? Find the answers to these questions and record them in your journal. Record what kinds of birds you frequently see in your areas.

Take two 30-second timings on each line. Focus on the technique at the left.

Keep your elbows in by your sides.

15 Type fast to reach the end of the line.
16 Keep your eyes on the copy as you type.
17 Tests are easy if you know the answers.
18 If they go to the zoo, invite them too.
| 1 | 2 | 3 | 4 | 5 | 6 | 7 | 8

F. PRETEST

Take a 1-minute timing on the paragraph. Note your speed and errors.

Remember to press ENTER only at the end of the paragraph.

19   As Inez roamed the ship, she told   7
20 fond tales. She slipped on that waxy   14
21 rung and fell to the deck. She hurt her   22
22 face and was dazed, but felt no pain.   30
| 1 | 2 | 3 | 4 | 5 | 6 | 7 | 8

G. PRACTICE

Type each line 2 times.

Check your posture.

23 waxy wavy wave save rave raze razz jazz
24 ship whip whop shop stop atop atoms At:
25 rung rang sang sing ring ping zing zinc
26 cure pure sure lure lyre byre bytes By:

27 tale kale Kate mate late lace face faze
28 fond pond bond binds bins inns Inez In:
29 gaze game fame same sale dale daze haze
30 roam loam loom zoom boom books took To:

H. POSTTEST

Repeat the Pretest. Compare your Posttest results with your Pretest results.

DATABASE APPLICATIONS

ACTIVITY 6
Database Table 2

Open the file DT2 and make the following changes:

1. Change the field name *Competition* to *Event*.
2. Add a new field named *Location;* specify 16 as the field size.
3. Position the *Location* field between the *Event* and *Start Time* fields.
4. Enter the locations for events as shown in the illustration.
5. Print the table.
6. Close the table window.

Speed Skating	The Oval
Luge	Metro Park
Figure Skating	Olympic Arena
Curling	The Coliseum
Downhill Skiing	Moose Mountain

ACTIVITY 7
Database Table 3

Open the file DT3 and make the following changes:

1. Change the field name *State Name* to *State*.
2. Change the field name *Capital City* to *Capital*.
3. Add a new field named *State Bird*; specify 28 as the field size.
4. Position the field *State Bird* as the last field.
5. Enter the birds for the states indicated in the first illustration.
6. Add the records from the second illustration to the table.
7. Print the table.
8. Close the table window.

LESSON 16

REVIEW

OBJECTIVES:

- Refine keyboarding skills.
- Type 25/1'/2e (25 words a minute for 1 minute with 2 errors).
- Learn to compose at the keyboard.

4 3 2 1   1 2 3 4

A. WARMUP

Type each line 2 times.

```
1  nest vote farm hail quid gaze coal waxy bake jeep
2  Gail must hold two jobs; she has had a hard life.
3  Kim, Ted has kept liquid oxygen frozen with care.
```

SKILLBUILDING

B. THIRD ROW KEYS

Type each line 2 times. Repeat if time permits.

```
4  pest west test rest guest roast yeast toast totes
5  yarn yard ward word worry hurry query quirt quilt
6  Try to get an aqua shirt to wear for the picture.
7  We took your tire to the shop, but it was ruined.
```

Take two 5-minute timings on the paragraphs. Note your speed and errors.

Goal: 40/5'/5e

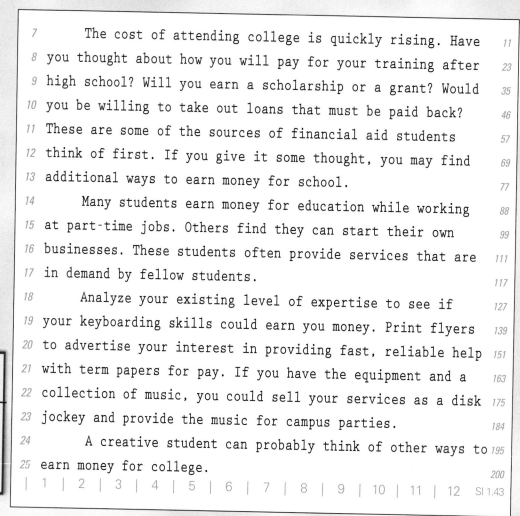

7   The cost of attending college is quickly rising. Have   11
8 you thought about how you will pay for your training after   23
9 high school? Will you earn a scholarship or a grant? Would   35
10 you be willing to take out loans that must be paid back?   46
11 These are some of the sources of financial aid students   57
12 think of first. If you give it some thought, you may find   69
13 additional ways to earn money for school.   77

14   Many students earn money for education while working   88
15 at part-time jobs. Others find they can start their own   99
16 businesses. These students often provide services that are   111
17 in demand by fellow students.   117

18   Analyze your existing level of expertise to see if   127
19 your keyboarding skills could earn you money. Print flyers   139
20 to advertise your interest in providing fast, reliable help   151
21 with term papers for pay. If you have the equipment and a   163
22 collection of music, you could sell your services as a disk   175
23 jockey and provide the music for campus parties.   184

24   A creative student can probably think of other ways to   195
25 earn money for college.   200

| 1 | 2 | 3 | 4 | 5 | 6 | 7 | 8 | 9 | 10 | 11 | 12   SI 1.43

MATH CONNECTIONS

Monitor the sports section of your local newpaper for a few days. Pick two or three sports events and track their scores.

FORMATTING

D. Software Features

GO TO

STUDENT MANUAL
Rename, Add, and Position Fields

Study Lesson 144 in your student manual. Complete all the practice activities while at your computer. Then complete the jobs that follow.

C. PUNCTUATION SPACING

Type lines 8–12 two times. Note the spacing before and after each punctuation mark. Repeat if time permits.

Space once after a colon, a semicolon, a period at the end of a sentence, and a period used with initials and titles.
Do not space after a period used within a.m. or p.m., geographic abbreviations, or academic degrees.

8 Robb passed the test; he studied about two hours.
9 These courses are open: marketing, band, and art.
10 Karel wishes to type. Her cat is on the computer.
11 Dr. E. O. Anton was given the award in the U.S.A.
12 Gretchen received her B.S. and M.B.A. in the a.m.

D. TECHNIQUE TIMINGS

Take two 30-second timings on each line. Focus on the technique at the left.

Press ENTER at the end of each line and continue typing smoothly.

13 Ask Brenda about the summer sale. It's in Tucson.
14 Wil could buy socks there. The price was minimal.
15 Today, stationery is half off. Help me buy paper.
16 Even the books are reduced. We want to read more.
| 1 | 2 | 3 | 4 | 5 | 6 | 7 | 8 | 9 | 10

E. PRETEST

Take a 1-minute timing on the paragraph. Note your speed and errors.

17   My cousin, Vera, has been exercising for at   8
18 least seven weeks. I did my best to keep up with   16
19 her for at least one hour today, but it was much   24
20 too difficult. She is very strong and very quick. 32
| 1 | 2 | 3 | 4 | 5 | 6 | 7 | 8 | 9 | 10

F. PRACTICE

SPEED: If you made 2 or fewer errors on the Pretest, type lines 21–28 two times each.

ACCURACY: If you made more than 2 errors on the Pretest, type lines 21–24 as a group two times. Then type lines 25–28 as a group two times.

Adjacent reaches are consecutive letters that are next to each other on the same row (weld).
Jump reaches are consecutive letters on the top and bottom rows typed with one hand (exam).

21 as base vases lasts haste taste fasts waste paste
22 po pole polar poems point poker polka spore spots
23 tr trade trips trace strut treat trend stray tray
24 re read real ream reel reeds breeds freed decreed

25 br bran brush brute broth bring break bread brain
26 mu must munch murky mushy musty music mumps mulch
27 ze amaze gauze dozen prize blaze craze glaze size
28 cr crate crater create crack crab crib crow croak

LESSON 144

DATABASES: RENAME, ADD, AND POSITION FIELDS

OBJECTIVES:

- Improve keyboarding skill.
- Type 40/5'/5e.
- Rename, add, and position fields in a database table.

A. WARMUP

Type each line 2 times.

Speed
Accuracy
Language Link
Numbers

1 I hope to have the first check by the second of next month.
2 Jack Bowman was very excited when my quilt won first prize.
3 His letter asked the personnel manager for a job interview.
4 Read pages 17, 20, 35, 46, and 89 to see the right answers.

| 1 | 2 | 3 | 4 | 5 | 6 | 7 | 8 | 9 | 10 | 11 | 12

SOCIAL STUDIES CONNECTIONS

The bravery and skill under fire of the 54th Volunteer Infantry from Massachusetts set an example for all. The 54th was an African American military unit that fought during the Civil War.

COME AND JOIN US BROTHERS.
PUBLISHED BY THE SUPERVISORY COMMITTEE FOR RECRUITING COLORED REGIMENTS
1210 CHESTNUT ST. PHILADELPHIA

SKILLBUILDING

B. PREVIEW PRACTICE

Type each line 2 times as a preview to the 5-minute timings that follow.

Accuracy
Speed

5 own analyze college probably creative equipment scholarship
6 grant could print still money their music start while think

G. POSTTEST

Repeat the Pretest. Compare your Posttest results with your Pretest results.

H. 1-MINUTE TIMINGS

Take two 1-minute timings on the paragraph. Note your speed and errors.

Goal: 25/1'/2e

```
29        It is good that you have learned all of the       9
30   alphabet keys. With just some extra practice, you      19
31   will zip through work quickly.                          25
     | 1 | 2 | 3 | 4 | 5 | 6 | 7 | 8 | 9 | 10  SI 1.22
```

LANGUAGE LINK

I. COMPOSING AT THE KEYBOARD

Keep your eyes on the screen as you type; do not worry about errors.

Composing at the keyboard enables you to create documents without having to write them by hand. As you compose at the keyboard, type at a comfortable pace. Do not look at your hands, and do not worry about errors. Get your thoughts recorded.

Answer each question with a single word.

32 Do you have a best friend?
33 What is your favorite sport?
34 Do you have a pet?
35 Have you ever ridden a horse?
36 What is your favorite color?

5. Close the table window.

16	16	
State Name	**Capital City**	**Date of Statehood**
Alabama	Montgomery	12/14/1819
Alaska	Juneau	1/3/1959
Arizona	Phoenix	2/14/1912
Arkansas	Little Rock	6/15/1836
California	Sacramento	9/9/1850
Colorado	Denver	8/1/1876
Connecticut	Hartford	1/9/1788
Delaware	Dover	12/7/1787

Social Studies
Connections

ACTIVITY 5
Database Table 2

Open the file DT2 and make the following changes:

1. Change the date for speed skating to February 12.
2. Change the start time for luge to 11:50 a.m.
3. Change the date for downhill skiing to February 14.
4. Add the following records as shown in the illustration.
5. Print the table.
6. Close the table window.

Date	**Competition**	**Start Time**
February 15	Speed Skating	9:15 a.m.
February 15	Luge	11:00 a.m.
February 16	Figure Skating	10:30 a.m.
February 17	Curling	7:00 p.m.
February 17	Downhill Skiing	1:15 p.m.

FACT FILE

Did you know that Alaska is the largest state with 591,004 square miles, and Rhode Island is the smallest state with 1,212 square miles. The last two states admitted to the Union were Alaska and Hawaii in 1959.

NEW KEYS: ? CAPS LOCK

OBJECTIVES:

- Learn the ? key.
- Use the caps lock key to type all-capital letters.
- Compose at the keyboard.

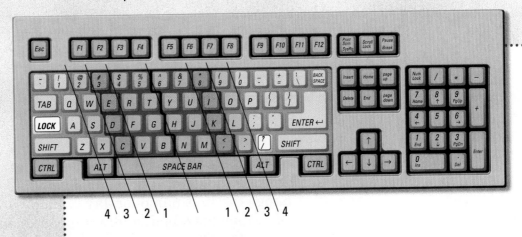

4 3 2 1   1 2 3 4

A. WARMUP

Type each line 2 times.

Hold those anchors.

1 herbs jinx gawk miff vest zinc ploy quad best zoo
2 Dozy oryx have quit jumping over the huge flocks.
3 Lax folks quickly judged the lazy dogs unfit now.

NEW KEYS

B. ? KEY

Type each line 2 times. Repeat if time permits.

Shift of /.
Use Sem finger and left shift key.
Anchor J.
Space once after a question mark.

4 ;;; ;/; ;/? ;?; ;?; ;;; ;/; ;/? ;?; ;?; ;;; ;/ ;?
5 ;/; ;?; now? now? ;?; how? how? ;?; who? who? ;?;
6 Who? What? Why? Where? When? Next? How many? Now?
7 How can Joe get there? Which way are the outlets?

 FORMATTING

F. SOFTWARE FEATURES

STUDENT MANUAL
Revise and Add Records
Date Fields

Study Lesson 143 in your student manual. Complete all the practice activities while at your computer. Then complete the jobs that follow.

 DATABASE APPLICATIONS

ACTIVITY 3
Database Table 1

Open the file DT1 and make the following changes:

1. Change the e-mail address for Jung Kim to *jkim6542@aol.com.*
2. Change the first name for Jay J. Baldwin to *James,* and change his e-mail address to *jbaldwin.*
3. Change the first name for Carla Davis to *Karly,* and change the e-mail address to *karlyd@aol.com.*
4. Change the e-mail address for Felix Gonzales to *felixg@buffalo.net* and the ZIP Code to *90145.*
5. Print the table.
6. Close the table window.

ACTIVITY 4
Database Table 3

Follow these steps to create Database Table 3 and name it DT3:

1. Define the three fields as shown in the illustration; identify the third field as a date field.
2. Specify the size of each field as shown above the columns.
3. Enter the records.
4. Print the table.

FACT FILE
The Gutenberg Bible, Old Testament, was the most expensive book ever sold. It was printed in Mainz, Germany, in 1455. Tokyo booksellers purchased this book for $5.39 million.

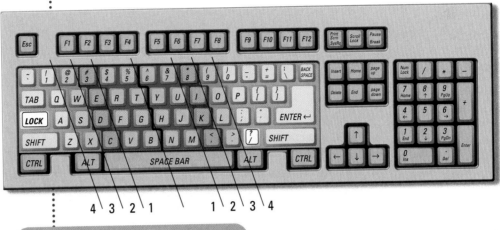

4 3 2 1   1 2 3 4

C. CAPS LOCK KEY

Use A finger.

Use the caps lock key to type letters or words in all-capital letters (all caps). You must press the shift key to type symbols appearing on the top half of the number keys.

Type each line 2 times. Repeat if time permits.

8 A COMPUTER rapidly scanned most AIRMAIL packages.
9 Another START/STOP safety lever was stuck lately.
10 Was JOSE elected CLASS PRESIDENT today or sooner?
11 You should not answer my door WHEN YOU ARE ALONE.

SKILLBUILDING

D. TECHNIQUE CHECKPOINT

Type each line 2 times. Repeat if time permits.

Quickly return fingers to home keys after reaching to other keys.

12 ;;; ;/; ;/? ;?; ;?; ;;; ;/; ;/? ;?; ;?; ;;; ;/ ;?
13 Did you see HELEN? Did you learn about her crash?
14 Her auto was hit by a TRAIN. She broke BOTH arms.
15 HOW will she manage while both arms are in casts?

E. TECHNIQUE TIMINGS

Take two 30-second timings on each line. Focus on the technique at the left.

Hold those anchors. Quickly return your fingers to home-key position.

16 Tony was a better friend than Hope was to Salena.
17 Lu and I were at Camp Piney Forest in early fall.
18 I rode the Rocky Ford train to San Juan in March.
19 Maya, Sue, and Grace were there. It was exciting.
  | 1 | 2 | 3 | 4 | 5 | 6 | 7 | 8 | 9 | 10

5 Which of these three carpets is the (more/most) practical?
6 Your layouts are the (more/most) appealing of any others in the display.
7 Both mountains have fantastic ski slopes; however, I prefer the slopes on the (higher/highest) one.
8 Of the two computers, the one that is networked is the (newer/newest).
9 Of the two movies you chose, the (shorter/shortest) one is the (more/most) interesting.
10 All three classes were difficult; however, math was the (lesser/least) challenging.

SKILLBUILDING

C. PRETEST

Take a 1-minute timing on the paragraph. Note your speed and errors.

11   You cannot build good skills while typing if you don't   12
12 practice various reaches on your keyboard. Practice all the   24
13 reaches that are especially difficult for you when you take   36
14 your timed writings. The more you type, the better you type.   48
| 1 | 2 | 3 | 4 | 5 | 6 | 7 | 8 | 9 | 10 | 11 | 12

D. PRACTICE

SPEED: If you made 2 or fewer errors on the Pretest, type lines 15–22 two times each.

ACCURACY: If you made more than 2 errors on the Pretest, type lines 15–18 as a group two times. Then type lines 19–22 as a group two times.

Up Reaches
15 daily card early away date earn fear fold argue baked cargo
16 page plus rise seat voted theft tape stand rules vary plead
17 meant gift large hold hours jury grade lets films made nest
18 reach hard build good don't your skill more timed take type

Down Reaches
19 very scope axle heavy cable value back calm cars sack bales
20 jobs each about disc badly cage cakes balk coach avid frank
21 taxi link packs rack reach palm score snack lack knee teach
22 wind vine blind came bland clans oxen column balm calm mine

E. POSTTEST

Repeat the Pretest. Compare your Posttest results with your Pretest results.

Take a 1-minute timing on the paragraph. Note your speed and errors.

```
20      The blind slats are broken. Can you fix the      9
21  broken ones? My WILY dog jumped out of the window    19
22  which is how this happened. There should be some     29
23  way to stop him. For a young dog, he is AMAZING.     38
    | 1 | 2 | 3 | 4 | 5 | 6 | 7 | 8 | 9 | 10
```

G. PRACTICE

Type each line 2 times.

```
24  slat slit skit suit quit quid quip quiz whiz fizz
25  LASS bass BASE bake CAKE cage PAGE sage SAGA sags
26  maze mare more move wove cove core cure pure pore
27  mix; fix; fin; kin; kind wind wild wily will well

28  cape cane vane sane same sale pale pals pats bats
29  jump pump bump lump limp limb lamb jamb jams hams
30  slow BLOW blot SLOT plot PLOP flop FLIP blip BLOB
31  mite more wire tire hire hide hive jive give five
```

H. POSTTEST

Repeat the Pretest. Compare your Posttest results with your Pretest results.

LANGUAGE LINK

I. COMPOSING AT THE KEYBOARD

Answer the following questions with a single word.

Keep your eyes on the screen as you type.

32 What day of the week is today?
33 What is your favorite animal?
34 What is your favorite food?
35 What is your favorite ice cream flavor?
36 What month is your birthday?

LESSON 143

DATABASES: REVISE AND ADD RECORDS

OBJECTIVES:

- Increase keyboarding skill.
- Learn about comparative and superlative adjectives and adverbs.
- Revise and add records to database tables.

A. WARMUP

Type each line 2 times.

Speed
Accuracy
Language Link
Numbers/Symbols

1 Jill has to take her time if she wants to do her best work.
2 Max quickly amazed Joan Bishop with five magic card tricks.
3 Amy came by at noon to pick me up; I had left much earlier.
4 We ordered 130# of #8 stock @ $42.65 on April 7 and July 9.
| 1 | 2 | 3 | 4 | 5 | 6 | 7 | 8 | 9 | 10 | 11 | 12

LANGUAGE LINK

B. COMPARATIVE AND SUPERLATIVE ADJECTIVES AND ADVERBS

Study the rule and examples below. Then edit lines 5–10 by choosing the correct word.

Rule 46:

Use **comparative** adjectives and adverbs, which use *-er, more,* and *less,* when referring to two nouns; use **superlative** adjectives and adverbs, which use *-est, most,* and *least,* when referring to more than two nouns.

Of the two players, Sam is more skillful at free-throw shooting.

She is looking for the most beautiful state to visit this summer.

LESSON 18

NEW KEYS: - _

OBJECTIVES:

- Learn the hyphen (-) and underscore (_) keys.
- Type 25/1'/2e.

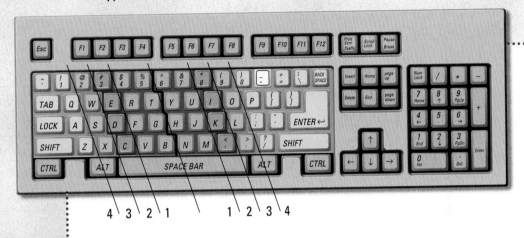

4 3 2 1   1 2 3 4

A. WARMUP

Type each line 2 times.

1 rave jinx tact safe mind glib quit yelp hawk doze
2 We all must be good friends to have good friends.
3 We have quickly gained sixty prizes for best jam.

NEW KEYS

B. — KEY (HYPHEN)

Type each line 2 times. Repeat if time permits.

Use Sem finger.
Anchor J.
Do not space before or after hyphens.

4 ;;; ;p; ;p-; ;-; -;- ;;; ;p; ;p-; ;-; -;- ;;; ;-;
5 ;p- ;-; self-made ;-; one-third ;p- one-sixth ;-;
6 ;p- ;-; part-time ;-; one-tenth ;p- two-party ;-;
7 Self-made Jim stopped at an out-of-the-way place.

ACTIVITY 2
Database Table 2

Follow these steps to create Database Table 2 and name it DT2:

1. Define the three fields as shown in the illustration; do not identify the first field as a date field.
2. Specify the size of each field as shown above the columns.
3. Enter the records.
4. Print the table.
5. Close the table window.

15	18	12
Date	**Competition**	**Start Time**
February 9	Speed Skating	10:30 a.m.
February 12	Luge	11:45 a.m.
February 13	Figure Skating	9:15 a.m.
February 14	Curling	3:30 p.m.
February 24	Downhill Skiing	2:45 p.m.

interNET CONNECTION

Search the Internet for the names of champions in each of the competitions listed above. Also search for information about other Olympic sports such as ice hockey. Determine when each sport became an Olympic event.

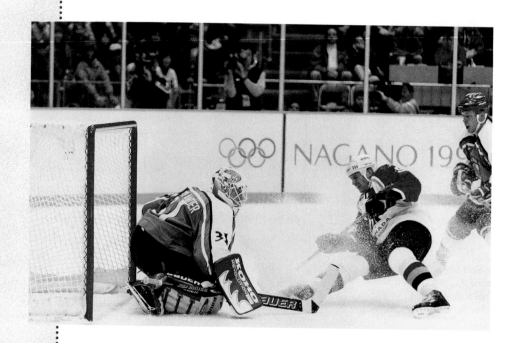

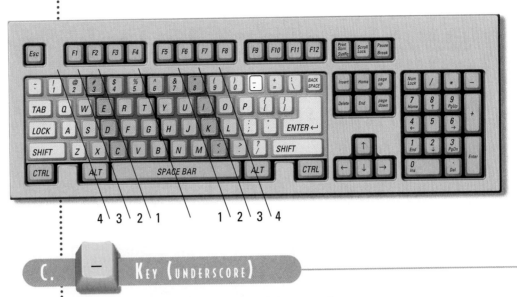

4 3 2 1   1 2 3 4

C. — KEY (UNDERSCORE)

Type each line 2 times. Repeat if time permits.

Use the Sem finger and the left shift key. Anchor J.

8 ;p; ;p⁻ ;⁻; ;⁻_; ;⁻_; ;p⁻_ _;_ ;p⁻_ ;⁻_; ;_; ;p⁻_
9 ;;; ;p; ;p_; ;_; _;_ ;;; ;p; ;p_; ;_; _;_ ;;; ;_;
10 Quick, create this seven-character line: _____.
11 Be sure to use her e-mail name, jennifer_cochran.

SKILLBUILDING

D. TECHNIQUE CHECKPOINT

Type each line 2 times. Repeat if time permits. Focus on the techniques at the left.

Keep your feet on the floor, back straight, elbows in.

12 ;;; ;p; ;p⁻; ;⁻; ⁻;⁻ ;;; ;p; ;p⁻; ;⁻; ⁻;⁻ ;;; ;⁻;
13 ;;; ;p; ;p_; ;_; _;_ ;;; ;p; ;p_; ;_; _;_ ;;; ;_;
14 Are you an easy-going person who gets along well?
15 The new name he now uses for e-mail is jute_rope.

E. TECHNIQUE TIMINGS

Take two 30-second timings on each line. Focus on the techniques at the left.

Sit up straight, keep your elbows in, and keep your feet flat on the floor.

16 Steward and Phon drove a car down to the shelter.
17 Ten people helped serve meals to thirty children.
18 They said it was hard work. Jung felt happy then.
19 This might help solve these problems in our city.
   | 1 | 2 | 3 | 4 | 5 | 6 | 7 | 8 | 9 | 10

FORMATTING

STUDENT MANUAL

Create Database Tables

Study Lesson 142 in your student manual. Complete all the practice activities while at your computer. Then complete the jobs that follow.

DATABASE APPLICATIONS

ACTIVITY 1
Database Table 1

Note: Paradox users simply create a table; name the table DTI.

Follow these steps to create Database Table 1. Name the file DT1.

1. Create a database and name it *Activities*.
2. Define the five fields as shown.
3. Specify the size of each field as indicated by the numbers above the columns.
4. Enter the records.
5. Print the table.
6. Close the table window.

12	12	32	5	7
First Name	**Last Name**	**E-mail Address**	**Area Code**	**ZIP Code**
Jung	Kim	jkim5642@aol.com	303	80015
Steven	Stein	steven-stein@ccsdl.shhs.k12.com	719	80012
Jay J.	Baldwin	jjbald@csn.com	790	82211
Carla	Davis	cdavis547@aol.com	303	80013
Jentry P.	Mitchell	jpmitchell@nesd.sbhs.k12.com	303	80215
Karey	Fletcher	12946@netserve.net	719	82211
Felix	Gonzales	felixg@landnet.com	818	90144
Osana	Kiux	ok5466@wallnet.com	818	90128

FACT FILE

The pteranodon was called the "flying reptile" and lived in Europe where its fossils were found in Germany in 1784.

Take a 1-minute timing on the paragraph. Note your speed and errors.

```
20        Look up in the western sky and see how it is    9
21  filled with magnificent pinks and reds as the sun     19
22  begins to set. As the sun sinks below the clouds,     29
23  you will see an amazing display of great colors.       39
    |  1  |  2  |  3  |  4  |  5  |  6  |  7  |  8  |  9  | 10
```

G. PRACTICE

SPEED: If you made 2 or fewer errors on the Pretest, type lines 24–31 two times each.

ACCURACY: If you made more than 2 errors on the Pretest, type lines 24–27 as a group two times. Then, type lines 28–31 as a group two times.

Left and right reaches are a sequence of at least three letters typed by fingers on either the left or the right hand. (lease, think)

```
24  was raged wheat serve force carts bears cages age
25  tag exact vases rests crank enter greet moves ear
26  was raged wheat serve force carts bears cages age
27  tag exact vases rests crank enter greet moves ear

28  get table stage hired diets gears wages warts rat
29  hop mouth union input polka alone moors tunic joy
30  him looms pumps nouns joked pound allow pours hip
31  lip mopes loose equip moods unite fills alike mop
```

H. POSTTEST

Repeat the Pretest. Compare your Posttest results with your Pretest results.

I.   1-MINUTE TIMINGS

Take two 1-minute timings on the paragraph. Note your speed and errors.

Goal: 25/1'/2e

```
32        We saw where gray lava flowed down a path.     9
33  At the exit, Justin saw trees with no bark and a     19
34  quiet, fuzzy duck looking at me.                     25
    |  1  |  2  |  3  |  4  |  5  |  6  |  7  |  8  |  9  | 10   SI 1.23
```

LESSON 142

DATABASES: CREATE DATABASE TABLES

OBJECTIVES:

- Improve keyboarding skill.
- Create database tables.

A. WARMUP

Type each line 2 times.

Speed
Accuracy
Language Link
Numbers/Symbols

1 I went to visit my aunt who lives down the street from Sue.
2 Max had a zest for quiet living and placed work before joy.
3 Leo was, of course, very surprised to hear his name called.
4 Do it now! Pay Bruce *(Adams) 10% and Pauline *(Drake) 15%.
| 1 | 2 | 3 | 4 | 5 | 6 | 7 | 8 | 9 | 10 | 11 | 12

SKILLBUILDING

B. 12-SECOND SPRINTS

Take three 12-second timings on each line. Try to increase your speed on each timing.

5 Take time to drop in on us if you are now in town sometime.
6 The girl is in the third grade and does fine work for them.
7 You have made the best use you could of all that free time.
8 If he visits with us, we shall call them at once from town.
| | | | 5 | | | |10| | | |15| | | |20| | | |25| | | |30| | | |35| | | |40| | | |45| | | |50| | | |55| | | |60

COMMUNICATION FOCUS

Learning another language takes practice and study. Ask a student from another country for tips he or she has used in learning another language.

LESSON 19

SKILLBUILDING

OBJECTIVES:
- Refine keyboarding skills.
- Use correct spacing before and after punctuation.

A. WARMUP

Type each line 2 times.

Words
Speed
Accuracy

1 fuzz busy flat apex gash avow junk quad czar mink
2 A good first impression must be made immediately.
3 Rob moved a psychology quiz to next week for Jay.

SKILLBUILDING

B. SPACE BAR

Type each line 2 times. Repeat if time permits.

Space between
words without
pausing.

4 up by rod hub cue dry mow zip elk jaw van era ark
5 do we fad wet tab boy hid lug mug zap box kid fog
6 in my car zoo tag pop vat jar lid yam fix war qua
7 so to add fun joy run sew lad man did nip was hop

C. SHIFT KEYS

Type each line 2 times. Repeat if time permits.

Type smoothly as you
use the shift keys.

8 Quinton Robert Farris Cheryl Eunice Xavier George
9 Juliet Noelle Ulysses Ingmar Hunter Yasmin Melvin
10 Tamara Zachary Quenna Aurora Bryant Dawson Salome
11 Mignon Jeffrey Yvette Olinda Harold Joanna Lionel

Take two 5-minute timings on the paragraphs . Note your speed and errors.

Goal: 40/5'/5e

13   As this world shrinks daily, we become neighbors to   11
14 people who live in nations across the oceans. One major   22
15 issue now facing the United States and the world is that of   34
16 global competition. Some college students will find that   45
17 work in a global environment is a part of their lives.   56
18   American students are less apt to be ready to work and   67
19 conduct business with those from different nations than are   79
20 students from other cultures. As countries continue to work   91
21 together, there is more and more demand to build skills for   103
22 this global marketplace.   108
23   More than half of the schools in the United States now   120
24 include the study of a foreign language as a requirement   131
25 for a degree, especially for students in their school of   143
26 business. According to a study done by the research office   154
27 of the Department of Education, some American corporations   166
28 require that graduates they employ possess some knowledge   177
29 of international affairs. This knowledge is essential for   189
30 those who are employed in banking and communications.   200

| 1 | 2 | 3 | 4 | 5 | 6 | 7 | 8 | 9 | 10 | 11 | 12 SI 1.54

Social Studies
Connections

FORMATTING

GO TO

STUDENT MANUAL

Database Tables   Windows
Navigating Within a Database   Selecting

Study Lesson 141 in your student manual. Complete all the practice activities while at your computer.

D. TAB KEY

Type each paragraph 2 times. Press the tab key to indent the first line; press ENTER only at the end of lines 13 and 15.

12   We read the daily newspaper to learn what is
13 going on in other countries. Do you also read it?

14   Do you read or watch the news? If you don't,
15 you should. How will you learn what is happening?

E. CONCENTRATION

Fill in the missing vowels as you type each line 1 time. Repeat if time permits.

16 E-ch d-y thos- fing-rs w-ll m-ve a l-ttl- f-st-r.
17 Y-u m-st le-rn to th-nk wh-re all thos- k-ys ar-.
18 D- y-u ke-p yo-r ey-s on th- c-py y-u ar- typ-ng?
19 On- d-y so-n yo-r f-ng-rs w-ll fly ov-r th- k-ys.

F. PUNCTUATION SPACING

Type lines 20–24 one time. Note the spacing before and after each punctuation mark. Repeat if time permits.

20 Accounting is a good course. I am taking it soon.
21 Dr. Tim Bellio, Ph.D., is in the U.S. or the U.K.
22 Please turn on the TV; my favorite program is on.
23 Mr. C. L. Brickmann and his son, T. J., are home.
24 We must talk to two people: Anthony and Consuela.

G. TECHNIQUE TIMINGS

Take two 30-second timings on each line. Focus on the techniques at the left.

Lines 25 and 26: Concentrate on efficient, smooth operation of the shift keys. Lines 27 and 28: Space quickly without pausing.

25 Jay and Ed were on time. Iva liked doing Tai Chi.
26 Alberto, set the clock. It is good to be on time.
27 Both Y. O. Fox and T. C. Ole had a Ph.D. in math.
28 Mr. Vasquez and Mr. Mayer were not in the office.

| 1 | 2 | 3 | 4 | 5 | 6 | 7 | 8 | 9 | 10

Rule 45: In all-capital abbreviations made up of single initials, do not use periods or internal spaces. (Exception: Keep the periods in most academic degrees and in abbreviations of geographic names other than two-letter state abbreviations.)

You will need to call the EEO office for clarification on that issue.

He earned an M.A. in business administration.

5 The meeting has been changed to 1 pm because of room conflicts.
6 Auditors said sales were understated in the June eom statement.
7 She enlisted in the U.S.M.C. after she received her PhD degree.
8 His old research paper deals with the early history of N A T O.
9 Denise said I should call about the paralegal position A.S.A.P.
10 We have consulted with A.A.A. about our upcoming European trip.

FACT FILE

Grizzly bears are surprisingly agile. They are also the fastest bears and can run at speeds up to 30 miles per hour. Adults may be 7 feet long and weigh 900 pounds.

SKILLBUILDING

C. PACED PRACTICE

Turn to the Paced Practice routine beginning on page SB7. Take three 2-minute timings, starting at the point where you left off the last time.

D. PREVIEW PRACTICE

Type each line 2 times as a preview to the timings that follow.

Accuracy
Speed

11 neighbors competition, economically international Americans
12 foreign conduct require people become world study major who

H. PRETEST

Take a 1-minute timing on the paragraph. Note your speed and errors.

```
29        Have you tried to get a project completed by     9
30   a deadline only to realize that you simply will       19
31   not be able to finish it? What you do next will       28
32   depend on the project and how soon you need it.       38
     |  1  |  2  |  3  |  4  |  5  |  6  |  7  |  8  |  9  |  10
```

I. PRACTICE

SPEED: If you made 2 or fewer errors on the Pretest, type lines 33–40 two times each.

ACCURACY: If you made more than 2 errors on the Pretest, type lines 33–36 as a group two times. Then type lines 37–40 as a group two times.

Up reaches are consecutive letters on the home row and third row typed by one hand. (task)

Down reaches are consecutive letters on the home row and bottom row typed by one hand. (call)

```
33   se seats seal pulse lease seams eases sedan mouse
34   gr great gray grows grain grade grass groan grave
35   lo love glove ploys clock locks flock block lobes
36   dr draft drift drive dress drama drums drab drape

37   av lava paved avert favor shave avoid brave raven
38   nk drink pink links crank plank sinks honks blank
39   sc scar scare scant scrap scent scoot scold scone
40   ba barks bare barns barb baby back bang bald bath
```

J. POSTTEST

Repeat the Pretest. Compare your Posttest results with your Pretest results.

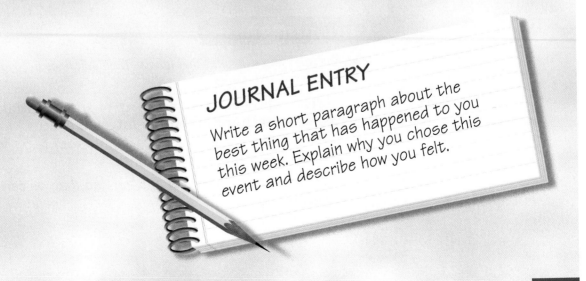

JOURNAL ENTRY

Write a short paragraph about the best thing that has happened to you this week. Explain why you chose this event and describe how you felt.

LESSON 141

DATABASES: DATABASE ORIENTATION

OBJECTIVES:

- Learn rules of abbreviation.
- Improve keyboarding skill.
- Navigate within a database.
- Learn about database tables, windows, and selecting.
- Type 40/5'/5e.

A. WARMUP

Type each line 2 times.

Speed
Accuracy
Language Link
Numbers/Symbols

```
1 She wanted low rates but did not want to lose any services.
2 I quickly explained that few big jobs involve many hazards.
3 Ned knew that he would soon need to return his dad's tools.
4 Tell each student to get his/her parents/guardians on 9/17.
  | 1 | 2 | 3 | 4 | 5 | 6 | 7 | 8 | 9 | 10 | 11 | 12
```

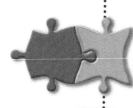

LANGUAGE LINK

B. ABBREVIATIONS

Study the rules and examples that follow. Then edit lines 5–10 to correct any abbreviation errors.

Rule 44:

In lowercase abbreviations made up of single initials, use a period after each initial but no internal spaces.

> *We will include several states in our tour (e.g., Maine, New Hampshire, and Vermont).*

> *We will begin our travel at 8 a.m. so that we can see everything.*

LESSON 20

SKILLBUILDING

OBJECTIVES:

- Refine keyboarding skills.
- Use correct spacing before and after punctuation.
- Type 25/1'/2e.

A. WARMUP

Type each line 2 times.

Words
Speed
Accuracy

```
1 itch plum jilt waxy fizz next clod quad brag skit
2 It is good to meet new people as soon as you can.
3 Cover the cozy liquid wax before Jack mops again.
```

SKILLBUILDING

B. ALPHABET REVIEW

Type each line 2 times. Repeat if time permits.

```
4 baffle quartz toxic veins major whack gaudy equip
5 banjo wizard rhyme heaven steep affix laugh quack
6 matrix shady squaw venom jacket spill zebra fudge
7 Be quick to move them up/down; jinx lazy fingers.
```

C. SHIFT KEYS

Type each line 2 times. Repeat if time permits.

Type smoothly as you use the shift keys.

```
8  Querida Arthur Donata Regina Gwynne Warden Samuel
9  Leilani Ursula Javier Margot Phoebe Irving Oliver
10 Timothy Carlos Elliot Felice Zenina Vernon Winona
11 Nokomis Isabel Hayley Pascal Justin Latham Kameko
```

WORDS TO LEARN

database table

database table
   report

date fields

formulas

monetary fields

navigate

numeric fields

position fields

query

records

sort

windows

CAREER BIT

COMPOSER   Composers create original music such as symphonies, operas, sonatas, or popular songs. They transcribe ideas into musical notations using harmony, rhythm, melody, and tonal structure. Many songwriters now compose and edit music using computers. Also, they may play the composition into the computer, which can record and play it back. Arrangers transcribe and adapt musical composition to a particular style for orchestras, bands, ballets, choral groups, or individuals. Components of music—including tempo, volume, and the mix of instruments needed—are arranged to express the composer's message. While some arrangers write directly into a musical composition, others use computer software to make changes. Compositions created with computer software can also be mailed electronically or placed on an Internet site.

D. TAB KEY

Type each line 1 time. Repeat if time permits.

Press the tab key to begin each sentence, and press ENTER at the end of each sentence.

12 Did you meet your goals? I did not. They all did.
13 My car is stuck. I need it towed. Will you do it?
14 Let's see a movie. What's playing? I do not know.
15 Look at that. It is quite amazing. I am thrilled.

E. CONCENTRATION

Fill in the missing vowels as you type each line 1 time. Repeat if time permits.

16 K--p all f-ng-rs curv-d -nd y--r wr-sts up a b-t.
17 Ke-p yo-r b-ck er-ct, b-t le-n yo-r b-dy forw-rd.
18 Ke-p y-ur elb-ws r-lax-d and cl-se to y-ur s-des.
19 K-ep y-ur h-ad up -nd t-rned tow-rd th- textb--k.
20 K-ep b-th fe-t on th- flo-r, on- aft-r th- oth-r.

F. PUNCTUATION SPACING

Type lines 21–25 one time. Note the spacing before and after each punctuation mark. Repeat if time permits.

21 Tom's flowers--especially the tulips--are lovely.
22 Have you seen her gloves? Are they in the drawer?
23 If Leilani can go tomorrow, we will go then also.
24 Estes Park has roads as well as hike/bike trails.
25 That fly-by-night business was selling old disks.

UNIT 8
Lessons 141–150

DATABASES

OBJECTIVES

- Demonstrate keyboarding speed and accuracy on straight copy with a goal of 40 words a minute for 5 minutes with 5 or fewer errors.

- Demonstrate the ability to create, navigate, and sort databases.

- Demonstrate the ability to create charts and tables and incorporate them into other applications.

G. Technique Timings

Take two 30-second timings on each line. Focus on the technique at the left.

Try to type smoothly as you operate the shift keys.

```
26 Oliver let Margo answer the Gopher Internet quiz.
27 Connecting with the World Wide Web was difficult.
28 Janice learned about URLs, FTP, and Gopher sites.
29 Sam, Jo, and Di were fluent in German and French.
   | 1 | 2 | 3 | 4 | 5 | 6 | 7 | 8 | 9 | 10
```

H. PRETEST

Take a 1-minute timing on the paragraph. Note your speed and errors.

```
30      There are fewer golf courses in Clark County    9
31 than in Milton County. One reason is the need for   19
32 rich soil to grow grass. Clark County has mostly    29
33 clay soil, which does not absorb water well.        38
   | 1 | 2 | 3 | 4 | 5 | 6 | 7 | 8 | 9 | 10
```

I. PRACTICE

SPEED: *If you made 2 or fewer errors on the Pretest, type lines 34–41 two times.*

ACCURACY: *If you made more than 2 errors on the Pretest, type lines 34–37 as a group two times. Then type lines 38–41 as a group two times.*

Discrimination reaches are keys that are commonly substituted and easily confused. (wear)

```
34 asa aside sadly flask sails saved trash masks sas
35 fgf fight goofs golfs fugue gaffe foggy frogs gfg
36 wew weans sweet swell sweat sewer fewer weeks ewe
37 rtr art part port sort fort worth trade title rtr

38 klk kilns kilts kills keels flock block locks lkl
39 nmn means lemon minor numbs names money hymns mnm
40 oio boils soils joins coins lions toils spoil ioi
41 jhj joy jewels judge huge hugs jugs just jury jhj
```

J. POSTTEST

Repeat the Pretest. Compare your Posttest results with your Pretest results.

Open the file SS47, save it as SS48, and create a pie chart by doing the following:

1. Select cell range A4 through B11, and create a pie chart.
2. Type in bold the title *A Sample of Occupational Earnings.*
3. Add a border to the chart.
4. Display a percentage in each piece of the chart.
5. Select the slice of highest earnings and set it off from the rest of the chart.
6. Preview the chart and make any necessary changes.
7. If your teacher has given you instructions for printing, print the spreadsheet. Otherwise, save the changes and close the file.

*inter*NET CONNECTION

Make a list of three or four career choices in which you are interested. Search the Internet for information about the salary that you might expect from each of these career choices. Also, search for statistics on the availability of jobs in the careers you have chosen. Compare information with your classmates.

PORTFOLIO
Activity

Choose one of the spreadsheets and one of the charts you have created in this unit. Print them and add them to your portfolio as a sample of your work.

K. 1-Minute Timings

Take two 1-minute timings on the paragraph. Note your speed and errors.

Goal: 25/1'/2e

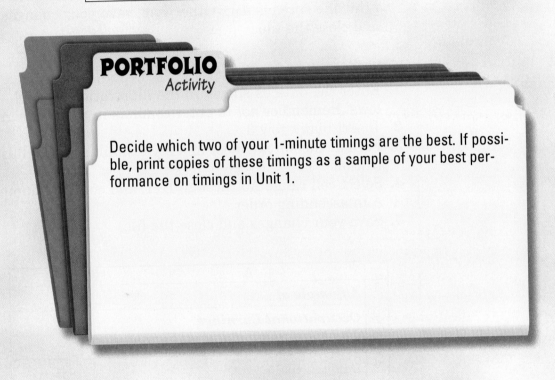

42   Paul bought five quartz watches. He expects   9
43 to give me one just to show his thanks. He will   19
44 also give me a large dog today.   25
   | 1 | 2 | 3 | 4 | 5 | 6 | 7 | 8 | 9 | 10   SI 1.16

PORTFOLIO Activity

Decide which two of your 1-minute timings are the best. If possible, print copies of these timings as a sample of your best performance on timings in Unit 1.

Open the file SS45, save it as SS46, and create a chart following these steps:

1. Select cell range A4 through E8 and create a horizontal bar chart.
2. Type in bold the title *Appliance Bids.*
3. Type the labels for each appliance and each store.
4. Be sure the chart is easy to understand; a separate legend is optional.
5. Add a border and gridlines.
6. Preview the spreadsheet and check for any errors.
7. If your teacher has given you instructions for printing, print the spreadsheet. Otherwise, save your changes and close the file.

Create a new spreadsheet and save it as SS47.

1. Enter the data as shown in the illustration that follows. Remember *not* to enter commas in the numbers.
2. Insert blank row 3.
3. Format the spreadsheet in a style similar to the illustration.
4. Select cell range A5 through B11, and sort by column A in ascending order.
5. Save your changes and close the file.

	A	B
1	*A Sample of*	
2	*Occupational Earnings*	
3		
4	*Occupations*	*Salaries*
5	Air Traffic Controller	63,000
6	Computer Programmer	78,000
7	Lawyer	114,000
8	Registered Nurse	48,000
9	Secretary	25,750
10	Teacher	32,000
11	US Vice President	171,500

WORDS TO LEARN

caret	Internet address	tilde
edit	Num Lock	

CAREER BIT

GEOLOGIST Geologists study the physical aspects and history of Earth. They identify and examine rocks, study information collected by remote sensing instruments in satellites, conduct geological surveys, construct field maps, and use instruments to measure Earth's gravity and magnetic field.

Many geologists and geophysicists search for oil, natural gas, minerals, and groundwater. Some geologists use two- or three-dimensional computer modeling to portray water layers and the flow of water or other fluids through rock cracks and porous materials. Other geological scientists play an important role in preserving and cleaning up the environment.

LESSON 140
SPREADSHEETS: REVIEW

OBJECTIVES:

- Improve keyboarding skills.
- Reinforce skill on up and down reaches.
- Strengthen spreadsheet concepts.

A. WARMUP

Type each line 2 times.

Speed
Accuracy
Language Link
Numbers/Symbols

1 Lee felt he could read five books by the end of this month.
2 Five or six dozen clubs may sign up with Karl for jonquils.
3 Will you please make 200 copies of the agenda for tomorrow.
4 Within 5% error, I can guess the prices of #32 and #48 now.
| 1 | 2 | 3 | 4 | 5 | 6 | 7 | 8 | 9 | 10 | 11 | 12

FACT FILE

One proven relaxation exercise is to visualize being
on vacation in the mountains or at the beach.
Listening to the sound of water is very soothing.

SKILLBUILDING

B. PRETEST

Take a 1-minute timing on the paragraph. Note your speed and errors.

5   You cannot build good skills while typing if you don't   11
6 practice various reaches on the keyboard. Practice all the   23
7 reaches that are especially difficult for you while you are   35
8 taking your timings.   40
| 1 | 2 | 3 | 4 | 5 | 6 | 7 | 8 | 9 | 10 | 11 | 12

LESSON 21

NEW KEYS: 4 $ 7 &

OBJECTIVES:

- Learn the 4, $, 7, and & keys.
- Refine keyboarding techniques.
- Type 27/2'/4e.

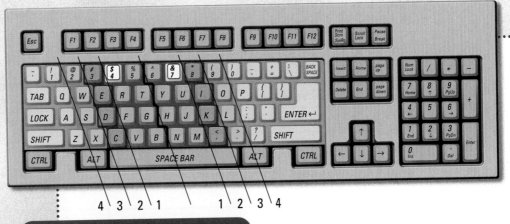

4 3 2 1   1 2 3 4

A. WARMUP

Type each line 2 times.

Words
Speed
Accuracy

1 shot idea jobs corn quip give flex whey maze elks
2 It is not a good idea to play ball in the street.
3 My joke expert amazed five huge clowns in Quebec.

NEW KEYS

B. 4 AND $ KEY

Type each line 2 times. Repeat if time permits.

Use F finger.
Anchor A.

4 frf fr4f f4f 444 f4f 4/44 f4f 44.4 f4f 44,444 f4f
5 44 films, 44 foes, 44 flukes, 44 folders, or 4.44
6 I saw 44 ducks, 4 geese, and 4 swans on the lake.
7 Today, our team had 4 runs, 4 hits, and 4 errors.

$ is the shift of 4.
Do not space
between the $
and the number.

8 frf fr4 f4f f4$f f$f f$f $4 $44 $444 f$f f4f $444
9 $444, 44 fish, 4 fans, $44, 444 fellows, $4, $444
10 Jo paid $44 for the oranges and $4 for the pears.
11 They had $444 and spent $44 of it for 4 presents.

14. Place a double line under cell range A3 through E3 and a single line under cell range A5 through E5.
15. Shade rows 7, 9, and 11.
16. Add a border around cell range A15 through E15, and bold the cells.
17. If your instructor has given you instructions for printing, print the spreadsheet. Otherwise, save your changes and close the file.

	A	B	C	D	E
1	Comprehensive Healthcare				
2	Statement of Benefits for Your Name				
3			Benefits	Amount	Payment
4	Dates	Procedures	Paid	Submitted	Rate
5	1/12	X-Ray/Testing		187	0.8
6				96	0.8
7				242	
8				23	
9				117	
10	Totals				
11	Patient's Responsibility				

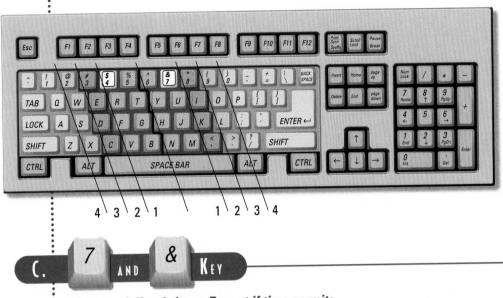

4 3 2 1   1 2 3 4

C. 7 AND & KEY

Type each line 2 times. Repeat if time permits.

Use J finger.
Anchor ;.

12 juj ju7j j7j 777 j7j 7/77 j7j 77.7 j7j 77,777 j7j
13 77 jokers, 77 joggers, 77 jets, or 7.77, 77 jumps
14 Hank will perform July 4 and 7, not June 4 and 7.
15 On July 4, we celebrated; on August 7, we rested.

Use J finger and left
shift.
Anchor ;.
Space before and
after the ampersand.

16 juj ju7 j7j j7&j j&j j&j j& &j& ju7& j&j j7j ju7&
17 7 jugs & 7 jars & 7 jewels & 7 jurors & 7 jungles
18 He thinks he paid $44 & $77 instead of $47 & $74.
19 B & C ordered 744 from Dixon & Sons on January 7.

SKILLBUILDING

D. TECHNIQUE TIMINGS

**Take two 30-second timings on each line. Focus on the techniques at
the left.**

Lines 20 and 21: Keep
your eyes on the
copy.
Lines 22 and 23:
Space without
pausing.

20 Kara saw a ship as she was walking over the hill.
21 Ned says he can mend the urn that fell and broke.
22 The five of us had to get to the bus before noon.
23 Lou said he would be at the game to see us later.

	A	B	C	D	E
1	Great Music Composers				
2	Prepared by Your Name				
3	Tchaikovsky, Piotr Ilych	1840–1893	Russia	Russian Folk Songs	
4	Haydn, Franz Joseph	1732–1809	Austria	Classical	Voice
5	Beethoven, Ludwig van	1770–1827	Germany		Organ
6	Chopin, Frederic	1810–1849	Poland	Polish Dances	Piano
7	Debussy, Claude	1862–1918	France	Impressionism	
8	Gershwin, George	1898–1937	America	Musical Comedy	
9	Mozart, Wolfgang Amadeus	1756–1791			Violin
10	Schubert, Franz	1797–1828			
11	Bach, Johann Sebastian	1685–1750		Baroque	

ACTIVITY 51
Spreadsheet 44

Create a new spreadsheet and save it as SS44. Then complete the following steps:

1. Enter the data as shown in the illustration.
2. Insert blank rows 3, 6, 12, and 14.
3. Make the following font changes: cell A1, 16-point; cell A2, 12-point italic.
4. Move cell range C4 through C5 to F4 through F5.
5. Move cell range D4 through F11 to C4 through E11.
6. Italicize cell range A4 through E5, and align cell range C4 through E5 at the right.
7. Format the date in cell A7 to *MM/DD/YY*.
8. Automatically set the width of columns A4 through E11.
9. Fill the following: from cell A7, fill down through cell A11. The dates should increase by 1. From cell B7, fill down through B11; from cells D7 through D8, fill down through cell D11.
10. In cell E7, enter a formula to multiply C7 by D7; then fill down through cell E11.
11. In cell C13, use SUM to add cell range C7 through C11; then copy the formula to cell E13.
12. In cell E15, enter a formula to subtract E13 from C13.
13. Format numbers as follows: in columns C and E, format numbers for 2 decimal places; in column D, format numbers as percentages with no decimal places.

E. PRETEST

Take a 1-minute timing on the paragraph. Note your speed and errors.

```
24        Each of us should try to eat healthful food,    9
25   get proper rest, and exercise moderately. All of     19
26   these things will help each of us face life with     29
27   more enthusiasm and more energy.                      35
     | 1 | 2 | 3 | 4 | 5 | 6 | 7 | 8 | 9 | 10
```

F. PRACTICE

SPEED: *If you made 2 or fewer errors on the Pretest, type lines 28–35 two times.*

ACCURACY: *If you made more than 2 errors on the Pretest, type lines 28–31 as a group two times. Then type lines 32–35 as a group two times.*

Adjacent Reaches

```
28   tr train tree tried truth troop strum strip stray
29   op open slope opera sloop moped scoop hoped opine
30   er were loner every steer error veers sewer verge
31   po port porter pole pods potter potion pound pout
```

Jump Reaches

```
32   on onion ozone upon honor front spoon phone wrong
33   ex exams exist exact flex exits exalt vexed Texas
34   ve even veers vests verbs leave every verge heave
35   ni nine ninth night nimble nifty nice nickel nigh
```

G. POSTTEST

Repeat the Pretest. Compare your Posttest results with your Pretest results.

H. 1-MINUTE ALPHANUMERIC TIMING

Take a 1-minute timing on the paragraph. Note your speed and errors.

```
36        Luke sent a $47 check to Computers & Such to    9
37   get a disk with 44 games & 4 special programs for    19
38   7 friends. He saw 47 of his friends at 4 p.m.        28
     | 1 | 2 | 3 | 4 | 5 | 6 | 7 | 8 | 9 | 10
```

SKILLBUILDING

C. 30-SECOND TIMINGS

Take two 30-second timings on lines 9–10. Then take two 30-second timings on lines 11–12. Try to increase your speed on each paragraph.

9	One of the best ways to learn from past mistakes is to	11
10	study what has taken place in the journal of man's history.	23
11	It is a wise person who can learn from the mistakes of	11
12	others and not have to learn those lessons from experience.	23

| 1 | 2 | 3 | 4 | 5 | 6 | 7 | 8 | 9 | 10 | 11 | 12

SPREADSHEET APPLICATIONS

ACTIVITY 50
Spreadsheet 43

FACT FILE

As early as 1914, a group of songwriters led by Victor Herbert met in New York. They established the American Society of Composers, Authors, and Publishers (ASCAP). This society protects the copyrighted musical compositions of its members.

Create a new spreadsheet, and save it as SS43. Then complete the following steps:

1. Enter the data as shown in the illustration.
2. Insert blank rows 3, 4, and 5.
3. Center and type in bold the following column headings beginning in cell A4: *Composer, Life Span, Country, Music, Specialty.*
4. Copy the following cells to these locations: C7 to C12 and C13; C8 to C14; D7 to D8, D12, and D13; E9 to E6, E10, E11, and E13; E8 to E14.
5. Select cells A6 through E14, and sort column B in descending order.
6. Select cells A4 through E14 and automatically widen the columns.
7. Change the following fonts: cell A1 to 14-point bold; cell A2 to 12-point bold.
8. Center cells A1 and A2 across the spreadsheet.
9. Shade cells A1 through E5, and place a line under row 5.
10. Shade the odd rows beginning with row 7.
11. Place a border around the spreadsheet and interior gridlines in A6 through E14.
12. Preview the spreadsheet; then change the orientation to landscape.
13. If your instructor has given you instructions for printing, print the spreadsheet. Otherwise, save your changes and close the file.

Unit 7 Lesson 139   **507**

Take two 2-minute timings on lines 39–44. Note your speed and errors.

Goal: 27/2'/4e

39	Have you been to our zoo? This is a great	9
40	thing to do in the summer. Bring your lunch to	18
41	eat in the park by the lake. You can watch a bear	28
42	cub perform or just view the zebras. Then explore	38
43	this spot and see the many quail and ducks. Take	48
44	some photos to capture the day.	54

| 1 | 2 | 3 | 4 | 5 | 6 | 7 | 8 | 9 | 10 SI 1.12

FACT FILE

In 1947, photographer Edwin Land demonstrated a
new invention. He developed a camera that could
take a picture, develop it, and print it in about a
minute. His invention became known as the
Polaroid camera.

MOOSE
HOLDING
YARD

LESSON 139

SPREADSHEETS: REVIEW

OBJECTIVES:

- Learn abbreviation rules for common nouns.
- Improve keyboarding skills.
- Strengthen spreadsheet concepts.

A. WARMUP

Type each line 2 times.

Speed
Accuracy
Language Link
Numbers/Symbols

1 Our school band played in the show for four years in a row.
2 Our squad was amazed that Xenia would quarrel with a judge.
3 He enjoys three types of music: popular, country, and jazz.
4 My check on 11/30 for $279.81 should have been for $305.06.
| 1 | 2 | 3 | 4 | 5 | 6 | 7 | 8 | 9 | 10 | 11 | 12

LANGUAGE LINK

B. ABBREVIATIONS

Study the rule and examples that follow. Then edit lines 5–8 to correct any abbreviation errors.

Rule 43:

In nontechnical writing, do not use abbreviations for common nouns (such as *dept.* or *pkg.*), compass points, and units of measure, or for the names of months, days of the week, cities, or states (except in addresses).

> *Our sales department will meet on Tuesday, March 7, in Tempe, Arizona.*

5 The new co. fleet cars are averaging about 21 miles per gal.
6 The remaining men will be transferred in Jan. to Athens, Ga.
7 On Mon., the trustee and auditor will meet with the co. pres.
8 The new product pkg. was colorful; the book was over 33 pgs.

LESSON 22

NEW KEYS: 3 # 8 *

OBJECTIVES:

- Learn the 3, #, 8, and * keys.
- Refine keyboarding skills.
- Type 27/2'/4e.

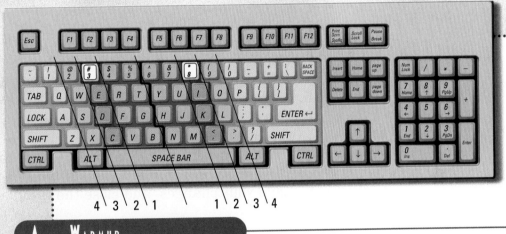

4 3 2 1   1 2 3 4

A.   WARMUP

Type each line 2 times.

Speed
Accuracy
Numbers
Symbols

1 The time for Andrew to stop is when the sun sets.
2 Ten foxes quickly jumped high over twelve zebras.
3 Lines 47, 77, and 44 were right; line 74 was not.
4 Bakes & Deli pays $4, $4.77, and $7.44 for dimes.

NEW KEYS

B.   3   AND   #   KEY

Type each line 2 times. Repeat if time permits.

Use D finger.
Anchor A or F.

5 ded de3d d3d 333 d3d 3/33 d3d 33.3 d3d 33,333 d3d
6 33 dimes, 33 dishes, 33 dots, 33 daisies, or 3.33
7 Draw 33 squares, 3,333 rectangles, and 3 circles.
8 They had 333 dogs in 33 kennels for over 3 weeks.

The # (number or
pound sign) is the
shift of 3.
Anchor A or F.
Do not space between
the number and #.

9 ded de3 d3d d3#d d#d d#d #3 #33 #333 d#d d3d #333
10 #3, 3 dots, #33, 33 dogs, #333, 333 ditches, #333
11 Is Invoice #373 for 344#, 433#, or 343# of fruit?
12 The group used 43# of grade #3 potatoes at lunch.

7. Change the page orientation to landscape and preview the document.
8. Adjust the size of the chart or make any other changes that are necessary so that all titles and labels can be read.
9. If your teacher has given you instructions for printing, print the spreadsheet. Otherwise, save your changes and close the file.

ACTIVITY 48
Spreadsheet 41

Open the file SS29, save it as SS41, and then follow these steps:

1. Delete rows 3 and 4.
2. Delete columns C, D, E, and F.
3. Change rows 1 and 2 to 10-point bold.
4. Adjust column A so that it is 20 points wide.
5. Align cell A4 at the left; align cell B4 at the right.
6. Place interior and exterior gridlines on cells A4 through B10.
7. Place a border around cell range A1 through B10.
8. Change the print orientation to landscape.
9. Save your changes, and close the file.

ACTIVITY 49
Spreadsheet 42

Open the file SS41, save it as SS42, and create a pie chart following these steps:

1. Select cell range A6 through B10 and create a pie chart.
2. Type in bold the title *Size of Small Caribbean Islands.*
3. Type in bold the subtitle *In Square Miles.*
4. Add the series labels as shown in column A. Have the actual values displayed on the chart instead of percentages.
5. Add a border around the chart.
6. Place the chart to the right of the spreadsheet if your software has that capability.
7. Preview the file and make any necessary adjustments.
8. If your teacher has given you instructions for printing, print the spreadsheet. Otherwise, save your changes and close the file.

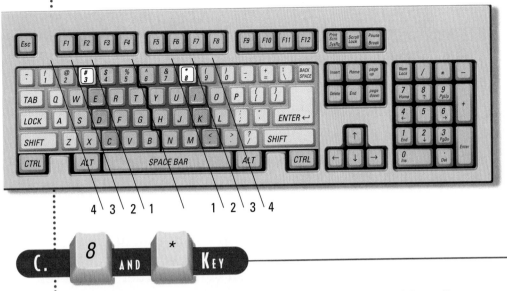

C. 8 AND * KEY

Type each line 2 times. Type smoothly as you use the shift keys. Repeat if time permits.

Use K finger.
Anchor ;.

13 kik ki8k k8k 888 k8k 8/88 k8k 88.8 k8k 88,888 k8k
14 88 kegs, 88 kilns, 88 knocks, 88 kickers, or 8.88
15 Our zoo has 88 zebras, 38 snakes, and 33 monkeys.
16 The house is at 88 Lake Street, 8 blocks farther.

The * (asterisk) is the shift of 8.
Do not space between the word and *.

17 kik ki8 k8k k8*k k*k k*k *8 *88 *888 k*k k8k *888
18 *8, 88 kits, *88, 88 keys, *888, 88 kimonos, *888
19 This manual* and this report* are in the library.
20 Reports* are due in 8 weeks* and should be typed.

SKILLBUILDING

D. PRETEST

Take a 1-minute timing on the paragraph. Note your speed and errors.

21   Do you brood when you make errors on papers?   9
22 It would be better to figure out what causes the   19
23 errors and to look for corrective drills to help   29
24 you make fewer errors in the future.   36
    | 1 | 2 | 3 | 4 | 5 | 6 | 7 | 8 | 9 | 10

SPREADSHEET APPLICATIONS

ACTIVITY 46
Spreadsheet 39

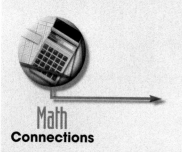

Math
Connections

Create a new spreadsheet, and save it as SS39. Then follow these steps to complete the spreadsheet and a correlated pie chart.

1. Type the data as shown in the illustration.
2. Bold cells A1 through B4.
3. Align cell B4 at the right.
4. Adjust column A to be 30 points wide.
5. Center cells A1 through A2 across the spreadsheet.
6. Sort cells A5 through B10 alphabetically in ascending order (A–Z).
7. Shade rows 6, 8, and 10.
8. Place 1 line under row 4.
9. Place an outline border around cell range A1 through B10.
10. Save your changes and close the file.

MATH CONNECTION

Using the data from Spreadsheet 39, calculate the amount of snow in feet rather than inches.

	A	B	C
1	Annual Snowfall at Popular Ski Resorts		
2	Prepared by Your Name		
3			
4	Resort	Inches	
5	Squaw Valley, Calif.	450	
6	Taos, N.M.	312	
7	Aspen, Colo.	400	
8	Jackson Hole, Wyo.	400	
9	Snowbird, Utah	500	
10	Sun Valley, Idaho	220	

ACTIVITY 47
Spreadsheet 40

Open the file SS39, save it as SS40, and create a pie chart following these steps:

1. Select cell range A5 through B10, and create a pie chart similar to the illustration that appears earlier in this lesson. Note that your spreadsheet may not create a separate legend.
2. Type in bold the title *Annual Snowfall at Popular Ski Resorts.*
3. Type in bold the subtitle *Inches Per Year.*
4. Add the series labels as shown in cells A5 through A10. Have the actual values displayed on the chart instead of percentages.
5. Add a border around the chart.
6. Place the chart to the right of the spreadsheet if your software has that capability.

E. PRACTICE

SPEED: *If you made 2 or fewer errors on the Pretest, type lines 25–32 two times.*

ACCURACY: *If you made more than 2 errors on the Pretest, type lines 25–28 as a group two times. Then type lines 29–32 as a group two times.*

Double Reaches

```
25 rr errs hurry error furry berry worry terry carry
26 ll bill allay hills chill stall small shell smell
27 tt attar jetty otter utter putty witty butte Otto
28 ff stuff stiff cliff sniff offer scuff fluff buff
```

Alternate Reaches

```
29 is this list fist wish visit whist island raisins
30 so sons some soap sort soles sound bosses costume
31 go gone goat pogo logo bogus agora pagoda doggone
32 fu fun fume fund full fuel fuss furor furry fuzzy
```

F. POSTTEST

Repeat the Pretest. Compare your Posttest results with your Pretest results.

G. NUMBER AND SYMBOL PRACTICE

Type each line 1 time. Repeat if time permits.

```
33 83 doubts, 38 cubs, 37 shrubs, 33 clubs, 34 stubs
34 87 aims, 83 maids, 88 brains, 73 braids, 84 raids

35 78 drinks, 48 brinks, 43 inks, 83 minks, 33 links
36 88 canes, 78 planes, 73 manes, 34 cans, 84 cranes

37 #7 blue, 4# roast, $3 paint, 77 books,* 3 & 4 & 8
38 7# boxes, 38 lists, $4 horse, #8 tree,* 7 & 3 & 4

39 Seek & Find Research sells this book* for $37.84.
40 The geometry test grades were 88, 87, 84, and 83.
```

FORMATTING

C. CREATING PIE CHARTS

A **pie chart** uses a circle divided into pieces or slices to visually show the relationship among values in a spreadsheet. Each piece of the pie represents one of the values in the spreadsheet; the whole circle represents the total. Pie charts are especially appropriate for displaying percentages of a whole, and the software will automatically calculate the percentages for you. In the following illustration, each slice of the pie chart represents a percentage of the total acres used for planting the top five crops in Texas. The labels and percentages make it easy to see which are the largest crops.

Top Five Crops Planted in Texas	
Crops	**Acres**
Cotton	6,400,000
Wheat	5,800,000
Grain Sorghum	2,700,000
Corn	2,100,000
Oats	650,000
Total	**17,650,000**

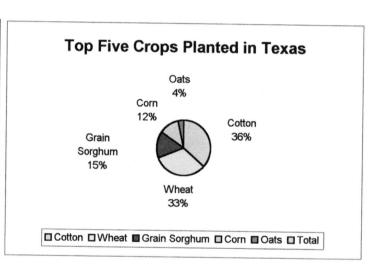

D. SOFTWARE FEATURES

STUDENT MANUAL

Pie Charts

Study Lesson 138 in your student manual. Complete all the practice activities while at your computer. Then complete the jobs that follow.

Take a 1-minute timing on the paragraph. Note your speed and errors.

41	B. Warmsly & J. Barnet paid the $847 charges — 9
42	for the closing costs of their home at 3487 Cliff — 19
43	Road; claim #47* shows the charge. — 26

| 1 | 2 | 3 | 4 | 5 | 6 | 7 | 8 | 9 | 10

I. 2-Minute Timings

Take two 2-minute timings on lines 44–49. Note your speed and errors.

Goal: 27/2'/4e

44	We just want to stay all day in the store to — 9
45	see the very new shoe styles. Sue quickly saw the — 19
46	mix of zany colors. Jo put on a yellow and green — 29
47	pair and looked in a mirror. The shoes had wide — 39
48	strips on the soles. We were certain of the good — 48
49	brand, so I bought two pair. — 54

| 1 | 2 | 3 | 4 | 5 | 6 | 7 | 8 | 9 | 10   SI 1.12

LESSON 138

SPREADSHEETS: CREATING PIE CHARTS

OBJECTIVES:

- Improve keyboarding skills.
- Create pie charts.

A. WARMUP

Type each line 2 times.

Speed
Accuracy
Language Link
Numbers/Symbols

1 The boy ran for the toys as fast as his short legs let him.
2 Squeeze that liquid gel into an opaque jar sealed with wax.
3 The computer now works--she finally had it repaired Friday.
4 Horses #29, #35, #17, and #48 are racing at 2:30 Wednesday.
| 1 | 2 | 3 | 4 | 5 | 6 | 7 | 8 | 9 | 10 | 11 | 12

SKILLBUILDING

B. 30-SECOND TIMINGS

Take two 30-second timings on lines 5–6. Then take two 30-second timings on lines 7–8. Try to increase your speed on each paragraph.

5   Some kinds of birds sleep with one half of their brain   11
6 at a time, with one eye closed and one open to spy enemies.   23

7   Dolphins sleep with only half their brains, also. They   11
8 need to remember to surface for air since they are mammals.   23
| 1 | 2 | 3 | 4 | 5 | 6 | 7 | 8 | 9 | 10 | 11 | 12

FACT FILE

Workers in the laboratories of Nippon Telephone and Telegraph Corp. have invented a microchip capable of identifying fingerprints. This chip can identify a fingerprint in a half second with 99 percent accuracy.

LESSON 23

NEW KEYS: 2 @ 9 (

OBJECTIVES:

- Learn the 2, @, 9, and (keys.
- Refine keyboarding skills.
- Type 27/2'/4e.

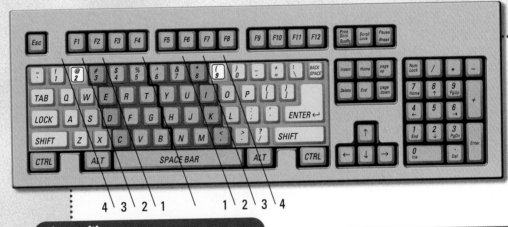

4 3 2 1   1 2 3 4

A. WARMUP

Type each line 2 times.

Speed
Accuracy
Numbers
Symbols

1 The big lake was filled with many ducks and fish.
2 Lazy Jaques picked five boxes of oranges with me.
3 The answer is 78 when you add 44 and 34 together.
4 Invoices #73 and #48 from C & M Supply were $438.

NEW KEYS

B. 2 AND @ KEY

Type each line 2 times. Repeat if time permits.

Use S finger.
For 2 and @, anchor F.

5 sws sw2s s2s 222 s2s 22.2 s2s 2/22 s2s 22,222 s2s
6 22 sips, 22 swings, 22 signals, 22 sites, or 2.22
7 Our class used 22 pens, 23 disks, and 24 ribbons.
8 There were 22 people waiting for Bus 22 on May 2.

@ (at) is the shift of 2.
Space once before
and after @ except
when it is used in an
e-mail address.

9 sws sw2 s2s s2@s s@s s@s @2 @22 @222 s@s s2s @222
10 @2, 2 sons, @22, 22 sets, @222, 222 sensors, @222
11 Paul said his e-mail address was smith@acc.co.us.
12 She bought 2 @ 22 and sold 22 @ 223 before 2 p.m.

ACTIVITY 45
Spreadsheet 38

Open the file SS37, save it as SS38, and create a chart by following these steps:

1. Select cell range A6 through D13 and create a vertical bar chart.
2. Type in bold the title *Baseball Game Attendance*.
3. Type in bold the subtitle *June 5–6, [Year]*.
4. Type the Y-axis label *Attendance*.
5. Type the X-axis label *Stadiums*.
6. Add the legend labels *Capacity; June 5; June 6*.
7. Place the chart to the right of the spreadsheet if your software has that capability. Otherwise, the spreadsheet and chart will be two separate documents.
8. Preview the file in landscape orientation. You may need to adjust the size of the chart or make changes in the font sizes so that all titles and labels can be read. For example, the font size of the stadium names may need to be smaller.
9. If your teacher has given you instructions to print, print the chart. Otherwise, save your changes and close the file.

*inter*NET CONNECTION

Search the Internet for other statistics about the capacity of stadiums around the country. Search for information on what kinds of events the stadiums are used for and whether any are home to professional sports teams. Share your findings with the class.

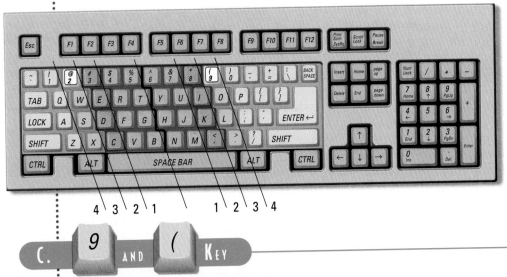

C. 9 AND (KEY

Type each line 2 times. Repeat if time permits.

Use L finger.
For 9 and (, anchor J.

13 lol lo91 191 999 191 9/99 191 99.9 191 99,999 191
14 99 laps, 99 loops, 99 lilies, 99 lifters, or 9.99
15 He said 99 times not to ask for the 99 fair fans.
16 They traveled 999 miles on Route 99 over 9 weeks.

The ((opening paren-
thesis) is the shift of
9. Space once before
an opening parenthe-
sis; do not space
after it.

17 lol lo9 191 19(1 1(1 1(1 (9 (99 (999 1(1 191 (999
18 (9, 9 lots, (99, 99 logs, (999, 999 latches, (999
19 lo9((99((9 lo9(1 lo(9(9(9 (9(9(9 1(lo9(1 9(
20 lo9(19(1 9(91 1((1 (9ol 99 lambs, (999, 999 lads

SKILLBUILDING

D. TECHNIQUE CHECKPOINT

Type each line 2 times. Focus on the technique at the left.

Keep your eyes on
the copy when
typing numbers and
symbols.

21 sws sw2s s2s 222 s2s 22.2 s2s 2/22 s2s 22,222 s2s
22 sws sw2 s2s s2@s s@s s@s @2 @22 @222 s@s s2s @222
23 lol lo91 191 999 191 9/99 191 99.9 191 99,999 191
24 lol lo9 191 19(1 1(1 1(1 (9 (99 (999 1(1 191 (999

E. PRETEST

Take a 1-minute timing on the paragraph. Note your speed and errors.

25   Were you in the biology group that mixed the   9
26 ragweed seeds with some vegetable seeds? Jon and   19
27 Kim sneezed all month because of that. All of us   29
28 agreed that we must be more careful in the lab.   38

| 1 | 2 | 3 | 4 | 5 | 6 | 7 | 8 | 9 | 10

2. Bold cell range A1 through D6.
3. Center cells A1 through A3 across the spreadsheet.
4. Center cells A5 through D6.
5. Automatically change the column width in cell range A5 through D12.
6. Place a border under A6 through D6.
7. Format all numbers to have commas and no decimal places.
8. Sort cell ranges A7 through D12 to alphabetize the park names in ascending order (A–Z).
9. Insert a blank row 12. Type the following information beginning in cell A12: *The Ball Park; 48100; 43917; 34866*.
10. Shade the odd-numbered rows beginning with row 7 through row 13.
11. Place a border around cell range A1-D13.
12. Save your changes and close the file.

	A	B	C	D
1	Baseball Game Attendance			
2	June 5-6, {year}			
3	Prepared by Your Name			
4				
5		Stadium	Attendance	Attendance
6	Park	Capacity	June 5	June 6
7	Shea Stadium	55600	15872	53210
8	Fenway Park	33870	20187	18992
9	Wrigley Field	38760	17438	38760
10	Dodger Stadium	56000	55110	30031
11	Jacobs Field	42400	42310	22764
12	Anaheim Stadium	64590	27321	58542

F. PRACTICE

SPEED: *If you made 2 or fewer errors on the Pretest, type lines 29–36 two times each.*

ACCURACY: *If you made more than 2 errors on the Pretest, type lines 29–32 as a group two times. Then type lines 33–36 as a group two times.*

Left Reaches

```
29  tab wards grace serve wears farce beast crate car
30  far weeds tests seeds tread graze vexed vests saw
31  bar crest feast refer cease dated verge bread gas
32  car career grasses bread creases faded vested tad
```

Right Reaches

```
33  you Yukon mummy ninon jolly union minim pylon hum
34  mom nylon milky lumpy puppy holly pulpy plink oil
35  pop oomph jumpy unpin nippy imply hippo pupil nip
36  you union bumpy upon holly hill moon pink ill mop
```

G. POSTTEST

Repeat the Pretest. Compare your Posttest results with your Pretest results.

H. 1-MINUTE ALPHANUMERIC TIMING

Take a 1-minute timing on the paragraph. Note your speed and errors.

```
37       The planned ski tour #4 begins at 2:43 p.m.,    9
38  and tour #3 begins at noon. Every tour costs $43,   19
39  and everyone will end at 7:38 p.m.                  26
    | 1 | 2 | 3 | 4 | 5 | 6 | 7 | 8 | 9 | 10
```

I. 2-MINUTE TIMINGS

Take two 2-minute timings on lines 40–45. Note your speed and errors.

Goal: 27/2'/4e

```
40       It is a joy to end a term with good grades.    9
41  Fall term could be very nice if it were not for    19
42  exams and quizzes. Jan, though, likes to study to  29
43  show how much she has learned. She places great    38
44  value in having high marks. She knows her peers    48
45  admire the grades she achieved.                    54
    | 1 | 2 | 3 | 4 | 5 | 6 | 7 | 8 | 9 | 10  SI 1.15
```

A bar chart uses vertical or horizontal bars to represent the values in the spreadsheet. In the illustration, the **Y axis,** or vertical scale, displays the values from the spreadsheet, which range from 0 to 6,000. The **X axis,** or horizontal scale, displays the labels or names of the schools. The legend on the right identifies the data being charted through the use of color or shading. This chart makes it very easy to see the enrollment changes in each school over a three-year period.

Three-Year Student Enrollment Barker County Schools

Schools	2000	2001	2002
Buffalo	2,165	2,298	3,147
Edna	1,834	1,054	1,576
Santa Rosa	3,009	3,641	3,880
Seminole	5,316	5,203	4,921

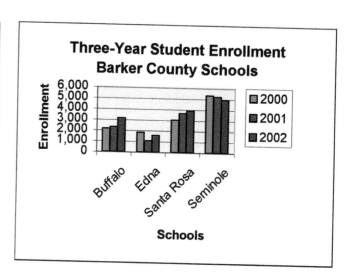

F. SOFTWARE FEATURES

STUDENT MANUAL
   Bar Charts

Study Lesson 137 in your student manual. Complete all the practice activities while at your computer. Then complete the jobs that follow.

SPREADSHEET APPLICATIONS

ACTIVITY 44
Spreadsheet 37

Create a new spreadsheet, and save it as SS37.

1. Type the data as shown in the illustration on the next page. Enter the dates in cells C6 and D6 as labels. To do this, type an apostrophe before the date (*'June 5*). The apostrophe indicates that the value is to be treated like a label; it will not be visible in the cell after you press ENTER.

LESSON 24 REVIEW

OBJECTIVES:

- Improve keyboarding skill.
- Type 27/2'/2e.
- Compose at the keyboard.

A. WARMUP

Type each line 2 times.

Speed
Accuracy
Numbers
Symbols

1 The first time Alf drove a car, he hit a pothole.
2 Zigzag through the zebu with zip to avoid injury.
3 Room 43 holds 87 people, but only 29 are present.
4 Buy 78 gross* of #2 pencils @ $3.94 at the store.

SKILLBUILDING

B. TAB KEY

Type each paragraph 2 times. Press the tab to indent the first line; press ENTER only at the end of lines 6 and 8. Repeat if time permits.

5   We found 99 gnats, 44 flies, 33 fleas, and
6 77 seals beside the 33 trees at the 2-acre beach.

7   Bo & Son bought 88 axles @ $42.98. They said
8 Rule #37 on page 88 was now Rule #42 on page 93.

C. ENTER KEY

Type each line 2 times. Press ENTER at the end of every sentence. Continue typing smoothly. Repeat if time permits.

Remember to press
ENTER at the end of
every sentence.

9 Study all of Chapter 29. It covers pages 234-249.
10 Chelsea lives at 778 Cherokee. That's in Paducah.
11 Write Jo at pets@coyote.com. Jo's address is new.
12 That text* is at B & B Printing. It is makeready.

Take two 5-minute timings on the paragraphs. Note your speed and errors.

Goal: 40/5'/5e

Social Studies
Connections

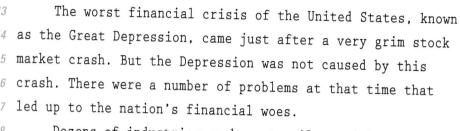

13	The worst financial crisis of the United States, known	11
14	as the Great Depression, came just after a very grim stock	23
15	market crash. But the Depression was not caused by this	34
16	crash. There were a number of problems at that time that	46
17	led up to the nation's financial woes.	54
18	Dozens of industries such as textiles and lumber and	64
19	the railroad began to slow down. Wages were cut and the	76
20	demand for consumer goods decreased. This then led to a	87
21	decline in auto plants and building trades, which forced	98
22	more layoffs and wage cuts.	104
23	Credit spending was also a big factor in the Great	114
24	Depression. Farmers bought land, equipment, and supplies	126
25	with funds they had borrowed. People used credit to buy	137
26	cars and homes. Investors borrowed money to buy stocks. As	149
27	more and more people became unable to repay the money they	160
28	had borrowed, more and more banks began to fail.	170
29	The nation's economy grew weaker, and foreign markets	181
30	felt the effects as they lost their buyers and main source	193
31	of loans.	195

| 1 | 2 | 3 | 4 | 5 | 6 | 7 | 8 | 9 | 10 | 11 | 12SI 1.38

FORMATTING

E.   Bar Charts

Information in a spreadsheet can be used to create bar charts. A **bar chart** is a type of picture or graph that shows the relationships among values. The bars may be different colors or patterns and different shapes such as lines, circles, stacks, cones, pyramids, or three-dimensional variations. In some programs the spreadsheet and chart are two separate documents; other programs enable you to place the chart inside the spreadsheet.

D. TECHNIQUE TIMINGS

Take two 30-second timings on each line. Focus on the technique at the left.

Keep elbows in.

```
13  She works for Mr. D. N. Logan at Logan Locksmith.
14  Is the May/June issue late? My copy has not come.
15  Find these colors: pink, blue, green, and purple.
16  My hoity-toity behavior was rude, extremely rude.
    |  1  |  2  |  3  |  4  |  5  |  6  |  7  |  8  |  9  |  10
```

E. PRETEST

Take a 1-minute timing on the paragraph. Note your speed and errors.

```
17         Ed's prize-winning ewe stays on Mario's farm    9
18  until the petting zoo opens. Every day Skip takes    19
19  that ewe and her lamb to the fair. It's amazing      29
20  to see how much time is spent caring for animals.    39
    |  1  |  2  |  3  |  4  |  5  |  6  |  7  |  8  |  9  |  10
```

F. PRACTICE

SPEED: *If you made 2 or fewer errors on the Pretest, type lines 21–28 two times each.*

ACCURACY: *If you made more than 2 errors on the Pretest, type lines 21–24 as a group two times. Then type lines 25–28 as a group two times.*

Adjacent Reaches
Jump Reaches
Double Reaches
Up Reaches

```
21  io trio riot pious Mario ew ewes mews sewer views
22  un tune dune under bound ze zeal zest prize seize
23  ss hiss boss dress gloss ll fall tall small jolly
24  dr drip drive dream drab ho hope hole hold hollow
```

Alternate Reaches
Left Reaches
Right Reaches
Down Reaches

```
25  ro rode rote crows throw do doze judo kudos docks
26  fa farm fast favor fazed er errs were erase terms
27  ki kiln skip skill skimp pl plot plum plows plugs
28  ca call caps cards caper ni niece nine nick night
```

G. POSTTEST

Repeat the Pretest. Compare your Posttest results with your Pretest results.

Rule 41: Use a dash instead of a comma, semicolon, colon, or parentheses when you want to convey a more forceful separation of words within a sentence.

> *At the meeting, the speakers—and topics—were superb.*

> *The icy road—slippery as a fish—was a hazard.*

Rule 42: Use a period at the end of a sentence that is a polite request. (Consider a sentence a polite request if you expect the reader to act or do as you ask rather than give you a yes- or no-answer.)

> *Will you please fax us a copy of the insurance policy today.*

> *Will you please close the door before you are seated.*

5 Her birthday present a World Atlas was finally delivered.
6 Since you are going to the pharmacy, will you buy vitamins.
7 Will you please send Guy your resume by e-mail before 11 a.m. today?
8 Several brands of soaps are on sale Zest, Dial, and Ivory.
9 The radio station not my favorite was giving the weather.
10 Living in the country has advantages quiet, calm, and tranquil days.

SOCIAL STUDIES CONNECTIONS

President Andrew Jackson was the first U.S. president to become a victim of an assassination attempt. Luckily, the guns fired by Richard Lawrence misfired and the President was not injured.

SKILLBUILDING

C. PREVIEW PRACTICE

Type each line 2 times as a preview to the timings that follow.

11 slow Dozens textile borrowed equipment financial Depression
12 layoffs markets lumber demand crash grew main cars fail pay

Take a 1-minute timing on lines 29–31. Note your speed and errors.

```
29        Our black cat, Beauty, weighed 9#. She had a       9
30 checkup at Paws & Claws on June 23. Her shots and       19
31 exam cost $48, but she's worth it all.                  27
   | 1 | 2 | 3 | 4 | 5 | 6 | 7 | 8 | 9 | 10
```

I. 2-Minute Timings

Take two 2-minute timings on lines 32–37. Note your speed and errors.

Goal: 27/2′/4e

```
32        Why use proper grammar when you speak? One        9
33 of the best reasons is that others judge you            19
34 by your speech. Fair or not, people examine the         28
35 words you use and how you use them. You have to         38
36 speak well each day. Avoid buzzwords and slang.         48
37 People will be quick to judge you.                      54
   | 1 | 2 | 3 | 4 | 5 | 6 | 7 | 8 | 9 | 10  SI 1.19
```

LANGUAGE LINK

J. Composing at the Keyboard

Answer each question with a few words or a short phrase.

38 Who is your best friend?
39 Who are two people who have been in the news this week?
40 Are you a licensed driver?
41 What is your favorite type of music?
42 What is your favorite song?

LESSON 137

SPREADSHEETS: CREATING BAR CHARTS

OBJECTIVES:

- Learn about colons, dashes, and periods with polite requests.
- Learn to create a bar chart.
- Type 40/5'/5e.

A. WARMUP

Type each line 2 times.

Speed
Accuracy
Language Link
Numbers/Symbols

1 A friend would like to go to the school play with me later.
2 The banquet speaker, James Carvings, analyzed a few hoaxes.
3 The flight attendant got huge, soft pillows for her and me.
4 Flight #1389 arrived late--7 p.m. (It was due at 6:45 p.m.)

| 1 | 2 | 3 | 4 | 5 | 6 | 7 | 8 | 9 | 10 | 11 | 12

LANGUAGE LINK

B. COLONS, DASHES, AND PERIODS

Study the rules and examples that follow. Then edit lines 5–10 to correct any errors in the use of colons, dashes, and periods.

Rule 40:

Use a colon to introduce explanatory material that follows an independent clause. (An **independent clause** is one that can stand alone as a complete sentence.)

The computer satisfies three criteria: speed, cost, and power.

There are many fine poets: Shelley, Keats, and Frost.

LESSON 25

NEW KEYS: 1 ! 0)

OBJECTIVES:

- Learn the 1, !, 0, and) keys.
- Refine keyboarding skills.
- Type 27/2'/4e.

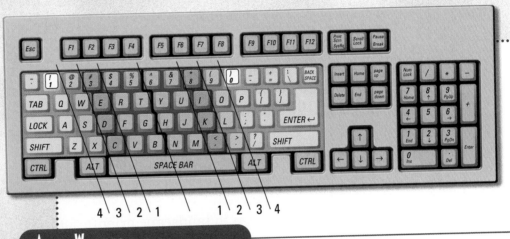

4 3 2 1   1 2 3 4

A. WARMUP

Type each line 2 times.

Speed
Accuracy
Numbers
Symbols

1 The goal of trade schools is to teach job skills.
2 Jess Mendoza quickly plowed six bright vineyards.
3 Nate took this new order: 78, 74, 83, 29, and 23.
4 Purchase 32# of grass seed today @ $2.98 a pound.

NEW KEYS

B. **1** AND **!** **KEY**

Type each line 2 times. Repeat if time permits.

For 1 and !, anchor F.
Use A finger. Do not
use the lowercase
letter l (el) for 1.

5 aqa aq1a a1a 111 a1a 1/11 a1a 11.1 a1a 11,111 a1a
6 11 arms, 11 areas, 11 adages, 11 animals, or 1.11
7 My 11 aides can type 111 pages within 11 minutes.
8 Joann used 11 gallons of gas to travel 111 miles.

! is the shift of 1.
Space once after an
exclamation point.

9 aqa aq1 a1a a1!a a!a a!a 1! 11! 111! a!a a1a 111!
10 1!, 1 ant, 11! 11 acres, 111! 111 adverbs, 1 area
11 Listen! There was a cry for help! They need help!
12 Look! It's moving! I'm frightened! Run very fast!

ACTIVITY 43
Spreadsheet 36

Create a new spreadsheet and save it as SS36.

1. Type the data as shown in the illustration.
2. Extend the numbers in cells B4 and C4 to M4. The last number should be *12*.
3. Bold the numbers.
4. Extend the numbers in cells A5 and A6 to A16. The last number should be *12*.
5. Bold the numbers.
6. Extend the numbers in cells B5 through C6 to D5 through M6.
7. Extend the numbers in cells B5 through M6 to B7 through M16. The number in M16 should be *144*.
8. Change cell A1 to 16-point bold.
9. Change cell A2 to 12-point bold.
10. Center cells A1 through A2 across the spreadsheet.
11. Shade cells B4 through M4 and A5 through A16.
12. Select cell range B5 through M16. Place a thin-line border around each cell.
13. Place a heavy-line border around the entire spreadsheet.
14. Change to landscape orientation.
15. If your teacher has given you instructions on how to print, print the spreadsheet. Otherwise, save your changes and close the file.

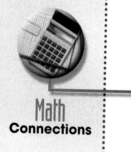

Math Connections

	A	B	C
1	Multiplication Tables		
2	Prepared by Your Name		
3			
4		1	2
5	1	1	2
6	2	2	4

COMMUNICATION FOCUS

Make a note in your journal to write a paragraph about the meaning of different expressions such as, "The grass is greener on the other side of the fence." What would this expression mean to a student from another country?

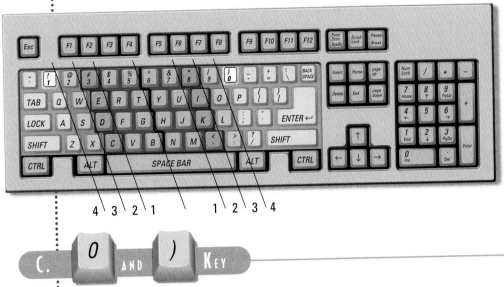

4 3 2 1   1 2 3 4

C. 0 AND) KEY

Type each line 2 times. Repeat if time permits.

Use Sem finger.
For 0 and), anchor J.
Do not use the capital letter O for 0.

) is the shift of 0 (zero).
Space once after a closing parenthesis except when it's followed by punctuation; do not space before it.

13 ;p; ;p0; ;0; 000 ;0; 1.00 ;0; 20.0 ;0; 30,000 ;0;
14 300 parts, 700 planks, 800 parades, 900 particles
15 Can you add these: 80, 10, 90, 40, 20, 70, & 130?
16 Some emoticons such as :-(or :(use parentheses.

17 ;p; ;p0 ;0; ;0); ;); ;););;);;; ;); ;0;);;; ;)
18 ;0; ;0) ;); ;); 10) 20) 30) 40) 70) 80) 90) 1001)
19 The box (the big red one) is just the right size.
20 My friend (you know which one) is arriving early.

SKILLBUILDING

D. TECHNIQUE CHECKPOINT

Type each line 2 times. Focus on the techniques at the left.

Keep eyes on copy; hold home-key anchors.

21 aqa aq1a a1a 111 a1a 1/11 a1a 11.1 a1a 11,111 a1a
22 aqa aq1 a1a a1!a a!a a!a 1! 11! 111! a!a a1a 111!
23 ;p; ;p0; ;0; 000 ;0; 1.00 ;0; 20.0 ;0; 30,000 ;0;
24 p;p p;0 ;0; ;0); ;); ;););;);;; ;); ;0;);;; ;)

E. PRETEST

Take a 1-minute timing on the paragraph. Note your speed and errors.

25   Dave and I took our backpacks and started up   9
26 the old mountain trail. Around sunset, we stopped   19
27 to set up camp and have a hot meal. We were very   29
28 tired after such a long day hiking uphill.   37

| 1 | 2 | 3 | 4 | 5 | 6 | 7 | 8 | 9 | 10

	A	B	C	D	E	F	G
1		January	February				
2							
3	Monday	8 a.m.-5 p.m.	8 a.m.-5 p.m.		7 a.m.-4 p.m.	7 a.m.-4 p.m.	7 a.m.-6 p.m.
4	Tuesday	8 a.m.-5 p.m.	8 a.m.-5 p.m.		7 a.m.-4 p.m.	7 a.m.-4 p.m.	7 a.m.-6 p.m
5							
6							
7							
8		Closed					Closed

ACTIVITY 42
Spreadsheet 35

Open the file SS34, save the file as SS35, and do the following:

1. In row 1, complete the months through June in column G.
2. In column A, complete the days through Sunday in row 12.
3. Use Fill Down or Copy and Paste to copy cells B6 through C7 to B8 through C10.
4. Use Fill Right to copy cell range C6 through C10 to D6 through D10.
5. Use Fill Down to copy cells E6 through F7 to E8 through F10.
6. Use Fill Down to copy cells G6 through G7 to G8 through G9.
7. Use Fill Right to copy cell B11 to C11 through G11.
8. Use Fill Down to copy cell range B11 through G11 to B12 through G12.
9. Bold and center the names of the months.
10. Bold the names of the days.
11. Select cell range A6 through G12 and automatically widen the columns.
12. Change cells A1 and A2 to 12-point bold and center each line above the block A1 through G1 and A2 through G2.
13. Shade cell range A1 through G2 and add a line at the bottom of cell range A2 through G2.
14. Shade cell ranges B3 through B12; D3 through D12; and F3 through F12.
15. Place a border around cell range A1 through G12.
16. Save your changes and close the file.

F. PRACTICE

SPEED: *If you made 2 or fewer errors on the Pretest, type lines 29–36 two times each.*

ACCURACY: *If you made more than 2 errors on the Pretest, type lines 29–32 as a group two times. Then type lines 33–36 as a group two times.*

Up Reaches

29 ho shock chose phone shove hover holly homes shot
30 st stair guest stone blast nasty start casts step
31 il lilac filed drill build spill child trail pail
32 de dear redeem warden tide render chide rode dead

Down Reaches

33 ab squab labor habit cabin cable abate about able
34 ca pecan recap catch carve cable scale scamp camp
35 av ravel gavel avert knave waved paved shave have
36 in ruin invent winner bring shin chin shrink pine

G. POSTTEST

Repeat the Pretest. Compare your Posttest results with your Pretest results.

H. 1-MINUTE ALPHANUMERIC TIMING

Take a 1-minute timing on lines 37–39. Note your speed and errors.

37   Joy wanted to get a dozen (12) baseball bats   9
38 @ $4.29 from the sports store at 718 Miner Place.   19
39 When I went, only 10 bats were left.   26
  | 1 | 2 | 3 | 4 | 5 | 6 | 7 | 8 | 9 | 10

I. 2-MINUTE TIMINGS

Take two 2-minute timings on lines 40–45. Note your speed and errors.

Goal: 27/2'/4e

40   In the fall of the year, I find pleasure in   9
41 zipping up to the hills to quietly view the trees   19
42 changing colors. Most all aspens turn to shades   29
43 of gold. Oak trees exude tones of red and orange.   39
44 The plants change colors each fall, but all these   49
45 changes are an amazing sight.   54
  | 1 | 2 | 3 | 4 | 5 | 6 | 7 | 8 | 9 | 10 SI 1.25

FORMATTING

C. FILL RIGHT, FILL DOWN, AND FILL SERIES

Spreadsheet fill commands reproduce or copy the same data down a column (**Fill Down**) or across a row (**Fill Right**). Fill commands can be used with text and values, including formulas. The **Fill Series** command is used to create data with a pattern. For example, if you type *Monday* and *Tuesday* in cells A1 and B1, you can use the fill command to fill cells C1 through G1 with the rest of the days. The same is true for months and numbers that have a pattern such as *5, 10, 15* or *15, 12, 9*. The fill commands generate data quickly and accurately and are great time-savers.

D. SOFTWARE FEATURES

STUDENT MANUAL

Fill Right   Fill Down
Fill Series

Study Lesson 136 in your student manual. Complete all the practice activities while at your computer. Then complete the jobs that follow.

SPREADSHEET APPLICATIONS

ACTIVITY 41
Spreadsheet 34

Create a new spreadsheet and save it as SS34. Then follow these steps:

1. Type the data as shown in the illustration, using Copy and Paste where applicable.
2. Insert 3 blank rows at row 1.
3. In cell A1, type the label *Proposed Work Schedule for Carlton, Inc.*
4. In cell A2, type *Prepared by* followed by your name.
5. Save your changes and close the file.

LESSON 26

NEW KEYS: 5 % 6 ^

OBJECTIVES:

- Learn the 5, %, 6, and ^ keys.
- Refine keyboarding skills.
- Type 27/2'/4e.

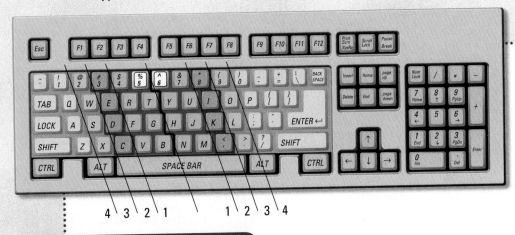

4 3 2 1   1 2 3 4

A. WARMUP

Type each line 2 times.

Speed 1 Our team at band camp did a new drill for guests.
Accuracy 2 Two jobs require packing five dozen axes monthly.
Numbers 3 Mark read the winning numbers: 190, 874, and 732.
Symbols 4 The shop (J & B) has #10 envelopes* @ $.24 a doz.

NEW KEYS

B. 5 AND % KEY

Type each line 2 times. Repeat if time permits.

Use F finger.
For 5 and %, anchor A.

5 ftf ft5f f5f 555 f5f 5/55 f5f 55.5 f5f 55,555 f5f
6 55 fins, 55 facts, 55 fields, 55 futures, or 5.55
7 Jo saw 55 bulls, 14 cows, 155 sheep, and 5 goats.
8 I just sold 55 items; his total for today is 555.

% is the shift of 5. The % (percent) is used in statistical data. Do not space between numbers and %.

9 ftf ft5 f5f f5%f f%f f%f 5% 55% 555% f%f f5f 555%
10 5%, 5 foes, 55%, 55 fees, 555%, 555 fiddles, 555%
11 The meal is 55% protein, 20% starch, and 25% fat.
12 On June 5, 55% of the students had 5% more skill.

LESSON 136

SPREADSHEETS: FILL RIGHT/FILL DOWN COMMANDS

OBJECTIVES:

- Improve keyboarding skill.
- Use Fill Right and Fill Down commands.
- Use Fill Series command.

A. WARMUP

Type each line 2 times.

Speed
Accuracy
Language Link
Numbers/Symbols

1 The boys will not go to the zoo as was said at the meeting.
2 Liza quit her job, packed six new bags, and moved far away.
3 The students hope that they can get passes to today's game.
4 You will set tabs for these jobs at 18, 24, 37, 42, and 54.
| 1 | 2 | 3 | 4 | 5 | 6 | 7 | 8 | 9 | 10 | 11 | 12

SKILLBUILDING

B. 30-SECOND OK TIMINGS

Take two 30-second OK (error-free) timings on lines 5–6. Then take two 30-second OK timings on lines 7–8. Goal: no errors.

5   Quinn was in a daze after watching six rented movies;   11
6 she wanted to jot down the plots before she forgot them.   23

7   Marvin went to buy zippers to fix the jeans, but then   11
8 he could not squeeze his vehicle into the parking place.   23
| 1 | 2 | 3 | 4 | 5 | 6 | 7 | 8 | 9 | 10 | 11 | 12

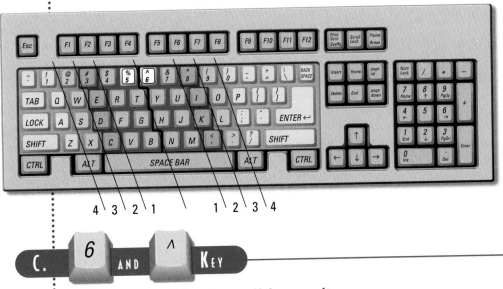

C. 6 AND ^ KEY

Type each line 2 times. Repeat if time permits.

Use J finger.
For 6 and ^, anchor ;.

13 jyj jy6j j6j 666 j6j 6/66 j6j 66.6 j6j 66,666 j6j
14 66 jaws, 66 jokes, 66 jewels, 66 jackets, or 6.66
15 Her averages were 76.46, 81.66, 86.56, and 96.36.
16 Multiply .66 by .51; the correct answer is .3366.

^ is the shift of 6. The ^ (caret) is used in some programming languages. Do not space between the caret and numbers.

17 jyj jy6 j6j j6^j j^j j^j ^j ^jj ^jjj j^j j6j ^jjj
18 6^, 6 jams, 66^, 66 jets, 666^, 666 jingles, 666^
19 The test problems included these: 75^2, 4^3, 8^6.
20 The ^ (caret) appeared 6 times in a line of code.

SKILLBUILDING

D. TECHNIQUE TIMINGS

Take two 30-second timings on each line. Focus on the technique at the left.

Sit up straight with your feet flat on the floor.

21 Snow leopards are graceful animals with soft fur.
22 They live in the high, rugged mountains of Tibet.
23 These big cats are adept at climbing and leaping.
24 They use their tails to balance on narrow ledges.

SPREADSHEET APPLICATIONS

ACTIVITY 39
Spreadsheet 32

Open the file SS18, save it as SS32, and follow these steps to clear formatting properties:

1. Select cell range A1 through E16 and clear the formatting. Note what happens to your spreadsheet.
2. If the format of the numbers in column C did not change, change them to numeric, general.
3. Move the contents of cells C1 and C2 to A1 and A2.
4. Change rows 1 and 2 to 10-point bold, and center cells A1 and A2 across the spreadsheet.
5. Clear the contents of cell range A7 through A16; then enter these numbers: *7, 15, 30, 37, 45, 51, 68, 77, 93, 105.*
6. Center and bold cell range A4 through E5.
7. Change the font in cells B5 and D5 to Wingdings.
8. Format cell range C7 through C16 for no decimal places.
9. Shade cell range A1 through E5 in a shade of your choice.
10. Shade the data in rows 7, 9, 11, 13, and 15 in a shade of your choice.
11. Add a border around the entire spreadsheet.
12. Save your changes and close the file.

ACTIVITY 40
Spreadsheet 33

Open the file SS24, save it as SS33, and follow these steps:

1. Delete column C. Notice that the grade averages are either recalculated or you get an error message indicating that you must recalculate or rewrite the formula.
2. Delete the rows containing data for Robin Flewharty, Logan Pfiel, and Priscilla Swafford.
3. Shade the data in rows 4, 6, 8, 10, 12, and 14 in a shade of your choice.
4. Place a border around the entire spreadsheet.
5. Place a line at the bottom of cell range A2 through F2.
6. Save your changes and close the file.

Take a 1-minute timing on lines 25–28. Note your speed and errors.

```
25       As a flock, the crows flew to some clumps of      9
26  stalks near the eddy. They seemed to eat the pods      19
27  joyfully as they fed in the field. We like to         28
28  watch them, especially in the morning.                36
    | 1  | 2  | 3  | 4  | 5  | 6  | 7  | 8  | 9  | 10
```

F. PRACTICE

SPEED: *If you made 2 or fewer errors on the Pretest, type lines 29–36 two times each.*

ACCURACY: *If you made more than 2 errors on the Pretest, type lines 29–32 as a group two times. Then type lines 33–36 as a group two times.*

Adjacent	29 po pods poem point poise lk hulk silk polka stalk
Jump	30 mp jump pump trump clump cr cram crow crawl creed
Double	31 dd odds eddy daddy caddy tt mitt mutt utter ditto
Consecutive	32 un unit punk funny bunch gr grab agree angry grip
Alternate	33 iv give dive drive wives gl glad glee ogled gland
Left/Right	34 fe fear feat ferns fetal jo joys join joker jolly
Up/Down	35 sw swan sway sweat swift k, ark, ask, tick, wick,
In/Out	36 lu luck blunt fluid lush da dash date sedan panda

G. POSTTEST

Repeat the Pretest. Then compare your Posttest results with your Pretest results.

H. 1-MINUTE ALPHANUMERIC TIMING

Take a 1-minute timing on lines 37–39. Note your speed and errors.

```
37       Kim ran the 7.96-mile race last week. Yanni     9
38  ran 14.80 miles. Zeke said the next 5K run will      19
39  be held on August 14 or August 23.                   25
    | 1  | 2  | 3  | 4  | 5  | 6  | 7  | 8  | 9  | 10
```

FORMATTING

E.   CLEARING CELLS

When you press delete or backspace in a cell or cell range, the contents of the cell are removed, but the formatting remains. To remove formatting properties from cells, use the clear commands. Clear usually removes basic formatting commands such as bold, italics, underline, and fonts. Some clear commands also remove shading, borders, alignments, and numeric formats. An option in the clear command is to remove both the contents and the formatting properties at the same time.

F.   DELETING ROWS AND COLUMNS

Spreadsheet rows and columns can be deleted by selecting the row number or column letter and using the delete command. If the spreadsheet contains formulas and a row or column is deleted, the software will adjust the addresses of the shifted cells. However, if a formula depends upon a cell that has been deleted, an error message will be displayed.

G.   SOFTWARE FEATURES

STUDENT MANUAL

Clear Commands
Delete Rows and Columns

Study Lesson 135 in your student manual. Complete all the practice activities while at your computer. Then complete the jobs that follow.

CULTURAL CONNECTIONS

Dates and time are expressed in different ways from one country to another. Ask a student from another country how he or she would write today's date on a letter.

Take two 2-minute timings on lines 40–45. Note your speed and errors.

Goal: 27/2′/4e

40	As you look for jobs, be quite sure that	9
41	the way you dress depicts the position that you	18
42	want. If you hope to obtain an office job, zippy	28
43	fashions are not for you. Expect to arrive in a	38
44	clean, pressed business suit. Your clothes should	48
45	match the job you are trying for.	54

| 1 | 2 | 3 | 4 | 5 | 6 | 7 | 8 | 9 | 10   SI 1.21

FACT FILE

E-mail acronyms are commonly used instead of phrases that you would otherwise type in full. Some of the most popular ones are these: IMHO (in my humble opinion), BTW (by the way), RTM (read the manual), LOL (laughing out loud), FWIW (for what it's worth), and ROFL (rolling on the floor laughing).

SKILLBUILDING

C. PREVIEW PRACTICE

Type each line 2 times as a preview to the timings that follow.

Accuracy
Speed

9 how extent impaired Alexander equipment surprised telephone
10 hearing speech moved wires help soon just grew live but was

D. 5-MINUTE TIMINGS

Take two 5-minute timings on the paragraphs. Note your speed and errors.

Goal: 39/5'/5e

Social Studies
Connections

Science
Connections

11   Throughout its history, America has prospered and   10
12 grown with the help of countless inventions. Although he   22
13 could not have realized the full extent of its effects at   33
14 the time, Alexander Graham Bell invented a device that led   45
15 to a change in the way we communicate not just in our own   57
16 country but in the entire world.   63

17   Bell grew up in a family that had a deep interest in   74
18 speech and deafness. He moved from Scotland to the United   86
19 States where he learned how to teach the hearing impaired   97
20 to speak. He also began to work with equipment that would   109
21 send several telegraph messages over one line. From this   121
22 interest, he started to try to send voices over electrical   132
23 wires. Soon the telephone was born.   140

24   Bell might be surprised at how his work has linked our   151
25 world together, but we can be sure he would be most proud   162
26 of the strides that have been made in helping the hearing   174
27 impaired. Bell's inventions have enabled those who cannot   186
28 hear to live richer lives in a hearing world.   195

| 1 | 2 | 3 | 4 | 5 | 6 | 7 | 8 | 9 | 10 | 11 | 12SI 1.42

LESSON 27

SPECIAL SYMBOLS

OBJECTIVES:

- Learn the <, >, \, +, =, {, }, [,], and ~ keys.
- Refine keyboarding skills.
- Type 27/2'/4e.

A. WARMUP

Type each line 2 times.

Speed	1 Brent hurt his arm today and is in a lot of pain.
Accuracy	2 The tax is zero on these dozen tax-exempt pizzas.
Numbers	3 The population of Cooper is 216,974, not 326,815.
Symbols	4 Stop & Shop has 25% off reams of 24# paper @ $13.

NEW KEYS

B. SPECIAL SYMBOLS

You have learned to type many frequently used symbols by touch. Other less frequently used symbols also appear on the keyboard. Although it is not necessary to learn these symbols by touch, you should know what they are, how they are used, where they are located, and what fingers to use.

LESSON 135

SPREADSHEETS: CLEAR CELLS, DELETE ROWS AND COLUMNS

OBJECTIVES:

- Learn nominative and objective pronoun use.
- Clear cells.
- Delete rows and columns.
- Type 39/5'/5e.

A. WARMUP

Type each line 2 times.

Speed
Accuracy
Language Link
Numbers/Symbols

```
1 That round key that you gave me will not fit into the door.
2 Buzz was pleased to qualify in the men's bike extravaganza.
3 Since school was called off, some of the students slept in.
4 Just 4% of the #156 ($2.36) on 3% of #78 ($1.90) were used.
 | 1 | 2 | 3 | 4 | 5 | 6 | 7 | 8 | 9 | 10 | 11 | 12
```

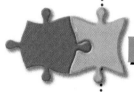 LANGUAGE LINK

B. PRONOUN USE

Study the rules and examples that follow. Then edit lines 5–8 to correct any errors in pronoun use.

Rule 38: Use **nominative** pronouns (such as *I, he, she, we,* and *they*) as subjects of a sentence or clause.
> *The programmer and he are reviewing that.*
> *It is she who likes this software.*

Rule 39: Use **objective** pronouns (such as *me, him, her,* and *them*) as objects in a sentence or clause.
> *The folders are for Susan and him.*
> *She went out with him and me.*

```
5 Rob knows art better than (she/her), but (she/her) can't add.
6 (She/Her) and (I/me) saw the new movie before (they/them) did.
7 My friends and (I/me) do not like (he/him) when (he/him) brags.
8 I'm sure (he/him) has more knowledge of cultures than (I/me).
```

4 3 2 1   1 2 3 4

Find each of the symbols shown below on your keyboard. Note which finger controls each key and the spacing used with the symbol. In the example column, study how the symbol is used.

Key	Name	Use	Finger	Spacing	Example
\	Back-slash	Naming files/ directories	Sem	No space before and after.	`a:\Medical\ Doctor.cgs`
<	Less Than	Math	K	One space before and after.	`15 < 25`
>	Greater Than	Math	L	One space before and after.	`31 > 19`
=	Equal	Math	Sem	One space before and after.	`A = 27`
+	Plus	Math	Sem	One space before and after.	`3 + 3 = 6`
[ ]	Left and Right Brackets	Enclose special text	Sem	No space after [or before].	`"He [Twain] wrote . . . "`
{ }	Left and Right Curly Braces	Math and Internet searches	Sem	No space after { or before }.	`{4, 2, 6}`
~	Tilde	Internet addresses	A	No space before and after.	`www.isp.com/~jon`

Open the file SS30, save it as SS31, and make the following changes:

1. Fill cell range A1 through G5 with a light shading or light horizontal lines.
2. Add a medium border at the top of cell range A15 through G15.
3. Using the same fill you used in step 1, shade the following cell ranges: A7 through G7; A9 through G9; A11 through G11; A13 through G13.
4. Save your changes and close the file.

FACT FILE

The spadefoot toad is a persistent desert dweller, digging with a projection on each hind foot. The toad experiences estivation, a type of hibernation, when drought sets in. This estivation can last eight or nine months.

PORTFOLIO
Activity

Write a short paragraph about the importance of accuracy in temperature conversions such as those in Activity 25. What can happen if you make an error? If you made any errors in your mathematical conversions, explain why you think you made the errors and what you can do to prevent such errors in the future.

Type each line 2 times. Repeat if time permits.

5 Dakota typed "C:\DATABASE\FRESHMEN\OFFICERS.SEP."
6 If X < Z and Y > X but < Z, then Z > X and Z > Y.
7 Please see if 7.13 + 5.21 = 12.34 and 9 + 2 = 11.

8 "They [Americans] captured Trenton [New Jersey]."
9 Search for these: {New York}, Ohio, {New Mexico}.
10 Use this format: http://www.server.com/~username.

SKILLBUILDING

C. PRETEST

Take a 1-minute timing on lines 11–14. Note your speed and errors.

```
11        A news report said that the trash will be     9
12 collected next week. Many county roads are still    19
13 covered with too much snow. The county officials    29
14 will discuss this problem for a few more days.      38
   | 1 | 2 | 3 | 4 | 5 | 6 | 7 | 8 | 9 | 10
```

D. PRACTICE

SPEED: If you made 2 or fewer errors on the Pretest, type lines 15–22 two times each.

ACCURACY: If you made more than 2 errors on the Pretest, type lines 15–18 as a group two times. Then type lines 19–22 as a group two times.

Discrimination reaches are keys that are commonly substituted and easily confused (wear).

```
15 asa flask aside sails saved masks sadly trash sas
16 fgf frogs foggy gaffe fugue golfs goofs fight gfg
17 ewe weeks fewer sewer sweat swell sweet weans wew
18 ded deal heeded dent need debate feed student ede

19 ioi spoil toils lions coins joins soils boils oio
20 mnm hymns money names numbs minor lemon means nmn
21 klk locks block flock keels kills kilts kilns lkl
22 yuy yule young unduly pulley bully ruby jumpy uyu
```

E. POSTTEST

Repeat the Pretest. Compare your Posttest results with your Pretest results.

SPREADSHEET APPLICATIONS

ACTIVITY 36
Spreadsheet 29

Open the file SS12, save it as SS29, and then follow these steps to change the spreadsheet:

1. Insert a blank column D.
2. In cell D6, center and type in bold the label *Transportation.*
3. In cell range D8 through D12, type the following entries: *Antilles Air; Ferry; Isle Air; Mailboat; Ferry.*
4. Automatically widen column D.
5. Select cell range A8 through F12, and sort column B in descending (high to low) order.
6. Follow your teacher's instructions for printing.
7. Save your changes and close the file.

ACTIVITY 37
Spreadsheet 30

Open the file SS20, save it as SS30, and follow these steps to change the spreadsheet:

1. Insert a blank column F.
2. In cell F5, type the label *Our Store.*
3. In cell range F7 through F12, enter the following values: *1.97; 1.03; 2.88; 0.99; 3.11; 1.78.*
4. Copy the formula in cell E14 to F14.
5. Select cell range A5 through G14, and automatically change the column width.
6. Insert a blank row 9.
7. In cell range A9 through G9, enter the following data: *Holstein Milk; 1 gal.; 1.56; 1.78; 1.89; 1.65; 1.49.*
8. Select cell range A7 through G13 and sort column A in ascending order.
9. If necessary, center cells A1 through A3 across the spreadsheet again.
10. Add a heavy border around cell range A1 through G15.
11. Add a border at the bottom of cell range A1 through G5.
12. Save your changes and close the file.

Type each line 1 time. Repeat if time permits.

```
23  aa alas also again after bb bake blow begin black
24  cc came coat charm clear dd drop door dream dated

25  ee ever each eager enemy ff five foal frame flute
26  gg game give grate guard hh hope hall heavy human

27  ii iced into ideal ionic jj jail joke jewel juice
28  kk keep kick knife knock ll long lace lower lever

29  mm mope mail merit music nn name none never night
30  oo over open order occur pp pure pain piece plump

31  qq quit quad quest quote rr roar rain rhyme rural
32  ss sing soap saber sense tt time talk tooth trait

33  uu us urge upon vv via vase vine ww wag west warm
34  xx ox axis exit yy yen year yank zz zoo zany zinc
```

Type each line 1 time. Repeat if time permits.

```
35  46 maps, 69 snaps, 65 traps, 15 drapes, 63 grapes
36  57 lots, 85 plots, 16 slots, 50 floats, 86 clocks

37  53 hams, 46 trams, 95 slams, 62 flames, 67 blames
38  58 ails, 60 sails, 96 nails, 45 snails, 47 trails

39  (1) 32% of $17, (2) 2^9, (3) 15 @ $.81, (4) Wait!
40  (5) the key,* (6) A & W, (7) 56 @ $.10, (8) 40^3*

41  Tony said 3^2 and 20% of 40 have the same answer.
42  He rented 56 vases, 239 tables, and 4,078 chairs.

43  A & Z billed us for 79 pens @ $.23 on Invoice #8.
44  Dan collected 98 flowers, 39 bugs, and 47 leaves.

45  Nice & Clean (formerly #1 Laundry) is in Memphis.
46  The 743 people were served 980 rolls by 12 girls.
```

C. INSERTING COLUMNS INTO A SPREADSHEET

Sometimes it may be necessary to insert additional columns into a spreadsheet. When you insert a column, all the columns following the insertion will be relettered, and formulas in the spreadsheet will be readjusted.

D. ADDING BORDERS AND SHADING

Spreadsheets can be made more attractive and readable by using lines, or **borders,** both in and around the worksheet and darker or color backgrounds called **shading.** Choose shading that does not interfere with reading the text. Also, do not use too many special treatments in a single spreadsheet. You may need to experiment with available options to find what works best.

Borders.
Lines placed around spreadsheet cells and/or cell ranges.

Shading.
Darkening or coloring the background of cells or cell ranges.

CONCESSION STAND ROSTER Tuesday, September 12				
5:30-6:30	**6:30-7:30**	**7:30-8:30**	**8:30-9:30**	**9:30-Cleanup**
Gray Aubrey	Bessonett, Teri	Diener, Darren	Corbin, Curt	Daehn, Sonja
Maddox, Roy	Horvath, Jessie	Katchinska, Ken	Estes, Edith	Feddon, Lee
McNeal, Mike	Ottwell, Dionne	Roark, Randa	Geitner, Gail	Gustafson, Gunther
Owen, Beverly	Rubio, Nan	Vega, Oscar	Hosea, Jim	Nix, Nita

E. SOFTWARE FEATURES

STUDENT MANUAL

Insert Columns
Add Borders and Shading

Study Lesson 134 in your student manual. Complete all the practice activities while at your computer. Then complete the jobs that follow.

H. 1-Minute Alphanumeric Timing

Take a 1-minute timing on lines 47–49. Note your speed and errors.

47	Jason paid Invoice #75 with Check #2301. He	9
48	mailed it June 24, but he forgot the $.39 stamp.	19
49	Stop & Go's bill needs to be paid July 1.	27

| 1 | 2 | 3 | 4 | 5 | 6 | 7 | 8 | 9 | 10

I. 2-Minute Timings

Take two 2-minute timings on lines 50–55. Note your speed and errors.

Goal: 27/2'/4e

Social Studies
Connections

50	The Cherokee had no desire to leave the land	9
51	of their fathers. Troops forced them to move to	19
52	the west. Many of them froze to death during the	28
53	brutal winter on the long journey. They could not	38
54	exist through the cold winter as they moved along	48
55	the tragic Trail of Tears.	54

| 1 | 2 | 3 | 4 | 5 | 6 | 7 | 8 | 9 | 10   SI 1.21

interNET CONNECTION

Use the Internet to search for additional information about the Cherokees and about the Trail of Tears. Report your findings to the class.

LESSON 134

SPREADSHEETS: INSERTING COLUMNS, BORDERS, AND SHADING

OBJECTIVES:

- Improve keyboarding skills.
- Insert columns into a spreadsheet.
- Add borders and shading.

A. WARMUP

Type each line 2 times.

Speed
Accuracy
Language Link
Numbers/Symbols

1 The four women spent the day on the lake in a fishing boat.
2 Ximenez may jeopardize the quality of those antique quilts.
3 None of the parents wanted their children out in the storm.
4 Those answers are: (a) $135, (b) $46, (c) $128, (d) $97.03.

| 1 | 2 | 3 | 4 | 5 | 6 | 7 | 8 | 9 | 10 | 11 | 12

SKILLBUILDING

B. PACED PRACTICE

Turn to the Paced Practice routine beginning on page SB7. Take three 2-minute timings, starting at the point where you left off the last time.

FACT FILE

The gray shark is a smaller version of a great white shark. Gray sharks are members of the Carcharhinidae or *man-eating* family of sharks. Gray sharks are most often found in the waters of the Mediterranean Sea and the Atlantic Ocean.

NUMERIC KEYPAD: 4 5 6 ENTER

OBJECTIVES:

- Learn the 4, 5, 6, and Enter keys on the numeric keypad.
- Learn capitalization rules.
- Refine keyboarding skills.
- Type 30/2'/4e.

A. WARMUP

Type each line 2 times.

Speed
Accuracy
Numbers
Symbols

```
1 We will be out for spring break in two more days.
2 Skip was quite vexed by the jazzman from Cologne.
3 Your fingers can now find 10, 29, 38, 47, and 56.
4 If T > Z, then explain (please!) why {T + H = Z}.
```

ACTIVITY 35
Spreadsheet 28

Open the file SS24, save it as SS28, and follow these steps to change the spreadsheet by inserting rows and sorting data:

1. Insert a blank row 1.
2. In cell A1, type in 12-point bold the label *Fifth-Period Junior English Class.*
3. Insert a blank row 2.
4. In cell A2, type in bold the label *Prepared by* followed by your name.
5. Insert a blank row 3.
6. In cell A3, type in bold the label *Beginning February 10,{year}.*
7. Center A1 across the spreadsheet. Repeat for A2 and A3.
8. Insert a blank row 4.
9. Bold and center cell range A5 through G6.
10. Select cell range A8 through G21, and sort the names in column A in ascending order.
11. Format all numbers to have no decimal places.
12. Insert gridlines and change the print orientation to landscape.
13. Follow your teacher's instructions for printing.
14. Save your changes and close the file.

 ***inter*NET** C O N N E C T I O N

Connect to the Internet. Search the World Wide Web for information on the skeletal structure of the blue whale. How does it compare with that of the dinosaur?

1 2 3 4

LANGUAGE LINK

B. CAPITALIZATION

Study the rules and the examples below. Then edit lines 5–8 to correct any errors in capitalization.

Rule 1: Capitalize the first word of a sentence.

> *The weather bureau predicted a winter storm. It was severe.*

Rule 2: Capitalize the names of the days of the week, months, holidays, and religious days. Do not capitalize the names of the seasons.

> *In the fall, we celebrate Thanksgiving on Thursday, November 24.*

Edit the lines to correct any errors in capitalization.

5 memorial day this year will fall on monday, may 27.
6 why wait until wednesday? we can leave later today.
7 during the Winter, they skied and skated every day.
8 Offices are closed on memorial day and on thursday.

NEW KEYS

C. KEYPAD HOME-KEY POSITION

The Num Lock key must be active before you can enter numbers on the keypad. If the Num Lock light is not on, press the Num Lock key.

The 4, 5, and 6 are the home keys for the numeric keypad.
1. Place your J, K, and L fingers on 4, 5, and 6 on the numeric keypad. You will feel a raised marker on the 5 key. This marker will help you keep your fingers on the home keys.
2. Place your Sem finger over the ENTER key. The ENTER key on the numeric keypad functions just like the ENTER key on the alphabetic keyboard.

SPREADSHEET APPLICATIONS

ACTIVITY 32
Spreadsheet 25

Open the file SS1, and save it as SS25. Then follow the steps below:

1. Insert a blank row 1.
2. In cell A1, type in 14-point bold the label *Fund-Raising Report*.
3. Insert a blank row 2.
4. In cell A2, type in 12-point bold the label *Prepared by* followed by your name.
5. Insert a blank row 3.
6. Save your changes and close the file.

ACTIVITY 33
Spreadsheet 26

Open the file SS25, save it as SS26, and follow these steps:

1. In cell A3, type in 12-point bold, the label *October 12-30, {year}*.
2. Insert a blank row 4.
3. Center cell range A1 through A3 across the spreadsheet.
4. Bold the contents of rows 19 and 20.
5. Change the print orientation to landscape.
6. If the contents of any column are not visible, adjust the width.
7. Save your changes and close the file.

ACTIVITY 34
Spreadsheet 27

Open the file SS26, save it as SS27, and follow these steps:

1. Select cell range A7 through E17.
2. Sort column E in descending order (from high to low). The names are no longer in alphabetic order but are arranged in order of highest to lowest total sales.
3. Follow your teacher's instructions for printing.
4. Save your changes and close the file.

FACT FILE

The dinosaur Mamenchisaurus had an extremely long neck. This type of dinosaur could have a neck as long as 49 feet, about 2 1/2 times as long as a giraffe's neck.

1 2 3 4

D. 4 5 6 Keys

Enter the following numbers column by column. Use the proper finger for each key. Press ENTER after the final digit of each number. Repeat if time permits.

Use J, K, and L fingers.

Keep your eyes on the copy.

Accuracy is very important when entering numbers.

9 444	456	454
10 555	654	464
11 666	445	546
12 455	446	564
13 466	554	654
14 544	556	645
15 566	664	666
16 644	665	555
17 655	456	444
18 456	654	456

SKILLBUILDING

E. Keypad Practice

Enter the following numbers column by column. Press ENTER after the final digit of each number. Keep your eyes on the copy. Repeat if time permits.

Use J, K, and L fingers.

Keep your eyes on the copy.

Accuracy is very important when entering numbers.

19	444	455	464	555	466	646	666	544	456	445	644
20	546	554	556	454	645	664	545	654	665	565	465
21	445	446	455	466	456	454	465	464	554	556	544
22	644	655	645	646	654	656	666	464	555	665	456
23	654	456	564	465	646	656	464	456	546	564	465

SKILLBUILDING

C. 30-Second Timings

Take two 30-second timings on lines 5–6. Then take two 30-second timings on lines 7–8. Try to increase your speed on each paragraph.

5   One type of report is an agenda; it is used to inform   *11*
6 people of items that may be discussed at a future meeting. *23*

7   Minutes of a meeting are another kind of report; they   *11*
8 are records of reference for what takes place in meetings. *23*

| 1 | 2 | 3 | 4 | 5 | 6 | 7 | 8 | 9 | 10 | 11 | 12

FORMATTING

D. Inserting Rows

Even when you carefully plan a spreadsheet, there will be times when you need to insert additional rows. When you insert a row, all of the rows after the insertion will be renumbered, and any formulas in the spreadsheet will be readjusted.

E. Sorting Data

Sorting data is arranging it in a certain order such as alphabetic or numeric. You can sort data in **ascending order** (from A to Z or low to high) or in **descending order** (from Z to A or high to low). You can also choose which column to sort first, second, and third. Before you sort data, it is a good idea to save your file. Your sort may not turn out the way you intended.

F. Software Features

STUDENT MANUAL

Insert Rows
Sort Data

Study Lesson 133 in your student manual. Complete all the practice activities while at your computer. Then complete the jobs that follow.

F. TECHNIQUE TIMINGS

Take two 30-second timings on each line. Focus on the techniques at the left.

Lines 24 and 25: Efficient and smooth operation of the shift keys.
Lines 26 and 27: Efficient and smooth operation of the ENTER key.

24 Will Zeb and Vern work Zone Two with Cam and Nic?
25 Miriam and Dolores saw Broadway and Main Streets.
26 Did Ben Milo fix that off/on switch? Did it work?
27 Ivan is grateful that it is ready for the winter.

G. DIAGNOSTIC PRACTICE: ALPHABET

Turn to the Diagnostic Practice: Alphabet routine on page SB1. Type one of the Pretest/Posttest paragraphs and identify any errors. Then type the corresponding drill lines on p. SB2 two times for each letter on which you made 2 or more errors and one time for each letter on which you made only 1 error. Finally, repeat the same Pretest paragraph and compare your performance.

H. 12-SECOND SPRINTS

Take three 12-second timings on each line. Try to increase your speed on each timing.

28 Walking can pick you up if you are feeling tired.
29 Your heart and lungs can work harder as you walk.
30 It may be that a walk is often better than a nap.
31 You will keep fit if you walk each and every day.
| | | |5| | | |10| | | |15| | | |20| | | |25| | | |30| | | |35| | | |40| | | |45| | | |50

I. 2-MINUTE TIMINGS

Take two 2-minute timings on lines 32–38. Note your speed and errors.

Goal: 30/2'/4e

32   Some senior students realize that once they   9
33 leave school, they must plan for more education.   19
34 Most will not know exactly what their first job   28
35 will be or what skills will equip them to move   38
36 ahead in a job or to change to another job. You   47
37 should make plans for your future now while you   57
38 have the time.   60
| 1 | 2 | 3 | 4 | 5 | 6 | 7 | 8 | 9 | 10   SI 1.25

LESSON 133

SPREADSHEETS: INSERTING ROWS/SORTING DATA

OBJECTIVES:

- Compose at the keyboard.
- Improve typing speed.
- Insert rows into a spreadsheet.
- Sort data in a spreadsheet.

A. WARMUP

Type each line 2 times.

Speed
Accuracy
Language Link
Numbers/Symbols

```
1 Three workers left early and were paid for only half a day.
2 Del and Wanda Quaid are great examples of quality citizens.
3 Everybody was warned to stay home due to the freezing rain.
4 18, 290, 27, 38, 851, 63, 94, 704, 91, 48, 532, 10, 76, 495
  | 1 | 2 | 3 | 4 | 5 | 6 | 7 | 8 | 9 | 10 | 11 | 12
```

LANGUAGE LINK

B. COMPOSING AT THE KEYBOARD

Compose the body of a one-page story which begins as follows:

"The last thing I remember was taking the dog for a walk. When I awoke, I found myself in a hospital room, but I couldn't remember . . ."

When you finish your story, proofread it carefully and correct any errors.

FACT FILE

The planet Neptune orbits the sun once in 164 years. That is a long orbit!

LESSON 29

NUMERIC KEYPAD: 7 8 9

OBJECTIVES:

- Learn the 7, 8, 9 keys on the numeric keypad.
- Refine keyboarding skills.
- Type 30/2'/4e.

1 2 3 4

A. WARMUP

Type each line 2 times.

Speed
Accuracy
Language Link
Numbers

1 No one can say that he is not giving full effort.
2 Alex was puzzled by the czar's quip about oxygen.
3 He and Molly traveled to Iowa on Saturday by bus.
4 Without looking I can type 67, 89, 23, 14, and 5.

FACT FILE

A leap second is inserted into the year (usually on New Year's Eve) to make up for the fact that Earth's rotation is slowing down. Scientists know when to insert a leap second by comparing Earth's rotation to an atomic clock.

Science
Connections

ACTIVITY 31
Spreadsheet 24

Create a new spreadsheet and save it as SS24. Then follow these steps:

1. Type the data as shown in the following table.
2. In cell G4, use the AVERAGE function to average Howard Joslin's grades.
3. Copy the contents of cell G4 to cell range G5 through G17.
4. Widen columns A, D, and F and the titles, so that you can read the names easily.
5. Save your changes and close the file.

	A	B	C	D	E	F	G
1	Students	Author	Portfolios	Persuasive	Narrative	Descriptive	Grade
2		Projects		Essays	Essays	Essays	
3							Averages
4	Joslin, Howard	88	92	78	83	75	
5	Calavan, Casey	97	99	91	93	89	
6	Petropoulos, Cheryl	73	81	80	65	77	
7	Figueroa, Miguel	79	90	87	82	80	
8	Vititow, Megan	75	55	81	73	69	
9	Mathis, Monica	98	94	88	95	96	
10	Quintero, Luis	84	76	66	89	92	
11	Kizer, Paula	90	87	94	88	91	
12	Yankey, Ottis	79	74	78	77	83	
13	Pfiel, Logan	95	89	96	92	87	
14	Locks, Andrea	100	97	99	98	100	
15	Flewharty, Robin	99	89	90	87	98	
16	Jimmerson, Gennifer	85	71	82	78	84	
17	Swafford, Priscilla	87	69	83	76	68	

interNET CONNECTION

Connect to the Internet. To learn more about ergonomic tips for office workers, search using the key words: workstation ergonomics.

1 2 3 4

NEW KEYS

B. **7 8 9** KEYS

Enter the following numbers column by column. Use the proper finger for each key. Press ENTER after the final digit of each number. Keep your eyes on the copy. Repeat if time permits.

Use J, K, and L fingers.

Be sure Num Lock is on.

Concentrate on accuracy as you enter the numbers.

5	474	585	696
6	747	858	969
7	774	885	996
8	447	558	669
9	744	855	966
10	477	588	699
11	444	555	666
12	747	858	969
13	774	885	996
14	747	858	969

SKILLBUILDING

C. KEYPAD PRACTICE

Enter the following numbers column by column. Press ENTER after the final digit of each number. Keep your eyes on the copy. Repeat if time permits.

Keep eyes on copy. Use proper fingers. Concentrate on accuracy.

15	456	556	474	699	477	577	677	748	847	947
16	654	664	585	747	488	588	688	749	849	948
17	445	665	696	858	499	599	699	758	857	957
18	446	456	477	969	478	578	678	759	859	958
19	554	654	588	789	489	589	689	767	868	969

STUDENT MANUAL
AVERAGE Function

Study Lesson 132 in your student manual. Complete all the practice activities while at your computer. Then complete the jobs that follow.

COMMUNICATION FOCUS

Write a short report on what you believe will be the advantages of working from home instead of from an office. Interview at least one person who has an office at home, perhaps a writer or an accountant in your city or town.

SPREADSHEET APPLICATIONS

ACTIVITY 29
Spreadsheet 22

Open the file SS1 and save it as SS22. Then follow these steps to change a spreadsheet by inserting the AVERAGE function.

1. Move cell range E1 through E16 to F1 through F16.
2. In cell E1, center and type in bold the label *Averages*.
3. In cell E3, find the average for weeks 1, 2, and 3.
4. Save your changes and close the file.

ACTIVITY 30
Spreadsheet 23

Open the file SS22, and save it as SS23. Then make the following changes:

1. In cell E4, find the average by typing the function name and selecting the cells to be averaged.
2. In cell E5, find the average by typing the function name and cell range.
3. Copy the contents of cell E5 to cell range E6 through E13.
4. Format all numbers to have two decimal places where necessary.
5. In cell E16, find the average of cell range E3 through E13.
6. Set the gridlines to print.
7. Automatically format the column width of cells E1 and F1.
8. Save your changes and close the file.

D. PACED PRACTICE

Turn to the Paced Practice routine beginning on page SB7. Take a 1-minute timing on the Entry Timing paragraph. Then follow the directions at the top of page SB7 for completing the activity.

E. 30-SECOND OK TIMINGS

Take two 30-second OK timings on lines 20–21. Then take two 30 second OK timings on lines 22–23. Goal: no errors.

```
20      He wants to work for a company that provides
21 benefits to workers. Jay's benefits are terrific.

22      Flat computer screen means that I can set up
23 my computer on my desk because the parts all fit.
   |  1  |  2  |  3  |  4  |  5  |  6  |  7  |  8  |  9  |  10
```

F. PRETEST

Take a 1-minute timing on the paragraph. Note your speed and errors.

```
24      Jenny loved most all of the opera music that      9
25 the kids sang. No one could deny how funny they       19
26 looked in muffs and emu feathers. Everyone had a      28
27 blast that afternoon.                                  33
   |  1  |  2  |  3  |  4  |  5  |  6  |  7  |  8  |  9  |  10
```

G. PRACTICE

SPEED: If you made 2 or fewer errors on the Pretest, type lines 28–35 two times each.

ACCURACY: If you made more than 2 errors on the Pretest, type lines 28–31 as a group two times. Then type lines 32–35 as a group two times.

Adjacent Reaches

```
28 as mast blast phase clash ashes atlas brash hasty
29 op crop opera flops opens poppy drops opals mopes
30 ds kids spuds grids bonds birds brads leads holds
31 lk milk talks walks balks milky silky bulky sulky
```

Jump Reaches

```
32 mu mute music muffs munch murky mulls musty muddy
33 ve cove verse serve curve verve wives chive sieve
34 ny deny funny phony shiny sunny irony corny agony
35 in sink blink slink whine shine winds pines inlet
```

H. POSTTEST

Repeat the Pretest. Compare your Posttest results with your Pretest results.

C. PRETEST

Take a 1-minute timing on the paragraph. Note your speed and errors.

9	It is essential that we get plenty of sleep so that we	11
10	are rested when we get up each morning. We must eat a good	23
11	breakfast to build up energy for the day. Physical exercise	35
12	is a must for stronger hearts and greater endurance.	45

| 1 | 2 | 3 | 4 | 5 | 6 | 7 | 8 | 9 | 10 | 11 | 12

Science

Connections

D. PRACTICE

In the chart below, find the number of errors you made on the Pretest. Then type each of the designated drill lines 2 times.

Pretest Errors	0–1	2	3	4+
Drill Lines	16–20	15–19	14–18	13–17

Accuracy

13 by friends families stronger breakfast minimize experienced
14 many rested problems run-down physical fatigued performance
15 build plenty energy increases endurance essential adversely
16 we quality morning exercise symptoms mentioned increasingly

Speed

17 hearts become energy there lives time each that when run we
18 levels active plenty tired these they good must felt our is
19 affect making crease limit spend with ways have down and it
20 friend affect rested sleep break days many just ever job of

E. POSTTEST

Repeat the Pretest. Compare your Posttest results with your Pretest results.

FORMATTING

F. Using the AVERAGE Function

AVERAGE (or AVG.) is a formula that automatically adds the values in a range of cells and divides by the number of values to find the average. The average can then be formatted to have the desired number of decimal places.

I. 2-MINUTE TIMINGS

Take two 2-minute timings on lines 36–42. Note your speed and errors.

Goal: 30/2'/4e

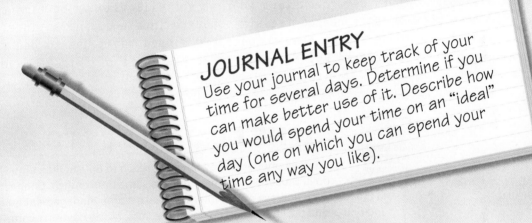

36 The end of a school program is a great feat	9
37 for most students. Some believe that it will be	18
38 the last time for a test; however, this may not	27
39 be so as a number of exams may be taken during a	37
40 lifetime. It is quite puzzling to some why tests	47
41 are given when their skills have been proved by	56
42 their achievements.	60

| 1 | 2 | 3 | 4 | 5 | 6 | 7 | 8 | 9 | 10   SI 1.21

JOURNAL ENTRY

Use your journal to keep track of your time for several days. Determine if you can make better use of it. Describe how you would spend your time on an "ideal" day (one on which you can spend your time any way you like).

LESSON 132

SPREADSHEETS: AVERAGE FUNCTION

OBJECTIVES:

- Improve keyboarding speed and accuracy.
- Use the AVERAGE function in a spreadsheet.

A. WARMUP

Type each line 2 times.

Speed
Accuracy
Language Link
Numbers/Symbols

1 Ruth sets her alarm so that she will wake up on time daily.
2 Zelda squeezed the six bouquets into a quaint antique vase.
3 Most of the area schools are closed today due to bad roads.
4 I ordered #6, #7, and #34 at discounts of 5%, 15%, and 20%.
| 1 | 2 | 3 | 4 | 5 | 6 | 7 | 8 | 9 | 10 | 11 | 12

interNET CONNECTION

Workers often find they have too much to do and little time to do it. Students, too, often feel the same time crunch. Connect to the following address on the Internet to take a time management quiz and find useful tips for managing your time: http://www.daytimer.com.

SKILLBUILDING

B. 12-SECOND SPRINTS

Take three 12-second timings on each line. Try to increase your speed on each timing.

5 The new desk and chair will be put in the back of the room.
6 Those boys were asked to cut and water the dry, brown lawn.
7 At long last I have a pen that will not leak on my fingers.
8 We need to turn off the light before they tell us to do it.
| | | 5 | | | 10 | | | 15 | | | 20 | | | 25 | | | 30 | | | 35 | | | 40 | | | 45 | | | 50 | | | 55 | | | 60

LESSON 30 REVIEW

OBJECTIVES:

- Refine numeric keypad skills.
- Refine keyboarding skills.
- Type 30/2'/4e.
- Compose at the keyboard.

A. WARMUP

Type each line 2 times.

Speed
Accuracy
Language Link
Numbers/Symbols

1 Tish dances with grace and seems to float on air.
2 Zudora and Javan are amazed by the tranquil pool.
3 We took Ms. Verhetsel to the airport on Thursday.
4 Movies 7 (on Highway 59) charges $2 on Thursdays.

SKILLBUILDING

B. KEYPAD REVIEW

Enter the following numbers column by column. Press ENTER after the final digit of each number. Keep your eyes on the copy. Repeat if time permits.

Use the correct fingers as you enter each set of numbers. Operate the numeric keypad smoothly.

5	444	999	657	547	557	985	968	897	766	687
6	555	489	658	548	558	986	969	898	768	697
7	666	589	659	549	559	964	894	899	769	567
8	777	689	654	554	987	965	895	764	684	459
9	888	789	655	556	984	967	896	765	685	648

C. TECHNIQUE CHECKPOINT

Type each line 2 times. Focus on the technique at the left.

Concentrate on smooth operation of the shift keys.

10 Benji typed a report on New Guinea and Australia.
11 Kodi said that all of us should meet after class.
12 I bought yards of flannel at Sew Easy this month.
13 Oren donated his profit to the Find-a-Child Fund.

	A	B	C	D	E	F
5	Item	Size	Cost Cutter	Family Foods	Food Queen	Paul Bunyon
6						
7	Egg Subs	16 oz	2.17	2.34	1.99	2.25
8	Bully Paper Towels	80.6 sq ft	0.96	1.07	1.14	0.99
9	Zippy Pasta Sauce	26 oz	2.89	2.53	2.67	2.73
10	Fizzy Cola	2 L	1.24	1.29	1.19	1.36
11	Fruit Crunch Cereal	16 oz	2.98	3.18	3.06	3.24
12	Buzzy Bee Honey	12 oz	1.98	1.99	1.83	1.91
13						
14	Total					

ACTIVITY 27
Spreadsheet 20

Open the file SS19, save it as SS20, and then make the following changes:

1. Select cell C14, and use AutoSum/QuickSum to get the total.
2. Select cell D14, and use Insert, Function to get the total.
3. Select cell E14, type = *SUM*, and select the cell range to be added to get the total.
4. Select cell F14, type = *SUM*, and select the cell range to be added to get the total.
5. Format cell range C14 through F14 with dollar signs and two decimals.
6. Save your changes and close the file.

ACTIVITY 28
Spreadsheet 21

Open the file SS20, save it as SS21, and make the following changes:

1. Bold and center row 5.
2. Select cell range A5 through F14, and automatically change the column width.
3. Align cell range B7 through B12 at the right.
4. Change cell A1 to 16-point bold.
5. Change cell A2 to 12-point bold.
6. Add gridlines so they will print.
7. Select cell range A1 through F3; center horizontally across the selection.
8. Change the height of row 4 to approximately 1.5 times the default height.
9. If your teacher has given you instructions for printing, print the spreadsheet. Otherwise, save your changes and close the file.

D. ALPHABET REVIEW

Type each line 1 time. Concentrate on efficient and smooth operation of the shift keys. Repeat if time permits.

```
14  A Anna Aram Alan B Bel Bern Beth C Curt Chan Cleo
15  D Desi Dino Dona E Ean Erin Egan F Fifi Finn Faye
16  G Gaby Gian Gena H Ham Hank Hedy I Ilse Ilya Iris

17  J Jess Jori Jojo K Kia Kern Kwan L Luke Lars Lyda
18  M Miki Marc Mara N Noe Niki Noel O Olin Otto Olga
19  P Pace Pita Powa Q Qam Quin Quan R Rani Reid Rory

20  S Suni Saul Shan T Tov Taio Tobi U Ulma Urie Ushi
21  V Vera Vick Vala W Web Wren Wilt X Xann Xela Xuxa
22  Y Yoki York Ynez Yusif Z Zizi Zane Zena Zeke Zara
```

E. TECHNIQUE TIMINGS

Take two 30-second timings on each line. Focus on the technique at the left.

Concentrate on smooth operation of the shift keys.

```
23  David and Ian still work at B. K. Dry Goods, Inc.
24  Mrs. R. K. Dunn taught Spanish at Jefferson High.
25  Rory, Anna, and Han ran the Mile-High Race today.
26  She is at the top in her new job at the car wash.
    |  1  |  2  |  3  |  4  |  5  |  6  |  7  |  8  |  9  |  10
```

F. PRETEST

Take a 1-minute timing on the paragraph. Note your speed and errors.

```
27       Buzz did research about the history of tidal    9
28  waves. The doom and gloom of his essay threw our    19
29  class into a tizzy. The wild storm outside didn't   29
30  help matters. We were all upset that day.           37
    |  1  |  2  |  3  |  4  |  5  |  6  |  7  |  8  |  9  |  10
```

E. USING FUNCTIONS

A **function** is a formula built into a spreadsheet that enables you to make calculations or text changes quickly and easily. The following list shows some of the most common functions available with most spreadsheets.

SUM	Adds values in a cell range	=SUM(A5:A16)
AVERAGE	Averages values in a cell range	=AVERAGE(D1:D9)
MAX	Finds largest value in a cell range	=MAX(F3:F91)
MIN	Finds smallest value in a cell range	=MIN(C12:C55)
ROUND	Rounds to a specified number of digits	=ROUND(SUM(B1:B3),2)
MEDIAN	Finds middle value in a cell range	=MEDIAN(L17:Q17)
SQRT	Finds square root of the value in a cell	=SQRT(Y54)
PROPER	Changes text to initial caps	=PROPER("kathy reeves")
UPPER	Changes text to all caps	=UPPER("jamal h. fowler")
NOW	Displays current time and/or date	=NOW()

F. SOFTWARE FEATURES

STUDENT MANUAL

SUM

Insert Functions

Horizontally Centering Across Cell Ranges

Study Lesson 131 in your student manual. Complete all the practice activities while at your computer. Then complete the jobs that follow.

SPREADSHEET APPLICATIONS

ACTIVITY 26

Spreadsheet 19

Create a new spreadsheet, save it as SS19, then follow the steps below:

1. In cell A1, type the label *Grocery Store Price Comparisons*.
2. In cell A2, type *Prepared by* followed by your name.
3. In cell A3, type the date as *February 14 {year}*, or *14 Feb., {year}* in bold. Note that your spreadsheet may automatically change the format of the date.
4. Type the data into the cells as shown below.
5. Save your changes and close the file.

G. PRACTICE

SPEED: *If you made 2 or fewer errors on the Pretest, type lines 31–38 two times each.*

ACCURACY: *If you made more than 2 errors on the Pretest, type lines 31–34 as a group two times. Then type lines 35–38 as a group two times.*

Double Reaches

```
31 ss pass floss guess essay lasso fussy abyss issue
32 oo doom gloom igloo roomy roost afoot bloom scoot
33 zz buzz pizza dizzy jazzy fuzzy dizzy tizzy fizzy
34 ll will silly hello jelly wells drill kills walls
```

Alternate Reaches

```
35 ti tidy ticks tight optic title tidal stick stiff
36 or fork odors storm world coral works adorn stork
37 wi wiry wield twice widow swift wicks swish twirl
38 sl slap slick isles aisle slant slams slips slows
```

H. POSTTEST

Repeat the Pretest. Compare your Posttest results with your Pretest results.

I.   2-MINUTE TIMINGS

Take two 2-minute timings on lines 39–45. Note your speed and errors.

Goal: 30/2'/4e

```
39      Good workers will be quick to discover what      9
40 others on the job like or dislike. Just a bit of    19
41 extra effort by them will make the office a more     29
42 pleasing place in which to work. A cheerful card     38
43 once in a while will bring a smile to one in need    48
44 of support at work. It is amazing how one kind       58
45 act spreads.                                         60
   | 1 | 2 | 3 | 4 | 5 | 6 | 7 | 8 | 9 | 10 SI 1.21
```

COMMUNICATION FOCUS

People who do not make eye contact when they speak are often thought by Americans to be unfriendly, insecure, inattentive, and impersonal. In Western cultures, not making eye contact means you cannot be trusted. In the South Pacific and Japan, lack of eye contact is a sign of respect.

5 All of the books in our catalog (is/are) categorized by
  subject.
6 Each of you (is/are) to bring two pencils to the test.
7 Neither one of us (is/are) likely to win the nomination.
8 One of the new cases storing books and tapes (was/were)
  damaged.

SKILLBUILDING

C. PREVIEW PRACTICE

Type each line 2 times as a preview to the timings that follow.

Accuracy
Speed

9 trend amazing relaxed quickly powerful employee communicate
10 leisure office small great home with that room work made by

D. 5-MINUTE TIMINGS

Take two 5-minute timings on the paragraphs. Note your speed and
errors.

Goal: 39/5'/5e

11 Businesses that are based in the home are booming as a	11
12 way to earn a good living. Also, more and more workers can	23
13 choose to stay at home and communicate with the company by	35
14 computer. An office in the home saves time and money spent	45
15 traveling to and from the office.	53
16 This trend is now possible because of the ease with	64
17 which workers can make use of small, powerful computers.	75
18 This means that the workplace does not need to be in the	89
19 corporate office building itself. Computers can fit into a	98
20 small part of a room in the home, and they have an amazing	110
21 power to communicate with each other. This ability has had	122
22 a great impact on where people do work. Projects worked on	134
23 by an employee on the computer at home can be sent quickly	145
24 over phone lines to the office through the use of modems,	157
25 faxes, and e-mail.	161
26 Today's workers want to have a more relaxed life and	172
27 to enjoy more leisure time than they could in the past.	183
28 Thanks to powerful computers, millions of people can do so.	195

| 1 | 2 | 3 | 4 | 5 | 6 | 7 | 8 | 9 | 10 | 11 | 12 SI 1.36

LANGUAGE LINK

Answer each question with a few words or a short phrase. Keep your eyes on the screen as you compose; do not look at your hands.

46 What career interests you?
47 What kind of animal do you think makes a good pet?
48 What are two states you would like to visit?
49 What are three things you would like to change about yourself?
50 Who are three people who have been in the news recently?

PORTFOLIO
Activity

Keep a copy of your best timing from the last ten lessons. Determine how much you have improved over the past few weeks, and explain why you have improved. Record some other things you can do to improve even more during the next few weeks.

LESSON 131

SPREADSHEETS: SUM FUNCTION, CENTER DATA

OBJECTIVES:

- Learn about verbs with pronouns.
- Use the SUM function.
- Center data across a spreadsheet selection.
- Type 39/5′/5e.

A. WARMUP

Type each line 2 times.

Speed
Accuracy
Language Link
Numbers/Symbols

1 The loan form asked for two proofs of a good credit record.
2 If prizes were given for anxiety, Ms. Jaquan would qualify.
3 An old adage says that a dog's bark is worse than its bite.
4 7/8, 4/5, 11/12, 1/2, 8/9, 10/11, 3/4, 6/7, 12/13, 5/6, 2/3
| 1 | 2 | 3 | 4 | 5 | 6 | 7 | 8 | 9 | 10 | 11 | 12

LANGUAGE LINK

B. SINGULAR AND PLURAL PRONOUNS

Study the rules and examples that follow. Then edit lines 5–8 by choosing the correct verb.

Rule 38:

Some pronouns (*anybody, each, either, everybody, everyone, much, neither, no one, nobody,* and *one*) are always singular and take a singular verb. Other pronouns (*all, any, more, most, none,* and *some*) may be singular or plural, depending on the noun to which they refer.

Everybody was glad to hear that we could leave early.

Most of the workers are going to get a large raise.

Each employee is responsible for summarizing reports.

Some of the gas is being pumped into the tank.

LESSON 31

NUMERIC KEYPAD: 1 2 3

OBJECTIVES:

- Learn the 1, 2, and 3 keys on the numeric keypad.
- Refine numeric keypad skills.
- Refine keyboarding skills.
- Type 30/2'/4e.
- Compose at the keyboard.

1 2 3 4

*inter*NET CONNECTION

Rain, sunshine, and earthquakes are physical phenomena present in our environmental system. We have virtually no control over their existence or non-existence in our environment. Search the Internet for definitions of these terms. Write a brief description of each term and what causes each to happen. Are these terms common throughout the world?

A. WARMUP

Type each line 2 times.

Speed
Accuracy
Language Link
Numbers/Symbols

1 The rain will stop soon; then the sun will shine.
2 Zeke exhibits exuberance on quizzes about quakes.
3 Shalena will meet us Saturday at Happy Rock Park.
4 Paige added 7 + 1 + 24 + 13 + 22 + 11 and got 78.

ACTIVITY 25
Spreadsheet 18

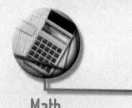

Math
Connections

6. In cell C4, type *Celsius*. Enter the following numbers below as shown from low to high (ascending order) into cell range A7 through A16.

    0, 10, 24, 32, 43, 57, 70, 86, 95, 100

7. In cell C7, enter the formula to convert Fahrenheit to Celsius: (A7-32)*5/9. To convert Fahrenheit to Celsius, you would subtract 32 from Fahrenheit degrees, multiply by 5, and divide by 9, or F-32*5/9.
8. Copy the formula from cell C7 into cell range C8 through C16.
9. Save your changes and close the file.

Open file SS17, save the file as SS18, and make the following changes:

1. In cell E7, enter the formula to convert Celsius to Fahrenheit: C7*9/5+32. To convert Celsius to Fahrenheit, you would multiply Celsius by 9, divide by 5, and add 32. Since the order of operations is correct, no parentheses are necessary.
2. Copy this formula to cell range E8 through E16.
3. Format the numbers in column C to have 1 decimal place.
4. Format the rest of the spreadsheet so that it is attractive and easy to read. Use Print Preview to see what adjustments are necessary.
5. Save your changes and close the file.

	A	B	C	D	E
1	Temperature Conversions				
2	Prepared by Your Name				
3					
4	Fahrenheit		Celsius		Fahrenheit
5	Temperatures	➜	Temperatures	➜	Temperatures
6					
7	0		-17.8		0
8	10		-12.2		10
9	24		-4.4		24
10	32		0.0		32
11	43		6.1		43
12	57		13.9		57
13	70		21.1		70
14	86		30.0		86
15	95		35.0		95
16	100		37.8		100

1 2 3 4

B. [1] [2] [3] KEYS

Enter the following numbers column by column. Use the proper finger for each key. Press ENTER after the final digit of each number. Keep your eyes on the copy. Repeat if time permits.

Use J, K, and L fingers.
Keep your eyes on
the copy.
Concentrate on
accuracy.

5	444	555	666
6	111	222	333
7	144	225	336
8	441	552	663
9	144	255	366
10	411	522	633
11	444	555	666
12	414	525	636
13	141	252	363
14	411	525	636

SKILLBUILDING

C. KEYPAD PRACTICE

Enter the following numbers column by column. Press ENTER after the final digit of each number. Keep your eyes on the copy. Repeat if time permits.

Keep your eyes on
the copy.

15	476	167	754	531	746	334	568	829	957	146
16	372	426	193	942	853	712	149	637	486	329
17	551	789	592	726	962	365	438	218	582	381
18	983	238	812	861	147	819	129	341	673	247
19	421	945	638	397	285	654	247	759	149	655

C. PRACTICE

In the chart below, find the number of errors you made on the Pretest. Then type each of the following designated drill lines two times.

Pretest Errors	0–1	2	3	4+
Drill Lines	12–16	11–15	10–14	9–13

Accuracy

9 men money enjoy living buffalo trapping moccasins Americans
10 fur spent called Oregon wearing adopted collected mountains
11 gun alone settle coffee trading because buckskin rendezvous
12 set would summer lodges friends country companies exchanged

Speed

13 native skins these traps call many wild quit try joy fur in
14 trader would Rocky times most time year with can for way of
15 friend first pelts their hers guns meet most end men and at
16 living where pants their buck good were they sum set met or

D. POSTTEST

Repeat the Pretest. Compare your Posttest results with your Pretest results.

SPREADSHEET APPLICATIONS

E. ENTERING FORMULAS

When you work with formulas, you may need to use several operators. Spreadsheet formulas are completed in a specific order called the **order of operations**. For example, multiplication and division are performed before addition and subtraction. If the operators are equal (such as + and −), they will be completed in the order in which they appear in the formula. To change the order, enclose what you want calculated first in parentheses.

ACTIVITY 24
Spreadsheet 17

Create a new spreadsheet and save it as SS17. Then, follow these steps:

1. In cell A1, type the label *Temperature Conversions*.
2. In cell A2, type *Prepared by* and your name.
3. In cell A4, type *Fahrenheit;* copy this label into cell E4.
4. In cell A5, type *Temperatures;* copy this into cells C5 and E5.
5. In cell B5, change the font to Wingdings. Hold down the Alt key and enter *0232* on the numeric keypad. This character should appear: → . Copy this to cell D5.

SKILLBUILDING

D. TECHNIQUE TIMINGS

Take two 30-second timings on each line. Focus on the technique at the left.

Keep your eyes on the copy.

```
20 The high school students will visit other places.
21 I toured an art museum that was west of the city.
22 Twenty letters were addressed to the three of us.
23 My car (the blue convertible) is hard to keep up.
   | 1 | 2 | 3 | 4 | 5 | 6 | 7 | 8 | 9 | 10
```

E. PRETEST

Take a 1-minute timing on the paragraph. Note your speed and errors.

```
24        Molly and Abe took water to the barn for the      9
25 horses to drink. Half an hour later, Ralph filled       19
26 the hay racks. It was he who discovered Star, our       29
27 very best horse, was ill.                               30
   | 1 | 2 | 3 | 4 | 5 | 6 | 7 | 8 | 9 | 10
```

F. PRACTICE

SPEED: If you made 2 or fewer errors on the Pretest, type lines 28–35 two times each.

ACCURACY: If you made more than 2 errors on the Pretest, type lines 28–31 as a group two times. Then type lines 32–35 as a group two times.

Left Reaches

```
28 Abe purse bases debts large match ocean nurse Tad
29 red urban water yearn Jerry trays racks horse set
30 war rated tubes upset verbs Xerox quart image cad
31 car fears raven carts froze graze exact grave sad
```

Right Reaches

```
32 Lon pilot linen Molly hours Louis zooms films Jim
33 mop jumps knows plugs Naomi quill flint drink hum
34 nip human flood Ralph mound joins yolks co-op poi
35 mop polka plums homey plump mound limps money Lou
```

G. POSTTEST

Repeat the Pretest. Compare your Posttest results with your Pretest results.

LESSON 130

SPREADSHEETS: ENTERING FORMULAS

OBJECTIVES:

- Improve keyboarding skill.
- Enter formulas into a spreadsheet.

A. WARMUP

Type each line 2 times.

Speed
Accuracy
Language Link
Numbers/Symbols

1 Do not try to blame anyone else when you are late for work.
2 Mr. Jakman found exactly a quarter in the woven zipper bag.
3 The towels in the Mallen's house said his and hers on them.
4 Olo saw apples @ $1.09, pears @ $1.29, and oranges @ $1.49.
| 1 | 2 | 3 | 4 | 5 | 6 | 7 | 8 | 9 | 10 | 11 | 12

SOCIAL STUDIES CONNECTIONS

On March 1, 1961, then President John F. Kennedy signed an executive order establishing the Peace Corps, a volunteer organization that is still in operation today.

SKILLBUILDING

B. PRETEST

Take a 1-minute timing on the paragraph. Note your speed and errors.

5   Fur traders were the first Americans to settle in the   11
6 part of the country we now call Oregon. Because they spent   23
7 most all of their time in the mountains, they were called   34
8 mountain men. Many adopted the ways of Native Americans.   46
| 1 | 2 | 3 | 4 | 5 | 6 | 7 | 8 | 9 | 10 | 11 | 12

Social Studies
Connections

H. 2-Minute Timings

Goal: 30/2'/4e

Take two 2-minute timings on lines 36–42. Note your speed and errors.

```
36        A good way to earn extra money is by taking      9
37 care of children. It is not a job for the lazy.      19
38 Being in charge of a small child requires hard      28
39 work and savvy. You can take workshops to learn      38
40 the basics of child care, and you should take a      47
41 course in first aid so you are prepared for any      57
42 medical crisis.                                       60
   | 1 | 2 | 3 | 4 | 5 | 6 | 7 | 8 | 9 | 10  SI 1.22
```

LANGUAGE LINK

I. COMPOSING AT THE KEYBOARD

Answer each question with a short phrase. Keep your eyes on the screen as you compose.

43 What are three things you should know before you agree to baby-sit?

44 Why should you keep your eyes on the copy when you type?

45 What three things do you admire most about your best friend?

ACTIVITY 21
Spreadsheet 14

Open the file SS13, save it as SS14, and make the following changes:

1. Select cell E10 and enter a formula to multiply cells C10 and D10.
2. Enter the appropriate formula into cell E11.
3. Select cell E15 and enter a formula to multiply cells C15 and D15.
4. Enter the appropriate formula into cell E16.
5. Select cell F7 and enter a formula to add cells E5 and E6.
6. Select cell F12 and enter a formula to add cells E10 and E11.
7. Save your changes and close the file.

ACTIVITY 22
Spreadsheet 15

Open the file SS14, save it as SS15, and then do the following:

1. Enter the appropriate formula into cell F17.
2. Enter a formula into cell F19 to add cells F7, F12, and F17. Change the font to 12-point bold.
3. Format the numbers in columns E and F for currency with the dollar sign and 2 decimals.
4. Increase the height of row 3 until it is about 1.5 times the default height.
5. Select column E and change the width to 12.
6. Save your changes and close the file.

ACTIVITY 23
Spreadsheet 16

Open the file SS15, save it as SS16, and then do the following:

1. Preview the spreadsheet.
2. Change the page orientation to landscape.
3. Set the gridlines to print.
4. Preview the spreadsheet again.
5. If your teacher has given you instructions for printing, print the spreadsheet. Otherwise, save your changes and close the file.

LESSON 32

NUMERIC KEYPAD: 0 .

OBJECTIVES:

- Learn the 0 and decimal keys on the numeric keypad.
- Refine numeric keypad skills.
- Refine keyboarding skills.
- Type 30/2′/4e.

1 2 3 4

A. WARMUP

Type each line 2 times.

Speed   1 To have more pep, walk one or two miles each day.
Accuracy   2 Zorba has cichlids imported from Lake Tanganyika.
Language Link   3 She watches while I write it out and he signs it.
Numbers/Symbols   4 S & A closed at 3 7/16, up 5/8, a +14.71% change.

FACT FILE

The hand is the most versatile part of the skeleton. The hand enables people to grasp and manipulate objects. The intricate hand movements are achieved by using small muscles that are contained entirely within the hand and the much larger forearm muscles.

SPREADSHEET APPLICATIONS

ACTIVITY 20
Spreadsheet 13

Create a new spreadsheet, and save it as SS13.

1. In cell A1, type the label *Expense Report for November*.
2. In cell A2, type *Prepared by* and your name.
3. Type the data as shown in the illustration. Use the copy feature when it is appropriate.
4. Change the font in cells A1 and A2 to 12-point bold.
5. Move A1 through A2 to C1 through C2. Center the text in rows 1 and 2.
6. Bold and center the data in rows 4, 9, and 14.
7. Select cell range A4 through E17, and automatically widen the columns.
8. Align cells A7, A12, and A17 at the right.
9. Change the font in cell A19 to 12-point bold.
10. Select cell E5 and enter a formula to multiply cells C5 and D5 (C5*D5).
11. Select cell E6 and enter a formula to multiply cells C6 and D6.
12. Save the changes and close the file.

	A	B	C	D	E
4	Travel	Dates	Miles	Per Mile	Mileage
5		November 7-9	500	0.31	
6		November 18-19	175	0.31	
7	Total Travel				
8					
9	Lodging	Dates	Nights	Per Night	Total
10		November 7-9	3	75	
11		November 18-19	2	80	
12	Total Lodging				
13					
14	Meals	Dates	Days	Per Day	Total
15		November 7-9	3	40	
16		November 18-19	2	40	
17	Total Meals				
18					
19	Total Expenses for November				

1 2 3 4

NEW KEYS

B. **0** KEY

Enter the following numbers column by column. Press ENTER after the final digit of each number. Keep your eyes on the copy. Repeat if time permits.

Use the right thumb. Keep your eyes on the copy. Concentrate on accuracy.

5	404	470	502
6	505	500	603
7	606	690	140
8	707	410	250
9	808	520	360
10	909	630	701
11	101	407	802
12	202	508	903
13	303	609	405
14	505	401	506

C. **.** KEY

Enter the following numbers column by column. Press ENTER after the final digit of each number. Keep your eyes on the copy. Repeat if time permits.

Use L finger. Keep K finger anchored on the 5 key as you reach down to the decimal.

15	4.5	7.8	1.2
16	6.5	9.8	3.2
17	4.4	7.7	1.1
18	4.4	7.7	1.1
19	5.5	8.8	2.2
20	5.5	8.8	2.2
21	6.6	9.9	3.3
22	6.5	9.9	3.3
23	4.5	7.8	1.2
24	6.5	8.9	1.3

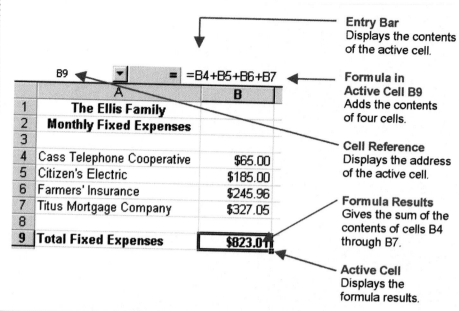

Entry Bar
Displays the contents of the active cell.

B9   ▼   =   =B4+B5+B6+B7

Formula in Active Cell B9
Adds the contents of four cells.

	A	B
1	The Ellis Family	
2	Monthly Fixed Expenses	
3		
4	Cass Telephone Cooperative	$65.00
5	Citizen's Electric	$185.00
6	Farmers' Insurance	$245.96
7	Titus Mortgage Company	$327.05
8		
9	Total Fixed Expenses	$823.01

Cell Reference
Displays the address of the active cell.

Formula Results
Gives the sum of the contents of cells B4 through B7.

Active Cell
Displays the formula results.

E. SOFTWARE FEATURES

STUDENT MANUAL

Formulas

Study Lesson 129 in your student manual. Complete all the practice activities while at your computer. Then complete the jobs that follow.

interNET CONNECTION

Connect to the Internet. Search the World Wide Web for information on income and expenses. You may want to include search words such as income, expenses, forms, capital, and gains/losses.

SKILLBUILDING

D. KEYPAD PRACTICE

Enter the following numbers column by column. Press ENTER after the final digit of each number. Keep your eyes on the copy. Repeat if time permits.

25	1.7	7.5	7.6	5.0	6.2	6.0	6.7	4.5	3.0	6.4
26	5.8	2.4	2.3	2.8	3.5	9.1	5.1	3.0	7.6	2.8
27	1.6	8.3	1.7	9.9	5.0	2.7	1.6	9.3	1.3	5.9
28	3.0	4.2	3.4	8.1	7.4	1.8	2.8	8.0	8.2	5.1
29	6.9	9.0	6.5	4.0	4.6	8.9	7.2	4.9	4.7	9.0

E. 12-SECOND SPRINTS

Take three 12-second timings on each line. Try to increase your speed on each timing.

```
30 If nothing nice can be said, do not say anything.
31 Be kind if you want others to be kind toward you.
32 You won't smell like roses if you play with pigs.
33 Keep the dog away from the cats to avoid a fight.
   | | | |5| | | |10| | | |15| | | |20| | | |25| | | |30| | | |35| | | |40| | | |45| | | |50
```

F. PRETEST

Take a 1-minute timing on lines 34–37. Note your speed and errors.

```
34        Unless they are crazy, most humans prefer to    9
35 be free, not in jail. That is why laws that take      19
36 away our freedom for illegal acts we perform are      29
37 created and are effective.                            34
   | 1 | 2 | 3 | 4 | 5 | 6 | 7 | 8 | 9 | 10
```

SKILLBUILDING

C. 30-Second OK Timings

Take two 30-second OK (error-free) timings on lines 9–10. Then take two 30-second OK timings on lines 11–12. Goal: no errors.

```
 9        A quick leap from a taxi caused Gavez to hurt his arm.    11
10  He fell down and hurt his shoulder, which was already sore.    23

11        Jay's six long vans zipped quickly down the wet roads,    11
12  but they were not able to finish the entire route in time.    23
    | 1 | 2 | 3 | 4 | 5 | 6 | 7 | 8 | 9 | 10 | 11 | 12
```

FORMATTING

D. Spreadsheet Formulas

Math
Connections

A **spreadsheet formula** simply instructs the spreadsheet to perform various calculations. For example, if you create a spreadsheet for your budget, you can enter formulas to add your income, add your expenses, and subtract your expenses from your income.

To enter a formula in a spreadsheet, you must use the cell names and the following **mathematical operators:**

- + (plus sign) for addition
- - (hyphen) for subtraction
- * (asterisk) for multiplication
- / (slash) for division
- ^ (caret) for exponentiation

When you enter a formula into a cell and press ENTER, only the answer will appear in the cell. The formula will be displayed in the entry bar. (See the example on the next page.)

To enter a formula, select the cell where you want the formula. Begin formulas with an equal sign (=) to indicate you are going to type a value, not a label. Formulas are typed without spaces.

Study the formula displayed in the entry bar on the next page. It adds the contents of cells B4 through B7 and displays the answer in the active cell, B9.

G. PRACTICE

SPEED: *If you made 2 or fewer errors on the Pretest, type lines 38–45 two times each.*

ACCURACY: *If you made more than 2 errors on the Pretest, type lines 38–41 as a group two times. Then type lines 42–45 as a group two times.*

Up Reaches

```
38  hu hunt shuts churn hunch human husky huffs hulls
39  de deck bride depth order wader adept video decay
40  fr free frock frame frost fryer fruit frail fresh
41  li line flies blind click slick limes light flier
```

Down Reaches

```
42  ac acre poach whack acrid actor tract slack enact
43  l. pal. hill. jail. nail. yowl. dial. peel. till.
44  az raze graze craze glaze dazed blaze gazed jazzy
45  on once ponds fonts stone clone alone don't front
```

H. POSTTEST

Repeat the Pretest. Compare your Posttest results with your Pretest results.

I. 2-MINUTE TIMINGS

Take two 2-minute timings on lines 46–52. Note your speed and errors.

Goal: 30/2'/4e

```
46      Poachers hunt and kill game against the law.    9
47  Many species such as big cats, caimans, quetzal    19
48  birds, and whales may become extinct from being    28
49  killed for their fur, hides, or feathers. Laws     38
50  have been passed to help save wildlife. Parks are  48
51  jointly set up in all parts of the world to be     57
52  havens for game.                                   60
    | 1 | 2 | 3 | 4 | 5 | 6 | 7 | 8 | 9 | 10  SI 1.24
```

Science
Connections

LESSON 129

SPREADSHEETS: ENTERING FORMULAS

OBJECTIVES:

- Learn the rules for apostrophes and possessives.
- Improve keyboarding skills.
- Learn to enter formulas into a spreadsheet.

A. WARMUP

Type each line 2 times.

Speed
Accuracy
Language Link
Numbers

```
1 Bill has worked as a short order cook in a small town cafe.
2 Ziggy James quickly paid us for the five new Rambler taxis.
3 Sara's car required four hundred dollars' worth of repairs.
4 Old Models 75, 83, and 96 are now Models 121, 344, and 500.
| 1 | 2 | 3 | 4 | 5 | 6 | 7 | 8 | 9 | 10 | 11 | 12
```

LANGUAGE LINK

B. APOSTROPHE

Study the rules and examples below. Then edit lines 5–8 by inserting apostrophes where appropriate.

Rule 35:   Use apostrophe *s* (*'s*) to form the possessive of indefinite pronouns.

  She was instructed to select anybody's paper for a sample.

Rule 36:   Do not use an apostrophe with possessive personal pronouns.

  Each computer comes carefully packed in its own container.

```
5 The new house was hers, but now it is yours.
6 Somebodys lottery ticket is going to be worth millions.
7 Our company recycles its paper, and everyones support is
  needed.
8 No ones desktop is running, so the laptops are ours for today.
```

LESSON 33 REVIEW

OBJECTIVES:

- Refine keyboarding skills.
- Type 30/2'/4e

A. WARMUP

Type each line 2 times.

Speed
Accuracy
Language Link
Numbers/Symbols

1 Think about this: If it is to be, it is up to me.
2 Vladimir Kosma Zworykin made the television tube.
3 Syd catches a plane at O'Hare Airport in Chicago.
4 Nashville has *985,026 people; Miami, *1,192,582.

SKILLBUILDING

B. KEYPAD PRACTICE—3-DIGIT NUMBERS

Enter the following numbers column by column. Press ENTER after the final digit of each number. Keep your eyes on the copy, and use the proper finger for each key. Repeat if time permits.

Enter numbers smoothly.
Use correct fingers.
Keep eyes on copy.

5 136	964	806	295	597	628	728	627	959	172
6 940	250	275	407	426	519	546	341	241	859
7 852	173	394	718	618	537	639	730	862	931
8 710	982	180	363	304	405	410	859	730	604
9 788	829	903	120	311	441	349	555	668	776

C. KEYPAD PRACTICE—DECIMAL NUMBERS

Enter the following numbers column by column. Press ENTER after the final digit of each number. Keep your eyes on the copy, and use the proper finger for each key. Repeat if time permits.

Enter numbers smoothly.
Use correct fingers.
Keep eyes on copy.

10 1.97	5.08	6.19	3.52	4.33	17.44	52.28	68.61
11 3.85	6.44	9.37	8.10	2.19	14.20	23.85	60.97
12 6.55	6.65	7.87	9.00	3.10	20.49	88.47	19.39
13 2.10	2.81	2.33	7.06	7.68	67.99	44.53	45.54
14 8.83	7.90	4.16	8.20	1.49	55.20	15.62	37.39

SPREADSHEET APPLICATIONS

ACTIVITY 16
Spreadsheet 5-B

Open the file SS5-B; then follow these steps:

1. Preview the file using Print Preview. Notice that the page orientation is portrait and there are no gridlines in the spreadsheet.
2. Change the page orientation to landscape.
3. Set the gridlines to print.
4. Preview the file, and note the changes that you made.
5. If your teacher has given you instructions for printing, print the spreadsheet. Otherwise, close the file without saving your changes.

ACTIVITY 17
Spreadsheet 3-B

Open the file SS3-B; then follow these steps:

1. Preview the file.
2. Change the orientation to landscape.
3. Select cell range A13 through G13, and print-preview that range.
4. Set the gridlines and row and column headings to print, and preview the spreadsheet again.
5. If your teacher has given you instructions for printing, print the selected cell range. Otherwise, close the file without saving your changes.

ACTIVITY 18
Spreadsheet 6

Open the file SS6; then follow these steps:

1. Preview the file.
2. Select cell range A1 through E8, and preview that range.
3. Deselect the cell range.
4. Close the file without saving your changes.

ACTIVITY 19
Spreadsheet 7

Open the file SS7; then follow these steps:

1. Change the page orientation to landscape.
2. Set the gridlines and row and column headings to print.
3. Preview the spreadsheet.
4. If your teacher has given you instructions for printing, print the spreadsheet. Otherwise, close the file without saving your changes.

Take two 30-second timings on each line. Focus on the techniques at the left.

Lines 15–16: Type without pauses.

Lines 17–18: Type end-of-sentence punctuation smoothly.

15 Roy and Bob did their best to study for the test.
16 My two cats are eager to sit in my lap as I work.
17 If you are to make friends, you must be friendly.
18 Who me? Oh no! I can. What time? Look out! Did I?
| 1 | 2 | 3 | 4 | 5 | 6 | 7 | 8 | 9 | 10

E. PRETEST

Take a 1-minute timing on lines 19–22. Note your speed and errors.

19   Joy's niece darted in front of a car, but   8
20 the driver was able to stop quickly. She was only   18
21 dazed. She did not want us to cheer or make a   27
22 fuss over her.   30
| 1 | 2 | 3 | 4 | 5 | 6 | 7 | 8 | 9 | 10

F. PRACTICE

SPEED: If you made 2 or fewer errors on the Pretest, type lines 23–30 two times each.

ACCURACY: If you made more than 2 errors on the Pretest, type lines 23–26 as a group two times. Then type lines 27–30 as a group two times.

Adjacent Reaches
Jump Reaches
Double Reaches
In Reaches

23 rt sort part heart start ui quit suit quiet quick
24 mo most move among money ce aced race cease niece
25 ee glee weed keeps cheer ss sass fuss grass cross
26 st stay stop stray state pi pint pile pines spine

Alternate Reaches
Left/Right Reaches
Up/Down Reaches
Out Reaches

27 to tofu torn storm torso pa paid pals pause pants
28 da dart dabs dazed dates jo joys join enjoy jolly
29 st star stop first coast h? ash? huh? Noah? dish?
30 fa fall sofa loofa farms ho hose hone hoist phone

G. POSTTEST

Repeat the Pretest. Compare your Posttest results with your Pretest results.

FORMATTING

D. Printing Spreadsheets

Many spreadsheets are too wide to print on a standard 8.5-inch-wide page. However, spreadsheets can be printed on an 11-inch-wide page. **Page orientation** is the direction of the page on which the spreadsheet is printed. The default page orientation (standard 8.5 × 11 inches) is called **portrait**. When the orientation is changed to print across the 11-inch width of a page it is called **landscape**.

Study the following illustrations.

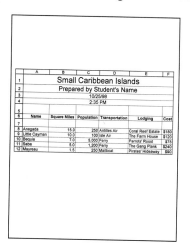
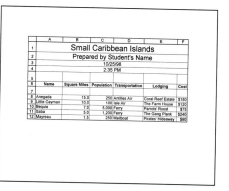

Spreadsheets often consist of multiple pages. However, you can print only a portion of a spreadsheet. In addition, you can print spreadsheets with or without the gridlines and with or without the row and column headings. Before you print a spreadsheet, use Print Preview to ensure you are printing what you want.

E. Software Features

STUDENT MANUAL

Print Spreadsheets   Print Cell Ranges

Print Gridlines   Print Row and Column Headings

Study Lesson 128 in your student manual. Complete all the practice activities while at your computer. Then complete the jobs that follow.

Social Studies
Connections

Take a 1-minute timing on lines 31–34. Note your speed and errors.

31 In 1929 stock prices passed $350 per share.	9
32 By 1932, they had dropped under $100, forcing	18
33 9,000 banks to close. People without jobs climbed	28
34 above 25%.	30

| 1 | 2 | 3 | 4 | 5 | 6 | 7 | 8 | 9 | 10

Take two 2-minute timings on lines 35–41. Note your speed and errors.

Goal: 30/2'/4e

35 Zebras are members of the horse family and	9
36 are well known for their unique stripes. They	18
37 enjoy life on the plains and mountains of Africa	28
38 where they feed on grass and shrubs. Attempts to	38
39 use them for work and to ride have failed. The	47
40 quagga, which is now extinct due to hunting, was	57
41 kin to the zebra.	60

| 1 | 2 | 3 | 4 | 5 | 6 | 7 | 8 | 9 | 10 *SI 1.25*

Science
Connections

LESSON 128

SPREADSHEETS: PRINTING

OBJECTIVES:

- Improve keyboarding speed and accuracy.
- Print a worksheet and cell ranges.
- Print with and without gridlines.
- Print with and without row and column headings.

A. WARMUP

Type each line 2 times.

Speed
Accuracy
Language Link
Symbols

```
1 The girls had fun playing games in the park near our house.
2 A sequence of jobs, or queue, is held in auxiliary storage.
3 The building's exterior was so worn, he questioned its age.
4 less than = <; greater than = >; backslash = \; a tilde = ~
  | 1 | 2 | 3 | 4 | 5 | 6 | 7 | 8 | 9 | 10 | 11 | 12
```

SKILLBUILDING

B. 30-SECOND TIMINGS

Take two 30-second timings on lines 5–6. Then take two 30-second timings on lines 7–8. Try to increase your speed on each timing.

```
5      A resume must be entirely free of errors; an employer    11
6 will view it as a reflection of how you will do on the job.  23

7      Before you go to an interview, learn all you can about   11
8 that company by spending some time in your public library.   23
  | 1 | 2 | 3 | 4 | 5 | 6 | 7 | 8 | 9 | 10 | 11 | 12
```

C. DIAGNOSTIC PRACTICE: ALPAHBET

Turn to the Diagnostic Practice: Alphabet routine on page SB1. Type one of the Pretest/Posttest paragraphs and identify any errors made. Then type the corresponding drill lines 2 times for each letter on which you made 2 or more errors and 1 time for each letter on which you made only 1 error. Finally, repeat the same Pretest and compare your performance.

LESSON 34

SKILLBUILDING

OBJECTIVES:

- Refine numeric keypad skills.
- Refine keyboarding skills.
- Type 31/3'/5e.

A. WARMUP

Type each line 2 times.

Speed
Accuracy
Language Link
Numbers/Symbols

1 All of us have bad days now and then, but they do not last.
2 The quetzal, a superb green and gold bird, lives in Mexico.
3 The exchange students arrived in winter and left in spring.
4 When Tip & Toe has a sale, buy 24 pairs of socks @ 25% off.

FACT FILE

One of the best known birds of the desert is the roadrunner. This bird spends almost its entire life on the ground running, attaining speeds up to 40 kilometers (over 25 miles per hour). How does this speed compare with that of the best athletes today?

SKILLBUILDING

B. KEYPAD PRACTICE—4-DIGIT NUMBERS

Enter the following numbers column by column. Press ENTER after the final digit of each number. Keep your eyes on the copy, and use the proper finger for each key. Repeat if time permits.

Use correct fingers.
Keep eyes on copy.
Input accurately.

5 8964	8073	6182	8090	2401	3159	5361	6047
6 3103	2619	5079	9324	5561	8252	6873	7984
7 5295	5302	6416	7451	8564	2785	9790	1021
8 7206	6195	2840	5327	4963	7548	2080	1976
9 1847	8443	3594	1686	1378	9029	4303	4267

6. Save your changes and close the file.

	A	B	C	D	E
8	Name	Square Miles	Population	Lodging	Cost
9					
10					
11					
12	Anegada	15	250	Coral Reef Estate	180
13	Beguia	7	5000	Parrot's Roost	78
14	Little Cayman	10	100	The Farm House	120
15	Mayreau	1.5	250	Pirate's Hideaway	90
16	Saba	5	1200	The Gang Plank	240

ACTIVITY 14
Spreadsheet 11

Open the file SS10, save it as SS11, and make the following changes:

1. Select row 1, and change the point size to 16.
2. Move cell A5 to A2.
3. Select cell A3, and format the date as *MM/DD/YY*.
4. Select cell A4, and format the time as *H:MM PM*.
5. Change rows 3 and 4 to 12-point size.
6. Move cell range A8 through E8 to A6 through E6.
7. Save your changes and close the file.

ACTIVITY 15
Spreadsheet 12

Open the file SS11, save it as SS12, and make the following changes:

1. Bold row 6.
2. Move cell range A12 through E16 to A8 through E12.
3. Format cell range B8 through B12 to have 1 decimal place.
4. Format cell range C8 through C12 to have commas and no decimals.
5. Format cell range E8 through E12 to have dollar signs and no decimals.
6. Select cell range A6 through E12, and automatically widen the columns.
7. Horizontally center the text in rows 1 through 4 between columns A through E.
8. Change row 5 to double the default height.
9. Change row 7 to 1.5 times the default height.
10. Save your changes and close the file.

C. KEYPAD PRACTICE—DECIMAL NUMBERS

Enter the following numbers column by column. Press ENTER after the final digit of each number. Keep your eyes on the copy, and use the proper finger for each key. Repeat if time permits.

10	80.5	9.72	67.04	4387.90	98.10	86.17
11	724.16	15.39	904.32	128.50	6524.01	349.05
12	7512.41	4607.09	583.55	95.63	141.16	2508.96
13	1204.78	672.80	808.23	379.94	6.39	677.28
14	339.45	453.92	1.62	4.63	7813.25	1.96

D. 12-SECOND SPRINTS

Take three 12-second timings on each line. Try to increase your speed on each timing.

15 You must repress your fears, or you will not be in control.
16 Our failures can teach us good lessons if we will let them.
17 When you have a dream, you must never, never give up on it.
18 You should give your best effort to everything that you do.
| | | | 5 | | | | 10 | | | | 15 | | | 20 | | | | 25 | | | 30 | | | 35 | | | | 40 | | | | 45 | | | | 50 | | | | 55 | | | | 60

E. TECHNIQUE TIMINGS

Take two 30-second timings on each line. Focus on the technique at the left.

Keep your eyes on the copy.

19 Lau went to the cafe in the city to have a good dinner out.
20 She and Travis left the band and saw the parade in Detroit.
21 Isau moved the desk over to my right side during our class.
22 People who work at the desk like to keep paper on the left.
| 1 | 2 | 3 | 4 | 5 | 6 | 7 | 8 | 9 | 10 | 11 | 12

FORMATTING

A **value** is a spreadsheet entry that begins with a number or a mathematical sign. Because spreadsheets are designed to work with values, you can format numbers, dates, and times in many different ways. For example, the number *15.75* can be formatted as *15¾*, *$15.75*, *15.8*, or *16*. The date *November 13, 2002*, can be formatted *11/13/02*. Remember that if a value is too wide to fit in a column, you will see only number signs (#####). When you widen the column, the value will be displayed.

F. SOFTWARE FEATURES

STUDENT MANUAL

Formatting Values

Study Lesson 127 in your student manual. Complete all the practice activities while at your computer. Then complete the jobs that follow.

FACT FILE

Abraham Lincoln met with Confederate vice president Alexander H. Stephens on February 3, 1865, in an attempt to end the Civil War. Because Lincoln would not yield on the subjects of emancipation and reunion, the conference was a failure, and the war continued for three more months.

SPREADSHEET APPLICATIONS

ACTIVITY 13
Spreadsheet 10

Create a new spreadsheet and save it as SS10. Then follow these steps to format the values:

1. In cell A1, type the label *Small Caribbean Islands*.
2. In cell A3, type the date as *10/25*.
3. In cell A4, type the time as *2:35:49 PM*.
4. In cell A5, type *Prepared by* and your name.
5. Enter the data as shown in the illustration on the next page into the correct cells.

Type each line 1 time. Repeat if time permits.

23 Alf is able to add; Bill bikes by Beth; Cal can call Carli.
24 Darla's dad is Dale; Evi eats eggs; Flo's farm is far away.
25 Gary's grass is green; Hans has his hats; Ilse is innocent.

26 Just jump, Jeff; Kylie knows knives; Lyle loves Louisville.
27 Marta manages a mall; Nona noted nothing; Orion owns opals.
28 Pat pinches pennies; Quinn quietly quit; Rez reads rapidly.

29 Suni serves sushi; Tara tells tall tales; Uriah uses umber.
30 Val visits Vermont; Wilma washes windows; Xan x-rays Xylia.
31 Yvonne yearns for a yellow yo-yo; Zachariah's zest is zero.

G. PACED PRACTICE

Turn to the Paced Practice routine beginning on page SB7. Take three 2-minute timings, starting at the point where you left off the last time.

H. 3-MINUTE TIMINGS

Take two 3-minute timings on lines 32–40. Note your speed and errors.

Goal: 31/3'/5e

32	A rain forest and a jungle are not quite the same.	10
33	A rain forest has very lofty trees that form a canopy for	22
34	shorter trees as well as vines and other plants that grow	34
35	in the shade. The floor is more or less open. A jungle, on	45
36	the other hand, is the dense, scrubby brush that exists	57
37	on the floor after a rain forest has been cut.	66
38	Large rain forests can be found in the Amazon basin.	77
39	Rain forests give us timber and sites for crops like tea	88
40	and house many species.	93

| 1 | 2 | 3 | 4 | 5 | 6 | 7 | 8 | 9 | 10 | 11 | 12 *SI 1.26*

Science
Connections

SKILLBUILDING

C. PREVIEW PRACTICE

Type each line 2 times as a preview to the timings that follow.

Accuracy
Speed

5 hazard produced expansion equipment inventions refrigerated
6 shipped comfort tracks vital fuel wood rail raw one air car

D. 5-MINUTE TIMINGS

Take two 5-minute timings on the paragraphs. Note your speed and errors.

Goal: 39/5'/5e

7   After the Civil War, the railroad played a vital role   11
8 in the growth of America. Expansion of the railroads helped   23
9 the iron and coal mining and lumber industries grow through   35
10 the need for iron tracks, engines, fuel, and wood railway   47
11 ties. New jobs were opened for people who built stations,   58
12 laid tracks, and produced equipment.   66

13   At the start, each train line built tracks of varied   76
14 widths. This made long-distance travel slow and difficult.   88
15 Later, rail widths were set to a standard size. This meant   100
16 that goods could be shipped more quickly using just one   111
17 train to cross the country. Trains shipped produce, raw   122
18 materials, and finished goods from place to place.   133

19   Four inventions improved rail transport a great deal.   144
20 Air brakes decreased the hazard of stopping a train. The   155
21 Janney car coupler made it simpler to link one car to the   167
22 next. Pullman sleeping cars increased the comfort of long   178
23 trips, and refrigerated cars allowed food to be shipped   189
24 without the risk of spoiling.   195

| 1 | 2 | 3 | 4 | 5 | 6 | 7 | 8 | 9 | 10 | 11 | 12 SI 1.45

Social Studies
Connections

LESSON 35

SKILLBUILDING

OBJECTIVES:

- Refine numeric keypad skills.
- Refine keyboarding skills.
- Learn capitalization rules.
- Type 31/3'/5e.

A. WARMUP

Type each line 2 times.

Speed
Accuracy
Language Link
Numbers/Symbols

1 Set your goals, and then make plans to achieve those goals.
2 The bombastic flibbertigibbit was bedizened in a bombazine.
3 We plan to travel on Tuesday to Baltimore for Thanksgiving.
4 Try this: 1 1/3 cup milk, 4/5 cup bananas, 1/8 cup raisins.

LANGUAGE LINK

B. CAPITALIZATION

Study the rule and the examples below. Then edit lines 5–8 to correct any errors in capitalization.

Rule 3:

Capitalize proper nouns and adjectives derived from proper nouns.

Tara and I always watch the Thanksgiving Day parade in Chicago.

Our supervisor, Mrs. Jazarian, is going to Tibet next year.

5 lou and darian saw chicago from the top of the sears tower.
6 we saw the american flag flying at our embassy in scotland.
7 mr. and mrs. haber wrote that they had visited san antonio.
8 president abraham lincoln did write the gettysburg address.

Social Studies
Connections

LESSON 127

SPREADSHEETS: FORMATTING VALUES

OBJECTIVES:

- Compose at the keyboard.
- Format values in a spreadsheet.
- Type 39/5'/5e.

A. WARMUP

Type each line 2 times.

Speed	1	If you find the small blue ball, please toss it to our dog.
Accuracy	2	Gwyn exceeds the speed limit by zigzagging through traffic.
Language Link	3	The teacher's day was full of her children's fun and games.
Numbers	4	Dale should use cars 47, 38, 29, or 10 if 56 laps are left.

| 1 | 2 | 3 | 4 | 5 | 6 | 7 | 8 | 9 | 10 | 11 | 12

LANGUAGE LINK

B. COMPOSING AT THE KEYBOARD

Compose the body of a letter to a large computer or software company and ask them for information on their latest developments. Explain that you are studying the future of computing and that you need to write a report on the topic of how computing is going to change the future.

COMMUNICATION FOCUS

A letter is an important type of business communication. A letter requesting information should be easy to follow so that the receiver can include all the requested information quickly. One way to make it easy is to put each requested item in a separate paragraph or bullet each item to be checked off by the receiver.

SKILLBUILDING

C. KEYPAD REVIEW

Enter the following numbers column by column. Press ENTER after the final digit of each number. Keep your eyes on the copy, and use the proper finger for each key. Repeat if time permits.

Use correct fingers. Keep eyes on copy. Be accurate.

9	3221	8997	5446	7114	2558	9336	5991	3775	4665	79.13
10	7987	6465	1323	4065	3120	9078	4005	7009	2003	10.05
11	5217	8469	1356	2007	3062	9940	1517	1492	1943	99.49
12	1541	1556	1603	1632	1689	1714	1763	1774	1775	18.04
13	6.59	2.58	37.4	20.0	9.48	7.11	30.6	51.2	8.83	25.67

D. PRETEST

Take a 1-minute timing on lines 14–17. Note your speed and errors.

```
14      The meadow is covered with sweet vetch and daisies. I   11
15  saw a covey of quail popping in and out of the shade and    22
16  a herd of cows foraging lazily among the bees. Soon it      38
17  will be too cold to walk in the meadow.                     41
    | 1 | 2 | 3 | 4 | 5 | 6 | 7 | 8 | 9 | 10 | 11 | 12
```

E. PRACTICE

SPEED: *If you made 2 or fewer errors on the Pretest, type lines 18–25 two times each.*

ACCURACY: *If you made more than 2 errors on the Pretest, type lines 18–21 as a group two times. Then type lines 22–25 as a group two times.*

Discrimination reaches *are keys that are commonly substituted and easily confused (wear).*

```
18  dsd sides dense shade dress daisy squad sedan dispel sedate
19  pop poise opens poach optic power piano opals proper option
20  wew wedge sweet weave tweed wreck vowel elbow twelve wealth
21  klk klutz bulky milky kilns slick click block plucky molusk

22  yuy dusky yours bumpy juicy murky truly query purify luxury
23  fgf gifts feign graft fling foggy fight grief forage fringe
24  vcv civil cover vicar covey havoc evict vetch vacate victor
25  mnm mania money numbs mines woman mints gnome sampan nomads
```

F. POSTTEST

Repeat the Pretest. Compare your Posttest results with your Pretest results.

Unit 2 Lesson 35

ACTIVITY 11
Spreadsheet 8

Open the file SS7 and save it as SS8. Then follow these steps:

1. Select cell range A3 through F3, and center the cell contents.
2. While cell range A3 through F3 is still selected, move the contents to cells A4 through F4.
3. Select cell range A16 through F16, and move the contents to A8 through F8.
4. Select cell range A8 through F15, and move the contents to A6 through F13.
5. Select cell range C4 through C13, and move the contents to B4 through B13.
6. Select row 4, and change the point size to 16.
7. Change row 3 to approximately 2 times the default height.
8. Change row 5 to approximately 1.5 times the default height.
9. Select row 4, and automatically widen the columns.
10. Save your changes and close the file.

ACTIVITY 12
Spreadsheet 9

Open the file SS8 and save it as SS9. Then follow these steps to move cell contents and change row heights:

1. Select cell range E4 through E13, and move the contents to C4 through C13.
2. Select cell range F4 through F13, and move the contents to E4 through E13.
3. Select cell range B6 through E13, and align the cell contents on the right.
4. Select cell range A4 through E13, and automatically widen the columns.
5. In cell A1, delete the words *for Tours of Summer*.
6. Select row 1, and change the point size to 20.
7. Select row 2, and change the point size to 18.
8. Select cell range A1 through A2, and move the contents to C1 and C2. Then center the column data.
9. Save your changes and close the file.

COMMUNICATION FOCUS

Spreadsheets and other graphics are important aids to communication. Ask an office worker if he or she uses spreadsheets or other graphics in reports or other documents.

Type each line 2 times. Note the spacing before and after each punctuation mark. Repeat if time permits.

Keep your eyes on the copy.

26 The shift of number 9 is (; be sure to hold anchor fingers.
27 Joy shops at Mann & Sons; she spent $72.33 today on slacks.
28 Add these numbers: 22, 33, 44, 77, 88, and 99. Answer: 363.

29 Paula owes Kim these amounts: $2.78, $3.47, $19.82, $21.42.
30 Sonja bought 44# of seed from Mrs. R. G. Herrera yesterday.
31 Look up Route #9 on the U.S.A. map for Ms. Lucky instantly.

32 Have you seen Perry? I think he went to 738 Mainard Street.
33 I need some #2 pencils. Will you get them for me at Paul's?
34 Belle and/or Jay will go to the airport tomorrow afternoon.

H. 3-MINUTE TIMINGS

Take two 3-minute timings on lines 35–43. Note your speed and errors.

Goal: 31/3'/4e

35   Life on the Oregon Trail was not easy. The pioneers   10
36 had to leave in the spring and arrive before the winter   21
37 freeze blocked the passes. They packed their wagons with   32
38 all they owned and then walked beside them. Only those who   44
39 were sick or old or young rode on the journey. The plains   55
40 seemed endless, and the rivers that had to be crossed were   67
41 swift and raging. If a wagon fell behind, it might have to   79
42 be lightened quickly by taking off excess goods and leaving   91
43 them there.   93
    | 1 | 2 | 3 | 4 | 5 | 6 | 7 | 8 | 9 | 10 | 11 | 12   *SI 1.25*

Social Studies
Connections

STUDENT MANUAL

Moving Spreadsheet Data
Changing Row Heights

Study Lesson 126 in your student manual. Complete all the practice activities while at your computer. Then complete the jobs that follow.

SPREADSHEET APPLICATIONS

ACTIVITY 10
Spreadsheet 7

Create a new spreadsheet and save it as SS7. Add the necessary data by following these steps.

1. In cell A1, type the label *Flight Departure Schedule for Tours of Summer*.
2. In cell A2, type the label *Prepared by* and your name.
3. Enter the data into the correct cells as shown in the illustration.
4. Select cell range A1 through F3, and bold the cell contents.
5. Save your changes and close the file.

	A	B	C	D	E	F
1	Flight Departure Schedule for Tours of Summer					
2	Prepared by Your Name					
3	Carrier		Boston	Phoenix	Omaha	Seattle
4						
5						
6						
7						
8						
9	American		4:50 p.m.	3:25 p.m.	3:10 p.m.	6:20 p.m.
10	Continental		7:10 p.m.	4:30 p.m.	2:45 p.m.	3:35 p.m.
11	Delta		6:25 p.m.	2:50 p.m.	4:17 p.m.	5:50 p.m.
12	Northwest		NA	3:50 p.m.	5:30 p.m.	NA
13	Southwest		NA	4:15 p.m.	2:15 p.m.	4:15 p.m.
14	United		5:45 p.m.	6:45 p.m.	2:15 p.m.	5:55 p.m.
15	US Airways		4:40 p.m.	7:25 p.m.	3:55 p.m.	5:55 p.m.
16	America West		NA	6:30 p.m.	NA	5:35 p.m.

LESSON 36

ORIENTATION TO WORD PROCESSING

OBJECTIVES:

- Refine keyboarding skill.
- Refine techniques on adjacent and jump reaches.
- Learn word processing features.

A. WARMUP

Type each line 2 times.

Speed
Accuracy
Language Link
Numbers/Symbols

1 Tom and Shelley may wish to sell this house if they own it.
2 While Sylvie waited, Jacques quickly fixed a dozen zippers.
3 Winifred will accept delivery of paper from Brown Paper Co.
4 Joel Paxon got a 15% discount on the 24# of bread at B & B.

SKILLBUILDING

B. KEYPAD PRACTICE

Enter the following numbers column by column. Press ENTER after the final digit of each number. Keep your eyes on the copy, and use the proper finger for each key. Do not type the commas.

Numbers with 4 or more digits often contain commas to make the numbers easier to read. When entering numbers using the keypad, do not type the commas.

5	45.12	56.89	8,505	1,303	.89	404	975	488	312	38
6	36.78	74.04	9,606	5,238	.24	101	606	577	250	56
7	56.23	52.38	1,404	2,953	.72	232	491	186	598	71
8	90.46	58.52	2,505	1,404	.94	494	638	904	756	32
9	69.63	87.42	3,606	2,505	.62	456	240	496	387	97

Take a 1-minute timing on the paragraph. Note your speed and errors.

```
 9      You may get a better grade in your courses if you will   11
10  allow enough time to find and fix any errors in a paper as   23
11  you prepare the final draft. A neat paper will impress most   35
12  people who read it.                                          39
    | 1 | 2 | 3 | 4 | 5 | 6 | 7 | 8 | 9 | 10 | 11 | 12
```

D. PRACTICE

SPEED: *If you made 2 or fewer errors on the Pretest, type lines 13–20 two times each.*

ACCURACY: *If you made more than 2 errors on the Pretest, type lines 13–16 as a group two times. Then type lines 17–20 as a group two times.*

Left Reaches

```
13  fad bar bag era few best data acted beads brass cards caves
14  get raw sat sea tea cage case debts defer edges erase faces
15  bed beg eve fat war debt rest fewer grade refer seats state
16  cat fed tar tab rat vest star gages water fever waste taxes
```

Right Reaches

```
17  him hop ill boil clip coil cool fill full allow ample ankle
18  ink inn joy gulp hill hold hole hook hope built child chips
19  mop oil pin hung hunt jump like lime lips clips color drill
20  pin pop hop kiln pump poll joke loan lump plump jolly plums
```

E. POSTTEST

Repeat the Pretest. Compare your Posttest results with your Pretest results.

FORMATTING

F. MOVING SPREADSHEET DATA

At times, you may need to move the contents of a cell to a different location within a spreadsheet. Unlike copying, which duplicates the cell contents, moving removes the contents from the original cell and inserts the contents into the new cell. Moving replaces the contents of the new cell. Be careful not to overwrite data that you still need.

G. CHANGING ROW HEIGHT

The height of a spreadsheet row automatically adjusts to fit the size of the font being used. For example, if you change to 18-point, the row height will automatically be adjusted to fit the new font. However, you may want to adjust the height of a row. Adjusting rows with values or labels in them will not affect font size.

C. PRETEST

Take a 1-minute timing on lines 10–13. Note your speed and errors.

```
10        If they have any extra fruit and milk, can you please    11
11 deliver them to the annex? I must buy twenty stamps before      23
12 tomorrow to mail my food-drive flyers. If I don't get these     35
13 in the mail quickly, we will not meet our goal.                 44
   | 1 | 2 | 3 | 4 | 5 | 6 | 7 | 8 | 9 | 10 | 11 | 12
```

D. PRACTICE

SPEED: *If you made 2 or fewer errors on the Pretest, type lines 14–21 two times each.*

ACCURACY: *If you made more than 2 errors on the Pretest, type lines 14–17 as a group two times. Then type lines 18–21 as a group two times.*

Adjacent Reaches

```
14 ui suits fruit guilt quilt quint squid fluid guide build ui
15 we weigh swept tweed tower power dowel jewel fewer vowel we
16 lk caulk yolks talks hulks sulks stalk balky silky chalk lk
17 as vases masts tasks lasts pasta gases aspen cases bases as
```

Jump Reaches

```
18 ex excel exact exert exile exist extra annex vexed index ex
19 mp skimp mumps stamp plump imply champ ample swamp crimp mp
20 mo lemon month money movie mouse emote smoke among model mo
21 ce cents mince paces cease piece slice fence place faces ce
```

E. POSTTEST

Repeat the Pretest. Compare your Posttest results with your Pretest results.

FORMATTING

F. SOFTWARE FEATURES

STUDENT MANUAL

New File   Close File
Open File   Quit word processor

Study Lesson 36 in your student manual. Complete all of the steps while at your computer.

LESSON 126

SPREADSHEETS: MOVING DATA, CHANGING ROW HEIGHT

OBJECTIVES:

- Reinforce skill on left and right reaches.
- Move data in a spreadsheet.
- Change row heights in a spreadsheet.

A. WARMUP

Type each line 2 times.

Speed
Accuracy
Language Link
Numbers/Symbols

1 The road to the left is the right one to take on our drive.
2 Wolf gave Jake an extra dozen quarts, but he can't pay him.
3 Ruth's sister went to the Women's Center to look for a job.
4 I can guess the prices for #32 and #48 within 5% error now!
| 1 | 2 | 3 | 4 | 5 | 6 | 7 | 8 | 9 | 10 | 11 | 12

SKILLBUILDING

B. 12-SECOND SPRINTS

Take three 12-second timings on each line. Try to increase your speed on each timing.

5 We will stop to rest as soon as we finish the last section.
6 The roof on our old shed is in need of repair at this time.
7 The cafe down the road has both good food and good service.
8 Chuck says rain is likely during the early part of the day.
| | | |5| | | |10| | | |15| | |20| | |25| | | |30| | | |35| | | |40| | | |45| | | |50| | | |55| | | |60

LESSON 37

ORIENTATION TO WORD PROCESSING

OBJECTIVES:

- Learn about special symbols.
- Learn word processing features.
- Type 31/3'/5e.

A. WARMUP

Type each line 2 times.

Speed | 1 We may make a nice profit if all of the work is done right.
Accuracy | 2 From the tower Dave saw six big jet planes quickly zoom by.
Language Link | 3 May saw her uncle at the Ohio State football game Saturday.
Numbers | 4 Please buy 50 paper clips, 9 pencils, 7 pens, and 4 stamps.

SKILLBUILDING

B. SPECIAL SYMBOLS

Many keys on the keyboard can be used to represent special symbols. The most common of these special symbols are shown below.

Symbols	Keystrokes	Examples
Roman numerals	Capital letters: I, V, X, L, C, D, and M	Chapters VII-XV
Feet and inches	Apostrophe, feet; quotation mark, inches	Marion is 5' 2".
Minutes and seconds	Apostrophe, minutes; quotation mark, seconds	My time: 3' 15"
Multiply	Small letter x with a space before and after	What is 58 x 12?
Subtract	Single hyphen with a space before and after	240 − 106 = 134
Ellipsis	Three periods (space before, between and after); four periods if words are omitted at the end of the sentence.	He . . . and no

ACTIVITY 9
Spreadsheet 6

Create a new spreadsheet file and save it as SS6. Then follow these steps:

1. In cell A1, type the label *Favorite Amusement Parks*.
2. In cell A2, type *Prepared by* and your name.
3. Enter the remaining data as shown in the illustration, copying cell contents whenever possible.
4. Select cell range A1 through D4 and bold the cell contents.
5. Select cell range A4 through D4 and center the cell contents.
6. Select cell range A6 through D14 and change the width of columns so that all information is displayed.

	A	B	C	D
1	**Favorite Amusement Parks**			
2	**Prepared by Your Name**			
3				
4	**State**	**City**	**Park**	**Attraction**
5				
6	California	Anaheim	Disneyland	Indiana Jones Adventure
7	California	Hollywood	Universal Studios	Back to the Future—The Ride
8	Florida	Orlando	Universal Studios	Back to the Future—The Ride
9	Florida	Orlando	Universal Studios	Terminator 2 3-D
10	New York	Lake George	The Great Escape	Comet
11	Ohio	Sandusky	Cedar Point	Raptor
12	Pennsylvania	Elysburg	Knoebels Amusement Resort	Haunted House
13	Pennsylvania	Hershey	Hersheypark	Wildcat
14	Texas	Arlington	Six Flags Over Texas	Texas Giant

CULTURAL CONNECTIONS

Learning to add, subtract, multiply, and divide are important skills that students learn early in life. Ask a student from another country how old he or she was when these skills were taught to him or her.

C. SYMBOL PRACTICE

Type each line 1 time. Notice the spacing with the symbols and how the symbols are used.

```
5  Dr. Karl told us to read Chapters II and IV from Volume XX.
6  At 6' 3", Mike was able to beat the record time of 10' 32".
7  Does Satbir know the answer to this: 480 x 120 — 150 x 307?
8  During a long, hot summer . . . water was extremely scarce.
```

D. 12- SECOND SPRINTS

Take three 12-second timings on each line. Try to increase your speed on each timing.

```
9   As you read a map, bear in mind that the top part is north.
10  If the top of a map is north, then the right of it is east.
11  Maps have legends that tell what the symbols and codes are.
12  When you can read maps, you possess a skill of great value.
    | | | |5| | | |10| | | |15| | |20| | |25| | | |30| | |35| | | |40| | |45| | | |50| | | |55| | |60
```

E. PREVIEW PRACTICE

Type each line 2 times as a preview to the 3-minute timings that follow.

```
13  zips expect Quaker January conference excitement basketball
14  finals their shown eight they this goal when ends the to if
```

SPREADSHEET APPLICATIONS

ACTIVITY 8
Spreadsheet 5

Open the file SS5, save it as SS5-B, and follow these steps:

1. Type your name after the words *Prepared by* in cell A2.
2. Center and bold the column headings (*Teachers, Period 1, Period 2,* and so on).
3. Add the names as shown from the illustration that follows. Copy the name in cell B6 to the other columns as shown.
4. Copy other names that are repeated in other columns.
5. Proofread your work carefully.

	A	B	C	D	E	F	G
1	Teacher Assistant Schedule						
2	Prepared by						
3							
4	**Teachers**	**Period 1**	**Period 2**	**Period 3**	**Period 4**	**Period 5**	**Period 6**
5							
6	Akins, Jason	Bunnell, N.					
7	Bailey, Karen			Graham, T.			
8	Brawner, Seth					Graham, T.	
9	Carter, Crystal					Walker, O.	
10	Clawson, Anna		Graham, T.				
11	Cowley, Rhonda			Bunnell, N.			
12	Green, Brad				Graham, T.		
13	Holloway, Nicholas	Graham, T.					
14	Ivie, Karla				Bunnell, N.		
15	Lane, Kathleen						Bunnell, N.
16	Morrison, Molly		Walker, O.				
17	Parish, James				Walker, O.		
18	Quillian, Harris		Bunnell, N.				
19	South, Suzette						Graham, T.
20	Sprock, Daniel			Walker, O.			
21	Turner, Wilson						Walker, O.
22	Williams, Virginia					Bunnell, N.	
23	Zobel, Adrian	Walker, O.					Walker, O.

Take two 3-minute timings on lines 15–23. Note your speed and errors.

Goal: 31/3'/5e

15	Those five members of the basketball team hope to be	11
16	chosen as part of the main team. They will need a lot of	22
17	practice to attain this goal. However, they know what the	34
18	excitement will be if they are chosen for the finals.	45
19	They expect that their team will be in first place in	56
20	its conference when the season ends. The team has shown a	67
21	lot more zip since February. Only eight more away games	78
22	have yet to be played. They must not lose the last game to	90
23	Quaker State.	93

| 1 | 2 | 3 | 4 | 5 | 6 | 7 | 8 | 9 | 10 | 11 | 12   SI 1.23

FORMATTING

G. SOFTWARE FEATURES

STUDENT MANUAL

Moving Around in a Document
Spelling Check
Correcting Errors

Backspacing
Saving Files

Study Lesson 37 in your student manual. Complete all the practice activities while at your computer.

inter**NET** CONNECTION

A Website dictionary is often an excellent place to start to locate the spelling of obscure words or new words that may not be in a standard printed dictionary yet. Use the Internet site http://www.onelook.com and look up various words such as *spam*, *netiquette*, and *smiley*.

FORMATTING

E. COPYING SPREADSHEET DATA

Sometimes it is necessary to enter the same information in several cells. Copying a cell's contents is faster and more accurate than typing the same information repeatedly. However, you must be sure that the information you are going to copy is correct before you copy it.

F. CHANGING COLUMN WIDTHS

When you enter data into a spreadsheet, some data may be hidden because the column is too narrow to display the data. When this occurs, you will have to adjust the width of the column to fit the data.

G. SOFTWARE FEATURES

STUDENT MANUAL

Copying Data   Changing Column Widths

Study Lesson 125 in your student manual. Complete all the practice activities while at your computer. Then complete the jobs that follow.

JOURNAL ENTRY

Write a short entry in your journal about the importance of keeping track of your income and expenses. Remind yourself by a note in your tickler file.

LESSON 38

ORIENTATION TO WORD PROCESSING

OBJECTIVES:

- Learn about confusing words.
- Refine techniques on typing symbols.
- Learn word processing features.

A. WARMUP

Type each line 2 times.

Speed
Accuracy
Language Link
Symbols

1 Tom kept his bank records for both last year and this year.
2 Braxton's wacky quip amazed but vexed his girlfriend, Thuy.
3 Svetlana will change planes at Kennedy Airport in New York.
4 He saw Jan's new car. It's not "up" but "down"! (I'm sure.)

interNET CONNECTION

Some cultures consider being on time important. Other cultures are more flexible about time. For example, in Central and South America, it is common to arrive 30 minutes late for an appointment.

Search the Internet for other examples of time-related cultural diversity. How do businesspeople in the United States value time when appointments are made?

To research the protocol for meetings in Russia, which are very different from meetings in other countries, search using the keywords: business protocol Russia.

5 At the customers request, she sent a copy of the companys report.
6 The mens watches and the womens shoes are on sale today.
7 The childs boots were a gift from her friends parents.
8 The secretaries computers were purchased with funds from the governments retraining program.

SKILLBUILDING

C. PREVIEW PRACTICE

Type each line 2 times as a preview to the timings that follow.

Accuracy
Speed

9 handles quality favorable vacations experience achievements
10 their might after when late cite pact job few for can up by

D. 5-MINUTE TIMINGS

Take two 5-minute timings on the paragraphs. Note your speed and errors.

Goal: 39/5'/5e

11   Job seekers can get a head start by starting their   10
12 search in late summer. This can be a good time to start a   22
13 job hunt because by late August, most managers have taken   34
14 their vacations and are back at work, sizing up the quality   46
15 of their staff. It also might be easier to get an interview   58
16 in the late summer when business is somewhat slower. Most   69
17 job openings are found by referrals or through personal   80
18 contacts. Meeting someone in person will sometimes give you   92
19 the best chance to make the most favorable impression.   103
20   When you search for a job, you will need a resume. It   114
21 should include a list of what you have done in your career.   126
22 Realize that you are trying to make a positive impact. You   138
23 can cite a few of your achievements. Also, you should send   150
24 a cover letter with a resume to the person who does the   161
25 hiring for the firm where you wish to work. Your letter and   173
26 resume should list each of your unique abilities and skills   185
27 and include all of your experience and training.   195

| 1 | 2 | 3 | 4 | 5 | 6 | 7 | 8 | 9 | 10 | 11 | 12 SI 1.44

LANGUAGE LINK

B. CONFUSING WORDS

Easily confused words include homonyms *(words spelled and pronounced alike) and* homophones *(words pronounced alike but spelled differently). Study the confusing words and their meanings shown below. Read each sentence carefully and determine which word should be used. Then edit lines 5–8 by choosing the correct word.*

accept (v.)   to take willingly
except (prep.)   other than

stationary (adj.)   fixed, immovable
stationery (n.)   paper, writing materials

I will accept the award. Everyone attended except Jo.

The boat remained stationary while I wrote my letter on nautical stationery.

5 Why did she (except/accept) all of the programs (except/accept) the one entry?

6 Our motto will be, "We will (except/accept) nothing (except/accept) the best."

7 A (stationary/stationery) wall unit is used to store our new (stationary/stationery).

8 While he designed our new (stationary/stationery), he remained (stationary/stationery).

SKILLBUILDING

C. TECHNIQUE TIMINGS

Take two 30-second timings on each line. Focus on the techniques at the left.

Keep your fingers curved and your elbows in.

9 You should know how you would use a computer before buying.
10 Decide what kinds of programs you will be using most often.
11 Will you be using database or spreadsheet programs with it?
12 Choose a computer that will meet all of your current needs.

| 1 | 2 | 3 | 4 | 5 | 6 | 7 | 8 | 9 | 10 | 11 | 12

LESSON 125

SPREADSHEETS: COPYING DATA, CHANGING COLUMN WIDTHS

OBJECTIVES:

- Learn the rules for apostrophes and possessives.
- Copy data within a spreadsheet and change column width.
- Type 39/5'/5e.

A. WARMUP

Type each line 2 times.

Speed
Accuracy
Language Link
Numbers

```
1 They may end the big fight by the lake by the usual signal.
2 Jody typed white requisitions for moving large-sized boxes.
3 Follow the advice of your legal counsel to sign the papers.
4 Read Chapters 129 and 374 and summarize Chapters 48 and 56.
  | 1 | 2 | 3 | 4 | 5 | 6 | 7 | 8 | 9 | 10 | 11 | 12
```

LANGUAGE LINK

B. APOSTROPHES AND POSSESSIVES

Study the rules and examples below. Then edit lines 5–8 by deciding whether an apostrophe or an apostrophe and s *are needed.*

Rule 32:   Use 's to form the possessive of singular nouns.

The hurricane caused major damage to Georgia's crops.

Rule 33:   Use only an apostrophe to form the possessive of plural nouns that end in *s*.

The investors' goals were outlined in the annual report.

Rule 34:   Use 's to form the possessive of plural nouns that do not end in *s*.

The women's offices were next door to the gym.

Type each line 1 time. Repeat if time permits.

$
@

13 Buy 11 blue @ $.79, 43 purple @ $.85, and 17 green @ $1.19.
14 Our e-mail addresses are david@xyz.com or larry@netnow.com.

#
%

15 Carpet remnants #3, #16, and #37 sell for 25% and 35% less.
16 Their #7, #8, and #9 sizes are from 36% to 46% higher here.

&
:

17 Pair them as follows: 10 & 29, 38 & 47, 56 & 65, 135 & 780.
18 What is the correct date: 1919* or 1943* or 1955* or 2002*?

*
=

19 S & L* left at 10:30 and arrived at 11:45. Peter* was late.
20 The answers are: 91 + 82 = 173; 14 + 76 = 90; 24 + 36 = 60.

+
()

21 Lisa, did you know that (3 + 4)(2 + 6)(5 + 7) = 7 x 8 x 12?
22 Bella labeled items (10), (21), (65), (74), (83), and (92).

[]
{}
<>

23 Their [Aztec] houses were [very] old and expensive [$400K].
24 Mrs. Gibson assigned this: ({7^2} {4^3}) + ({17^4} {13^5}).
25 In ASCII, G < H and J < K. Are T > S and W > V and Z > A-Y?

FORMATTING

E. SOFTWARE FEATURES

STUDENT MANUAL

Font Styles   Print/Page Preview
Font Sizes   Print

Study Lesson 38 in your student manual. Complete all the practice activities while at your computer.

Social Studies
Connections

FACT FILE

Abraham Lincoln wrote the Gettysburg Address; however, he did not sign the Declaration of Independence.

	A	B	C	D
1	Budget for the Month of July			
2	Your Name			
3				
4	Income			
5		Allowance	$30.00	
6		Baby-sitting	$80.00	
7		Lawn Care	$20.00	
8				$130.00
9				
10	Expenses			
11		Clothes	$50.00	
12		Movies	$20.00	
13		Loan from Dad	$10.00	
14		Savings	$15.00	
15				
16	Total Expenses			$95.00
17				
18	Money for Misc. Expenses			$35.00

ACTIVITY 7
Spreadsheet 4

Open SS3-B and save it as SS4. Enter the data from the following "what if" questions and see what changes result in the spreadsheet.

1. What if your allowance was increased to $55? (Your total income increases to $155, and miscellaneous money increases to $60.)
2. Type the original amount of $30 in cell C5 before continuing.
3. What if you do extra baby-sitting and earn $95?
4. What if rain reduces your lawn care income to $10?
5. What if you spend $75 on clothes?
6. What if you put $30 in savings?
7. Save the file.
8. Now try some of your own "what if" situations.
9. Close the file without saving your changes.

LESSON 39

ORIENTATION TO WORD PROCESSING

OBJECTIVES:

- Learn about confusing words.
- Refine skills on double letters and alternate reaches.
- Learn word processing features.

A. WARMUP

Type each line 2 times.

Speed 　1 I did not see her take the pencil, but I know that she did.
Accuracy 　2 Taxi drivers are quick to zip by the huge jumble of wagons.
Language Link 　3 It's the secretary who accepted the stationery on Thursday.
Numbers/Symbols 　4 Lee cut the pieces of twine 9 1/2, 7 3/4, and 6 5/8 inches.

COMMUNICATION FOCUS

To avoid confusing people, choose your words carefully. Some words are often misunderstood and misused. Which of the following words give you difficulty?

　accept—except　　access—excess　　than—then　　cite—sight—site

Look up the definitions of these words in a dictionary or thesaurus. Use each of them in a sentence. You may want to start a list of confusing words to review regularly.

SPREADSHEET APPLICATIONS

ACTIVITY 5
Spreadsheet 2

Create a new spreadsheet and save it as SS2.

1. In cell A1, type the label *Paint Inventory*. Notice that the portion of the label that doesn't fit in cell A1 displays in cell B1 because that cell is empty.
2. In cell A2, type *Prepared by* followed by your full name.
3. Type the labels and values as shown in the illustration.
4. Select cells A1 through C4 and bold the contents.
5. Select cells A4 through C4 and center the contents.

	A	B	C
4	Colors	Gallons	Cost
5	Black	8	5.79
6	Blue	13	3.99
7	Green	9	6.88
8	Pink	11	9.75
9	Red	7	4.89
10	White	5	5.95
11	Yellow	6	4.97

ACTIVITY 6
Spreadsheet 3

Open the file SS3. Save it as SS3-B. Then complete the following steps:

1. In cell A2, enter your name.
2. Enter the information shown in the illustration on page 447 that is missing from the spreadsheet into the correct cells. The amounts in column D will change because formulas have been entered into these cells. Remember, you do not need to type the dollar signs or decimals. The column has been formatted to insert them automatically.
3. When you finish typing the data, proofread carefully and correct any errors. If you have entered the correct numbers, cell D18 will show $35.00.
4. Save the file with your changes.

LANGUAGE LINK

B. CONFUSING WORDS

Study the confusing words and their meanings shown below. Read each sentence carefully to determine which word should be used. Then edit lines 5–8 by choosing the correct word.

principle (n.)   rule, code of conduct
principal (adj.)   chief, leading
                (n.)   a person in a leading position

it's   contraction meaning "it is"
its   possessive pronoun, belonging to it

The students consider the coach a man of principle.
The school principal treats all students fairly.
It's a challenge to hold a job after school and study.
The coach praised the team for its leadership.

5 The (principle/principal) upon which this (principle/principal) was hired is clear.
6 Does the (principle/principal) know what (principle/principal) affected the choice?
7 (It's/Its) good to see that the firm is improving (it's/its) poor image.
8 (It's/Its) quiet movement is a sign that (it's/its) operating very well.

SKILLBUILDING

C. 30-SECOND OK TIMINGS

Take two 30-second OK (errorless) timings on lines 9–10. Then take two 30-second OK timings on lines 11–12. Goal: No errors.

9 The students begin to excel when they have peace and quiet.
10 Analyze your study habits and learn to be successful daily.
11 When you type, try moving your fingers quickly to the keys.
12 I think I have answered all of your questions at this time.
    | 1 | 2 | 3 | 4 | 5 | 6 | 7 | 8 | 9 | 10 | 11 | 12

LESSON 124

SPREADSHEETS: CREATE, ALIGN COLUMNS

OBJECTIVES:

- Improve keyboarding speed.
- Create a spreadsheet and align columns.
- Enter data into a spreadsheet.

A. WARMUP

Type each line 2 times.

Speed
Accuracy
Language Link
Technique

1 Jane and the man got five fish and kept them on the island.
2 Maizie quickly paid Jane for the five new taxis she bought.
3 If you follow your counsel's advice, you will plea-bargain.
4 Saul Kent Dora Mary Alva Paul Ruth Kate Zora Lena Rick Juan
| 1 | 2 | 3 | 4 | 5 | 6 | 7 | 8 | 9 | 10 | 11 | 12

SKILLBUILDING

B. PACED PRACTICE

Turn to the Paced Practice routine beginning on page SB7. Take three 2-minute timings, starting at the point where you left off the last time.

FORMATTING

C. SOFTWARE FEATURES

STUDENT MANUAL

Create a Spreadsheet   Align Columns

Study Lesson 124 in your student manual. Complete all the practice activities while at your computer. Then complete the jobs that follow.

D. PRETEST

Take a 1-minute timing on lines 13–16. Note your speed and errors.

```
13      When the food fight began, we all laughed. But Coach    11
14  Parr took one look and ushered all eight guilty students     22
15  to the office for mops and scrubbing supplies. All of them   31
16  were very quiet as they cleaned up the mess.
    | 1 | 2 | 3 | 4 | 5 | 6 | 7 | 8 | 9 | 10 | 11 | 12
```

E. PRACTICE

SPEED: *If you made 2 or fewer errors on the Pretest, type lines 17–24 two times each.*

ACCURACY: *If you made more than 2 errors on the Pretest, type lines 17–20 as a group two times. Then type lines 21–24 as a group two times.*

Double Reaches

```
17  ff offer cliff stuff bluff affix scuff cliff sniff whiff ff
18  oo goose looks shoot loose noose scoop boost swoop roost oo
19  rr error carry tarry berry merry worry sorry furry hurry rr
20  ee cheer jeers trees sleep keeps weeps breed creek deeds ee
```

Alternate Reaches

```
21  tight fight hairy eight sight bland rigid girls laugh Blair
22  chair girls chant clams flame worms their maybe prowl Chris
23  signs usher heist other growl light gowns proxy prism Diana
24  vigor field anvil bugle dozen quake names right soaps Jamel
```

F. POSTTEST

Repeat the Pretest. Compare your Posttest results with your Pretest results.

FORMATTING

G. SOFTWARE FEATURES

STUDENT MANUAL

Alignment
Show/Hide, Reveal Codes
Selecting Text

Study Lesson 39 in your student manual. Complete all the practice activities while at your computer.

The positioning of data at the left, center, or right of a cell is called **alignment**. The default alignment for labels is left, and the default alignment for values is right. Alignment can be easily changed.

Study the spreadsheet illustration below. Note that the contents of cells A1 through E1 are displayed in bold. Labels (words) are aligned at the left. Values (numbers) are aligned at the right. A formula was entered into cells B15–E15 to calculate the total sales.

	A	B	C	D	E
1	**Class Members**	**Week 1**	**Week 2**	**Week 3**	**Total Sales**
2					
3	Finzer, Nick	$15.35	$22.00	$32.89	$70.24
4	Follman, Jadie	$21.98	$18.55	$29.98	$70.51
5	Fowler, Eric	$13.50	$29.19	$24.35	$67.04
6	Glosup, Margaret	$20.00	$14.75	$28.05	$62.80
7	Grimes, Kelley	$19.00	$23.80	$18.15	$60.95
8	McCoy, Andres	$24.25	$18.85	$33.97	$77.07
9	Parker, Kent	$29.88	$28.10	$23.54	$81.52
10	Spoeder, Dustin	$25.79	$21.95	$20.65	$68.39
11	Spradlin, Sherry	$11.15	$16.65	$35.50	$63.30
12	Stanley, Ronnie	$33.35	$27.99	$19.94	$81.28
13	Wright, Mary	$16.50	$31.00	$22.75	$70.25
14					
15	Total Sales	$230.75	$252.83	$289.77	$773.35
16	Average Sales	$20.98	$22.98	$26.34	$70.30

SPREADSHEET APPLICATIONS

ACTIVITY 4
Spreadsheet 1

Open the file SS1 and save it as SS1-B. Then do the following:

1. In cell A1, change the label to *Students*.
2. In cell A7, change the name *Grimes, Kelly* to *Grimes, Kerry*.
3. In cell A10, type the name *Soeder, Dean*.
4. In cell A12, type *Stanley, Robert*.
5. In cell A13, type *Wright, Wendy*.
6. Type the following numbers in cells C3 through C13: C3, 15.05; C4, 22.37; C5, 13.75; C6, 20.02; C7, 17.54; C8, 24 (notice what happens after you press ENTER); C9, 31.53; C10, 23.88; C11, 18.51; C12, 22.52; C13, 26.60. You do not need to type the dollar sign. Notice how the numbers in cells C15, C16, E15, and E16 change as you type the new numbers. Formulas have been entered into these cells to recalculate the sums and averages. If you enter the numbers correctly, cell E16 will show 68.75.

ORIENTATION TO WORD PROCESSING

OBJECTIVES:

- Learn word processing features.
- Type 32/3'/5e.

A. WARMUP

Type each line 2 times.

Speed
Accuracy
Language Link
Numbers/Symbols

1 I like to read about Lewis and Clark as they traveled west.
2 Sacagawea was the Shoshone who helped navigate the terrain.
3 The expedition included gunsmiths and carpenters in winter.
4 After 18 months and 4,000 miles, the journey ended in 1805.

Social Studies
Connections

SKILLBUILDING

B. DIAGNOSTIC PRACTICE: NUMBERS

Turn to the Diagnostic Practice: Numbers routine on page SB4. Type one of the Pretest/Posttest paragraphs and identify any errors made. Then type the corresponding drill lines, on p. SB5 and p. SB6, 2 times for each number on which you made 2 or more errors and 1 time for each number on which you made only 1 error. Finally, repeat the Pretest and compare your performance.

C. PREVIEW PRACTICE

Type each line 2 times as a preview to the 3-minute timings that follow.

5 in Civil maize Quapaw Arkansas smallpox Oklahoma eighteenth
6 migrate topped homes beans tribe clay went East and War the

5 The student sought (advise/advice) from the school's (counsel/council) president.

6 I (advise/advice) you not to answer until you have retained reputable (counsel/council).

7 The AMA (Counsel/Council) on Aging (advises/advices) people to stop smoking.

8 Her (advise/advice) is based on years of experience giving (advise/advice) to others.

9 The archeologist (advised/adviced) the town (counsel/council) to take action quickly.

10 The Tribal (Counsel/Council) gave the group good (advise/advice).

SKILLBUILDING

C. 30-Second OK Timings

Take two 30-second OK (error-free) timings on lines 11–12. Then take two 30-second OK timings on lines 13–14. Goal: no errors.

11   It is not just the size of fingers but their quickness   11
12 that builds every extra word per minute in a timed writing.   23

13   Exercise maintains good health and gives you zest when   11
14 you adjust for the pace required to keep your body healthy.   23

| 1 | 2 | 3 | 4 | 5 | 6 | 7 | 8 | 9 | 10 | 11 | 12

FORMATTING

D. Entering Spreadsheet Data

Words entered into a spreadsheet are called **labels**. Numbers, dates, or times entered into a spreadsheet are called **values**. Mathematical calculations that are entered into a spreadsheet cell are called **formulas**. You can use formulas to add, subtract, multiply, or average the contents of cells.

Changing how information is displayed in a spreadsheet cell is called **formatting**. Data can be displayed in bold or italics and with different font styles and sizes. Numbers, times, and dates can also be displayed in a variety of formats.

Take two 3-minute timings on lines 7–15. Note your speed and errors.

Goal: 32/3'/5e

Social Studies
Connections

7	The Quapaw Indians first lived on the East Coast. They	11
8	moved to the prairies of the Midwest and later went to the	23
9	Arkansas River where they built and lived in homes of earth	35
10	topped with tree bark. They grew maize and beans and were	47
11	noted for their red and white clay jars.	55
12	In the eighteenth century, much of the tribe was wiped	66
13	out by smallpox. Floods and the Civil War caused the Quapaw	78
14	to migrate many times. Today, although the tribe has few	89
15	members, they live in Oklahoma.	96

| 1 | 2 | 3 | 4 | 5 | 6 | 7 | 8 | 9 | 10 | 11 | 12   SI 1.27

FORMATTING

STUDENT MANUAL
Help

Study Lesson 40 in your student manual. Complete all the practice activities while at your computer.

LESSON 123

SPREADSHEETS: ENTERING DATA

OBJECTIVES:

- Learn about confusing words.
- Improve keyboarding accuracy.
- Enter and change spreadsheet data.

A. WARMUP

Type each line 2 times.

Speed
Accuracy
Language Link
Numbers/Symbols

1 Their firm is paid to paint half the signs for those towns.
2 Jacqueline of Hainaut lost Zeeland and Holland to a cousin.
3 You need these personal traits: tact, quick wit, and humor.
4 Certain sales are 15% or 20% off and one is $10 or $15 off.
| 1 | 2 | 3 | 4 | 5 | 6 | 7 | 8 | 9 | 10 | 11 | 12

LANGUAGE LINK

B. CONFUSING WORDS

Study the confusing words and their meanings shown below. Then edit lines 5–10 by choosing the correct word.

advice (n.)   An opinion, recommendation, information, or notice given

advise (v.)   To give information or advice to; to counsel

council (n.)   An organization or group

counsel (v.)   To give advice as a result of a consultation
       (n.)   A policy or plan of action or behavior; a lawyer

UNIT 3

Lessons 41–60

WORD PROCESSING

OBJECTIVES

- Demonstrate keyboarding speed and accuracy on straight copy with a goal of 33 words a minute for 3 minutes with 5 or fewer errors.

- Demonstrate correct use of word processing features.

- Demonstrate an understanding of proofreaders' symbols by editing copy marked for revision.

- Demonstrate basic formatting skills on a variety of reports, correspondence, and envelopes from a variety of copy—arranged, unarranged, rough draft, and handwritten.

- Compose phrases and sentences at the keyboard.

4. Select a group of cells by clicking cell D3 and dragging down through cell D13. Note that the entry bar shows only cell D3 and its contents.
5. Deselect cells D3 through D13 by clicking outside the shaded area.

ACTIVITY 2
Spreadsheet 1

If necessary, open the file SS1, and follow these steps:

1. Select cells A3 through E3.
2. Deselect cells A3 through E3.
3. Select cells A3 through E9.
4. Deselect cells A3 through E9.
5. Move the cell pointer to cell E5. Note the formula in the entry bar and the results in cell E5.

ACTIVITY 3
Spreadsheet 1

If necessary, open the file SS1, and do the following:

1. Move the cell pointer to cell C16 and note the formula in the entry bar.
2. Move the cell pointer to cell C15 and note the formula in the entry bar.
3. Select all of column D by clicking once on the letter D.
4. Deselect column D.
5. Select all of row 11 by clicking once on the number 11.
6. Deselect row 11.
7. Select the entire spreadsheet by clicking once on the Select All button in the upper-left corner where the row and column headings meet. Note what is displayed in the entry bar.
8. Deselect the spreadsheet.
9. Close the file.

*inter*NET CONNECTION

Connect to the Internet. In the location text box of your browser, enter the name(s) of two-year colleges or universities in which you are interested. You may want to search using the key words: two-year college and the state, or city in which you are interested.

WORDS TO LEARN

bold
center page
cut/copy/paste
date insert

envelopes
italic
line spacing

numbering command
page break

page numbering
underline
widow/orphan control

CAREER BIT

RESERVATION AGENT

Reservation agents help people plan trips and make reservations. They answer telephone inquiries and offer suggestions on travel arrangements such as routes, time schedules, rates, and types of accommodation. They quote fares and room rates, make and confirm transportation and hotel reservations, and sell tickets. Agents use computerized systems to quickly obtain information needed to make, change, or cancel reservations for customers.

C. PRACTICE

In the chart below, find the number of errors you made on the Pretest. Then type each of the following designated drill lines 2 times.

Pretest Errors	0–1	2	3	4+
Drill Lines	12–16	11–15	10–14	9–13

Accuracy

9 those seize whether require advanced training opportunities
10 two- high capable colleges graduates finishing communicates
11 want watched getting complete employers carefully coworkers
12 up judged failing criterion four-year essential exceptional

Speed

13 degree demand others after often while open many for can go
14 finish judged worker there doors these wish also who but on
15 people person school right thing prime find jobs may the is
16 listed reason skills along going being will than one get of

D. POSTTEST

Repeat the Pretest. Compare your Posttest results with your Pretest results.

FORMATTING

E. SOFTWARE FEATURES

STUDENT MANUAL

Select Cells   Deselect Cells

Study Lesson 122 in your student manual. Complete all the practice activities while at your computer. Then complete the jobs that follow.

SPREADSHEET APPLICATIONS

ACTIVITY 1
Spreadsheet 1

Open the file SS1 and practice selecting and deselecting cells.

1. Click on cell A3, *Finzer, Nick*.
2. Use the arrow keys to move to cell A7, *Grimes, Kelly*. Check the entry bar at the top of the spreadsheet to be sure you are in the correct cell.
3. Use the arrow keys to move to cell C1, *Week 2*.

LESSON 41

ONE-PAGE ACADEMIC REPORTS

OBJECTIVES:

- Learn word processing features.
- Format one-page academic reports with titles.
- Improve keyboarding skill.

A. WARMUP

Type each line 2 times.

Speed
Accuracy
Language Link
Numbers/Symbols

1 Nancy came into the room knowing that we were hiding there.
2 Voltaire wrote about Zadig, a Babylonian forced into exile.
3 Please buy oranges, apples, and bananas when you have time.
4 Go to the store (M & W Feed) and buy 9# of #7 corn* @ $.43.
　| 1 | 2 | 3 | 4 | 5 | 6 | 7 | 8 | 9 | 10 | 11 | 12

SKILLBUILDING

B. 12-SECOND SPRINTS

Take three 12-second timings on each line. Try to increase your speed on each timing.

5 He did see my two dogs walk along the road to the red barn.
6 The dogs went into the barn to eat their meals and to rest.
7 The cat was in the barn and did not want the dogs in there.
8 It was calm in the barn while the cat hid in the dark silo.
　| | | |5| | | |10| | | |15| | | |20| | | |25| | | |30| | | |35| | | |40| | | |45| | | |50| | | |55| | | |60

LESSON 122

SPREADSHEETS: NAVIGATING

OBJECTIVES:

- Improve keyboarding speed and accuracy.
- Move around within a spreadsheet.

A. WARMUP

Type each line 2 times.

Speed
Accuracy
Language Link
Numbers

1 The firm sent the forms over an hour after she called them.
2 These women quietly gave back the prizes of the six judges.
3 They're planning to eat there for their brother's birthday.
4 Those five passengers are 10, 29, 38, 47, and 56 years old.
| 1 | 2 | 3 | 4 | 5 | 6 | 7 | 8 | 9 | 10 | 11 | 12

FACT FILE

A high school diploma or General Equivalency
Diploma (GED) is required for entry into almost
every job you can name today. Along with the high
school diploma and each level of education that you
complete thereafter, you usually have an increase
in salary.

SKILLBUILDING

B. PRETEST

Take a 1-minute timing on the paragraph. Note your speed and errors.

5   Finishing high school can open up many doors for those   11
6 who wish to go on to complete a two- or four-year degree in   23
7 college. It may also open up opportunities for those who   35
8 wish to find jobs after high school.   42
| 1 | 2 | 3 | 4 | 5 | 6 | 7 | 8 | 9 | 10 | 11 | 12

FORMATTING

C. ONE-PAGE ACADEMIC REPORTS

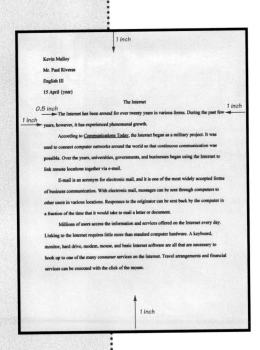

There are many different formats for reports. Academic reports, however, are usually formatted in the MLA (Modern Language Association) style. To format a report in MLA style:

1. Use 1-inch top, bottom, and side margins.
2. Double-space the entire report, including the heading information.
3. Type the heading information (your name, your teacher's name, the class name, and the date) at the left margin.
4. Type the date in military style: 15 April {year}.
5. Center and type the title with initial capital letters for each important word.
6. Indent paragraphs 0.5 inch.

D. SOFTWARE FEATURES

STUDENT MANUAL

Line Spacing   Underline   Margins

Study Lesson 41 in your student manual. Complete all the practice activities while at your computer. Then complete the jobs that follow.

will be taking a major test and want to know what your final grade would be if you received a test grade of 85. You could enter the 85 and have the spreadsheet recalculate your grade average.

Spreadsheets consist of rows and columns. Vertical columns are identified with letters of the alphabet. Horizontal rows are identified with numbers. The rectangle where a column and row meet is called a **cell**. A cell name or address is the column letter and row number. For example, the cell name of the highlighted cell in the example is D10.

Entry Bar
Area where the text, number, or formula in the active cell is displayed. The entry bar is called the formula bar in some programs.

Cell name or address
Column and row of a cell; for example, cell D10 means Column D, Row 10.

Row
Horizontal data identified by numbers.

Cell
Box where a row and column intersect.

Active Cell
Cell currently in use or selected.

Column
Vertical data identified by letters.

D10   ▪ 20.65

	A	Week 1	Week 2	Week 3	Total Sales
1	Class Members	Week 1	Week 2	Week 3	Total Sales
2					
3	Finzer, Nick	$15.35	$22.00	$32.89	$70.24
4	Follman, Jadie	$21.98	$18.55	$29.98	$70.51
5	Fowler, Eric	$13.50	$29.19	$24.35	$67.04
6	Glosup, Margaret	$20.00	$14.75	$28.05	$62.80
7	Grimes, Kelley	$19.00	$23.80	$18.15	$60.95
8	McCoy, Andres	$24.25	$18.85	$33.97	$77.07
9	Parker, Kent	$29.88	$28.10	$23.54	$81.52
10	Spoeder, Dustin	$25.79	$21.95	$20.65	$68.39
11	Spradlin, Sherry	$11.15	$16.65	$35.50	$63.30
12	Stanley, Ronnie	$33.35	$27.99	$19.94	$81.28
13	Wright, Mary	$16.50	$31.00	$22.75	$70.25
14					
15	Total Sales	$230.75	$252.83	$289.77	$773.35
16	Average Sales	$20.98	$22.98	$26.34	$70.30

F. SOFTWARE FEATURES

STUDENT MANUAL
Spreadsheets

Study Lesson 121 in your student manual. Complete all the practice activities while at your computer.

Type this report in MLA format. Underline the magazine title in the second paragraph.

Kevin Malloy

Mr. Paul Riveras

English III

15 April {year}

The Internet

The Internet has been around for over twenty years in various forms. During the past few years, however, it has experienced phenomenal growth.

According to <u>Communications Today</u>, the Internet began as a military project. It was used to connect computer networks around the world so that continuous communication was possible. Over the years, universities, governments, and businesses began using the Internet to link remote locations together via e-mail.

E-mail is an acronym for electronic mail, and it is one of the most widely accepted forms of business communication. With electronic mail, messages can be sent through computers to other users in various locations. Responses to the originator can be sent back by the computer in a fraction of the time that it would take to mail a letter or document.

SKILLBUILDING

Take two 5-minute timings on the paragraphs. Note your speed and errors.

Goal: 39/5'/5e

Social Studies
Connections

7	During the Second World War, world leaders knew that	11
8	something had to be done to prevent another war. They met	22
9	and came up with the idea for the United Nations, which has	34
10	served as a forum for many international disputes.	45
11	Almost all the countries in the world have joined this	56
12	organization. The United Nations has several groups that	67
13	help to solve crises and keep peace between countries.	78
14	Even though this quality organization does not pass	89
15	laws, it has worked for over fifty years to help keep world	101
16	peace, offer a place where people can meet and work out	112
17	their problems, and help nations cooperate among themselves	124
18	in fixing the problems that bother them. The members of the	136
19	United Nations work to protect human rights and improve	147
20	standards of living all over the world.	155
21	Like any big family, this one is not without problems.	166
22	The United Nations has some money woes and is denounced for	178
23	the way it spends money. But while there are problems, most	190
24	people agree that we do need it.	197

| 1 | 2 | 3 | 4 | 5 | 6 | 7 | 8 | 9 | 10 | 11 | 12 SI 1.35

FORMATTING

A **spreadsheet** is an electronic worksheet or grid that is used to organize and analyze information and calculate projections (for instance, to answer "what ifs").

For example, suppose you have your English grades entered and averaged in a spreadsheet. On Friday, you

Millions of users access the information and services offered on the Internet every day. Linking to the Internet requires little more than standard computer hardware. A keyboard, monitor, hard drive, modem, mouse, and basic Internet software are all that are necessary to hook up to one of the many consumer services on the Internet. Travel arrangements and financial services can be executed with the click of the mouse.

REPORT 2
One-Page
MLA Format

Type this report in MLA format. Underline the book title in the last paragraph.

Lindy Alvarez

Mrs. Karen Schmidt

Computer Literacy II

13 November {year}

Software Ethics

Everyone who owns a computer uses software for various activities such as word processing, spreadsheets, and games.

That neat game your friend has would be great to add to your collection of games. Of course, you would also allow your friend to make a copy of one of your games. Before you copy software, be aware that you and your friend would be breaking the law.

LESSON 121

SPREADSHEETS: ORIENTATION

OBJECTIVES:

- Identify the basic parts of a spreadsheet.
- Compose at the keyboard.
- Type 39/5'/5e.

A. WARMUP

Type each line 2 times.

Speed
Accuracy
Language Link
Technique

1 Just see how well his fingers are flying over the keys now.
2 Kaz quickly mixed the two squeezed juices in the brown jug.
3 The personal note he got said they were on their way there.
4 Do NOT type any CAPITAL in lowercase; always use UPPERCASE.

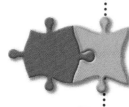

LANGUAGE LINK

B. COMPOSING AT THE KEYBOARD

Compose the body of a short letter requesting information from a nearby museum. Ask for a program of scheduled events, the hours of operation, and the cost of admission.

SKILLBUILDING

C. PREVIEW PRACTICE

Type each line 2 times as a preview to the timings that follow.

Accuracy
Speed

5 United dispute quality criticize organization international
6 fixing other over were most keep with came and not is to up

Illegal copying of software is called piracy. When you purchase software, you have the right to use the software only on your computer. New methods of preventing software piracy are being implemented every year. Soon every computer will have a "fingerprint" that will prevent a person from installing software on another person's computer.

The creators and writers of the software that you purchase in stores own what is called a copyright on their programs. A copyright is a legal right to exclusive publication, distribution, sale, or use of the copyrighted work. Musicians and authors own the same right for songs and books they write. The ease of copying software, even though it is illegal and unethical, has caused a real problem for the owners of software copyrights. Jane Ellis writes in her book, <u>Don't Share That Software!</u>, that what seems like a harmless thing to do is costing businesses and consumers millions, perhaps billions, of dollars.

FACT FILE

Microprocessors (computer chips) are the brains for personal computers. They are also used in many common items including microwave ovens, VCRs, and TV remote controls. Before the invention of microprocessors, machines could be programmed to do only one task at a time.

WORDS TO LEARN

AVERAGE

bar chart

cell ranges

fill down

fill right

fill series

formula

functions

gridlines

operators

pie chart

row height

sort

SUM

values

what if

worksheet

X axis

Y axis

CAREER BIT

METEOROLOGIST Meteorology is the study of the atmosphere. Meteorologists study the atmosphere's physical characteristics, motions, and processes, and the way it affects the rest of our environment. The best known application of this knowledge is in weather forecasting. Meteorologists study information on air pressure, temperature, humidity, and wind velocity, and apply physical and mathematical relationships to make short- and long-range weather forecasts. Their data come from weather satellites, weather radar, and remote sensors and observers in many parts of the world. Weather information and meteorological research are also applied in air-pollution control, agriculture, air and sea transportation, defense, and the study of trends in Earth's climate such as global warming or ozone depletion.

LESSON 42 ONE-PAGE BUSINESS REPORTS

OBJECTIVES:

- Improve keyboarding skill.
- Learn proofreaders' marks.
- Learn word processing features.
- Format a one-page business report with a title and byline.

A. WARMUP

Type each line 2 times.

Speed
Accuracy
Language Link
Numbers/Symbols

1 Have you been to the new cafe that is down on Marsh Street?
2 Egyptians carved the Sphinx to guard King Khafre's pyramid.
3 Please accept the stationery that Principal White gave you.
4 Bill paid $85 for 3 shirts and $197.50 for 2 pair of pants.
| 1 | 2 | 3 | 4 | 5 | 6 | 7 | 8 | 9 | 10 | 11 | 12

SKILLBUILDING

B. CONCENTRATION DRILLS

Type each line 1 time. Concentrate on keeping your eyes on the copy. Repeat if time permits.

5 accommodation lackadaisical weatherproofed environmentalist
6 objectionable bougainvillea characteristic hyperventilation
7 philosophical discombobulate identification thoughtlessness
8 filibustering noninvolvement reconnaissance departmentalize

C. TECHNIQUE CHECKPOINT

Type each line 2 times. Repeat if time permits. Focus on the technique at the left.

Do not hesitate before or after pressing the space bar.

9 I will not go to Joe Yen's home if he has gone to the mall.
10 You are the one to be at the home when all of us have gone.
11 It is a good idea to have me save all of my pay that I can.
12 Go get the cat and the dog so we can get to the park early.

UNIT 7
LESSONS 121–140

SPREADSHEETS

OBJECTIVES

- Demonstrate keyboarding speed and accuracy on straight copy with a goal of 39 words a minute for 5 minutes with 5 or fewer errors.

- Demonstrate knowledge of the basic parts of a spreadsheet.

- Demonstrate the ability to create a spreadsheet and manipulate the data.

- Demonstrate the ability to use spreadsheets to ask "what if" questions.

- Compose letters and short stories at the keyboard.

FORMATTING

D. PROOFREADERS' MARKS

Proofreaders' marks are used to indicate changes and corrections in a document (called a rough draft) that is being revised for final copy. Study the proofreaders' marks and examples that follow, and learn what each mark means.

Proofreaders' Marks	Draft	Final Copy
Omit space	data base	database
Insert	if he's going	if he's not going,
Capitalize	Maple street	Maple Street
Delete	a final draft	a draft
Insert space	allready to	all ready to
Change word	and if you	and when you
Use lowercase letter	our President	our president
Paragraph	¶ Most of the	Most of the
Bold	He did say	He **did** say
Don't delete	a true story	a true story

E. ONE-PAGE BUSINESS REPORT

The format of a business report is different from an academic report. To format a business report:
1. Use default side and bottom margins.
2. Double-space the entire report. Change the line spacing before you begin the report.
3. Leave an approximate 2-inch top margin (press ENTER 3 times).
4. Center and type the report title in all caps and bold.
5. Center and type the subtitle (a further description of the title) or the byline (the author's name) in initial caps.

¶Recycling has now become more important than ever. Business and industry are finding new ways to recycle waste products such as paper, plastics, glass, oil, animal by-products, tires, and other trash. In many places, trash is being burned to create electricity.

¶There is a wealth of information available on global environmental changes. There are CDs, videodiscs, and other materials available to help explore the various aspects of Earth's systems. Everyone needs to be aware of what he or she can do to help protect life on Earth.

REPORT 71
Invitation

Create an invitation to a formal dinner dance using the desktop publishing features that you have learned.

1. The dance is called the Washington Ball.
2. It will be held on September 23.
3. Dinner will begin at 7:30 p.m. and dancing will begin at 9 p.m.
4. The dance will be held at the Mt. Washington Hotel in Bretton, New Hampshire.
5. The cost is $60 per couple, and reservations must be made.
6. The telephone number is 603-555-0203, and all reservations must be received by September 1.

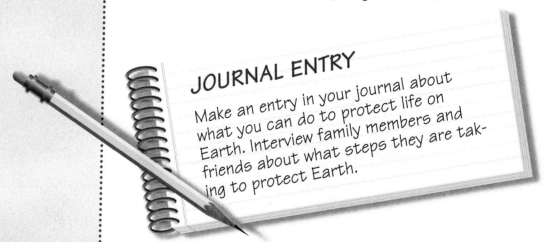

JOURNAL ENTRY

Make an entry in your journal about what you can do to protect life on Earth. Interview family members and friends about what steps they are taking to protect Earth.

STUDENT MANUAL

Bold   Cut/Copy/Paste
Italic

Study Lesson 42 in your student manual. Complete all the practice activities while at your computer. Then complete the jobs that follow.

WORD PROCESSING APPLICATIONS

REPORT 3

One-Page
Business
Report

Type the following one-page report. Make the corrections indicated by the proofreaders' marks.

THE AMAZING COMPUTER

by Gayle Todd

The computer is an amazing electronic device. It can compute complex calculations, store vast amounts of data, and process information with the stroke of a key. All this can take place within a matter of seconds.

Computers are a significant part of our lives, and new and exciting uses are continually being developed. Software is the fastest changing component of the computer. New and improved versions of software are frequently introduced that improve the capability and functions of the computer.

According to one of the monthly computer magazines, *Education Software*, what and how we learn has also been affected by the computer. Interactive software enables students and

REPORT 70
Newsletter

Create a newsletter by following these steps:

1. Use text/word art and Times New Roman 36-point to create the title *OUR WORLD*.
2. Type the body of the newsletter in two columns using Times New Roman 13-point and full justification. Insert a vertical line between the columns.
3. Indent paragraphs 0.25 inch.
4. Insert a graphic of a globe between the third and fourth paragraphs.
5. Type the heading *Promoting Conservation* so that the type reverses to white in a green box.
6. Add an appropriate page border to the newsletter.

¶When the first pictures from space appeared in *Life* magazine several decades ago, we gained a new perspective on the planet Earth. Science was not just the study of land, sea, air, and living things. It was also the study of an entire planet—the only one in our solar system—that so far has been found suitable for life.

¶Earth is the only planet where water is stable at the surface. Seas are important because water has been the catalyst for the development of life on our planet.

¶As the population of humanity continues to grow and use more and more of the world's resources, it is more important than ever that everyone realize the impact this is having and will continue to have on the environment.

¶Concern for the environment and ecology has led to the formation of about 3,000 environmental interest groups. Their goals range from protecting endangered natural resources to protecting endangered wildlife.

Promoting Conservation

¶The Forest Service has restored millions of acres of forests used for outdoor recreation, for timber, and for wildlife habitats.

¶The federal government created the Environmental Protection Agency to help clean up our air, water, land, and other natural resources.

Science
Connections

teachers to explore subject areas previously limited to text-books. Math and Science classes utilizes the computer to teach complex concepts using a hands-on approach. Language Arts and Literature classes write reports and creative assignments using computers. Business classes teach students to use the latest software currently ^being used in bus-inessses and colleges. Computers continue to become an integrated part of our lives. It would be hard, ^difficult if not impossible, to name an area of our life ^lives that has not been affected by this amazing device.

REPORT 4
One-Page
Business Report

Open Report 3 and revise it by moving the second paragraph to the beginning of the report. Move the last paragraph to before the third paragraph.

FACT FILE

To prevent damage to your computer screen, use a screen saver. A screen saver displays constantly moving images. These moving images prevent your screen from being etched by an image that does not change for a period of time. You can set the amount of time your computer is idle before the screen saver automatically appears. There are many different kinds of screen savers including graphics, photos, or animated characters.

LESSON 120

DESKTOP PUBLISHING REVIEW

OBJECTIVES:

- Improve keyboarding skill.
- Review desktop publishing features.

A. WARMUP

Type each line 2 times.

Speed
Accuracy
Language Link
Numbers/Symbols

1 It is now time for all of us to take the time to save more.
2 Pat quickly froze the gold mixtures in five old brown jars.
3 The personnel department sent out their recognition awards.
4 The total bill was $5.78 + $9.64 + $2.13, less 5% = $16.67.

| 1 | 2 | 3 | 4 | 5 | 6 | 7 | 8 | 9 | 10 | 11 | 12

SKILLBUILDING

B. 12-SECOND SPRINTS

Take three 12-second timings on each line. Try to increase your speed on each timing.

5 They will be able to amend the votes that were taken today.
6 She sent a note about an issue to four kind men who helped.
7 When you take a tour, you may see four new members at work.
8 The first court passed one new law today that we must read.

| | | |5| | | |10| | | |15| | |20| | | |25| | | |30| | | |35| | | |40| | | |45| | | |50| | | |55| | | |60

C. DIAGNOSTIC PRACTICE: ALPHABET

Turn to the Diagnostic Practice: Alphabet routine beginning on page SB1. Type one of the Pretest/Posttest paragraphs and identify any errors made. Then type the corresponding drill lines 2 times for each letter on which you made 2 or more errors and 1 time for each letter on which you made only 1 error. Finally, repeat the same Pretest paragraph and compare your performance.

LESSON 43

LISTS, OUTLINES, AND AGENDAS

OBJECTIVES:

- Learn word processing features.
- Compose at the keyboard.
- Format enumerations.
- Format outlines and agendas.
- Type 33/3'/5e.

A. WARMUP

Type each line 2 times.

Speed
Accuracy
Language Link
Numbers/Symbols

1 After the cats ate lunch, they bathed their paws and faces.
2 Quentin and Ynez Zbleski moved to Phoenix, Arizona, in May.
3 It's just weird how the kitten lost its red leather collar.
4 On August 23-25, A.D. 79, 19-23 feet of ash buried Pompeii.
| 1 | 2 | 3 | 4 | 5 | 6 | 7 | 8 | 9 | 10 | 11 | 12

LANGUAGE LINK

B. COMPOSING AT THE KEYBOARD

Answer each question with a few words or short phrases.

5 Which season is your favorite?
6 What is the most recent movie you have seen?
7 Where would you like to go on summer vacation?
8 Who is your favorite recording artist?

SKILLBUILDING

C. DIAGNOSTIC PRACTICE: ALPHABET

Turn to the Diagnostic Practice: Alphabet routine on page SB1. Type one of the Pretest/Posttest paragraphs and identify any errors made. Then type the corresponding drill lines 2 times for each letter on which you made 2 or more errors and 1 time for each letter on which you made only 1 error. Finally, repeat the Pretest and compare your performance.

Short-Term Parking Passes: Because of road repairs near Wesley Tower and Building H, additional parking has been arranged for employees. If you work in either building, you can obtain a special parking permit from Roger Loucks, Mail Code 1209.

¶The permits are valid for spaces in Lot A on the northwest corner of Logan and Beaubien Streets.

Theater Tickets: If there is sufficient interest by Welco employees in seeing *West Side Story,* which is coming to the Palm City Theater, the company will purchase a block of discount tickets for the Friday, March 16, performance. The show begins at 8 p.m. If you are interested in purchasing tickets, please call Diane Cohen, Civic Affairs Dept., Ext. 479, before March 2.

Las Vegas Night: The Five-Year Club is sponsoring a Las Vegas Night fundraiser on April 26 at 8 p.m. at the Town Line House. All proceeds from this event will be donated to those charities supported by the club. Please call Helen Oldhoff at Ext. 291 for details.

Community Service: Welco continues to support the local school system by providing employees with release time to speak at schools or career fairs with students who are making career decisions. If you are interested, please contact Diane Cohen, Ext. 479.

Credits: *THE REPORTER* is published weekly by Welco. Letters should be addressed to the editor at New Center Building, 609 Griswold, Room 703, Detroit, Michigan 48030. Editor: *Phillip S. DeRoy*; Reporters: *Gilbert Hall, Diane Novick, Anne Ricci, Collette Searle*; Designer/Desktop Specialist: *Betty Lynclyff.*

D. 30-Second OK Timings

Take two 30-second OK (error-free) timings on lines 9–10. Then take two 30-second OK timings on lines 11–12. Goal: no errors.

9	Exercise your fingers on these drill lines every day,	11
10	and watch them zip and bound over all of the keys quickly.	23
11	Exercise such as walking gives your body the zest it	11
12	needs to adjust to the pace needed to maintain good health.	23

| 1 | 2 | 3 | 4 | 5 | 6 | 7 | 8 | 9 | 10 | 11 | 12

E. Preview Practice

Type each line 2 times as a preview to the timings that follow.

13	worship weather freedom journey equipped Pilgrims craftsmen
14	disease friends native their north knew farm fish hunt guns

F. 3-Minute Timings

Take two 3-minute timings on the paragraphs. Note your speed and errors.

Goal: 33/3′/5e

15	The Pilgrims were a mix of people who wanted freedom	11
16	to worship and poor farmers and craftsmen who hoped for a	22
17	better life. They had guns but knew little about hunting.	34
18	They planned to fish but knew nothing about fishing.	44
19	When their journey took them north of their target,	55
20	it was winter, and they found they were not equipped for	66
21	the harsh weather. Almost half of the Pilgrims froze or	77
22	died of hunger and diseases. In the early spring, four	89
23	native friends taught them to farm, hunt, and fish.	99

| 1 | 2 | 3 | 4 | 5 | 6 | 7 | 8 | 9 | 10 | 11 | 12   SI 1.28

Social Studies
Connections

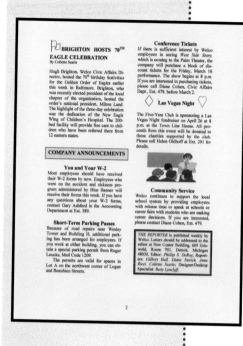

5. Type the body of the article in Times New Roman 12-point.
6. Insert a text box with a black border and yellow fill, and type *COMPANY ANNOUNCEMENTS* in bold Times New Roman 14-point. Center and type each announcement head in initial caps, bold, Times New Roman 14-point. Type the announcement text in 12-point Times New Roman, full-justified.
7. Add a diamond on one side of *Las Vegas Night,* and add a heart on the other side. Make both symbols red, 36 points. Insert a space between each symbol and the text. (Use WPIconic Symbols A, diamond = ", heart = !)
8. Insert an appropriate graphic above the community service article.
9. Insert a text box for the credits at the end of the second column. Add a double-line border, shade the box light yellow, and type the credits in Times New Roman 11-point.
10. Adjust the columns and text boxes so that your page looks similar to the illustration.
11. Number the page (2) at the bottom center of the page.

Headline: *BRIGHTON HOSTS 70TH EAGLE CELEBRATION*
Byline: By Collette Searle
¶Hugh Brighton, Welco Civic Affairs Director, hosted the 70th birthday festivities for the Golden Order of Eagles earlier this week in Baltimore. Brighton, who was recently elected president of the local chapter of the organization, hosted the order's national president, Milton Land. The highlight of the three-day celebration was the dedication of the New Eagle Wing of Children's Hospital. The 200-bed facility will provide free care to children who have been referred there from 12 eastern states.

Company Announcements:

You and Your W-2: Most employees should have received their W-2 forms by now. Employees who were on the accident and sickness program administered by Blue Banner will receive their forms this week. If you have questions about your W-2 forms, contact Gary Ashford in the Accounting Department at Ext. 589.

G. NUMBERED AND BULLETED LISTS

Use numbers or bullets to display items in a list. Numbers and bullets are automatically positioned at the left margin, and carryover lines are automatically indented to align with the text in the line above.

1. If the order of the items is important, use numbers; otherwise, use bullets.
2. If the list is part of a single-spaced document, single-space the list (press ENTER 2 times before and after the list). If the list is part of a double-spaced document, double-space the list (press ENTER only 1 time before and after the list).

H. OUTLINES

An outline is a plan for the organization of a document. It identifies the topics within the document and the sequence in which those topics are presented. To format an outline:

1. Use default side and bottom margins. Leave an approximate 2-inch top margin (press ENTER 6 times).
2. Center and type the title of the outline in all caps and bold.
3. Press ENTER 2 times; then turn on the numbering command and type each item.

I. AGENDAS

An agenda is a list of topics to be discussed at a meeting or a formal program of a meeting. To format an agenda:

1. Use default side and bottom margins. Leave an approximate 2-inch top margin (press ENTER 6 times).
2. Center and type the name of the committee or the company in all caps and bold.
3. Press ENTER 2 times; then center and type *Meeting Agenda* in initial caps.
4. Press ENTER 2 times; then center and type the date in initial caps.
5. Press ENTER 2 times; then turn on the numbering command and type each item.

SKILLBUILDING

C. PRETEST

Take a 1-minute timing on the paragraph. Note your speed and errors.

```
 9        It is our civic duty to vote for the mayor of this      10
10   city. We may also need to audit the books so that we have    22
11   proof that the manner in which we do business is correct.    34
12   We will have to go through channels for this to work out.     45
     | 1 | 2 | 3 | 4 | 5 | 6 | 7 | 8 | 9 | 10 | 11 | 12
```

D. PRACTICE

SPEED: *If you made 2 or fewer errors on the Pretest, type lines 13–20 two times each.*

ACCURACY: *If you made more than 2 errors on the Pretest, type lines 13–16 as a group two times. Then type lines 17–20 as a group two times.*

```
13  nn funny cannon cannot dinner manner runner winner channels
14  oo good wood room soon proof spoon foods tooth groom booths
15  tt kitty bottle button attach cattle fitted attacks attends
16  mm rummy tummy drummer summer simmer summit yummy hammer mm

17  duck duty bush busy city clay audit blend civic cycle field
18  dock down both bowl buck burn flaps girls goals panel risks
19  dial corn cork body also auto rocks spend their tight vivid
20  dark pens kept coal gyms pent fight right tight burnt socks
```

E. POSTTEST

Repeat the Pretest. Compare your Posttest results with your Pretest results.

DESKTOP PUBLISHING APPLICATIONS

REPORT 69

Complete the second page of the newsletter you created in Lesson 118. Follow these steps:

1. Set the top and bottom margins at 0.75 inch and the left and right margins at 1.2 inches.
2. Format the text in two columns, justify the text, and use automatic hyphenation.
3. Type the headline for the first article in all caps and bold at the left margin using Times New Roman 14-point. Add a flag to the left of the title (Wingdings, O), and make it red, 36 points. Insert a space after the flag.
4. Type the byline on the next line in Times New Roman 10-point.

STUDENT MANUAL

Numbers and Bullets

Study Lesson 43 in your student manual. Complete all the practice activities while at your computer. Then complete the jobs that follow.

WORD PROCESSING APPLICATIONS

REPORT 5

Agenda

Type the following agenda using the bullets and numbering feature for the numbered and bulleted items. Do not space before or after the diagonal.

ASSOCIATION OF COMPUTER USERS

Meeting Agenda

January 6, {year}

1. Access the World via the Internet/Alexander Room
   - Chris Melrose
   - Adam Chandler
2. Technology in the Workplace/Saturn Room
   - Karen Larsen
3. Lunch/Ballroom A
4. Virtual Reality: A Training Tool/Franklin Room
   - Willard Gallagher
   - Michael Laney
5. Teleconference Roundtables/Ballroom B

REPORT 6

Outline

Type this report using the outline feature.

PLAYING YOUR MUSIC

1) YOUR CHOICES
   a) CD players
   b) MP3 players
2) PERFORMANCE ISSUES
   a) Sound quality
   b) Shock resistance
   c) Battery life
      i) Chargeable or non-chargeable
      ii) AC adapter
3) PRICING

LESSON 119 NEWSLETTERS

OBJECTIVES:

- Improve keyboarding skill.
- Learn about confusing words.
- Complete the second page of a newsletter.

A. WARMUP

Type each line 2 times.

Speed
Accuracy
Language Link
Numbers

1 Andy may pay me for the bicycle if he is paid for the work.
2 Jacqueline was vexed by the folks who got the money prizes.
3 My savings account pays low interest of only 4 5/8 percent.
4 She sold 1,234 in June, 3,456 in July, and 7,890 in August.
| 1 | 2 | 3 | 4 | 5 | 6 | 7 | 8 | 9 | 10 | 11 | 12

LANGUAGE LINK

B. CONFUSING WORDS

Study the confusing words and their meanings shown below. Then edit lines 5–8 by selecting the correct word to complete each sentence.

personal (adj.)   private; of, relating to, or affecting a person;

personnel (n.)   employees; a staff making up a work-force; human resources workers

their (pron.)   possessive form of *they*

there (adv.)   at or in that place
     (pron.)   used to introduce a clause

5 The letters are (personal/personnel) and should not be read at (there/their) party.
6 All of the teachers expressed (their/there) (personal/personnel) concerns about the problems.
7 Over (their/there) are our neighbors; (their/there) family is very pleasant.
8 The (personal/personnel) staff are (their/there) to help you.

LESSON 44 — REPORTS WITH HEADINGS

OBJECTIVES:

- Improve keyboarding skill.
- Format reports with side headings and paragraph headings.

Type each line 2 times.

Speed
Accuracy
Language Link
Numbers/Symbols

1 I am quite sure that we have had rain every day this month.
2 Zanzibar, a part of Tanzania, exports cassava and coconuts.
3 Except for one, all students wanted to take a French class.
4 Pets & Paws will groom my dog for $45 (that's a lot) today.
| 1 | 2 | 3 | 4 | 5 | 6 | 7 | 8 | 9 | 10 | 11 | 12

SKILLBUILDING

B. 12-SECOND SPRINTS

Take three 12-second timings on each line. Try to increase your speed on each timing.

5 We all like to be able to have fun and get the chores done.
6 While we work, we may find more work that needs to be done.
7 As we work at a job, we know what to do and it gets easier.
8 The more you do the same task, the better you become at it.
| | | 5 | | | | 10 | | | | 15 | | | 20 | | | 25 | | | 30 | | | 35 | | | 40 | | | 45 | | | 50 | | | 55 | | | 60

C. PACED PRACTICE

Turn to the Paced Practice routine beginning on page SB7. Take three 2-minute timings, starting at the point where you left off the last time.

Article 2 headline: *SMART USERS KEEP PCs SECURE*
Byline: By Gilbert Hall
Article 2 text: When the topic of computer theft comes up, most people think only of "hackers," clever PC users who break into large computer systems and steal or manipulate information. However, Dave Devaney, Computer Systems Manager, thinks that employees should be far more concerned with another kind of theft—the physical removal of their equipment from the office.

¶"Right now we don't have a problem, but the situation bears watching," says Devaney. "Other companies have had instances where equipment has just disappeared. Employees must learn to think of their computers and their software in the same manner as other valuable office items."

¶Devaney strongly recommends two measures:

- Physically lock down the equipment using a special device available from the computer systems department.
- Lock all software in a drawer or specially designed case when not in use.

FACT FILE

Usually companies bring lawsuits against those who have stolen equipment or information from them. A court reporter may be used to record the testimony presented during the trial.

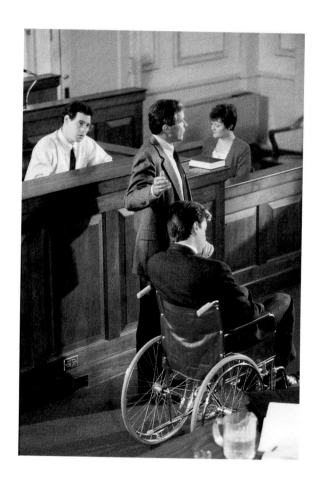

D. REPORTS WITH PARAGRAPH AND SIDE HEADINGS

Side Headings break a report into specific sections. Type side headings:
1. At the left margin in all caps and bold.
2. With a double space before and after.

Paragraph Headings are minor subdivisions of a report. Type paragraph headings:
1. Indented 0.5 inch.
2. In initial caps and bold.
3. Followed by a period (also in bold).
4. Followed by one space.

WORD PROCESSING APPLICATIONS

REPORT 7

One-Page Report With Side Headings

Social Studies
Connections

Type the following report with side headings. Double-space the report.

KENYA THE BEAUTIFUL
By Sharon Eldridge

The republic of Kenya is located near the equator on the east coast of Africa. One of the most beautiful places on earth, it's blessed with a rich assortment of wildlife and spectacular scenery. Kenya's most famous landmark, Mount Kilimanjaro, is located in Tanzania.

TOURISM

Visitors from all over the world come to see the variety of plant and animal species found here. Beautiful, uncrowded beaches are found along the coastline with snorkeling and diving being popular recreation activities.

WILDLIFE

The wildlife of Kenya is among the most populous and diversified in the world. Large herds of zebras, giraffes, elephants, gazelles, and other grazing animals are seen roaming

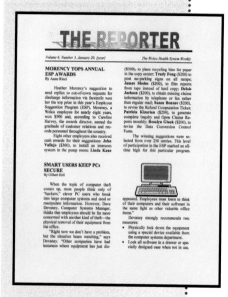

5. Add the date line below the nameplate. Align the volume number and date at the left; align the tag line at the right. Use Times New Roman 11-point italic. The line should read: *Volume 6, Number 3, January 20, {year}/The Welco Health System Weekly.*

6. Add a thin horizontal line from margin to margin below the date line.

7. Type the headline for article 1 in all capital letters and bold at the left margin using Times New Roman 14-point. Type the byline in Times New Roman 10-point.

8. Type the body of the article in Times New Roman 12-point. Indent paragraphs approximately 0.25 inch, justify the text, and use automatic hyphenation.

9. Type the names of the eight other winners in bold.

10. Balance the columns.

11. Follow steps 7–8 for the second article.

12. Add an appropriate graphic at the top of the second column of the second article. Balance the columns.

13. Adjust the spacing as necessary to fit everything on one page.

Article 1 headline: *MORENCY TOPS ANNUAL ESP AWARDS*
Byline: By Anne Ricci
Article 1 text: ¶Heather Morency's suggestion to send out-of-town requests for discharge information via facsimile won her the top prize in this year's Employee Suggestion Program (ESP). Morency, a Welco employee for nearly eight years, won $500 and, according to Caroline Harvey, the awards director, earned the gratitude of customer relations and records personnel throughout the country.
¶Eight other employees also received cash awards for their suggestions: John Vallejo ($300), to install an intercom system in the pump room; Linda Kane ($300), to place recycling bins for paper in the copy center; Trudy Fong ($200), to post no-parking signs on all ramps; James Sholes ($200), to film reports from tape instead of hard copy; Delois Jackson ($200), to obtain missing claims information by telephone or fax rather than regular mail; Susan Bonner ($200), to revise the Refund Computation Ticket; Patricia Kizarian ($200), to generate complete Inquiry and Open Claims Reports monthly; Rosalyn Gluck ($200), to revise the Data Conversion Control Form.
¶The winning suggestions were selected from more than 250 entries. This level of participation in the ESP marked an all-time high for the suggestion program.

the landscape in search of food. There is also an abundance of predator animals such as the leopard, the wild dog, and the cheetah.

LANDSCAPE

Both the deserts and highlands can be found in Kenya. The forests that once covered the highlands have been decreasing due to clearing the land for crops. The desert area has little in the way of trees, but grazing grasses cover the desert floor.

Type the following report with paragraph headings. Double-space the report, and remember to turn off bold after typing the period in the paragraph heading.

REPORT 8

One-Page Report With Paragraph Headings

Science
Connections

FACT FILE

The crested caracara is also known as the Mexican eagle. The crested caracara is often seen in the Sonoran Desert perched on giant saguaro or organ pipe cactus. This bird typically does not hunt for food; rather it eats carrion instead.

BIRD WATCHING IS FUN

By Thomas Chastain

Bird watching is the most popular and fastest growing outdoor activity for people of all ages. Both young and old delight in observing all kinds of birds from the common backyard bird to the majestic eagle. No special equipment is needed for bird watching; it is easily the most inexpensive outdoor activity today.

Birds are identified in two ways, either by sight or by sound. Learning to identify birds is challenging, educational, and fun. There is also a sense of accomplishment when the identification is correct.

Identification by Sight. When a bird is perched in a tree, it can be identified by its silhouette, by its movement, or by its flight pattern. The color and special markings of a bird also help to identify it.

Identification by Sound. Identifying birds by sound is an additional aid to identification and also adds fun to bird watching. Sound is also a way for the blind to participate in this fun activity. Birds sing for two reasons: to find a mate and to mark their territory. Many birds look alike making positive identification difficult. Sound is one way to distinguish between look-alikes. Birds that look alike generally have very different songs. Knowing the song of a particular bird can aid in positive identification.

Take two 5-minute timings on the paragraphs. Note your speed and errors.

Goal: 38/5'/5e

7	Almost everything we use today is made with the help	11
8	of machines. Technology has caused a great change in how we	23
9	produce our goods. People first invent and then run the	34
10	machines. They also come up with new ideas for all of the	46
11	quality items that these machines can produce.	55
12	Human hands never examine some goods. In some cases,	66
13	all workers have to do is push a button. But, employees do	78
14	need to know which button to push so that they can get the	89
15	job done.	91
16	The producers in our country realize they must sell	102
17	their goods abroad to stay competitive. It is said that we	114
18	are the world's biggest exporter. Our country offers a big	126
19	market for producers in other countries as well. For that	137
20	reason, foreigners want to sell their goods here. There is	149
21	strong competition from foreign products. We are reported	161
22	also to have the most productive workers in the world. Our	173
23	product worth has improved because our employees are well-	184
24	trained, diverse, and skilled.	190

| 1 | 2 | 3 | 4 | 5 | 6 | 7 | 8 | 9 | 10 | 11 | 12SI 1.42

DESKTOP PUBLISHING APPLICATIONS

REPORT 68

Create the first page of a newsletter following these directions:

1. Set the top and bottom margins at 0.75 inch and the left and right margins at 1.2 inches.
2. Press ENTER until you reach approximately 2.5 inches, then move the cursor to the top of the page.
3. Create the nameplate, *THE REPORTER,* using colorful word/text art. Use Arial Black 36-point for the font.
4. Add a thick horizontal line from margin to margin under the nameplate.

LESSON 45

MINUTES OF MEETINGS

OBJECTIVES:

- Learn the rule for subject-verb agreement.
- Learn additional proofreaders' marks.
- Format minutes of meetings.

A. WARMUP

Type each line 2 times.

Speed
Accuracy
Language Link
Symbol

```
1 The Pilgrims were brave, but they did not know how to live.
2 Samoset and Squanto, a Wampanoag, helped the Pilgrims farm.
3 The principle behind her actions was accepted; she was not.
4 If ({X + Y} < {A - B}), then ({A - B} > {X + Y}), isn't it?
  | 1 | 2 | 3 | 4 | 5 | 6 | 7 | 8 | 9 | 10 | 11 | 12
```

LANGUAGE LINK

B. SUBJECT-VERB AGREEMENT

Study the rule and examples below. Then edit lines 5–8 by choosing the correct verb to agree with the subject in each sentence.

Rule 4: Use singular verbs and singular pronouns with singular subjects and plural verbs and plural pronouns with plural subjects.

Singular subject and verb:

>   *The <u>doctor advised</u> his patients to stay in bed.*
>
>   *<u>She called</u> her doctor to see if she should get a flu shot.*

Plural subject and verb:

>   *Several <u>doctors were</u> able to agree on the prognosis.*
>
>   *<u>They were</u> relieved that Dad's chest pains were gone.*

```
5 The computer prices (has/have) greatly fallen in March.
6 Ed's past sales experiences (has/have) aided his growth.
7 Dan's method (was/were) not good for organizing supplies.
8 The volunteers' hard work (is/are) appreciated by all.
```

LESSON 118 NEWSLETTERS

OBJECTIVES:

- Improve keyboarding skill.
- Type 38/5'/5e.
- Complete the first page of a two-page newsletter.

A. WARMUP

Type each line 2 times.

Speed
Accuracy
Language Link
Numbers

1 Both of the men may go soon if he pays them for their work.
2 Brown jars would prevent the mixture from freezing quickly.
3 At 2 p.m. this afternoon, my 21-year-old son located a job.
4 There are 539 students and 68 faculty members at this camp.
| 1 | 2 | 3 | 4 | 5 | 6 | 7 | 8 | 9 | 10 | 11 | 12

*inter*NET C O N N E C T I O N

Connect to the Internet. Search the Web for the latest information on voice recognition technology. Go to your nearest office supply or computer store to learn which types of voice recognition software are in stock. Report to the class on the technology involved in this software.

SKILLBUILDING

B. PREVIEW PRACTICE

Type each line 2 times as a preview to the timings that follow.

Accuracy
Speed

5 new realize quality foreign exporter Technology competition
6 know with help stay use the job all our of is in to do we a

C. DIAGNOSTIC PRACTICE: ALPHABET

Turn to the Diagnostic Practice: Alphabet routine on page SB1. Type one of the Pretest/Posttest paragraphs and identify any errors made. Then type the corresponding drill lines 2 times for each letter on which you made 2 or more errors and 1 time for each letter on which you made only 1 error. Finally, repeat the Pretest and compare your performance.

FORMATTING

D. PROOFREADERS' MARKS

More proofreaders' marks are illustrated below. Study these proofreaders' marks and learn what each mark means.

Proofreaders' Marks	Draft	Final Copy
Transpose	how you can	how can you
Single-space	ss ┌first line └second line	first line second line
Double-space	ds ┌first line second line	first line second line
Spell out	keep ① copy	keep one copy
Don't delete	our ~~two~~ copies	our two copies
Move left	⌐ She fell	She fell
Move right	⌐Th⌐e final	The final
Move as shown	The two pages (extra)	The extra two pages
Italic	*ital* Vogue magazine	*Vogue* magazine
underline	u/ℓ Vogue magazine	Vogue magazine

REPORT 66

Open Report 65 and add the following text in two balanced columns as a separate section beginning below the first section.

¶Accountability involves asking for help when necessary to produce the desired results. It means knowing how to delegate and making sure each person knows exactly what needs to be done. Accountability is not saying, "It was all my fault." It is looking calmly at what caused a problem and determining how to prevent it from happening again. Accountability is promising only what can be delivered. It means constantly sorting out priorities and taking responsibility for ongoing communication about the status of projects. It involves asking questions in order to understand the big picture and what is expected. It is also acknowledging work that is well done. If your boss doesn't practice accountability, you must still be accountable.

REPORT 67

Open Report 66 and revise it as follows:

1. Create a masthead using text/word art and Arial 36-point type. The name of the newsletter is *Professional Journal*.
2. Add a heavy line beneath the masthead.
3. Before you press ENTER, change the font to Times New Roman 12-point; then press ENTER once.
4. Type the volume and number at the left and the current date at the right. This newsletter is *Vol. 6, No. 3*.
5. Add a lighter line beneath the date line and leave some space between this line and the headline type.
6. Add to the second article the title *ACCOUNTABILITY* in Times New Roman 22-point.
7. Add a byline in Times New Roman 10-point. Use your name in the byline.
8. At the end of the first article, insert a graphic of people working in an office. Size the graphic appropriately, and keep the columns balanced.

The secretary of an organization is responsible for taking and keeping minutes of meetings. Minutes are the official record of what happened at a meeting. To format minutes:

1. Use default side and bottom margins and single spacing.
2. Leave an approximate 2-inch top margin (press ENTER 6 times).
3. Center and type the name of the committee or the company in all caps and bold.
4. Press ENTER 2 times, then center and type *Minutes of the Meeting* in initial caps 2 lines below the title.
5. Press ENTER 2 times, then center and type the date in initial caps.
6. Type the side headings in all caps and bold at the left margin. Leave a blank line above and below the side headings.
7. After the last section, press ENTER 2 times and begin the closing at the left margin.
8. Then press ENTER 4 times and type the secretary's name and title at the left margin.

WORD PROCESSING APPLICATIONS

REPORT 9
Minutes of Meeting

Type these minutes. Remember to leave a blank line before and after the side headings.

LINCOLN HIGH PARENT ORGANIZATION

Minutes of the Meeting

(Current Date)

ATTENDANCE

The monthly meeting of the Lincoln High School Parent Organization was held in the school library with Mario Palazollo presiding. The meeting was called to order at 7 p.m. Forty-seven parents attended. All officers were present.

APPROVAL OF MINUTES

The secretary read the minutes of the last meeting. They were approved as read. The treasurer reported that there was $790 in the treasury as of the end of the month.

```
5  We bought 15 pairs of socks, seven jackets, and 23 scarves.
6  On the third of July, he made plans for the July 4th parade.
7  At nine a.m. we delivered the $500 rent check to the owner.
8  On the sixth of December, we got ten tickets for January 2.
```

SKILLBUILDING

C. PACED PRACTICE

Turn to the Paced Practice routine beginning on page SB7. Take three 2-minute timings, starting at the point where you left off the last time.

FORMATTING

D. NEWSLETTERS

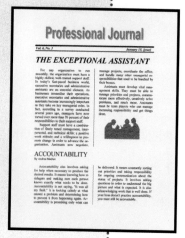

Newsletters are one of the best ways to communicate a variety of information to a wide range of people. A well-planned newsletter will be attractive and easy-to-read; it will use graphics to draw readers' attention and other DTP features to add interest and emphasize text. Most newsletters have these standard elements:

1. **Nameplate/masthead:** section located on the first page giving the name of the newsletter, the name of the organization, and possibly a logo. The nameplate sometimes includes a tagline that explains the newsletter's purpose.

2. **Date line:** line under the nameplate that includes the volume number, issue number, and the date of publication.

3. **Headline:** large-type title stating the subject of an article. (Some articles may also have a byline giving the name of the writer.)

4. **Body text**: the information in an article.

5. **Credits:** a list of the names and locations of the newsletter's staff.

ADJOURNMENT

There being no new business, the meeting was adjourned at 9 p.m.

Respectfully submitted,

Mary Upchurch, Secretary

Type these minutes. Remember to leave a blank line above and below the side headings.

REPORT 10
Minutes of Meeting

THE CHILDREN'S FOUNDATION
Minutes of the Meeting
November 16, {year}

CALL TO ORDER

The meeting was called to order by Elsie Russell at 11:30 a.m. in the Conference Room of the Foundation Building. The meeting was adjourned at 1 p.m. All members of the Board were present except Anne Laster.

UNFINISHED BUSINESS

The minutes of the October meeting were read and approved. The Treasurer's report was reviewed and accepted as submitted. The proposed budget was presented and discussed. There was agreement that the amount listed in from grants the budget as income should be should be decreased from $40,000 to $20,000. The proposed budget was approved as revised.

The Executive Director's report was read and accepted. Ms. Russell shared that we need to expend our Big Brother/Big Sister outreach program. Suggestions for accomplishing this were discussed.

NEW BUSINESS

Mrs. Costa suggested that there is a need to establish a publicity plan for the work being done by the foundation. This would help with fund-raising efforts.

Motion carried to accept 4 new prospective members as members of the Board of Directors--Richard Bates, Wanda Rudd, Florence Loucks, and Melvin Hearns.

Respectfully submitted,
Arlene Porter, Secretary

LESSON 117

DESKTOP PUBLISHING: NEWSLETTERS

OBJECTIVES:

- Improve keyboarding speed.
- Learn rules for typing numbers.
- Create a newsletter.

A. WARMUP

Type each line 2 times.

Speed
Accuracy
Language Link
Numbers/Symbols

1 If they pay me for the emblem, I may make it to the social.
2 Six big men quickly won over Jeff despite his greater size.
3 The students working on the project will resolve the issue.
4 With the 8% increase, Ed bought 29# of #134 and #56 for $7.

| 1 | 2 | 3 | 4 | 5 | 6 | 7 | 8 | 9 | 10 | 11 | 12

LANGUAGE LINK

B. NUMBER EXPRESSION

Study the rules and examples that follow. Then edit lines 5–8 to correct any errors in number usage.

Rule 30: Use figures for dates (use *st, d,* or *th* with a date only if it precedes the month) and all numbers if two or more related numbers both above and below ten are used in the same sentence.

Rule 31: Use figures for measurements (time, money, distance, weight, and percentage) and mixed numbers.

She ordered 2 printers, 3 keyboards, and 12 printer cartridges on May 1 at 10 a.m.

On the 4th of July, we spent $65 to buy 20 pounds of meat for the picnic, which was being held 3⅝ miles away.

LESSON 46

MULTIPAGE REPORTS

OBJECTIVES:

- Practice the top-row number keys.
- Learn word processing features.
- Format multipage reports.

Type each line 2 times.

Speed
Accuracy
Language Link
Numbers/Symbols

1 Check our lists to be sure that we are ready for this trip.
2 Zachariah analyzed the situation and queried the witnesses.
3 One box of staplers and tape dispensers was shipped Monday.
4 Our seat assignments are 30-41, 56-72, 88-109, and 111-114.
| 1 | 2 | 3 | 4 | 5 | 6 | 7 | 8 | 9 | 10 | 11 | 12

CULTURAL CONNECTIONS

A chemical engineer, Mae Jemison, became the first African American woman to go into space in 1992.

SKILLBUILDING

B. 30-SECOND TIMINGS

Take two 30-second timings on lines 5–6. Then take two 30-second timings on lines 7–8. Try to increase your speed on each timing.

5   Before you drive a car, adjust your seat and mirrors.   11
6 Lock the doors and buckle your seat belt. Drive with care.   23

7   Eating like a bird could mean drilling trees for ants   11
8 or diving in water for fish or probing mud for marine life.   23
| 1 | 2 | 3 | 4 | 5 | 6 | 7 | 8 | 9 | 10 | 11 | 12

¶Assistants must develop vital management skills. They must be able to manage priorities and projects, communicate effectively, creatively solve problems, and much more. Assistants must be team players who can manage increasing responsibility and get things done.

REPORT 65

Open Report 64 and revise it as follows:

1. Add the title *THE EXCEPTIONAL ASSISTANT* in a font that resembles a newspaper heading (for example, Times New Roman Bold Italic or Arial Black. Place it at the top of the page and increase the font size so that the title spans both columns.
2. Arrange the report into two balanced newspaper columns.
3. Add a line between the columns.

JOURNAL ENTRY

Make an entry in your journal or tickler file for the birthdays or anniversaries of your friends for the current month. Check them off as you plan the event and send a card or wish them a happy day.

Take a 1-minute timing on lines 9–12. Note your speed and errors.

Number diagnostic

```
 9        We serviced 11 phones at 2:22 p.m. in offices 3-13 at    11
10  4455--the headquarters of Outlook 77. They had not replaced    23
11  their equipment since 1988. It was not difficult for them       34
12  to spend $9,000--$1,660 more than they had estimated.           45
    | 1 | 2 | 3 | 4 | 5 | 6 | 7 | 8 | 9 | 10 | 11 | 12
```

D. PRACTICE

Type lines 13–22 one time. Then repeat any lines that stress the digits on which you made errors in the Pretest.

```
1   13  At 11 a.m. on 10-11-01, there were 11 ducks at 1011 Redbud.
2   14  Paul says that 1/2 of 2424 is 1212; now figure 1/2 of 1212.
3   15  Please get the names of players 33, 34, 38, 53, 73, and 93.
4   16  Lu made 14 copies of Chapter 4 in Volume 44, pages 424-443.
5   17  Timothy's number is 513-555-2505; Philip's is 513-555-5250.

6   18  The 6:15 train arrived at 6:56, so the 63 guests were late.
7   19  Tina is 7; Tia is 17; their mother is 37; her mother is 67.
8   20  Sue was born August 8, 1988, so write 8-8-1988 on the form.
9   21  This hat costs $9.99, but I have only $9. Do you have $.99?
0   22  He counts by tens: 10, 20, 30, 40, 50, 60, 70, 80, 90, 100.
```

E. POSTTEST

Repeat the Pretest. Compare your Posttest results with your Pretest results.

FORMATTING

F. MULTIPAGE REPORTS

To format a multipage report:

1. Use default side margins for all pages of the report.
2. Leave an approximate 2-inch top margin on page 1; leave a 1-inch top margin on continuing pages.
3. Leave an approximate 1-inch bottom margin on all pages. A soft page break will be inserted automatically at the bottom of each page as you type the report.
4. Turn on widow/orphan protection.
5. Do not number the first page. However, number all continuing pages at the top right.

FORMATTING

D. COLUMNS

In desktop publishing, columns are often used to create documents such as brochures and newsletters. Arranging text in columns often makes the text easier to read and provides more visual interest. In addition, the length and width of columns can be varied and lines and boxes can be added to columns.

E. SOFTWARE FEATURES

STUDENT MANUAL
Columns

Study Lesson 116 in your student manual. Complete all the practice activities while at your computer. Then complete the jobs that follow.

DESKTOP PUBLISHING APPLICATIONS

REPORT 64

Single-space the following copy. Begin at the top margin, and indent paragraphs 0.5 inch. Do not leave a blank line between paragraphs.

¶For any organization to run smoothly, the organization must have a highly skilled, well-trained support staff. In today's fast-paced business world, executive secretaries and administrative assistants are an essential element. As businesses streamline their operations, executive secretaries and administrative assistants become increasingly important as they take on key managerial roles. In fact, according to a survey conducted several years ago, managers have now turned over more than 70 percent of their responsibilities to their support staff.
¶Support staff must have a combination of finely tuned management, interpersonal, and technical skills; a positive work attitude; and a willingness to promote change in order to advance the organization. Assistants now negotiate, manage projects, coordinate the office, and handle many other managerial responsibilities that used to be handled by their bosses.

STUDENT MANUAL

Page Breaks   Page Numbering
Widow/Orphan Control

Study Lesson 46 in your student manual. Complete all the practice activities while at your computer. Then complete the following jobs.

WORD PROCESSING APPLICATIONS

REPORT 11

Multipage
Report

Social Studies
Connections

Type the following multipage report with side and paragraph headings. Remember to turn on widow/orphan protection.

A VISIT TO A JAPANESE HOME

By Matthew Stedman

Japan is one of the most urbanized nations in Asia. The use of modern equipment and facilities has changed the traditional way of life. While most Japanese people live in the city, over one-fourth of the population still live in the countryside where the traditional way of life still prevails.

CITY LIFE

Most city dwellers live in high-rise apartments with modern conveniences such as electric appliances and central heat. Many Japanese city dwellers use public bath houses, while others prefer the privacy of their own baths. City life in Japan is much like that of the western world with mass transit, restaurants, entertainment, and shopping located close by.

LESSON 116 COLUMNS

OBJECTIVES:

- Improve keyboarding skill.
- Learn to format text in columns.

A. WARMUP

Type each line 2 times.

Speed
Accuracy
Language Link
Numbers

1 Sue is to pay the man to fix the bicycle for the six girls.
2 Pete quickly froze the egg mixtures in five old brown jars.
3 One of the students rides the bus all the way from Fordham.
4 The 10 men lived 29 days at 3847 Bluff Way and 5 days here.

| 1 | 2 | 3 | 4 | 5 | 6 | 7 | 8 | 9 | 10 | 11 | 12

SKILLBUILDING

B. 30-SECOND TIMINGS

Take two 30-second timings on lines 5–6. Then take two 30-second timings on lines 7–8. Try to increase your speed on each timing.

5   Ida will go to the movie with Jay and take her small   11
6 dog to a vet today. Tom will also be there with his dog.   22

7   We had the box of new books in our office and got the   11
8 new pens before he did. My boss gave us a ride to the city.   23

| 1 | 2 | 3 | 4 | 5 | 6 | 7 | 8 | 9 | 10 | 11 | 12

C. DIAGNOSTIC PRACTICE: ALPHABET

Turn to the Diagnostic Practice: Alphabet routine on page SB1. Type one of the Pretest/Posttest paragraphs and identify any errors made. Then type the corresponding drill lines 2 times for each letter on which you made 2 or more errors and 1 time for each number on which you made only 1 error. Finally, repeat the same Pretest paragraph and compare your performance.

COUNTRY LIFE

The countryside dwellers of Japan live quite differently than city dwellers. They live in small houses built out of bamboo. Since Japan is prone to earthquakes, these bamboo structures hold up better in earthquakes than heavier structures.

Rooms in the House. Traditional houses generally have three to four rooms that serve as both living and sleeping quarters. A kitchen is also part of the house but does not serve as the living or sleeping quarters. The kitchen has a stove made of clay or brick and is heated with straw. In some homes the stoves are heated with compressed gas.

Floor Coverings. The floor of Japanese homes is covered with woven straw mats that measure six feet by three feet. The mats are woven by hand by the women of the house, typically the mother and grandmother. In order to keep the mats clean, they remove their shoes before entering the house.

Furniture. The furniture found in most traditional homes consists of little in the way of decoration with the exception of some embellished parchment doors and flower arrangements.

Outside the House. The Japanese love to grow flowers, and their homes are usually surrounded by flowering plants. They are avid gardeners and are masters at creating beautiful gardens with ponds and ornate statues.

CULTURAL CONNECTIONS

Kangi is a Japanese system of writing that uses characters that have been adapted from Chinese writing. The writing is so beautiful it is considered a kind of art. Learning to use this system takes many years of practice.

4. Adjust the size of the word/text art so that it extends from the top margin to the bottom margin of the page.
5. Insert a text box below the clip art and horizontally center it.
6. Select an attractive, easy-to-read font style and size; then type the copy as illustrated in the text box horizontally centered, breaking the lines as shown. Type the graduate's name in bold in a slightly larger type size. Double-space before and after the graduate's name and between the separate sections (see the illustration).
7. If you have additional clip art available, you may want to add it to the bottom of the invitation.
8. Size the box so that the bottom aligns evenly with the text on the right and left. If necessary, adjust the font style and/or size to fit all of the text in the box.

You are cordially invited
to join family and friends
in a celebration to honor
our graduate
Faye Marie Themus

Date: Sunday, June 2, {year}
Time: 5 p.m. to 8 p.m.
Place: 21337 Kenwyck Circle
West Columbia, SC 29170

Please respond before May 22.
Call 803-555-3219.

REPORT 63

Design an invitation to your own birthday party, which will be held at your house.

FACT FILE

Ethical employees always apply the rules of proper business etiquette and always treat their colleagues and customers with respect.

LESSON 47 REVIEW

OBJECTIVES:

- Learn the rules for correct subject-verb agreement.
- Review reports and minutes of meetings.
- Type 33/3′/5e.

A. WARMUP

Type each line 2 times.

Speed
Accuracy
Language Link
Technique

```
1 The Sun is center of our solar system and our closest star.
2 The Aztecs built Tenochtitlan on an island in Lake Texcoco.
3 The seas of Australia include the Tasman Sea and Coral Sea.
4 Ada Bob Cam Don Evi Fay Gil Hal Ian Joy Kay Lon Mya Nan Ola
```

| 1 | 2 | 3 | 4 | 5 | 6 | 7 | 8 | 9 | 10 | 11 | 12

LANGUAGE LINK

B. SUBJECT/VERB AGREEMENT

Study the rule and examples below. Then edit lines 5–8 by choosing the correct verb for subject/verb agreement.

Rule 5: The subject *the number* takes a singular verb; *a number* takes a plural verb.

> *The number of children riding in the bus <u>was</u> minimal.*
>
> *The number of dogs and cats <u>is</u> astronomical.*
>
> *A number of pages <u>were</u> missing from the file.*
>
> *A number of women <u>were</u> to meet for lunch.*

```
5 A number of students in the class (is/are) working on a
  project.
6 The number of men attending the convention (was/were) greater
  than expected.
7 The number of cars to be parked (exceeds/exceed) the number of
  spaces available.
8 A number of workers (was/were) waiting for word about that.
```

Take two 5-minute timings. Note your speed and errors.

Goal: 38/5'/5e

Science
Connections

```
10        Many leaves change colors in the fall. The two main    11
11  types of trees are evergreens and broadleafs. Evergreen      22
12  trees have green needles all year round. The needles form a  34
13  quality heavy waxy cover that protects them. They also have   46
14  natural antifreeze inside that will usually protect them.     57
15        Broadleaf trees are just as the name implies. These    68
16  trees have leaves that are flat and wide. They do not have    80
17  a wax covering or natural antifreeze that will protect them   92
18  from being zapped by winter's cold. When the weather gets     103
19  cold enough and the leaves die, they usually fall off.        114
20        Some broadleaf trees are considered to be evergreens,   125
21  such as holly. They are green all year. In warmer areas,      136
22  some broadleaf trees do not turn colors. Those trees that     148
23  turn beautiful fall colors are where the weather gets below   160
24  freezing. Usually, they turn fall colors just before the      171
25  leaves fall off the trees. The usual season to see fall       182
26  foliage is September through October.                         190
```

| 1 | 2 | 3 | 4 | 5 | 6 | 7 | 8 | 9 | 10 | 11 | 12 SI 1.40

DESKTOP PUBLISHING APPLICATIONS

REPORT 62
Invitation

Follow these steps to create an invitation similar to the one in the illustration on the next page:

1. Select a piece of clip art that has something to do with either graduation or a celebration.
2. Adjust the size of the clip art to form a 2.5-inch square, and horizontally center it on the page.
3. Using word/text art and an attractive font set for 30 or 32 points, arrange the words *GRADUATION TIME!* vertically down the left side of the page. Insert *CELE-BRATION TIME!* vertically down the right side of the page.

SKILLBUILDING

C. PREVIEW PRACTICE

Type each line 2 times as a preview to the timings that follow.

9 an Vail quickly amazing however wrought telegraph seventeen
10 inventing artist dashes short text long code dots sent that

D. 3-MINUTE TIMINGS

Take two 3-minute timings on the paragraphs. Note your speed and errors.

Goal: 33/3′/5e

11   Samuel Morse was an artist. Today, however, he is   10
12 known not for his major works of art but for inventing   21
13 the telegraph and the code it uses. With the help of his   33
14 friend, Alfred Vail, Morse made up a code of dashes and   44
15 dots that stood for numbers and letters. Text could be   55
16 sent with this Morse Code by using long and short signals.   66
17   Seventeen years before the Civil War began, Morse   77
18 tapped out his first message, "What hath God wrought."   88
19 It was quickly received an amazing thirty-five miles away.   99

| 1 | 2 | 3 | 4 | 5 | 6 | 7 | 8 | 9 | 10 | 11 | 12 SI 1.34

Social Studies ↑

Connections

FACT FILE

During the past several decades, engineers have created more advanced technology than at any other time in history.

LESSON 115

DESIGNING AN INVITATION

OBJECTIVES:

- Compose at the keyboard.
- Type 38/5'/5e.
- Create a party invitation.

A. WARMUP

Type each line 2 times.

Speed
Accuracy
Language Link
Symbols

1 The profit she got for the corn and hay may make them rich.
2 Jim saw five dozen extra quilts by peeking under the truck.
3 The cost is one's own even if somebody's hat was left here.
4 Mr. Edward C. Jones joined Smith & Smythe, Inc., last June.

LANGUAGE LINK

B. COMPOSING AT THE KEYBOARD

Choose one of the following topics and compose a short, three-paragraph report. Use the topic as the report title.

5 My Most Embarrassing Moment
6 My Favorite Relative
7 My Favorite Memory

SKILLBUILDING

C. PREVIEW PRACTICE

Type each line 2 times as a preview to the 5-minute timings that follow.

8 waxy zapped needles quality September antifreeze broadleafs
9 enough leaves change types green where that name all the to

REPORT 12

One-Page Report With Numbered List

Remember to double-space the report.

TELEPHONE TECHNIQUES FOR THE JOB

When you answer the telephone, remember that you represent the company. Make the first impression of your business a good one by following these techniques:

1. Greet the caller by identifying your company and yourself. Ask how you may assist or direct the call.
2. Use a friendly tone, speak clearly and distinctly, and avoid slang or mumbling.
3. Listen carefully to be sure you understand everything the caller is saying.
4. Be professional if you have to place a caller on hold while you get files or if you need to transfer the call to someone else.
5. If you place a caller on hold, periodically return to the caller and ask if he or she wishes to continue holding, to speak with someone else, or to leave a message.
6. Offer to take a message or have someone return the phone call.
7. Record messages accurately. Include the caller's name and telephone number and any other important information such as when they called and why. Repeat the telephone number to be sure you wrote it correctly.
8. Close the call by expressing appreciation to the caller. Be sure you and the caller agree on what action is to be taken. Then say goodbye.

REPORT 13

Minutes of Meeting

Remember to use the BACKSPACE key to delete one or a few characters.

PLANNING COMMITTEE

Minutes of *the* Meeting
November 13, {year}
ATTENDENCE
The Planning Committee met on (Nov.) 13, {year}, at the Board Room of the Douglas County Courthouse. Members present were Ronald Horton, Lakisha Lopez, Tonnetta McCoy, Chris Ngyen, Martha Ristau, and Steve Vanderhoff. Ronald Horton, chairperson, called the meeting to order at 7:15 p.m.

CERTIFICATE OF PROFICIENCY

This certifies that

Jonathan Riley

has successfully completed the requirements of the
Level 1 Desktop Publishing Training
offered by
Rodgers Career Technical Center

_____
RCTC Training Specialist

_____
Date

CULTURAL CONNECTIONS

Interview customs may vary from country to country. Select someone from another country to interview about the types of questions a prospective employee is asked by an interviewer.

UNFINISHED BUSINESS

Arbor Mall Station construction began on Nov. 10. Martha Ristau moved that land parcels on the east side of the construction site be auctioned to prospective new businesses, since those parcels are zoned E-5. Chris Ngyen seconded the motion. After a lengthy discussion, the motion was passed unanimously.

NEW BUSINESS

Kendall Construction Company presented a blue print for developing the land parcels across Douglas boulevard from Arbor Station Mall. Mr. Kevin O'Rourke from Kendall Construction Company proposed the building of several "big box" stores in those parcels. After several questions arose concerning the environmental impact of developing these parcels, a motion was made to table a vote until the corps of Engineers could conduct land impact studies on the area. *This item will be discussed at the December meeting.*

ADJOURNMENT

The meeting was adjourned at 9:30 p.m. The next meeting for December 10 is scheduled {year}, in the Conference Room at Douglas County High School. Respectfully submitted, J. D. Harper, Secretary

REPORT 14

Two-Page Report With Paragraph Headings

CHOOSING THE RIGHT COLLEGE
By Carl Klees

Choosing a college is one of the big decisions a student makes in life. Careful planning and thoughtful consideration can make this decision easier for you.

Match Your Interests. Finding a college that matches your interests is an important factor in your choice. Several colleges, not just one, can offer you an opportunity to match your interests with those of other students. Choosing a college just because it's popular or because your parents went there could result in the loss of time spent at a college that best suits your needs.

9 is exist message selection computer comparison presentation
10 are common variety software referred supported relationship
11 it's because writers although choosing recognize frequently
12 pie format written graphic excellent information understand

Speed

13 reader sliced number chart their order items they most line
14 manner pieces change kinds graph looks right will used work
15 better reveal period today three often makes that when want
16 support report choice print forms parts like this show over

D. POSTTEST

Repeat the Pretest. Compare your Posttest results with your Pretest results.

DESKTOP PUBLISHING APPLICATIONS

REPORT 61
Certificate

Create a certificate similar to the illustration on the next page.

1. Change your page orientation to landscape (11 × 8½ inches).
2. Vertically center the page.
3. Using text/word art, select a slightly curved style of type and an interesting font. Change the type size to 40-point, and center and type the certificate title.
4. Center and type the text of the certificate using a script font set at 24 points. Type the name of the student in a heavier but complementary 24-point font.
5. Below the certificate title, insert a graphic that relates to academic achievement, such as the seal in the illustration.
6. Change to 12-point type, and create a table for the signature and date line at least 1 inch below the last line of the text.
7. Type the signer's title, *RCTC Training Specialist,* beneath the signature line, and type the word *Date* beneath the date line.

Academic Programs. The offering of specific academic programs is one of the most important reasons for choosing a college. Some colleges specialize in particular majors while others offer a broad range of majors. Determine what your academic needs are in order to aid your decision.

Size. Consider the size of the college when making your decision. Perhaps you like small classes where you know the professor and other classmates rather than classes held in lecture hall situations with hundreds of other students. Many people do better in small situations as opposed to large ones.

Extracurricular Activities. The extracurricular offerings of a college deserve a special look. Consider whether the college offers activities that you enjoy and whether these activities are available to people of your skill level. Also determine whether these activities will interfere with your class and study obligations. The activities offered outside the college in the surrounding community should also be considered.

Financial Considerations. Cost, of course, is an important consideration in college choice. Public versus private school will impact cost as will attending school in state or out of state. Tuition for out-of-state students is double or triple the cost of in-state students.

Plan a Visit. Once you have narrowed the choice down to a few colleges, plan to visit the campus. A visit to the campus can give you a better picture of the college, the students, the community, and whether the overall picture suits you. The earlier you begin considering colleges, the more time you will have to visit them.

LESSON 114 DESIGNING A CERTIFICATE

OBJECTIVES:

- Improve keyboarding skill.
- Design a certificate.

A. WARMUP

Type each line 2 times.

Speed
Accuracy
Language Link
Numbers/Symbols

1 When did he go to the city and pay them for the world maps?
2 Five brown ibexes quickly zipped up among the jagged rocks.
3 My best friend, Carlene, liked the new soft leather saddle.
4 Ronda knew that 3/4 of $84 = $63 and that 30% of $90 = $27.
| 1 | 2 | 3 | 4 | 5 | 6 | 7 | 8 | 9 | 10 | 11 | 12

FACT FILE

The word *pandemonium* is used to refer to a situation that is chaotic or in a state of uproar.

SKILLBUILDING

B. PRETEST

Take a 1-minute timing on the paragraph. Note your speed and errors.

5   Information that is presented in a graph or a chart is   11
6 frequently referred to as graphics. Many writers like this   23
7 manner of presentation because they recognize that a reader   35
8 will best understand a message when it includes graphics.   46
| 1 | 2 | 3 | 4 | 5 | 6 | 7 | 8 | 9 | 10 | 11 | 12

C. PRACTICE

In the chart below find the number of errors you made on the Pretest. Then type each of the designated drill lines 2 times.

Pretest Errors	0–1	2	3	4+
Drill Lines	12–16	11–15	10–14	9–13

LESSON 48   PERSONAL BUSINESS LETTERS

OBJECTIVES:

- Practice the top-row number keys.
- Learn word processing features.
- Format personal-business letters.

A. WARMUP

Type each line 2 times.

Speed
Accuracy
Language Link
Numbers/Symbols

1 Check our lists to be sure that we are ready for this trip.
2 Zachariah analyzed the situation and queried the witnesses.
3 A number of students were excused from their science class.
4 Buy 2# of pears (#1 Bartlett*) @ $1.98 at the Fruit & More.

FACT FILE

Engineers John Pierce and Harold Rosen designed successful communication satellites in the 1960s. Because of their developments, we can talk on the phone and watch television beamed up to satellites from places far away.

SKILLBUILDING

B. 30-SECOND OK TIMINGS

Take two 30-second OK (error-free) timings on lines 5–6. Then take two 30-second OK timings on lines 7–8. Goal: no errors.

5	Extend a burst of energy to your fingers as you force	11
6	them to zoom over the keys. Enjoy the rush of rapid typing.	23
7	People who routinely succeed squeeze value out of each	11
8	minute. They judge the best way to do a task and act on it.	23

6. Type the information into the text box as follows: Use Times New Roman 36-point for the first line, and insert a space between the letters; change to italic for the second line.
7. Press ENTER 2 times, change the font size to 24-point, and type the next sentence.
8. Press ENTER 2 times, type *HSK* in bold (no italic), then complete the rest of the sentence in italic (no bold).
9. Press ENTER 2 times and type the next line.
10. Press ENTER 2 times and center and type the Internet address in regular type.
11. Add a blank line between each line of text at the left of the text box, and position the text box so that the copy appears to be vertically centered beside the box.
12. Create another text box at the lower left of the page, and insert the text in Times New Roman 10-point. Position the box so that the bottom of both boxes align. The text for the text box is Member of Retail Career Association.

REPORT 60

Open Report 59 and make the following changes:

1. Change the color of the title to red, and add a shadow.
2. Change the text at the left of the text box to bold.
3. Add blue shading to the text box at the right.
4. Add a shadow to the first two lines of text in the text box at the right.

*inter*NET CONNECTION

The Internet is an excellent source of information and can be used to locate people and businesses. Enter the following URL to locate information about a business in a particular city: http://yp.yahoo.com

Take a 1-minute timing on lines 9–12. Note your speed and errors.

Social Studies
Connections

9	Wyoming was the first state to give women the right to	11
10	vote. The other states in the West joined the cause in the	23
11	next two decades. After New York and Illinois gave women	34
12	the right to vote, Congress began to debate the issue.	45

| 1 | 2 | 3 | 4 | 5 | 6 | 7 | 8 | 9 | 10 | 11 | 12

D. PRACTICE

Type each line 2 times.

Build speed on repeated word patterns.

```
13  road toad load loam loan moan moat goat coat coal cowl cows
14  vows bows rows tows tons tone zone cone come comb tomb bomb

15  quip quit suit suet sued sues cues cued coed toed toes does
16  dogs bogs cogs logs lots loss boss moss most cost lost post

17  noon soon loon boon boot soot spot spat scat swat swam swim
18  swum scum scup scud stud stun shun shin chin thin then them

19  Tex. text test rest west lest lost last mast past fast cast
20  case vase base bask back tack pack hack hark mark dark dart

21  gaze haze faze daze raze race pace pate gate bate bade wade
22  ware hare mare more mode rode rote vote tote tope rope hope

23  Dora Lora Lara Mara Myra Myla Nyla Nola Nona Rona Rena Zena
24  Bill Will Wilt Walt Dalt Dale Kale Kole Cole Colt Cort Cory
```

E. POSTTEST

Repeat the Pretest. Compare your Posttest results with your Pretest results.

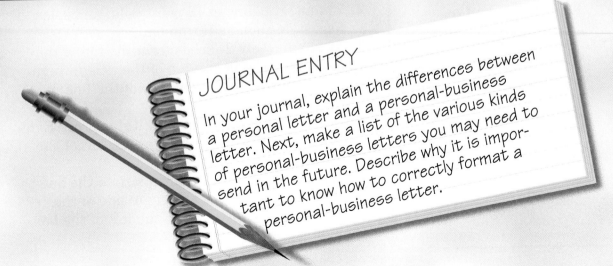

JOURNAL ENTRY

In your journal, explain the differences between a personal letter and a personal-business letter. Next, make a list of the various kinds of personal-business letters you may need to send in the future. Describe why it is important to know how to correctly format a personal-business letter.

5 He will therefore, take all precautions before proceeding.
6 Can she however be certain that all the reports are there?
7 I would under most circumstances approve the merger today.
8 Hillary is as you can see the perfect candidate for them.

SKILLBUILDING

C. 30-Second OK Timings

Take two 30-second OK (error-free) timings on lines 9–10. Then take two 30-second OK timings on lines 11–12. Goal: no errors.

9 Paula reviewed the subject before giving Raylynn and   11
10 Monte a quiz and quietly reviewed the next game with Buzz. 22

11 Even with all kinds of gripes, Maxine had a zest for   11
12 quiet living; Zeke examined all work and rejected most all. 22

| 1 | 2 | 3 | 4 | 5 | 6 | 7 | 8 | 9 | 10 | 11 | 12

DESKTOP PUBLISHING APPLICATIONS

REPORT 59

Create the flyer in the illustration following these steps:

1. At the top right of a page, insert a graphic element similar to the one shown in the illustration.
2. Change the font to 48-point bold, and select a font style such as Garamond.
3. Approximately 2 inches from the top of the page, type the beginning of the title in regular type; type the remainder of the line in italic.
4. Change the font to 28-point italic, press ENTER 3 times, and type the copy at the left of the page with initial caps.
5. Create a text box similar in size to the one shown, position it at the right side of the page, and set the wrap to the left of the box.

F. PERSONAL-BUSINESS LETTERS

Alternate
Block Style
Personal-Business

The writer's address is before the date, not after the signature.

To format a personal-business letter in alternate block style:

1. Type all lines beginning at the left margin.
2. Center the letter vertically, then type the writer's address. Type the date.
3-6. Follow Steps 3 to 6 as shown at the right.
7. Press Enter 4 times and type the writer's name. Do not type the address.

A letter from an individual to a business is called a personal-business letter. A personal-business letter should contain these parts:

Date Line. The month, day, and year the letter is typed.

Inside Address. The name and address of the person to whom the letter is being sent.

Salutation. An opening greeting such as *Dear Ms. Jones.*

Body. The text of the letter.

Complimentary Closing. A closing to the letter such as *Sincerely* or *Yours truly.*

Signature. The writer's signature.

Writer's Identification. The writer's typed name and address.

To format a personal-business letter in block style:

1. Type all lines beginning at the left margin.
2. Center the letter vertically, then type the date.
3. After the date, press ENTER 4 times and type the inside address. Leave 1 space between the state and the ZIP code.
4. After the inside address, press ENTER 2 times and type the salutation.
5. Press ENTER 2 times and begin the body of the letter. Single-space the body, but press ENTER 2 times between paragraphs.
6. After the last paragraph, press ENTER 2 times and type the complimentary closing.
7. Press ENTER 4 times and type the writer's name and address.

G. SOFTWARE FEATURES

STUDENT MANUAL

Center Page   Date Insert

Study Lesson 48 in your student manual. Complete all the practice activities while at your computer. Then complete the following jobs.

LESSON 113

DESKTOP PUBLISHING DESIGNS: FLYERS

OBJECTIVES:

- Improve keyboarding skill.
- Learn comma usage.
- Prepare documents using DTP features.

A. WARMUP

Type each line 2 times.

Speed
Accuracy
Language Link
Numbers/Symbols

```
1 The man got a snap of an authentic whale by the big island.
2 I quickly explained that few big jobs involve many hazards.
3 The twins' book had big print and the book's cover was red.
4 Ed had 789 birds there in 1982; but by 1992 there were 823.
  | 1 | 2 | 3 | 4 | 5 | 6 | 7 | 8 | 9 | 10 | 11 | 12
```

LANGUAGE LINK

B. COMMA USAGE

Study the rule and the examples below. Then edit lines 5–8 to correct any errors in comma usage.

Rule 29:

Use a comma *before* and *after* a nonessential expression. Nonessential expressions include words, phrases, or clauses that are not necessary for the meaning of a sentence. Names in direct address are also considered nonessential. Use one comma if a nonessential element appears at the end or at the beginning of a sentence.

> *We are willing, as you know, to renegotiate the offer.*
>
> *Therefore, the lease will be terminated next Thursday.*
>
> *Lisa requested, however, that she retain her position.*
>
> *You will be notified, Mr. Samuel, of our new location.*

LETTER 1
Block Style
Personal-Business

Type the following letter in block style. Vertically center the letter, and insert the current date. Use standard punctuation: a colon after the salutation and a comma after the complimentary closing.

2314 Oak Street
Scottsdale, AZ 85257
(Current Date)

Mrs. Joan L. Locke
2356 North Central Avenue
Phoenix, AZ 85004

Dear Mrs. Locke:

Thank you for helping our sponsor by assisting on our trip to Flagstaff last week. It was a pleasure to meet you and hear about the various trips you have made in southwestern United States. As you know, we just moved to Arizona. It's my intention to learn about and see more of my new state.

I was particularly interested in Flagstaff and its importance as a vacation area. The presentation by the Chamber of Commerce was very worthwhile. It surprised me to learn that skiing is one of Flagstaff's top winter tourist attractions. No one would think that skiers would come from such states as California, New Mexico, or Texas to ski in Arizona. I would have thought it was too warm in Arizona for such a winter sport.

My parents and I plan to go to the Grand Canyon this coming summer; I told them that Flagstaff was the gateway to the Canyon. They indicated to me that my grandparents had taken a train to Flagstaff and then, taken a bus to the Canyon. I hope I can do something similar.

Thanks again for helping us on our trip.

Sincerely yours,

Ms. Alice L. L'Huillier

Alternate
Block Style
Personal-Business

The writer's address is before the date, not after the signature.
   Type the writer's address before the date.
   Do not type the address after the sender's name.

(Current Date)

Mrs. Joan L. Locke
2356 North Central Avenue
Phoenix, AZ 85004

Dear Mrs. Locke:

Thank you for helping our sponsor by assisting on our trip to Flagstaff last week. It was a pleasure to meet you and hear about the various trips you have made in southwestern United States. As you know, we just moved to Arizona. It's my intention to learn about and see more of my new state.

I was particularly interested in Flagstaff and its importance as a vacation area. The presentation by the Chamber of Commerce was very worthwhile. It surprised me to learn that skiing is one of Flagstaff's top winter tourist attractions. No one would think that skiers would come from such states as California, New Mexico, or Texas to ski in Arizona. I would have thought it was too warm in Arizona for such a winter sport.

My parents and I plan to go to the Grand Canyon this coming summer; I told them that Flagstaff was the gateway to the Canyon. They indicated to me that my grandparents had taken a train to Flagstaff and then, taken a bus to the Canyon. I hope I can do something similar.

Thanks again for helping us on our trip.

Sincerely yours,

Ms. Alice L. L'Huillier
2314 Oak Street
Scottsdale, AZ 85257

REPORT 58
Survey Form

Create a customer survey form similar to the one shown below.

1. Use Times New Roman 36-point italic with a shadow for the title.
2. Choose an appropriate graphic for the upper right corner of the page.
3. Use Times New Roman 16-point for the remaining text except for the bottom box.
4. Add a drop cap to the first line.
5. Draw red check boxes that are large enough to write a number from 1 to 5 inside.
6. Leave an appropriate amount of space between the parts of the form.
7. Add a light shading to the bottom box and type the text in red Times New Roman 36-point italic bold.

What do you think?

Please rate our business today.

Excellent = 5   Poor = 1

You may use any number from 1 through 5. The higher the number, the more positive the rating. Use the boxes at the left to fill in your rating.

☐ How would you rate our overall service today?

☐ How friendly were our employees?

☐ Please rate the appearance of the store.

What can we do to make your next visit better?

_____

_____

Please write the names of any employees you feel were especially helpful to you.

_____

_____

Thank you for your help.

LETTER 2
Block Style
Personal-Business

Alternate
Block Style
Personal-Business

To prepare this personal-business letter in alternate block style, type the writer's address before the date.

Do not type the address after the sender's name.

Refer to pages 169–170, if needed.

Type the following letter in block style. The slash marks in the inside address and closing lines indicate line endings. Do not type the slashes.

The ¶ symbol indicates the start of a new paragraph. Do not indent a new paragraph. However, leave one blank line before beginning a new paragraph.

Current Date / Ms. Caroline Davis / 5200 Roselawn Avenue / Topeka, KS 67218 / Dear Ms. Davis: /

¶Your presentation at the Kentwood Business Club was one of the most enjoyable our club has ever had.

¶It is always a pleasure to have a professional like you speak on ways a graduate can seek a job. The follow-up question-and-answer period as well as your handouts were well received.

¶On the advice of our teacher, our accounting class has decided that one way we can follow up your presentation is to bring to class employment ads, and then write letters of application. Already the class has prepared twelve letters, which were sent to our teacher as the employer; thirteen more are all ready to be signed.

¶I believe this is one of the most interesting projects I have ever been assigned. Members of the class have learned to critique the letters without feeling self-conscious about their work.

¶Would you consider reviewing some of our letters and advise us which you think are the best? We hope you will say, "yes!" I will call you next Monday to discuss the details. Sincerely yours, / Brian K. Long / 347 Main Street / Topeka, KS 67209

FACT FILE

Virtual reality is the creation of images and tactile sensations by means of a computer, producing the illusion of reality. Images are often projected onto special goggles to strengthen the illusion.

LESSON 112

DESKTOP PUBLISHING REVIEW

OBJECTIVES:
- Improve keyboarding skill.
- Practice using desktop publishing features.

A. WARMUP

Type each line 2 times.

Speed
Accuracy
Language Link
Numbers/Symbols

1 The six forms she got from the firm may do for the problem.
2 Jack typed four dozen requisitions for hollow moving boxes.
3 He was always trying to be a helpful, courteous individual.
4 Type the problems: 100 - 74 = 26; 86 + 17 = 103; 4 - 3 = 1.
| 1 | 2 | 3 | 4 | 5 | 6 | 7 | 8 | 9 | 10 | 11 | 12

SKILLBUILDING

B. 30-SECOND TIMINGS

Take two 30-second timings on lines 5–6. Then take two 30-second timings on lines 7–8. Try to increase your speed on each timing.

5   Things seem to happen right for some people; they know   11
6 when a good chance comes along and can quickly seize it.   22

7   They are quick to get an exact vision of how this luck   11
8 can work for them; it may make their lives very different.   22
| 1 | 2 | 3 | 4 | 5 | 6 | 7 | 8 | 9 | 10 | 11 | 12

LESSON 49

REINFORCEMENT

OBJECTIVES:

- Practice typing with continuity.
- Strengthen skill in formatting personal-business letters.

A. WARMUP

Type each line 2 times.

Speed
Accuracy
Language Link
Numbers

1 If you want to be the best typist, then practice correctly.
2 Xavier is amazed by the two jazz artists' expert qualities.
3 The number of students involved in intramural sports is up.
4 We are scheduled for April 29, May 14, June 30, and July 7.
| 1 | 2 | 3 | 4 | 5 | 6 | 7 | 8 | 9 | 10 | 11 | 12

SKILLBUILDING

B. TECHNIQUE TIMINGS

Take two 30-second timings on each line. Focus on the technique at the left.

Type with continuity.

5 We would find life very different in a world without trees.
6 Trees provide us food, fuel, fibers, lumber, and chemicals.
7 Trees keep our soil from eroding and provide us windbreaks.
8 Even dead trees are useful by providing homes for wildlife.
| 1 | 2 | 3 | 4 | 5 | 6 | 7 | 8 | 9 | 10 | 11 | 12

Science
Connections

REPORT 57

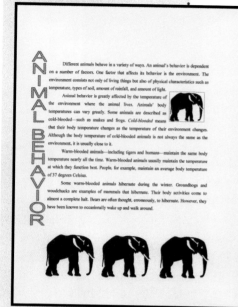

Open Report 51 and make the following changes:

1. Change the title to a vertical style at the left of the page.
2. Position the vertical type so that it extends from the top of the text to the bottom of the text.
3. Change the color of the type to green.
4. Move the graphic at the beginning of the first paragraph to the end of that same paragraph.
5. Change the wrap so that the text wraps to the left.
6. Move the graphic at the end of the last paragraph to just below the vertical text.
7. Adjust the size of the graphic and copy and paste it so that three of them extend from the left margin to the right margin.

FACT FILE

Hieroglyphics were used by the ancient Egyptians as a type of communication in pictorial characters. How do they compare with logos?

Type each line 2 times. Concentrate on keeping your eyes on the copy.

9 A proficient secretary manipulates microcomputers expertly.
10 Authorized institutions substitute experimental techniques.
11 The Mississippi and Missouri Rivers provide transportation.
12 Agricultural goods surpass manufactured industrial gadgets.

D. PACED PRACTICE

Turn to the Paced Practice routine beginning on page SB7. Take three 2-minute timings, starting at the point where you left off the last time.

WORD PROCESSING APPLICATIONS

LETTER 3
Block Style
Personal-Business

Alternate
Block Style
Personal-Business

To prepare this personal-business letter in alternate block style, type the writer's address before the date.

Do not type the address after the sender's name.

Refer to pages 169–170, if needed.

Type this letter in block style with standard punctuation. Insert the current date.

(Current Date) / Ms. Louise Feigleson / Personnel Director / Smith and Kovacs Agency / 7858 High Street / Columbus, OH 43216 / Dear Ms. Feigleson:

¶I was told there were job opportunities in your agency this summer, and I would like to apply for a job in your accounting department.

¶I am completing my junior year as an accounting major at Ohio State University. I have completed basic, intermediate, and advanced accounting. I will be available for employment from May 15 through August 1. During the year, I have been employed as a part-time bookkeeper at the Buckeye Lodge in Westerville. Mr. John Forte, manager of the lodge, has indicated that he would send you a letter of recommendation. My academic advisor, Dr. Josephine Craig, will be happy to make a recommendation if you wish.

¶You may, at your convenience, call me at my dorm telephone number, 555-0677, after 3:30 p.m. Monday through Friday. If you would like for me to come in for an interview, please let me know.

Yours truly, / May Kent / 234B Hayes Hall / Ohio State University / Columbus, OH 43210

F. SOFTWARE FEATURES

STUDENT MANUAL

Drawing Tools   Text/Word Art
Vertical Text

Study Lesson 111 in your student manual. Complete all the practice activities while at your computer. Then complete the jobs that follow.

DESKTOP PUBLISHING APPLICATIONS

REPORT 56

Open Report 37 and make the following changes:

1. Change the title to a wavy shape.
2. Adjust the width of the title to fit within the margins of the page.
3. Remove the bullets and begin each paragraph with a drop cap in a color that complements the title.
4. Add the following text to print vertically on the right side of the page: *GET THE JOB YOU WANT!* If necessary, change the color to complement the title and drop caps.
5. Add an appropriate graphic at the bottom center of the page and size it appropriately.

LETTER 4
Block Style
Personal-Business

Alternate
Block Style
Personal-Business

To prepare this personal-business letter in alternate block style, type the writer's address before the date.

Do not type the address after the sender's name.

Refer to pages 169–170, if needed.

inter**NET**
CONNECTION

Use the Internet to explore sites that provide career and job information. Some sites you may want to try are:

http://www.careermosaic.com/
http://www.stats.bls.gov.ocohome.htm
http://www.dbm.com/jobguide/

Type this letter in block style with standard punctuation. Make the corrections indicated by the proofreaders' marks.

(Current Date)

Mr. Jacob Reis, Manager
Longhorn Department Store
1366 South State St.
Chicago, IL 60616

Dear Mr. Reis:

Thank you for sending me an application for the position of a part-time clerk in your store.

I am currently working part time as a clerk at the One-A Supermarket. My cooperative education teacher assisted me in obtaining this position and I have been on this job for 2 years.

As is requested on the form, I am asking that the letters of recommendation be sent to you. You will receive letters from my cooperative teacher, current employer, and scout leader within the next few days. The high school office administration will send you a transcript of my grades.

As I indicated in my letter of application, I will be completing high school in June, and will enroll at Northern Illinois University in September. I am pleased with the position you are offering me, and I know the position will assist me in financing my college education.

I look forward to meeting you, my fellow employees, and our customers in June.

Sincerely yours,

Kyle Long
4578 Chicago Road
Evanston, IL 62242

The soft Angora kitten slept peacefully near the fireplace.
Roger purchased a noise shield for the loud, rapid printer.

5 Karen has what I would call a dynamic forceful presentation.
6 The sleek colorful tractor won first prize at the contest.
7 Last week they went to a long, boring movie at the theater.
8 The space shuttle is transported on a long sturdy vehicle.

SKILLBUILDING

C. 12-Second Sprints

Take three 12-second timings on each line. Try to increase your speed on each timing.

9 Mark can quickly type the words for, the, but, can, and go.
10 The four of them had to get to the bus by the time it left.
11 Sue says that she can fix the vase that fell from the desk.
12 Jane and the girl kept their title to the farm on the hill.

| | | | |5| | | |10| | | |15| | | |20| | | |25| | | |30| | | |35| | | |40| | | |45| | | |50| | | |55| | | |60

D. Diagnostic Practice: Numbers

Turn to the Diagnostic Practice: Numbers routine on page SB4. Type one of the Pretest/Posttest paragraphs and identify any errors made. Then type the corresponding drill lines 2 times for each number on which you made 2 or more errors and 1 time for each number on which you made only 1 error. Finally, repeat the same Pretest paragraph and compare your performance.

FORMATTING

E. Page Design

The design of a page can be made more exciting by creating special effects with text. **Text art** enables you to curve, distort, and twist text into a variety of shapes and sizes. In addition, you can shade the text and make it three-dimensional. Treating text as art is useful in creating unique company or personal logos on letterhead and business cards.

LESSON 50 ENVELOPES

OBJECTIVES:

- Improve keyboarding skills.
- Learn word processing features.
- Format envelopes.

A. WARMUP

Type each line 2 times.

Speed
Accuracy
Language Link
Technique

1 The true beauty of that diamond was brought out by its cut.
2 Aquilla told Bix the difference in a xylophone and marimba.
3 A number of fields of cotton and milo haven't been planted.
4 Paul Quan Rand Stan Trev Ulan Vern Ward Xerxes Yohann Zared
| 1 | 2 | 3 | 4 | 5 | 6 | 7 | 8 | 9 | 10 | 11 | 12

SKILLBUILDING

B. 30-SECOND OK TIMINGS

Take two 30-second OK (error-free) timings on lines 5–6. Then take two 30-second OK timings on lines 7–8. Goal: no errors.

5   Each of the students decided what he wanted to eat for   11
6 breakfast. Amazingly, just six bravely asked for ham quiche.   23

7   Both the dog and the fox were fat and lazy. They never   11
8 ran or jumped quickly. All they ever did was eat and sleep.   23
| 1 | 2 | 3 | 4 | 5 | 6 | 7 | 8 | 9 | 10 | 11 | 12

LESSON 111

TEXT/WORD ART

OBJECTIVES:

- Increase keyboarding speed.
- Learn comma usage rules.
- Learn about the drawing toolbar.
- Learn to use text/word art.

A. WARMUP

Type each line 2 times.

Speed
Accuracy
Language Link
Numbers/Symbols

1 The six girls held a social to pay for a visit to the lake.
2 Why would quick brown foxes want to jump over any lazy dog?
3 My cousin's winter ski jacket is much warmer than my parka.
4 Ed & Zoe sold 59# of sugar @ $1.67, for a total of $103.84.
| 1 | 2 | 3 | 4 | 5 | 6 | 7 | 8 | 9 | 10 | 11 | 12

B. COMMA USAGE

Study the rule and examples that follow. Then edit lines 5–8 to correct any errors in comma usage.

Rule 28:

Use a comma between two adjacent adjectives that modify the same noun. To determine whether the adjectives do describe the same noun, use the following test.

Read the sentence, "Chris gave a *short, emotional* speech." Now change the order to say, "A speech was short *and* emotional." If it makes sense, it proves that both adjectives describe *speech,* and a comma is necessary.

Read the sentence, "She mailed a *new spring* schedule. Now change the order to say, "A schedule is new *and* spring." It doesn't make sense, so no comma is needed.

C. PRETEST

Take a 1-minute timing on lines 9–12. Note your speed and errors.

Social Studies
Connections

9	Andrew Jackson, seventh President of our country, was	11
10	known as Old Hickory by his friends and King Andrew by his	23
11	foes. Born in Waxhaw, South Carolina, Jackson was left an	34
12	orphan in his teens and grew up poor.	41

| 1 | 2 | 3 | 4 | 5 | 6 | 7 | 8 | 9 | 10 | 11 | 12

D. PRACTICE

In the chart below, find the number of errors you made on the Pretest. Then type each of the following designated drill lines 2 times.

Pretest Errors	0–1	2	3	4+
Drill Lines	16–20	15–19	14–18	13–17

Accuracy

13 Old grew votes orphan fought common Andrew Jackson Carolina
14 King East Adams seventh federal citizens settlers self-made
15 known liked South workers instead Hickory country President
16 West fired plain teens bitter Waxhaw Quincy friends farmers

Speed

17 hired made race from dent poor drew king left our the in he
18 seven plain work jobs beat grew east foes was who try an of
19 liked farms self born when fire west mean and son for by up
20 south know those teen came held like vote most his old as a

E. POSTTEST

Repeat the Pretest. Compare your Posttest results with your Pretest results.

FACT FILE

You can remember the names of the departments in the President's Cabinet by remembering this mnemonic: See the dog jump vigorously in a circle; leave her here to entertain efficiently. (State, Treasury, Defense, Justice, Veterans Affairs, Interior, Agriculture, Commerce, Labor, Health and Human Services, Housing and Urban Development, Transportation, Energy, Education)

DESKTOP PUBLISHING APPLICATIONS

REPORT 54

Create informal personal stationery for yourself. Be sure to include your full name, your address including ZIP Code, and your telephone number.

1. Insert a shape of your choice from the shapes available in your word processor.
2. Center the shape at the top of the page.
3. Choose a font to use for your initials, which will be typed inside the shape.
4. Center your main initial (the first letter of your last name) between your first initial and your middle initial. Make the main initial twice as large as the others.
5. Center your name, address, telephone number, and e-mail address below the shape (either on one line with spaces between sections or on several lines).
6. Create a table in a footer and insert a series of shapes or symbols of your choice for the bottom of the page.

REPORT 55

Create a more formal letterhead for yourself.

1. Use Times New Roman 16-point.
2. Center and type your name.
3. Press ENTER once.
4. Change the font to Times New Roman 12-point, and center your address on 2 lines. Use initial caps.
5. Press ENTER once.
6. Center and type your telephone number, beginning with your area code.
7. Press ENTER once.
8. Center and type your e-mail address.
9. Add a heavy line above and below your name and address.

*inter***NET** CONNECTION

Companies often design a special logo to use on their letterhead stationery. Search the World Wide Web for information on logos and trademarks.

F. ENVELOPES

There are two commonly used envelope sizes: a No. 10 (large envelope) and a No. 6: (small envelope). The No. 10, which is the standard size for business letters, is 9 ½ by 4 ⅛ inches. A correctly addressed envelope should be typed as follows:

1. **Return Address.** The writer's name and address typed or printed in the upper left corner of the envelope (see the illustration that follows).

2. **Mailing Address.** The recipient's name and address beginning at least 2 inches from the top edge and 4 inches from the left edge of the envelope. The mailing address may be typed either in initial caps with punctuation (see the small envelope), or in all caps with no punctuation (see the large envelope).

HiTech Construction Associates
4200 Cedar Avenue, Minneapolis, MN 55404-1839

MS JOAN R HUNTER
BOLWATER ASSOCIATES
ONE PARKLANDS DRIVE
DARIEN CT 06820-3214

Roger J. Michaelson
901 East Benson, Apt. 3
Ft. Lauderdale, FL 33301

Mr. Joseph G. Jenshak
17032 Stewart Avenue
Augusta, GA 30904

Take two 5-minute timings on the paragraphs. Note your speed and errors.

Goal: 38/5′/5e

7	American companies used to be content with people who	11
8	showed up for work on time, performed their jobs, and did	23
9	as they were told. Now, managers want to find better ways	34
10	to run the business.	38
11	As they have in the past, workers still need to have	49
12	such skills as being able to read, to write, and to do	60
13	math. But those skills alone are not enough. Employers	71
14	want to hire workers who have creative ideas, good manners,	83
15	and confidence. Workers should also be strong in technical	85
16	areas. Other pluses are being willing to learn, a team	106
17	player, a good listener, and a quick thinker.	115
18	Although employers might provide training, they still	126
19	seek workers who have at least some of the above traits.	138
20	Employers also say that if they could hire enough bright,	149
21	able workers, middle management wouldn't be needed. They	161
22	realize this could lead to more profits. American companies	173
23	looked at the success of foreign rivals and found ways to	184
24	improve how they do business.	190

| 1 | 2 | 3 | 4 | 5 | 6 | 7 | 8 | 9 | 10 | 11 | 12   SI 1.40

FORMATTING

D. Designing Letterhead

When you are designing stationery, you should take into consideration how it will be used. For example, if you are designing a letterhead for writing letters to friends, you can use a less formal font and style. If the letterhead is going to be used to write a personal-business letter, such as a letter of application for employment, you should use a more traditional, formal style.

G. FOLDING LETTERS

To fold a letter for a large envelope: (see the illustration)
1. Place the letter face up and fold up the bottom third.
2. Fold the top third down to approximately 0.5 inch from the bottom edge.
3. Insert the last crease into the envelope first with the flap facing up.

To fold a letter for a small envelope: (see the illustration)
1. Place the letter face up and fold up the bottom half to 0.5 inch from the top.
2. Fold the right third over to the left.
3. Fold the left third over to 0.5 inch from the right edge.
4. Insert the last crease into the envelope first with the flap facing up.

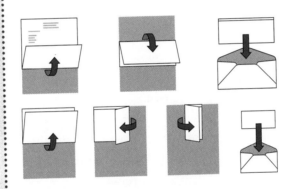

H. SOFTWARE FEATURES

STUDENT MANUAL
Envelopes

Study Lesson 50 in your student manual. Complete all the practice activities while at your computer. Then complete the jobs that follow.

WORD PROCESSING APPLICATIONS

ENVELOPE 1

Open the file for Letter 2, and prepare a No. 10 envelope. Use the correct return address and add/append the envelope to the letter.

ENVELOPE 2

Open the file for Letter 3, and prepare a No. 10 envelope. Use the correct return address and add/append the envelope to the letter.

LESSON 110

PERSONAL STATIONERY

OBJECTIVES:

- Improve keyboarding skill.
- Type 38/5'/5e.
- Create personal stationery.

A. WARMUP

Type each line 2 times.

Speed
Accuracy
Language Link
Numbers

1 The home row keys are easy to find as you type, type, type.
2 Why did Professor Black give you a quiz on the major texts?
3 Blue and red are very popular colors found on today's cars.
4 I saw on page 38 that 47 times 29 was much less than 1,560.
| 1 | 2 | 3 | 4 | 5 | 6 | 7 | 8 | 9 | 10 | 11 | 12

FACT FILE

Stationery comes in many colors, sizes, and qualities. Research the types of stationery for sale in a local supply store. Prepare a short report as your teacher directs.

SKILLBUILDING

B. PREVIEW PRACTICE

Type each line 2 times as a preview to the timings that follow.

Accuracy
Speed

5 team firms foreign creative Employers confidence management
6 able ways some the are how who and not key if do as to in a

ENVELOPE 3

LETTER 5
Block Style With
Envelope

Alternate
Block Style
Personal-Business

To prepare this personal-business letter in alternate block style, type the writer's address before the date.

Do not type the address after the sender's name.

Open the file for Letter 4, and prepare a No. 10 envelope. Use the correct return address and add/append the envelope to the letter.

Type the following letter in block style, and prepare a large envelope for the letter.

(Current Date) / Ms. Kaye Lincoln / Waldo Travel Bureau / 8900 Longwood Avenue / Suite 1304 / Boston, MA 02115 / Dear Ms. Lincoln:

¶I am interested in a trip to England, Holland, France, and Germany this coming summer. Do you have special packaged tours for students?

¶My financial resources are limited. I am looking for a trip that would take less than a month and cost less than $2,000. Currently, I am working as a waiter in a local restaurant; and I hope to save additional money for the trip.

¶What is the round trip airfare from Boston to London? Can I use trains from London to Amsterdam, Paris, and Frankfort? Can you recommend a hostel in each city and give me some idea of the daily costs? I would appreciate your sending me brochures on airlines, railroads, and hostels you recommend. I plan to apply for my passport, and I am aware that it takes more than a week for processing.

¶If you have further questions concerning my proposed trip, please let me know. You may call me at 781-555-2535. I can get released time from work to see you, and I can see you at your convenience.

Sincerely yours, / William Stoneman / 678 Main Street / Milton, MA 02186

PORTFOLIO
Activity

Decide which of the letters in this unit is your best one. Retype the letter using your name and address in place of the writer's name and address. Correct any errors, then print a copy and save the letter as an example of your work.

REPORT 53

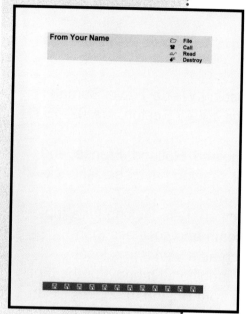

1. Create a boxed table with 1 column and 1 row, and apply a 20-percent color fill to the row.
2. Set tabs at 4.5 inches and 5 inches from the left margin.
3. Change the font to Arial Bold 20-point, and type *From* and your name. Then press CTRL + TAB to move to the first tab stop.
4. Change the font to Wingdings 14-point, and type the number *1* to create the file folder.
5. Press CTRL + TAB, change the font to Arial Bold 14-point, and type *File*. Then, press ENTER once.
6. Repeat steps 4–6 for the remaining words and symbols (= telephone; $ = glasses; M = bomb.
7. Create a footer, insert a 1-column, 1-row table, and apply a 100-percent color fill.
8. Change the font to Wingdings 18-point, space once, and type < to create a disk. Space once before creating the next disk. Type as many disks as needed to fill the row. Reverse the type to white.

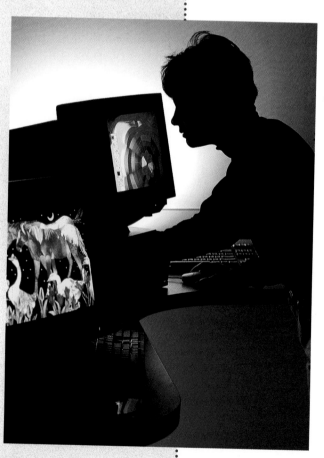

ART CONNECTIONS

Graphic artists and designers use computers and a variety of software programs in their work. They design everything from business logos to multi-media productions.

LESSON 51

BUSINESS LETTERS

OBJECTIVES:

- Compose at the keyboard.
- Format business letters.
- Type 33/3'/5e.

A. WARMUP

Type each line 2 times.

Speed
Accuracy
Language Link
Numbers/Symbols

1 We will be happy to see the sun after so many days of rain.
2 Janita and six friends quickly zipped by the two villagers.
3 The number of farmers helping their sick neighbor was huge.
4 Our 9 cakes, 45 pies, 60 doughnuts, and 72 cookies arrived.
| 1 | 2 | 3 | 4 | 5 | 6 | 7 | 8 | 9 | 10 | 11 | 12

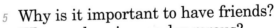

LANGUAGE LINK

B. COMPOSING AT THE KEYBOARD

Answer each of the following questions with complete sentences.

5 Why is it important to have friends?
6 Why are hurricanes dangerous?
7 What historical person would you most like to meet? Why?
8 Do you prefer team or individual sports?
9 Why is music important to you?

LANGUAGE ARTS CONNECTIONS

The word *skate* comes from the German word meaning bone. People first began skating more than 2,000 years ago. They would tie animal bones to their feet so that they could move or slide quickly across the ice.

DESKTOP PUBLISHING APPLICATIONS

REPORT 52

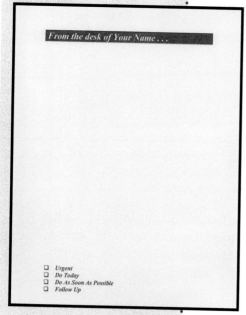

Create the notepad illustrated here by following these steps:

1. Create a boxed table with 1 column and 1 row.
2. Change the font to Times New Roman Bold Italic 24-point.
3. Type *From the desk of* and your name followed by a space and then by three periods. Leave a space between the periods.
4. Apply a 100-percent fill in the color of your choice to the box and reverse the type to white.
5. Create a footer.
6. Change the font to Wingdings 16-point, type the letter *q* to create a check box, and space once.
7. Change the font to Times New Roman Bold Italic 16-point, type *Urgent,* and press ENTER once.
8. Repeat steps 5–7 for the remaining lines, using the words indicated in the illustration.
9. Change the color of the text in the footer to match the color you chose for the top section.

CULTURAL CONNECTIONS

Writing styles and stationery used may vary from country to country. Interview someone from another country to find out how that country writes business letters. Ask what type of stationery is used and what style of letters they use.

SKILLBUILDING

C. 12-SECOND SPRINTS

Take three 12-second timings on each line. Try to increase your speed on each timing.

10 Ray looks nice in his new jacket, but he does not think so.
11 He finds it hard to accept nice words being said about him.
12 He should smile and thank the one who said the nice things.
13 Do you find you are ill at ease when a nice remark is made?
| | | | 5 | | | | 10 | | | 15 | | | 20 | | | 25 | | | 30 | | | 35 | | | 40 | | | 45 | | | 50 | | | 55 | | | 60

D. PREVIEW PRACTICE

Type each line 2 times as a preview to the timings that follow.

14 skills fixing machines produce equipped analyzing computers
15 every that free high have work data sure help you job it is

E. 3-MINUTE TIMINGS

Take two 3-minute timings on the paragraphs. Note your speed and errors.

16   Computers used today can help produce work that is   10
17 free from errors. These new machines are equipped to work   22
18 with data at high rates of speed. This means that errors   33
19 are processed at high speeds too. For this reason, it is   44
20 crucial that computer users have skills in analyzing and   55
21 fixing errors.   58
22   In every job, it is important to check your work to   69
23 be sure that what you have is what you wanted and that the   81
24 quality is acceptable. The computer is just a tool. If   92
25 used wisely, it can make your job a simpler one.   102
| 1 | 2 | 3 | 4 | 5 | 6 | 7 | 8 | 9 | 10 | 11 | 12 SI 1.35

SKILLBUILDING

C. PRETEST

Take a 1-minute timing on the paragraph. Note your speed and errors.

8 Reading a book during a weekend is a wise choice. You	10
9 can increase your word power even by reading popular books.	22
10 Enjoy yourself; join a number of those who choose to read a	33
11 good book. Invest your weekend time wisely by reading.	44

| 1 | 2 | 3 | 4 | 5 | 6 | 7 | 8 | 9 | 10 | 11 | 12 |

D. PRACTICE

SPEED: *If you made 2 or fewer errors on the Pretest, type lines 12–19 two times each.*

ACCURACY: *If you made more than 2 errors on the Pretest, type lines 12–15 as a group two times. Then type lines 16–19 as a group two times.*

Adjacent Reaches

12 we weak wean wept weave wedge sweat weigh weary dowel sweet
13 oi soil toil boil hoist point joist poise spoil avoid noise
14 po pond port pour pound pouch poach point polka power polar
15 rt tort sort dart short court party warts sorts forth mirth

Jump Reaches

16 ce cede cell cent cease hence sauce grace niece cedar cello
17 um numb jump lump chump mumps crumb gummy stump thumb bumpy
18 in bind find grin brain cabin cling brink drain faint grain
19 om come pomp some bloom romps domes homes tombs zooms rooms

E. POSTTEST

Repeat the Pretest. Compare your Posttest results with your Pretest results.

FORMATTING

F. SOFTWARE FEATURES

STUDENT MANUAL
Reverse Text

Study Lesson 109 in your student manual. Complete all the practice activities while at your computer. Then complete the jobs that follow.

F. BUSINESS LETTERS

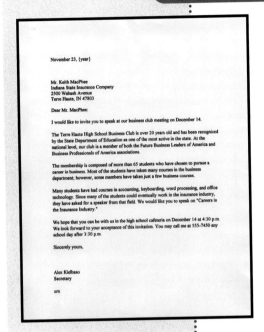

November 23, {year}

Mr. Keith MacPhee
Indiana State Insurance Company
2500 Wabash Avenue
Terre Haute, IN 47803

Dear Mr. MacPhee:

I would like to invite you to speak at our business club meeting on December 14.

The Terre Haute High School Business Club is over 20 years old and has been recognized by the State Department of Education as one of the most active in the state. At the national level, our club is a member of both the Future Business Leaders of America and Business Professionals of America associations.

The membership is composed of more than 65 students who have chosen to pursue a career in business. Most of the students have taken many courses in the business department; however, some members have taken just a few business courses.

Many students have had courses in accounting, keyboarding, word processing, and office technology. Since many of the students could eventually work in the insurance industry, they have asked for a speaker from that field. We would like you to speak on "Careers in the Insurance Industry."

We hope that you can be with us in the high school cafeteria on December 14 at 4:30 p.m. We look forward to your acceptance of this invitation. You may call me at 555-7450 any school day after 3:30 p.m.

Sincerely yours,

Alex Kielbaso
Secretary

urs

A business letter represents a company, not an individual. Business letters are usually printed on company stationery called letterhead. The letterhead usually includes the company's name, address, and telephone number. The differences between a business letter and a personal-business letter are these:

1. The writer's company name and address appear in the letterhead; therefore, they are not typed in the closing lines.
2. The writer's business title is typed below the name. A short title may be placed on the same line as the name, separated by a comma. The name and title are called the **writer's identification**.
3. The initials of the typist (called **reference initials**) are typed a double space below the writer's identification.

WORD PROCESSING APPLICATIONS

Type the following letter in block style. Use your own initials for the reference initials. Address a No. 10 envelope. Do not include a return address. Add/append the envelope to the letter.

LETTER 6
Block-Style
Business

November 23, {year} / Mr. Keith MacPhee / Indiana State Insurance Company / 2500 Wabash Avenue / Terre Haute, IN 47803 / Dear Mr. MacPhee:

¶I would like to invite you to speak at our business club meeting on December 14.

¶The Terre Haute High School Business Club is over 20 years old and has been recognized by the State Department of Education as one of the most active in the state. At the national level, our club is a member of both the Future Business Leaders of America and Business Professionals of America associations.

LESSON 109

PERSONAL NOTEPADS

OBJECTIVES:

- Compose at the keyboard.
- Improve keyboarding skill.
- Learn about reverse text.
- Create personal notepads.

A. WARMUP

Type each line 2 times.

Speed
Accuracy
Language Link
Technique

```
1 Nan said she may go back to her job by the end of the week.
2 Jane quickly seized the wax buffer and removed a big patch.
3 Bert lost his shoes Tuesday on Flight 567; they are size 9.
4 q z p / w x o . e c I , r v u m t b y n a ; s l d k f j g h
  | 1 | 2 | 3 | 4 | 5 | 6 | 7 | 8 | 9 | 10 | 11 | 12
```

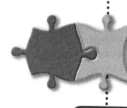

LANGUAGE LINK

B. COMPOSING AT THE KEYBOARD

Choose one of the following topics and compose a short three-paragraph report.

5 My Greatest Fear
6 My Proudest Moment
7 My Future Plans

FACT FILE

In 1987, astronomer Ian Shelton discovered a supernova (exploding star). This event was the first such discovery visible with the naked eye since 1604.

¶The membership is composed of more than 65 students who have chosen to pursue a career in business. Most of the students have taken many courses in the business department; however, some members have taken just a few business courses.

¶Many students have had courses in accounting, keyboarding, word processing, and office technology. Since many of the students could eventually work in the insurance industry, they have asked for a speaker from that field. We would like you to speak on "Careers in the Insurance Industry."

¶We hope that you can be with us in the high school cafeteria on December 14 at 4:30 p.m. We look forward to your acceptance of this invitation. You may call me at 555-7450 any school day after 3:30 p.m.

Sincerely yours, / Alex Kielbaso / Secretary / urs

Type the following letter in block style. Use your initials for the reference initials. Use the current date.

LETTER 7
Block-Style Business

(Current Date) / Ms. Elyse Demers / 2101 Market Street / York, PA 17404 / Dear Ms. Demers:

¶You have been scheduled for surgery next month by the Orthopedic Unit of St. Ann's Hospital. Within the next few days, you will receive a form that authorizes your physician to provide us with information on your medical history. This information is vital to us. It will help us to eliminate repeat tests and take into consideration any additional health problems you may have.

¶Please provide the name of your physician and your date of birth on the form. Then, sign and date the form and give it to your physician so that your medical history will be forwarded to us before your surgery.

¶If you have more than one physician from whom we need records or if you have any questions or concerns, please call us at 717-555-9000 and request additional forms.

Sincerely, / Marsha Cunningham / Administrator / urs

*inter*NET CONNECTION

Use the Internet to learn more about the Future Business Leaders of America and the Business Professionals of America. Explore information about other members of these organizations.

to do." "Frowns cause wrinkles; smile now—avoid wrinkles later." "Smile—everyone will wonder what you are up to." "Smile and the world smiles with you—cry and you cry alone." "Smiles beget smiles." "It takes fewer face muscles to smile than to frown." Why not give smiling a try?

REPORT 51

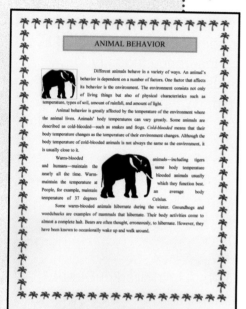

Open Report 49 and make the following changes:

1. Change the border of the title to a heavy line.
2. Resize the graphic at the top of the page to approximately 1.5 by 1.5 inches, and add a thin border the same color as the title border.
3. Move the graphic to the beginning of the first paragraph, and wrap the text to the right of the graphic.
4. Move the graphic at the end of the report to the end of the second paragraph, and size it to approximately 2 inches wide.
5. Wrap the text around both sides of the graphic.
6. To the entire page, add a fancy border that relates to the content of the report.

PORTFOLIO Activity

Using what you have learned so far about desktop publishing, create a document that incorporates this knowledge. Think of a theme relating to health, manners, careers, or other topics of interest. If necessary, search the Internet for information about your topic to include in your document. Print the final product and save it as an example of your work.

LESSON 52

BUSINESS LETTERS

OBJECTIVES:

- Improve keyboarding skill.
- Learn word processing features.
- Reinforce the skill of formatting business letters.

A. WARMUP

Type each line 2 times.

Speed
Accuracy
Language Link
Numbers/Symbols

```
1 It will help to put away worry and doubt about your skills.
2 The dozen extra blue jugs were quickly moved from the pool.
3 The number of items to remember to pick up is overwhelming.
4 (it is) [to the] {of a} 5 < 9 (in at) [by it] {be on} 7 > 1
  | 1 | 2 | 3 | 4 | 5 | 6 | 7 | 8 | 9 | 10 | 11 | 12
```

SKILLBUILDING

B. DIAGNOSTIC PRACTICE: ALPHABET

Turn to the Diagnostic Practice: Alphabet routine on page SB1. Type one of the Pretest/Posttest paragraphs and identify any errors made. Then type the corresponding drill lines 2 times for each letter on which you made 2 or more errors and 1 time for each letter on which you made only 1 error. Finally, repeat the Pretest and compare your performance.

C. PACED PRACTICE

Turn to the Paced Practice routine beginning on page SB7. Take three 2-minute timings starting at the point where you left off the last time.

FACT FILE

Silicon is a nonmetallic element from which semi-conductors are made. Next to oxygen, it is the most abundant element found in nature. Silicon, which is found in rocks and sand, is also used in the manu-facture of glass, concrete, brick, and pottery.

D. WRAPPING TEXT

Once a text or graphic box is inserted into a document, it can be positioned anywhere on the page. In order to keep the original text on the page readable, you may want to wrap the text around the box or have the text appear above, below, or beside the box.

E. SOFTWARE FEATURES

GO TO

STUDENT MANUAL

Wrapping Text

Study Lesson 108 in your student manual. Complete all the practice activities while at your computer. Then complete the jobs that follow.

DESKTOP PUBLISHING APPLICATIONS

REPORT 50

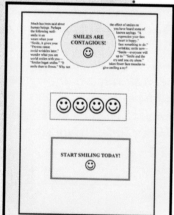

Open Report 46 and revise it as follows:

1. Type the paragraph following the numbered steps at the top of the page.
2. Wrap the text around the sides of the circle containing the words *SMILES ARE CONTAGIOUS*. Make any adjustments that may be necessary to attractively arrange the text and circle.
3. Add a 48-point smiley face symbol centered below the type in the circle.
4. Delete the graphic from the text box.
5. Insert four 78-point smiley face symbols in the text box, horizontally center them, and adjust the size of the text box as necessary.
6. Add a 48-point smiley face symbol centered below the text in the last text box.
7. Add a heavy black border to the page.

Much has been said about the effect of smiles on human beings. Perhaps you have heard some of the following well-known sayings. "A smile is an expression your face wears when your heart is happy." "A smile is your umbrella during stormy times." "A smile is a frown turned upside down." "Smile, it gives your face something

FORMATTING

D. SOFTWARE FEATURES

STUDENT MANUAL

Find and Replace

Study Lesson 52 in your student manual. Complete all the practice activities while at your computer. Then complete the jobs that follow.

WORD PROCESSING APPLICATIONS

Type the following letter in block style. Use your own initials for the reference initials. Address a No. 10 envelope. Do not include a return address, and add/append the envelope to the letter.

LETTER 8

Block-Style
Business

(Current Date) / Mrs. Alma Louise Yeu / President / Yeu & Yeu Associates / 4500 Elk Grove Avenue / Arlington Heights, IL 60004 / Dear Mrs. Yeu:

¶It is a pleasure to accept the task of chairperson for the United Fund campaign this fall.

¶As you are aware, I have been on the local United Fund board for the past eight years. I have had a great eight years; I look forward to at least four more years with the fund. Will I, as the new chairperson, have the responsibility of selecting the campaign committee? Jason Lewis, last year's chairperson, told me that it would be best if I could. He selected a committee composed of representatives from the business, industrial, educational, and lay communities. Last year's drive was the best yet; I think the results were due in large part to the committee.

¶Jason Lewis, Marsha Hunt, and Alex Garcia were on the committee last year; they were outstanding members. I plan to retain them if they are willing to serve again.

¶If you have questions about the proposed committee, please call me.

Sincerely yours, / Louise K. Fletcher / Production Engineer / urs

LESSON 108

BOXES: WRAPPING TEXT

OBJECTIVES:

- Improve keyboarding techniques.
- Learn to wrap text around boxes.

A. WARMUP

Type each line 2 times.

Speed
Accuracy
Language Link
Numbers/Symbols

```
1 Show her what a nice day it is so that she may take a walk.
2 Expert jockeys quickly led a horse away from a blazing van.
3 Because we stopped to eat, we got home well after midnight.
4 Jon & Bev paid for 674# of #95 glue @ $1.92 at Quill & Ink.
   | 1 | 2 | 3 | 4 | 5 | 6 | 7 | 8 | 9 | 10 | 11 | 12
```

SKILLBUILDING

B. 12-SECOND SPRINTS

Take three 12-second timings on each line. Try to increase your speed on each timing.

Keep your eyes on the copy.

```
5 Irene was to make the cake for the office party this month.
6 He bought a new computer from the dealer at the mall today.
7 My courses were given in the rooms of the old school house.
8 When you go to the dance, be sure to take her some flowers.
 | | | |5| | | |10| | | |15| | |20| | |25| | | |30| | |35| | | |40| | | |45| | |50| | | |55| | | |60
```

C. PACED PRACTICE

Turn to the Paced Practice routine beginning on page SB7. Take three 2-minute timings, starting at the point where you left off the last time.

COMMUNICATION FOCUS

A *smiley* or *emoticon* is sometimes used to mean a grin or some other emotion. Ask your friends and a few business associates how they feel about receiving these symbols in messages.

Type the following letter in block style. Use your own initials for the reference initials. Address a No. 10 envelope. Do not include a return address, and add/append the envelope to the letter.

(Current Date) / Mrs. Lottie Alexander / Personnel Director / Minneapolis Manufacturing Co. / 1700 University Avenue / Minneapolis, MN 55104-3020 / Dear Mrs. Alexander:

¶It is a pleasure to write a recommendation for John Saum for the position of word processor specialist with your company. John was in my accounting, computer, and multimedia classes; he was an outstanding student. He has an excellent background in grammar and spelling. He consistently received high grades in his production work on the computer.

¶Our advisory committee recommended him as the top student in the cooperative education program his senior year. John worked for the Miller Manufacturing Company as a word processor trainee in the mornings and attended afternoon classes. His supervisor consistently gave him exceptional ratings.

¶I am sure that John has asked the school to send you a copy of his transcript; it is outstanding. He indicates that he would like to attend a university once he has a job. I know that John Saum will be an excellent employee.

Sincerely yours, / Jose Sauceda / Business Instructor / urs

Open Letter 8 and make these revisions: Use find and replace to change Yeu to Yeun and Jason Lewis to Leonard Whilhite.

Open Letter 9 and make the following changes:
1. *Use find and replace to change John Saum to Maria Suma.*
2. *Use find and replace to change all the masculine pronouns to feminine pronouns (he, his, him to she, her).*
3. *Be sure to change all instances of John's given name with Maria's name.*

REPORT 48

Open Report 47 and modify it as follows:

1. Beginning with the first paragraph, change the line spacing to 1.5.
2. Add the page number at the bottom center.
3. Create a text box at the beginning of the first paragraph.
4. Choose an animal graphic and insert it into the box.
5. Resize the graphic and the text box so that the graphic remains proportional.
6. Position the text box so that it does not cover any text.
7. Delete the text box border.

REPORT 49

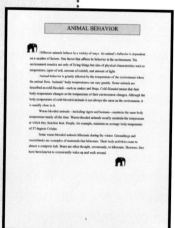

Open Report 48 and make the following changes:

1. Create a text box at the top of the report.
2. Horizontally center the text box.
3. Inside the text box, center and type in Times New Roman 20-point bold, *ANIMAL BEHAVIOR*.
4. Shade the text box with a 15-percent fill in a color that complements the graphic.
5. Change the body of the report to full justification.
6. Add the same animal graphic that appears at the beginning of the page after the last line of text.
7. Position the graphic so that it does not cause text to shift, and delete the border.

LESSON 53 REVIEW

OBJECTIVES:

- Improve skill in formatting personal-business letters, envelopes, and business letters.
- Learn to use commas in a series and with transitional expressions.

A. WARMUP

Type each line 2 times.

Speed
Accuracy
Language Link
Symbols

1 Emi would like to buy the dress if it comes in green denim.
2 Karl may sign up with five or six dozen clubs for jonquils.
3 When our order arrived, a number of lightbulbs were broken.
4 My brother-in-law gave Trev that you-know-what-I-mean look.
| 1 | 2 | 3 | 4 | 5 | 6 | 7 | 8 | 9 | 10 | 11 | 12

LANGUAGE LINK

B. LANGUAGE LINK

Study the rules and examples below. Then edit lines 5–8 to correct any errors in comma usage.

Rule 6: Use a comma between each item in a series of three or more.

> *I walked the beach, read novels, and ate well while on vacation.*

Rule 7: Use a comma before and after a transitional expression (such as *therefore* or *however*).

> *Our account, therefore, is current.*

5 The ball bat and glove were in the garage beside the car.
6 Meg told about big cities tall buildings and busy people.
7 My yard is full of leaves and therefore needs to be raked.
8 Lowering gas prices however does not affect costs of cars.

FORMATTING

E. SOFTWARE FEATURES

 STUDENT MANUAL

Fill   Borders

Study Lesson 107 in your student manual. Complete all the practice activities while at your computer. Then complete the jobs that follow.

DESKTOP PUBLISHING APPLICATIONS

REPORT 47

Type the following report single-spaced. Press ENTER 6 times to leave an approximately 2-inch margin. Do not include a title. Do not leave a blank line between paragraphs.

Different animals behave in a variety of ways. An animal's behavior is dependent on a number of factors. One factor that affects its behavior is the environment. The environment consists not only of living things but also of physical characteristics such as temperature, types of soil, amount of rainfall, and amount of light.
¶Animal behavior is greatly affected by the temperature of the environment where the animal lives. Animals' body temperatures can vary greatly. Some animals are described as cold-blooded—such as snakes and frogs. *Cold-blooded* means that their body temperature changes as the temperature of their environment changes. Although the body temperature of cold-blooded animals is not always the same as the environment, it is usually close to it.
¶Warm-blooded animals—including tigers and humans—maintain the same body temperature nearly all the time. Warm-blooded animals usually maintain the temperature at which they function best. People, for example, maintain an average body temperature of 37 degrees Celsius.
¶Some warm-blooded animals hibernate during the winter. Groundhogs and woodchucks are examples of mammals that hibernate. Their body activities come to almost a complete halt. Bears are often thought, erroneously, to hibernate. However, they have been known to occasionally wake up and walk around.

 Science
Connections

SKILLBUILDING

Take two 30-second timings on lines 9–10. Then take two 30-second timings on lines 11–12. Try to increase your speed on each timing.

```
 9        When you talk to customers on the phone, here are some    12
10   tips. Answer on the first ring, and identify the company.      24

11        Speak courteously. If you wear a smile, it will help      11
12   you have a friendly tone of voice. Try to be friendly.         22
     | 1 | 2 | 3 | 4 | 5 | 6 | 7 | 8 | 9 | 10 | 11 | 12
```

WORD PROCESSING APPLICATIONS

LETTER 12

Block-Style
Business

Type the following rough-draft business letter. Make the corrections indicated by the proofreaders' marks. Use your initials as the typist.

(Current Date)

Mrs. Stephanie Ackerman

3257 Lake Side Drive

Lake Oswego, OR 97053

Dear Mrs. Ackerman:

Thank you for asking for Pleasure Island Travel to plan your overseas trip. While we finalize your itinerary, you may want to apply for your passport. Often it takes weeks before you receive your passport in the mail.

A passport application can be obtained from your post office or from any federal or state court. There is a required fee, and two current, identical photos of you are needed to help prove who you

SKILLBUILDING

C. PREVIEW PRACTICE

Type each line 2 times as a preview to the timings that follow.

Accuracy
Speed

9 merit fortunate promotion beforehand experience individuals
10 a do be in the you not set are now own how why than what

D. 5-MINUTE TIMINGS

Take two 5-minute timings on the paragraphs. Note your speed and errors.

Goal: 38/5'/5e

11   If you feel fortunate to have a job today, this might   11
12 not be in your best interest. In fact, this feeling will   22
13 prevent some individuals from taking the risks needed to   34
14 keep up with salary trends in their field.   42

15   You should realize that getting a raise is harder now   53
16 than it was ten years ago. When you believe you merit one,   65
17 do not be afraid to seek it out. Usually, a promotion comes   77
18 with a raise. In this case, your good work already is being   89
19 recognized and rewarded. However, there are times when an   101
20 employee must take the initiative to seek what is due.   112

21   Take inventory of yourself. Be sure you know what your   123
22 strengths are and how your experience makes you a valuable   135
23 employee. Know why you deserve the raise so you can justify   147
24 it to your employer.   151

25   Requesting a raise on your own may mean you need to   162
26 meet a different set of job standards. Your employer might   173
27 expect something more from you. You might want to think   185
28 about a response beforehand.   190

| 1 | 2 | 3 | 4 | 5 | 6 | 7 | 8 | 9 | 10 | 11 | 12SI 1.36

interNET CONNECTION

Connect to the Internet and enter the following key words in a search engine: job interview. You may also want to do a search on: salary negotiation.

are. You will also need a document, such as a certificate birth to prove that you are a U.s. citizen. Instructions on the application detail the types of proof of citizenship that are accpetable. once your passport is issued, it will remain valid for five or ten years, depending on your age.

We would like to have your itinerary finalized in about two weeks. If there is any thing else we can do during that time to assist you, please give us a call.

Sincerely,

Margret Sagan

Agent
urs

LETTER 13

Block-Style Business

Type the following business letter in block style.

(Current Date) / Ms. Alexia Wilcox / 956 Second Avenue/ Seattle, WA 98101 / Dear Ms. Wilcox:

¶Thank you for your telephone call requesting information about the clothing we carry at Easygoing Wear. Under separate cover we have sent you a catalog which contains all of our clothing lines.

¶Our sales representative, Ms. Nelda Gomez, has received your name and address; she will be calling on you within the next few days. Ms. Gomez will answer any questions you have concerning purchases, credit, and deliveries. In addition, she will have an array of products we are featuring this year.

¶This week's ad for Jacobson's, a store that carries our line and advertises in *The Seattle Inquirer,* features clothing that could be worn this fall; the ad displays clothing for football games and hiking. Jacobson's tells us that our fall line is one of their best selling lines.

¶We hope that you will be impressed with our line and that you will consider purchasing some of our clothing. We believe that you will be pleased with the quality, the styling, and the price.

Sincerely yours, / Mr. Alexander Long / Sales Manager / urs

BOXES: FILL, BORDERS

OBJECTIVES:

- Type 38/5'/5e.
- Learn rules for commas.
- Learn to change box borders and fill.

A. WARMUP

Type each line 2 times.

Speed
Accuracy
Language Link
Numbers

1 I came to work for this firm and have been here since then.
2 Jacques picked five boxes of oranges while Diz stayed home.
3 The council gave advice; a counselor advised Flora to stay.
4 Please clean Rooms 4, 6, and 7 but not Rooms 9, 29, and 38.
| 1 | 2 | 3 | 4 | 5 | 6 | 7 | 8 | 9 | 10 | 11 | 12

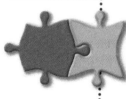

LANGUAGE LINK

B. COMMAS

Study the following rules and examples for comma usage. Then edit lines 5–8 to correct any errors.

Rule 26: Use a comma before and after the year in a complete date.

> *On December 7, 1996, the* Tribune *reviewed the Pearl Harbor events.*

> BUT: *The* News Monthly *printed December 1996 reviewed the same events.*

Rule 27: Use a comma before and after a state or country that follows a city, but not before a ZIP Code.

> *Sioux City, Iowa, is a lovely place in which to live.*

> BUT: *Sioux City, IA 51102, is where she plans to live.*

5 The warehouse buildings will be ready in September, 2000.
6 The lawyer told the clerk to use May 3, 1999 as the date.
7 The reports were sent to Nagoya, Japan on March 14, 1999.
8 The move to Toledo, Ohio, was scheduled for August, 2001.

LESSON 54　MODIFIED-BLOCK LETTERS

OBJECTIVES:

- Strengthen reaches.
- Learn word processing features.
- Format modified-block letters.

A.　WARMUP

Type each line 2 times.

Speed
Accuracy
Language Link
Numbers/Symbols

1　The boys will miss swim class for the first time this term.
2　The lazy judge was quick to pay my taxes on the five barns.
3　As soon as the facts are known, Hale will write the report.
4　$76.01 $13.02 $83.03 $92.04 $62.05 $30.06 $65.07 $82.08 $10

　| 1 | 2 | 3 | 4 | 5 | 6 | 7 | 8 | 9 | 10 | 11 | 12

SKILLBUILDING

B. PRETEST

Take a 1-minute timing on the paragraph. Note your speed and errors.

5　　　The blazing paint gave off toxic odors which gagged　　11
6　the nearby runners and joggers. Quickly the sunny sky grew　22
7　dimmer as it filled with the acrid smoke. Everyone ran　　33
8　even faster to get away from the spreading flames.　　43

　| 1 | 2 | 3 | 4 | 5 | 6 | 7 | 8 | 9 | 10 | 11 | 12

C. PRACTICE

SPEED: If you made 2 or fewer errors on the Pretest, type lines 9–16 two times each.
ACCURACY: If you made more than 2 errors on the Pretest, type lines 9–12 as a group two times. Then type lines 13–16 as a group two times.

Double Reaches

9　mm comma gamma gummy mummy dummy yummy jimmy tummy hammy mm
10　gg baggy leggy foggy soggy doggy muggy piggy buggy jaggy gg
11　nn inner annoy sunny funny bunny bonny gunny nanny runny nn
12　tt kitty ditty bitty catty nutty witty vitta patty motto tt

GO TO

STUDENT MANUAL

Text Boxes   Graphic or Figure Boxes

Study Lesson 106 in your student manual. Complete all the practice activities while at your computer. Then complete the jobs that follow.

DESKTOP PUBLISHING APPLICATIONS

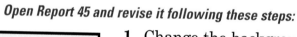

REPORT 45
Flyer

FACT FILE

The act of smiling apparently has some positive effect on the mood chemicals released from the brain, thereby making smiling a method to relieve stress.

REPORT 46
Flyer

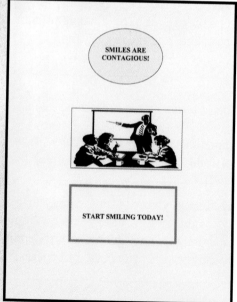

SMILES ARE CONTAGIOUS!

START SMILING TODAY!

Create a flyer following these steps:

1. Create a circle at the top of the page and horizontally center it.
2. In the circle, center and type in Times New Roman 18-point bold, *SMILES ARE CONTAGIOUS!*, and size the circle to fit the text on 2 lines.
3. Approximately 1 inch below the circle, insert a text box that is 4 inches wide and 2 inches high.
4. In the text box, vertically and horizontally center and type in Times New Roman 18-point bold, *HELP START AN EPIDEMIC!*
5. Approximately 1 inch below the text box, insert another text box and center and type in Times New Roman 18-point bold, *START SMILING TODAY!*

Open Report 45 and revise it following these steps:

1. Change the background of the circle to light yellow.
2. Replace the text in the first text box with a graphic of a group of people.
3. Adjust the size of the graphic and/or the text box so that the graphic looks proportionally correct and fills the text box without increasing the size of the text box.
4. Change the border of the bottom text box to a thick green border.

Alternate Reaches

```
13  toxic blame paint their towns bland panda theme tucks blend
14  panel throb turns flame pause throw tusks bogus proxy title
15  tutor boric prism tithe ticks bowls prowl tight bugle psych
16  rigor slept vigor quake chant flair shame snake right thigh
```

D. POSTTEST

Repeat the Pretest. Compare your Posttest results with your Pretest results.

E. 12-SECOND SPRINTS

Take three 12-second timings on each line. Try to increase your speed on each timing.

```
17  He bought the buns at the store for my friends in the park.
18  We went to the park to have a good time and play some ball.
19  The ball got lost in the water, and we had to find another.
20  None of us wanted to leave when it got dark, but we had to.
    | | | |5| | | |10| | | |15| | | |20| | | |25| | | |30| | | |35| | | |40| | | |45| | | |50| | | |55| | | |60
```

FORMATTING

F. MODIFIED-BLOCK STYLE LETTERS

In the modified-block style letter, the date and closing lines (complimentary closing, writer's name, and title) begin at the center point of the writing line. Paragraphs in a modified-block style letter may be blocked at the left margin (the preferred style) or indented 0.5 inch.

G. SOFTWARE FEATURES

GO TO

STUDENT MANUAL

Ruler and Tab Set

Study Lesson 54 in your student manual. Complete all the practice activities while at your computer. Then complete the jobs that follow.

LESSON 106

BOXES: TEXT AND GRAPHIC BOXES

OBJECTIVES:

- Improve keyboarding speed.
- Learn about text and graphic boxes.
- Learn to add text and graphics to boxes.

A. WARMUP

Type each line 2 times.

Speed
Accuracy
Language Link
Technique

1 All my friends met Tom at the mall and went on to the play.
2 Judy gave a quick jump as the zebra and lynx fought wildly.
3 She counseled and gave advice, but the advice did not work.
4 Anne saw RCA, BBS, US, and MTV written on the PTO brochure.
| 1 | 2 | 3 | 4 | 5 | 6 | 7 | 8 | 9 | 10 | 11 | 12

SKILLBUILDING

B. 30-SECOND OK TIMINGS

Take two 30-second OK (error-free) timings on lines 5–6. Then take two 30-second OK timings on lines 7–8. Goal: no errors.

5   Roxie picked yellow jonquils as Delbert watched; then   12
6 he zipped off to the cavern to tell of the amazing event.   24

7   Holly received a prize for jumping over six feet, and   12
8 Mac quickly explained that some big jumps involved risks.   24
| 1 | 2 | 3 | 4 | 5 | 6 | 7 | 8 | 9 | 10 | 11 | 12

FORMATTING

C. INSERTING BOXES

Boxes can be used to highlight text and graphics. Text inside a box can be formatted using different font styles and sizes. Whether a box contains text or graphics, its borders and fill can be changed, and it can be repositioned and resized.

LETTER 14
Modified-Block

Type the following letter in modified-block style. Use your initials.

(Current Date) / Mr. Weijun Zhao, President / All-Star Appliances / 2200 South Maybelle Avenue / Tulsa, OK 74107-2000 / Dear Mr. Zhao: / Welcome to the select group of Apex television dealers. ¶Your application has been approved and we look forward to many years of successful business for both your firm and ours. ¶We take pride in the fact that we have never rescinded a dealership agreement in our 40 years of manufacturing quality television sets. Every dealer will tell you that we are a family working together to improve the industry —both the manufacturing and servicing industry. ¶We are aware of the fine reputation of your company for service and sales in the greater Tulsa area; therefore, it would be a pleasure to have you visit our offices and plant at our expense as soon as you have an opportunity to do so. / Sincerely yours, / Amos Morgan / President / urs

LETTER 15
Modified-Block

Type the following letter in modified-block style. Use your initials.

(Current Date) / Mr. William J. Gross, President / National Training and Development Association / 3500 Collingwood Boulevard / Toledo, OH 43624 / Dear Mr. Gross: / It is a pleasure to accept your invitation to speak at the National Training and Development Association's Annual Convention in Cleveland next April. I will be glad to speak either on the current status of word processing or the skills needed by a beginning word processor. ¶As you know, I have spent considerable time in advising various firms on how a quality word processing center affects the total communication system of the firm. The effects of a good center bring increased revenues and result in a better image of the firm. ¶If you wish, I would be most happy to discuss with your members the importance of hiring well-trained word processors. I have taught technology administration at the local university as well as developed in-house training programs for firms. I could include in the speech the need for highly developed technical, human relations, and personal skills. ¶You or your members may desire another topic in the area of word processing or its personnel; if so, please let me know. ¶Again, thank you for an invitation to speak at your annual meeting. / Sincerely yours, / David G. Morgan / Consultant / urs

FORMATTING

F. CIRCLES, ELLIPSES (OVALS), AND OTHER SHAPES

By using a variety of shapes such as circles, rectangles, and ellipses (ovals), you can make page layouts more interesting. Once these shapes are inserted into a document, they can be repositioned and resized.

G. SOFTWARE FEATURE

STUDENT MANUAL

GO TO

Inserting/Drawing Shapes
Sizing   Moving

Study Lesson 105 in your student manual. Complete all the practice activities while at your computer. Then complete the jobs that follow.

DESKTOP PUBLISHING APPLICATIONS

REPORT 43

Follow these directions to create a snowperson similar to the illustration at the left.

1. Draw an oval approximately 3 inches wide and 2.5 inches high.
2. Drag the oval to the lower half of the page.
3. Create a circle and size it so that it is approximately 2 inches in diameter.
4. Place this circle on the top of the oval and center it.
5. Create another circle and size it so that it is approximately 1 inch in diameter.
6. Place this circle on top of the other circle in the approximate horizontal center.
7. Add the face, arms, and other features using drawing tools.

REPORT 44

Open Report 35 and make the following changes:

1. Insert a right arrow beside the title. Size the arrow so that it is approximately the height of the title and does not overlay the text.
2. Add a 100-percent red fill to the arrow.
3. Insert a rounded rectangle approximately 4 inches wide and 0.25 inch high at the end of the document.
4. Change the border to red.

LESSON 55

LETTERS WITH INDENTED PARAGRAPHS

OBJECTIVES:

- Compose at the keyboard.
- Improve keyboarding skill.
- Format letters with indented paragraphs.

A.   WARMUP

Type each line 2 times.

Speed
Accuracy
Language Link
Symbols

1 I could not read the small print on the map she sent to me.
2 A dozen jumpy zebras quickly zipped over the six big gates.
3 Because I had good grades, my scholarship has been renewed.
4 it's hasn't we'll aren't they'll couldn't you've don't I've
   | 1 | 2 | 3 | 4 | 5 | 6 | 7 | 8 | 9 | 10 | 11 | 12

LANGUAGE LINK

B.   COMPOSING AT THE KEYBOARD

Answer each of the following questions with complete sentences.

5 If you could invent something to improve the quality of our lives, what would it be?
6 Why did you choose to invent what you did?
7 What can pets teach us?
8 If you could travel anywhere in the world, where would you go? Why?

FACT FILE

On March 16, 1926, Robert H. Goddard became the first man to build a liquid-fueled rocket and to fire the rocket.

5 The interest rates were discussed in the November 24 Tribune.
6 Types of Life Insurance is an excellent chapter in your text.
7 Her proposed title for the report was Vacations Versus Trips.
8 The December 2 issue of "Newsweek" had most excellent coverage.

SKILLBUILDING

C. PRETEST

Take a 1-minute timing on the paragraph. Note your speed and errors.

9 Regardless of the type of job you have or the work you	12
10 do, it is most important that you manage your time so that	24
11 you can get more work accomplished. It is not possible for	36
12 us to reuse time; therefore, we should organize our days.	47

| 1 | 2 | 3 | 4 | 5 | 6 | 7 | 8 | 9 | 10 | 11 | 12 |

D. PRACTICE

In the chart below find the number of errors you made on the Pretest. Then type each of the designated drill lines 2 times.

Pretest Errors	0–1	2	3	4+
Drill Lines	16–20	15–19	14–18	13–17

Accuracy

13 possible organize important beginning accomplish regardless
14 remember employed recognize improving particular prioritize
15 activity powerful therefore essential difficult suggestions
16 quite borrows maximum example another critical accomplished

Speed

17 manage should reuse can't type have work that the you of or
18 stolen others never first your time more from can not do it
19 moment saving write items once gone back good for may so us
20 placed employ those above down jobs wish this top use to we

E. POSTTEST

Repeat the Pretest. Compare your Posttest results with your Pretest results.

SKILLBUILDING

C. 30-Second OK Timings

*Take two 30-second OK (error-free) timings on lines 9–10. Then take
two 30-second OK timings on lines 11–12. Goal: no errors.*

9	Bea majored in zoology after she qualified for a large 12
10	research grant. She must speak with her adviser, Dr. Haver. 24
11	I am anxious because I have a dozen errands and cannot 12
12	be late for class. Have Paula adjourn this meeting quickly. 24

| 1 | 2 | 3 | 4 | 5 | 6 | 7 | 8 | 9 | 10 | 11 | 12 |

FACT FILE

One of the greatest problems for humans in space
is weightlessness. On long missions, astronauts
often come back in weakened physical state.
Russian cosmonauts, who have spent the most time
in space—up to a year, are sometimes so weak that
they need help to get out of their space capsule.

FORMATTING

D. Letters With Indented Paragraphs

A variation of the modified-block style letter is to indent
the first line of each paragraph, usually 0.5 inch.

When using the indented paragraph style, set two
tabs—one for the paragraph (at 0.5 inch from the left
margin) and one for the date and closing lines (at the
center point of the line).

LESSON 105

DRAWING

OBJECTIVES:

- Improve keyboarding skills.
- Learn about quotation marks and italics.
- Learn to insert various shapes into documents.

A. WARMUP

Type each line 2 times.

Speed
Accuracy
Language Link
Numbers/Symbols

1 Norma may go for a walk on this nice day to visit that boy.
2 A dozen big witches quickly jumped over six long red sofas.
3 Their friends saw the footballs over there in Dave's field.
4 They bought #2 lead pencils @ $.24 each at Penzey's Papers.
| 1 | 2 | 3 | 4 | 5 | 6 | 7 | 8 | 9 | 10 | 11 | 12

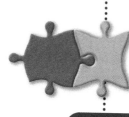

LANGUAGE LINK

B. QUOTATION MARKS AND ITALICS

Study the following rules and examples. Then edit lines 5–8 to correct any errors in the use of quotation marks and italics.

Rule 24: Use quotation marks around the titles of newspaper articles, magazine articles, chapters in a book, conferences, and similar items.

> The next assignment is to read the chapter entitled "The Kennedy Years."
>
> Kurt read and reread the article, "An Interview With Joe Montana."

Rule 25: Italicize (or underline) the titles of books, magazines, newspapers, and other complete published works.

> *The Fifties* by David Halberstam gives an excellent portrait of the decade.
>
> The article in <u>Sports Illustrated</u> covered the new basketball rules changes.

LETTER 16

Modified-
Block With
Indented
Paragraphs

Type the following letter in modified-block style with indented paragraphs. Remember to set 2 tabs.

(Current Date) / Ms. Barbara Cole / One North 79 Avenue / Chicago, IL 60635 / Dear Ms. Cole:

¶Congratulations on completing the requirements for your undergraduate degree! As you look forward to joining the workforce on a full-time basis, you are probably trying to determine how you can stretch your budget to include reliable transportation. We can be of help to you!

¶ During the next three months, we are offering a special discount package. This package is available only to members of this year's college graduating class who will be purchasing a new car for the first time. In addition, we can arrange financing at a rate lower than the rates available at most banks.

¶Call us toll free at 1-800-555-5295. Our customer service representative will put you in touch with your nearest Astra dealer. Act now! This special offer will be available for a limited time.

Sincerely, / Madonna Chavez / Marketing Manager / urs

PORTFOLIO
Activity

If you made any errors in Letter 16, correct them. Then print a copy of the letter and add it to your portfolio. In addition to the letter, write a short paragraph about the importance of proof-reading all documents carefully and the need to learn a variety of formats.

REPORT 42
Flyer

Open Report 40 and make the following changes.

1. Change the listed items so that they left-align approximately 1.5 inches from the margin.
2. Adjust the geometric shape so that it still wraps around the list.
3. Delete the line at the bottom of the page.
4. Add a thick horizontal line from margin to margin below the section containing the telephone number.
5. Change the color of the rules above and below the title to red.
6. Change the border of the geometric shape to red.

JOURNAL ENTRY

Study the photograph; then write about the importance of correct position while working at a keyboard. Answer: Why is it important? What is the correct position? What are some results of incorrect position?

Type the following letter in modified-block style with indented paragraphs, making the corrections indicated by the proofreaders' marks. Use your initials for reference.

(Current Date)

↓4

Mr. Marvin Estawick
Lawton Industries
5492 warren Avenue
Detroit, MI 48207-9602

Dear Mr. Estawick:

Mrs. Barbara Cole, who was an employee by your company as a summer intern, has applied for credit. Since Ms. Cole does not have a credit record, we will need a data sheet to be completed by her most recent employer.

Will you please fill out and return the form that was sent to you so we that we may process Ms. Cole's request for an automobile loan. A release statment has been signed giving you permission to disclose the requested information.

If you have any questions regarding this form can be answered by calling me at 312-555-9672, Ext. 40. Please FAX the form to me at 312-555-9677.

Sincerely,

Ms. Madonna Chavez
Marketing Manager

urs

FORMATTING

C. GRAPHIC LINES/RULES

Vertical and/or horizontal lines, or rules, can be used to enhance the appearance of a printed page or to separate text to make it more readable. There are many line styles from which to choose. Lines may be light, heavy, solid, broken, double, and so on. In addition, lines can be positioned in different ways to make your document visually appealing.

D. SOFTWARE FEATURES

STUDENT MANUAL

Lines	Line Position
Line Size	Line Style

Study Lesson 104 in your student manual. Complete all the practice activities while at your computer. Then complete the jobs that follow.

DESKTOP PUBLISHING APPLICATIONS

REPORT 40
Flyer

Open and revise Report 33 as follows:

1. Add a heavy line the length of the heading above and below the heading.
2. Add a heavy line the length of the longest text line approximately 0.5 inch below the last line of text.
3. Delete the Wingdings diamonds and extra spaces from both sides of each item in the list.
4. Draw a geometric shape around the items in the list.

REPORT 41
Flyer

Open Report 38. Give it a new look by following these steps:

1. Delete the border around the title.
2. Delete the page border.
3. Change the page layout so that the title starts approximately 2 inches from the top of the page.
4. Change the title to Times New Roman 20-point blue.
5. Add a thick horizontal blue line beneath the title.
6. Change the bullets to 20-point red.
7. Add a 5-inch horizontal double blue line 0.5 inch below the last line of text.

LESSON 56

LETTERS WITH ENCLOSURES AND ATTACHMENTS

OBJECTIVES:

- Improve keyboarding skill.
- Format modified-block letters with enclosures and attachments.
- Type 33/3'/5e.

A. WARMUP

Type each line 2 times.

Speed
Accuracy
Language Link
Technique

1 James was not here when all of us signed the card for Rita.
2 Jacqueline was glad her family took five or six big prizes.
3 The picnic is always Labor Day (first Monday in September).
4 Will students use the SHIFT LOCK to type in SOLID CAPITALS?
| 1 | 2 | 3 | 4 | 5 | 6 | 7 | 8 | 9 | 10 | 11 | 12

SKILLBUILDING

B. PRETEST

Take a 1-minute timing on the paragraph. Note your speed and errors.

Social Studies
Connections

5   The fight for women's suffrage took quite a few years.   11
6 One zealous leader of the battle was a Quaker named Alice   22
7 Paul who used protest marches and hunger strikes to fight   33
8 for the right to vote.   37
| 1 | 2 | 3 | 4 | 5 | 6 | 7 | 8 | 9 | 10 | 11 | 12

LESSON 104

GRAPHIC LINES/RULES

OBJECTIVES:

- Refine keyboarding skill.
- Learn to select, size, and position lines.
- Learn about line styles.

A. WARMUP

Type each line 2 times.

Speed
Accuracy
Language Link
Numbers/Symbols

1 Clair may wish to blame me for both of these big work jams.
2 By quietly giving back six tops, we amazed the four judges.
3 The French student will visit the Grand Canyon in February.
4 Rick sold 64 tickets on 10/23/99, and then he sold 75 more.
| 1 | 2 | 3 | 4 | 5 | 6 | 7 | 8 | 9 | 10 | 11 | 12

SKILLBUILDING

B. 30-SECOND TIMINGS

Take two 30-second timings on lines 5–6. Then take two 30-second timings on lines 7–8. Try to increase your speed on each timing.

5   I think that we might cut down our staff loss if you   11
6 will make a pay scale that shows all are being paid fairly.   23

7   We have not been able to cut costs. We do not know how   11
8 a boss set up the pay scale to show we are all paid fairly.   23
| 1 | 2 | 3 | 4 | 5 | 6 | 7 | 8 | 9 | 10 | 11 | 12

*inter*NET CONNECTION

Connect to the Internet. Enter the following URL: http://www.almaz.com/nobel/literature.html. Prepare a short report from the information you have read.

In the chart below, find the number of errors you made on the Pretest. Then type each of the following designated drill lines two times.

Pretest Errors	0–1	2	3	4+
Drill Lines	13–16	11–15	10–14	9–12

Accuracy

9 not fight women named until marches battle zealous Illinois
10 did leader states joined strikes protest suffrage Amendment
11 was after begin issue quite hunger decades Wyoming Congress
12 New their first debate Alice woman thirty Quaker Nineteenth

Speed

13 decades state years next pass took nine York the and did in
14 protest right named vote last test mend gave for was but to
15 strikes cause first lead them West used teen win who few of
16 fight other march rage Paul join zeal give two one not at a

D. **POSTTEST**

Repeat the Pretest. Compare your Posttest results with your Pretest results.

FORMATTING

E.   ENCLOSURE AND ATTACHMENT NOTATIONS

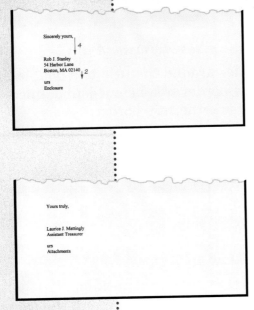

To show that an item is enclosed with a letter, type the word *Enclosure* at the left margin on the line below the reference initials. If the item is stapled or clipped to the letter, type the word *Attachment* on the line below the reference initials.

    If more than one item is enclosed or attached, type *Enclosures* or *Attachments*.

¶When you arrive for an interview, be sure to introduce yourself to the receptionist or assistant. Be pleasant and courteous. You can be assured that the manager will receive feedback on your manners and appearance from this person.

¶Once you are in the interviewer's office, wait until you are invited to sit. This shows that you have respect for the interviewer's position. If someone comes into the office during the interview, stand up and be prepared to shake hands with this person—it might be the interviewer's boss.

REPORT 37

Open Report 36 and make the following changes:

1. Center and type in all caps and bold the title *GOOD MANNERS FOR JOB INTERVIEWS* approximately 2 inches from the top of the page.
2. Add a thin border around the title.
3. Add a drop shadow to the title border.
4. Add a 10-percent fill inside the border.
5. Add a thick border to the entire page.
6. Change the paragraphs to a bulleted list.

REPORT 38

Open Report 37 and revise it following these steps:

1. Change the border around the title to a double line.
2. Change the page border to a heavy double line.
3. Delete the fill inside the title border.
4. Change the justification of the paragraphs to full justification.
5. Vertically center the page.

REPORT 39

Open Report 33 and make these changes:

1. Add a heavy border around the heading.
2. Add a heavy, double-line border around the page.
3. Add a broken-line border to the last line.
4. Add a 5-percent fill/shading to the last line.

LETTER 18
Modified-Block With Indented Paragraphs

Type this letter in modified-block style with indented paragraphs. Be sure to include an enclosure notation.

(Current Date) / Mr. and Mrs. Marvin Carson / Circle Route, Box 318 / Elk City, OK 73644 / Dear Mr. and Mrs. Carson: ¶Congratulations on becoming the owner of a Model L350 dishwasher! The TurboKleen name on your dishwasher identifies it as a top-quality kitchen appliance.

¶For the past 25 years, we have produced appliances that are reliable—products that will help America's busy families better manage their limited time. Because we are so certain of the reliability of our appliances, every TurboKleen appliance comes with a ten-year warranty. Your warranty is enclosed with this letter. If your dishwasher should need servicing before that time, a call to our dealer will bring a service technician to your door within 24 hours.

¶Welcome to our family of satisfied customers. When we can be of any assistance to you, please let us know. /Cordially yours, / William Clifford / President / urs

LETTER 19
Modified-Block With Indented Paragraphs

Type this letter in modified-block style with indented paragraphs. Remember to type your reference initials and an enclosure notation.

May 17, [year]

Mrs. Rosa Ortez

39 McFarland Lane

Madison, WI 53714

Dear Mrs. Ortez:

We are pleased to answer the question of your science students about allergy testing. The test takes two days. This includes food allergy tests as well as the usual tests for plants, animals, and old spores, etc. Technicians in our labs must be able to conduct these tests.

You were interested in having your class visit our labs. This would be a good time to plan to have your students visit. I would be willing to come in early on the Thursday morning you specify to work with your students and you. When you have decided upon a date, please give me a call. Use the enclosed form to select the best time for your students to visit our labs.

Sincerely,

Hans Rosen

Clinic Manager

FORMATTING

F. BORDERS, DROP SHADOW, FILL

In addition to different fonts and colors, there are other special formatting techniques that will make documents more eye-catching. For example, you can use **borders** (frames), around text or pages; **drop shadows** (shading), to make text look three-dimensional; or **fill** (shading), options to call attention to text.

G. SOFTWARE FEATURES

STUDENT MANUAL

Borders   Drop Shadows   Fill

Study Lesson 103 in your student manual. Complete all the practice activities while at your computer. Then complete the jobs that follow.

DESKTOP PUBLISHING APPLICATIONS

REPORT 36

Type the following report single-spaced. Use the default top margin. Leave a blank line between paragraphs.

¶It is important to display good manners at all times. Manners are especially important during a job interview. Good manners show that you are sociable and civilized and may be a potentially good member of the company's team.

¶Arriving for an interview on time is one way to demonstrate your good manners. This indicates that you are reliable and will be on time for work. Being late for an interview could harm your chances of being hired.

¶Go to your interview alone. Even if someone must drive you to the interview, do not have him or her accompany you to the interview site. If possible, leave your hat and coat in the outer office. Carrying or wearing them into the interviewer's office may be awkward, and it may give the interviewer the impression that you are anxious to leave!

LETTER REINFORCEMENT

OBJECTIVES:

- Improve keyboarding skill.
- Strengthen skill in formatting business letters.

A. WARMUP

Type each line 2 times.

Speed
Accuracy
Language Link
Symbols

1 It was a good idea to start to write your report this week.
2 My ax just zipped through the fine black wood quite evenly.
3 The accident was distressing; however, no one was impaired.
4 What a sight! Good luck! Watch out! At last! No way! Never!
| 1 | 2 | 3 | 4 | 5 | 6 | 7 | 8 | 9 | 10 | 11 | 12

SKILLBUILDING

B. TECHNIQUE TIMINGS

Take two 30-second timings on each line. Focus on the techniques at the left.

Use the correct shift keys.
Type without pausing.

5 Dr. and Mrs. Wynans won tickets to the Hula Bowl in Hawaii.
6 The Gas & Go was first named Your Place and then Shop Stop.
7 Mr. Ulan is taking us to the Museum of Fine Arts in Boston.
8 I turned right on Lemon, left on Davis, and left on Fuller.
| 1 | 2 | 3 | 4 | 5 | 6 | 7 | 8 | 9 | 10 | 11 | 12

C. PACED PRACTICE

Turn to the Paced Practice routine beginning on page SB-7. Take three 2-minute timings, starting at the point where you left off the last time.

CULTURAL CONNECTIONS

Did you know that students in Japan go to school five or six days a week? The school day usually begins about 8:30 a.m. and ends about 3:30 p.m. Saturday classes are usually over by noon. Most students begin studying English in the seventh grade and continue until they finish school.

C. PRETEST

Take a 1-minute timing on the paragraph. Note your speed and errors

```
15      You should join those who have learned how to use      10
16 their typing skill on the job. This skill can be used in     22
17 many walks of life, and it is just what you will need to     33
18 help you succeed. Most jobs now require computer typing.      44
   | 1 | 2 | 3 | 4 | 5 | 6 | 7 | 8 | 9 | 10 | 11 | 12
```

D. PRACTICE

SPEED: *If you made 2 or fewer errors on the Pretest, type lines 19–26 two times each.*

ACCURACY: *If you made more than 2 errors on the Pretest, type lines 19–22 as a group two times. Then type lines 23–26 as a group two times.*

Left-Hand Reaches

```
19 ded den dear deaf dread greed horde stead adept defer dried
20 wew wet week weed weave swear where worse weigh wheat wheel
21 cdc cod clad cord cedar crowd cloud cadet child crude cider
22 rtr art wart cart track train start trail tramp parts troop
```

Right-Hand Reaches

```
23 uyu your duly yule duty lucky young youth dusty yucca murky
24 jhj just huge join harm joist hunch jumpy house judge heart
25 klk milk folk walk silk silky balky milky links polka stalk
26 opo pop poor stop snoop whoop spoon ponds pound polka scope
```

E. POSTTEST

Repeat the Pretest. Compare your Posttest results with your Pretest results.

FACT FILE

Silly putty was originally known as "gupp." This popular material was invented in 1945 by engineers at GE.

LETTER 20

Block-Style
Personal-Business

Alternate
Block-Style
Personal-Business

To prepare this personal-business letter in alternate block style, type the writer's address before the date.

Do not type the address after the sender's name.

Refer to pages 169–170, if needed.

Format the personal-business letter below in block style; prepare a No. 10 envelope. Use the writer's name and address for the return address on the envelope. Add/append the envelope to the letter.

(Current Date) / Ms. Zoe Albright / Merkel Realtors, Inc. / 150 E. Ponce De Leon / Decatur, GA 30032 / Dear Ms. Albright:

¶My family and I are moving to Decatur from Indianapolis in October, and I would like your help in finding our new home. Friends in Decatur have told me that you know which homes best suit your clients; no one can do better. I am employed by the Albertson Corporation as an accountant, and I would like to drive less than 10 miles to work.

¶We are interested in a four-bedroom home with three and a half baths, a family room, a double-car garage, and a pool, if possible. We would like either a brick ranch or two-story colonial home. My wife prefers the ranch style, and I prefer the colonial style. I have attached some pictures of similar homes that appeal to us.

¶As we have two children, a boy and a girl, two of the four bedrooms would be for their use. One bedroom and bath would be for guests. We would like a large master bedroom overlooking the rear of the property.

¶Please send me any available information on such a home including the location, price, taxes, closing costs, and other such fees. As soon as we hear from you, we will make an appointment to visit you and see the homes you suggest.

¶You may call me at work at 317-555-2900 or my wife at home at 317-555-8957.

Sincerely yours, / Lewis K. Lincoln / 3350 Carson Avenue / Indianapolis, IN 46227/Attachments

*inter*NET CONNECTION

Use the Internet to search for sites that provide information about available properties for sale, information about a particular area, and financial information such as selling prices and mortgage rates.

LESSON 103

BORDERS AND FILL

OBJECTIVES:

- Improve keyboarding skill.
- Compose at the keyboard.
- Learn about borders and fill.
- Learn about drop shadows.

A. WARMUP

Type each line 2 times.

Speed
Accuracy
Language Link
Technique

```
1 The six forms she got from the firm may do for the problem.
2 The judge quickly gave six of the prizes to the able woman.
3 There at the bank their personnel gave personal statements.
4 I need TWO or THREE or FOUR, but ONE or FIVE are good also.
  | 1 | 2 | 3 | 4 | 5 | 6 | 7 | 8 | 9 | 10 | 11 | 12
```

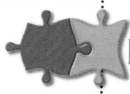

LANGUAGE LINK

B. COMPOSING AT THE KEYBOARD

To make your writing easier to read and understand, use concise wording. Replace lengthy phrases such as *due to the fact that* with *because*.

Revise the following paragraph to eliminate the redundant wording.

```
5      Last week I completed my term paper in a satis-
6  factory manner. The paper was six pages in length and
7  was written for the purpose of describing what happened
8  during the Civil War. For the simple reason that I had
9  done my research for the purpose of completing this
10 report, I know that my grade will meet with my approval.
11 It would appear that my instructor plans to extend to
12 me an invitation to read the report to the class. Due
13 to the fact that I am not a good speaker, I am experi-
14 encing nervousness about doing this.
```

Format the business letter below in modified-block style with blocked paragraphs. Make the corrections indicated by the proofreaders' marks, and prepare a large envelope. Append/add the envelope to the document.

(Current Date)

Mr. William J. Gross President

National WordProcessing Association

3500 Collingwood Boulevard

Toledo, Oh 43624

Dear Mr. Gross:

¶ Thank you for you letter of last week telling me that you

believe a talk on the skills needed by a word processor

would be a great intrest to your associatoin member.

¶ I have taken the liverty of developing a talk and have

entitled it "The Well-trained Word Processor." The talk will

take approximate one hour. I will need an over head

projector, a screen, and a mike. Its my intent to have them

microphone   members

involve during the talk, and I will need assistance in

it be possible for

distributing handouts to the audience. Would you please to

have two assistants available to help me?

¶ Enclosed is an outline of my talk also I have enclosed a

also

synopsis of the talk. I thought you might be interested in

what I was planning to discuss. If you have suggestions for

any

other points which should be included please let me know.

¶The next step is to prepare a draft of your resume. Start with your name, address, and telephone number. You may want to include an objective such as "Obtain a position that utilizes my skills and provides an opportunity for growth." Next, include your educational background. Include school names, dates, special courses, and your grade point average.

¶Next, list your work experience, if any. This list should be arranged in chronological order, with the most recent experience first. Include the name and address of your employer, your supervisor's name, and a brief description of your duties. If you have no work experience, you may want to describe activities in which you participated that have provided you with valuable skills.

¶Finally, develop a list of references. Before doing so, ask people for permission to use their names. References should consist of teachers, employers, supervisors, or other people who can vouch for your work ethics and other important traits.

¶Once you determine what should be on your resume, type the final copy. Be sure to proofread carefully. Your resume will often make the first impression an employer will have of you, and you want it to be perfect. Then, print your resume on high-quality paper that matches the paper you will use for your cover letter and the envelope.

¶While sending a perfect resume will maximize your chances of securing a job, it does not guarantee that everyone to whom you send your resume will interview you.

PORTFOLIO
Activity

Choose a card file or an address book and begin to ask people if you may use their names as references. If a person agrees, write his or her name, title, address, telephone number, and a few brief words about what kind of information they could provide a prospective employer. Next, begin recording information about yourself that you will need to prepare a resume. Update this information every few months.

¶ I plan to make my air plane reservations next week. Is there an exact time you would like me to arrive on the first day of the meeting? I plan to attend as many sessions as possible.

Sincerely yours,

David G. Moran,
Consultant

urs
Enclosures

LETTER 22

Modified-
Block Style
With
Indented
Paragraphs

Open Letter 21, and revise it as follows:

1. Change the format to modified-block style with indented paragraphs.
2. Replace all instances of *talk* with *presentation*.

PORTFOLIO
Activity

Revise Letter 22 if you made any errors. Print a copy for your portfolio. Then compose a short paragraph describing the differences between block-style and modified-block style business letters. Decide which style you would prefer to use, and explain why you chose that style.

STUDENT MANUAL

Font Color   Drop Caps

Study Lesson 102 in your student manual. Complete all the practice activities while at your computer. Then complete the jobs that follow.

DESKTOP PUBLISHING APPLICATIONS

REPORT 35

Follow these directions to format the report that follows:

1. Turn on widow/orphan control.
2. Center and type the title in a 20-point sans serif font, such as Arial, approximately 2 inches from the top of the page.
3. Add a diamond symbol to either side of the title with Wingdings (t).
4. Change the title color to red.
5. Center and type your name in a 16-point sans serif font. Leave a blank line between the title and your name.
6. Type the body of the report in Times New Roman 16-point, single-spaced with full justification. Leave a blank line between paragraphs, but do not indent the paragraphs.
7. Use a blue drop cap for the first letter of each paragraph.
8. Number the pages at the bottom center.

AN EFFECTIVE RESUME / By Your Name

¶The main goal of a resume is to create enough interest to secure an interview for a job. A resume should be brief—no more than one page. It should reflect your education, skills, accomplishments, and experience in a positive way.

¶Before you begin writing your resume, do a self-evaluation. Determine your abilities and your goals and ensure that they are compatible. Know what you want to do, why you want to do it, and why someone should hire you to do this.

LESSON 58

RESUMES

OBJECTIVES:

- Refine keyboarding skill.
- Learn about resumes.
- Type 33/3'/5e.

A. WARMUP

Type each line 2 times.

Speed
Accuracy
Language Link
Numbers/Symbols

1 Building typing skill seems easier if you type short words.
2 Maxine will become eloquent over a zany gift like jodhpurs.
3 Evi went to math, history, and art; but she missed English.
4 She decided that 1/3 of $36 = $12 and that 20% of $30 = $6.

| 1 | 2 | 3 | 4 | 5 | 6 | 7 | 8 | 9 | 10 | 11 | 12

SKILLBUILDING

B. PREVIEW PRACTICE

Type each line 2 times as a preview to the 3-minute timings that follow.

Accuracy
Speed

5 co-op solved picture resume training opportunity experience
6 learn other will give when some work stay you job not do or

C. 3-MINUTE TIMINGS

Take two 3-minute timings on lines 7–15. Note your speed and errors.

Goal: 33/3'/5e

7   Picture this. You go to look for work. You do not get   11
8 the job since you have no work experience. You cannot get   23
9 work experience. No one will give you the opportunity. It   34
10 may seem like a big problem to you, but students who enroll   46
11 in a co-op work class have solved it. While still in high   58
12 school, they earn as they learn. Some stay on the job full   70
13 time. Some go on to college or other training. In any case,   81
14 they will have work experience to list on their resumes   92
15 when they complete high school.   99

| 1 | 2 | 3 | 4 | 5 | 6 | 7 | 8 | 9 | 10 | 11 | 12 SI 1.27

Take two 5-minute timings on the paragraphs. Note your speed and errors.

Goal: 38/5'/5e

```
7        You can realize many benefits from using a computer      11
8   calendar program. At times, however, even with computers,     22
9   there still may be a need for a desk calendar. A desk         32
10  calendar can be quite useful if entries are neatly written    45
11  in pencil so that you can change them quickly as you need     56
12  to. If your calendar is visible on the desk and your notes    68
13  are clear, your coworkers and your boss can extract needed    80
14  details of your schedule when you are out of the office. Do   92
15  not jot your private notes on the calendar.                   101

16       A daily planner can also help you manage your time.      111
17  This record might have ruled or blank paper with places to    123
18  mark each hour of your day. Some people prefer to use a       134
19  weekly planner, which shows the schedule for a whole week.    146
20  The pages are split into parts and may have a blank space     158
21  for routine entries.                                          162

22       Another daily reminder tool is a tickler file. The       172
23  tickler file uses dated index cards. You can then place       184
24  reminders behind the correct date.                            190
```

| 1 | 2 | 3 | 4 | 5 | 6 | 7 | 8 | 9 | 10 | 11 | 12 SI 1.39

FORMATTING

D. FONT COLORS AND DROP CAPS

In addition to changing font sizes and styles, you can also create special effects by using color throughout a document and by using special treatments such as drop caps at the beginning of paragraphs. Keep in mind that you should limit the number of font styles and colors to keep your document readable.

D. RESUMES

Once you decide to apply for a job, you will need to prepare a resume. A resume is a summary of your training, background, and qualifications for the job. There are many acceptable formats for resumes, but there is basic information that should be included no matter which format you choose.

1. **Heading.** Your name, address, telephone number (with area code), and e-mail address if you have one.
2. **Objective.** A statement about the type of job you are seeking.
3. **Education.** A list of your educational background beginning with the highest level of and most recent education first. Include the school name and address, any diplomas or degrees, the year you earned them, the year you graduated, and your major area of study.
4. **Experience.** A list of your work experience beginning with the most recent. Include the name, address, and telephone number of the company; dates of employment; your job title(s); and the name and title of your supervisor. You may also want to include a brief description of your duties.
5. **Honors, Awards, and Activities.** Any special activities or achievements that relate to the position for which you are applying. (These may give you an "edge" over other applicants.)
6. **References.** A list of at least three people who can tell a prospective employer about what kind of worker you are. Include their names, job titles, addresses, and telephone numbers. You may want to use teachers, former supervisors, and former employers as references. Before you use a person's name as a reference, you *must* get permission from that person. Another option for references is to include the statement, "References will be furnished upon request."

FACT FILE

The Internet is being used more and more by companies and individuals to match available jobs to the people who have the required skills. You can now post your resume on the Internet at a variety of sites. When you prepare a resume for electronic posting, you should keep it simple. Use a minimum number of fonts, do not use bold or italic, and use a minimum number of other special features.

LESSON 102

FONT COLORS AND FEATURES

OBJECTIVES:

- Learn to change font color.
- Learn to use drop caps.
- Type 38/5'/5e.

A. WARMUP

Type each line 2 times.

Speed
Accuracy
Language Link
Numbers/Symbols

1 They may go to town for the pens if they are not both busy.
2 We amazed six judges by quietly giving back the four pages.
3 He told Aunt Joan to buy Major Michael an anniversary gift.
4 Jo & Don bought 20 cookies @ $.25 from the You & Me Bakery.
| 1 | 2 | 3 | 4 | 5 | 6 | 7 | 8 | 9 | 10 | 11 | 12

interNET CONNECTION

Keeping track of dates and required information should be simple and easy. Search the World Wide Web for types of tickler files. You may want to start with a search using the key words: time management.

SKILLBUILDING

B. PREVIEW PRACTICE

Type each line 2 times as a preview to the timings that follow.

Accuracy
Speed

5 extract planner realize penciled calendar reminder benefits
6 on if of as may day for use the can jot your each with help

This is one example of a formatted resume. There are many acceptable styles.

Martina Valdez
4101 Fuller Apartments
Clio, MI 48240
313-555-2714
E-mail: martina@valdez.net

OBJECTIVE

To obtain an office position with word processing responsibilities.

EDUCATION

Clio High School, Clio, MI 48420

Graduated: June 1998
Major: Office Technology
Grade Point Average: 3.66

Business Subjects: Accounting, keyboarding (75 wam), word processing (Word and WordPerfect)

Honors and Activities: Student Council president during senior year; concert choir for four years; Business Student of the Year in 1998

EXPERIENCE

Rathjen Moving Co., 471 Vienna Road, Flushing, MI 48433
Telephone: 313-555-5420

June 1998 to present
Position: General Office Assistant
Supervisor: Joyce Wiesnewski, Administrative Assistant

Duties: Composing and typing routine correspondence; preparing invoices

REFERENCES

References will be furnished upon request.

REPORT 34

When my ☺ rang, I was ☹. I turned on some ♫ to make me ☺; then I read the paper. There were several articles I ✂ out to send to my friends. Of course, that meant I had to ✎ to them first. As someone ☞ out, ✉ may be the ☀ in someone's day.

Follow these steps to type the paragraph:

1. Change the font size to 24 points.
2. Change the font to WPIconicSymbolsA (or something comparable); replace the words in brackets; then use the following keystrokes to create the symbols. (Before you continue typing, be sure to change the font back to Times New Roman.)

clock	@	cut	C
unhappy	;	write	N
		pointed	L
music	+	letters	J
happy	(	sunshine	z

When my [alarm clock] rang, I was [unhappy]. I turned on some [music] to make me [happy]; then I read the paper. There were several articles I [cut] out to send to my friends. Of course, that meant I had to [write] to them first. As someone [pointed] out, [letters] may be the [sunshine] in someone's day.

REPORT 15

Resume

Type the resume that is illustrated on page 206 using the same format. Follow these steps:

1. Use default side and bottom margins.
2. Vertically center the page.
3. Center and type the name in bold.
4. Center and type each line in the heading; then press ENTER 2 times.
5. Type the side heading *OBJECTIVE* in all caps and bold; then press ENTER 2 times.
6. Align the remaining text at the left margin. Leave a blank line between sections.
7. Leave a blank line before and after the bold side headings.

REPORT 16

Resume

Prepare a resume for yourself using the guidelines in this lesson. Include all sections that are applicable to your background. Do not include a section if you have no entries to place in that section.

PORTFOLIO
Activity

Once you create your resume, continue to "fine-tune" it as you continue taking courses or gaining additional work experience. Prepare a list of people you want to use as references, and ask those people for permission to list their names. Create a sheet with their names, titles, addresses, and telephone numbers. Update the list periodically so that when you are looking for a job you have the most complete, up-to-date information.

REPORT 33
Flyer

Create the flyer in the illustration following these steps:

1. Center the text vertically and horizontally.
2. Type the heading using Arial 36-point.
3. Add the symbols on either side of the heading using Wingdings 36-point (8).
4. Double-space after the heading.
5. Change to Arial 20-point and type the remaining text. Quadruple-space before and after the list; double-space before typing the last line.
6. Add the diamond shapes to the listed items using Wingdings (t). Leave a space after the symbol at the beginning of a line and before the symbol at the end of a line.

⌐CompuTrain, Inc.⌐

Learn with the best trainers in the country!

◆ Upgrade your skills. ◆
◆ Improve your efficiency. ◆
◆ Create exciting publications. ◆
◆ Learn at your own pace. ◆
◆ Attend a live seminar. ◆

To schedule a live training seminar or to order video training, call 800-555-5555.

Don't wait! Call us now!

LESSON 59

APPLICATION LETTERS

OBJECTIVES:

- Improve keyboarding skill.
- Learn to format application letters.

A. WARMUP

Type each line 2 times.

Speed
Accuracy
Language Link
Numbers/Symbols

1 Janet works after school four hours a day at the town bank.
2 Buzz quickly designed five new projects for the wax museum.
3 I waited for my best friend, and she was late getting here.
4 Interest charged on the $7,000 loan is 15% (down from 17%).
  | 1 | 2 | 3 | 4 | 5 | 6 | 7 | 8 | 9 | 10 | 11 | 12

FACT FILE

Thanksgiving is celebrated around the world throughout the year. Thanksgiving in the United States is the fourth Thursday of November. Thanksgiving in Canada is the second Monday in October. In the Virgin Islands, Thanksgiving is celebrated on October 25, which marks the end of the hurricane season.

SKILLBUILDING

B. 12-SECOND SPRINTS

Take three 12-second timings on each line. Try to increase your speed on each timing.

5 The time had come for Bev to study for college final exams.
6 Be sure to relax, rest, and have a good meal before a test.
7 Sean scored better on this test than on the test last week.
8 This drill was written to be easy to read and fast to type.
  | | | 5 | | | 10 | | | 15 | | | 20 | | | 25 | | | 30 | | | 35 | | | 40 | | | 45 | | | 50 | | | 55 | | | 60

FORMATTING

C. ORIENTATION TO DESKTOP PUBLISHING

Desktop publishing (DTP) is the process of using special word processing features to make your documents fun and visually appealing. Through the use of different font styles, colors, boxes, and graphics, you can create a variety of special documents such as letterheads, flyers, and newsletters.

For documents to be effective, however, they should be fairly simple, have a limited number of different font styles, and contain a lot of white space.

D. SOFTWARE FEATURES

GO TO

STUDENT MANUAL
Special Characters

Study Lesson 101 in your student manual. Complete all the practice activities while at your computer. Then complete the jobs that follow.

DESKTOP PUBLISHING APPLICATIONS

REPORT 32

Follow these steps to type the paragraph:

1. Change the font size to 20 points.
2. Type the paragraph below in Times New Roman, but replace the words in brackets with Wingdings. To do this, change the font to Wingdings; then use the following keystrokes to create the symbols. (Before you continue typing, be sure to change the font back to Times New Roman.)

letter	+ (plus)
mailbox	- (hyphen)
air	Q (capital *Q*)
telephoned	((left parenthesis)
happy	J (capital *J*)

I wrote a [letter] and rushed to get it into the [mailbox]. I was sending it by [air] to get it delivered quickly. Once the [letter] was sent, I [telephoned] my friend, who was [happy] to learn it was coming.

Take a 1-minute timing on the paragraph. Note your speed and errors.

9	Most people work hard to improve their writing skills.	11
10	They make the nucleus of what they wish to say more clear	23
11	by poring over their rough drafts. They bring home their	34
12	point by rewriting, if necessary, and replacing some words.	46
	| 1 | 2 | 3 | 4 | 5 | 6 | 7 | 8 | 9 | 10 | 11 | 12	

D. PRACTICE

SPEED: *If you made 2 or fewer errors on the Pretest, type lines 13–20 two times each.*

ACCURACY: *If you made more than 2 errors on the Pretest, type lines 13–16 as a group two times. Then type lines 17–20 as a group two times.*

Adjacent Reaches

13 tr trip trade trait strain trolls truck strive tromp trials
14 po polka potter pomp point pot pork power poster poker pore
15 re renter remember resting rewrite reptiles referees recite
16 sa sample sank salmon sap sack saws sags sable savor sabers

Jump Reaches

17 mo money motor motley most mock mower mop mobile monkey moo
18 br break brake brain bracket brick brook broke brat bramble
19 nu nut number nurture nude null nurse nuclear knuckle nutty
20 ce recede center cellular celery cement certain censor celt

E. POSTTEST

Repeat the Pretest. Compare your Posttest results with your Pretest results.

COMMUNICATION FOCUS

The purpose of an application letter is to get an interview. When you go for an interview, dress neatly and appropriately. Be prepared to answer questions such as: Why do you think we should hire you for this job? How would you best describe yourself? What experience do you have? In addition, listen carefully to the interviewer, look at the interviewer when you speak, avoid nervous gestures, speak clearly, and answer questions honestly.

LESSON 101

DESKTOP PUBLISHING: SPECIAL CHARACTERS

OBJECTIVES:

- Improve keyboarding speed.
- Learn about desktop publishing.
- Learn about special characters.

A. WARMUP

Type each line 2 times.

Speed
Accuracy
Language Link
Numbers

```
1 The goal of the rich girls is to fix a bike for an old man.
2 Dave froze the mixtures in the deep brown jugs too quickly.
3 One runner from our high school races in the June 12 event.
4 Fabra will mark the board at 10, 29, 38, 47, and 56 inches.
 | 1 | 2 | 3 | 4 | 5 | 6 | 7 | 8 | 9 | 10 | 11 | 12
```

SKILLBUILDING

B. 12-SECOND SPRINTS

Take three 12-second timings on each line. Try to increase your speed on each timing.

```
5 She said the four girls can swim across the lake with ease.
6 Please take one of these big boxes down to the post office.
7 May we go to the game with you, or do you have other plans?
8 The short words are often typed faster than the long words.
| | | |5| | | |10| | | |15| | |20| | |25| | |30| | |35| | |40| | |45| | |50| | | |55| | | |60
```

FACT FILE

Opals are made up of many spheres of silica mole-
cules. They are not, however, crystals.

F. APPLICATION LETTERS

An application letter is written to apply for a position. Your resume should be enclosed with the letter. Since this may be the first impression an employer has of you, be sure that your letter and resume are each a single page, neat, accurate, and contain all essential information.

An application letter should contain the following paragraphs:

Paragraph 1: The purpose of the letter, the job for which you are applying, and how you learned of the opening.

Paragraph 2: The qualifications that make you especially suited for the position. Mention skills you have that can help the employer and the company. Refer to the resume you are enclosing.

Paragraph 3: Special skills that will set you apart from other applicants. For example, do you work well with other people? Are you very well organized? Are you proficient at using various machines?

Paragraph 4: A request for an interview. Restate your interest in the job and indicate when you will be available. Include a telephone number where an employer can easily reach you.

WORD PROCESSING APPLICATIONS

LETTER 23
Block Style

Alternate
Block Style

To prepare this application letter in alternate block style, type the writer's address before the date. Use the writer's address shown on page 211.

Format the following application letter in block style. Review the format of a personal-business letter in Lesson 48.

June 12, {year}

Mrs. Carlotta Drain
Richardson Insurance Agency
One Washington Boulevard
Fort Worth, TX 76126

Dear Mrs. Drain:

One of the participants in a career fair at my high school, Mr. Curtiss Hall, mentioned that you have an opening for an office assistant in your downtown office. I would like to be considered as an applicant for that position.

WORDS TO LEARN

automatic hyphenation

clip art

drawing tools

drop caps

graphics

newspaper columns

special characters

text color

text/word art

vertical lines

vertical text

CAREER BIT

GRAPHIC ARTIST Graphic artists may create promotional copy for new products, visual designs for annual reports and other corporate literature, or distinctive logos for products or businesses. Graphic artists use a variety of print, electronic, and film media to create art. Most graphic artists now use computer software to design new images; some of this work appears on the Internet and CD-ROM. Artists may be assigned to create the overall layout and design of magazines, newspapers, journals, and other publications. They may also be asked to create graphics for television and computer-generated media, for example, home pages on the Internet.

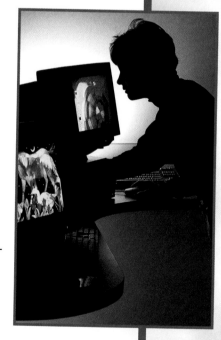

My extensive training and experience in the use of various software programs will enable me to serve Richardson Insurance Agency as a competent employee. As you will see on my enclosed resume, my computer skills helped me win two awards in competitions at the regional and state levels. Also, I have excellent grades in all of my high school business courses.

I have taken an active leadership role in school. I was president of our local chapter of Future Business Leaders of America, and I served as secretary of my class during my junior and senior years. These activities have provided me with valuable leadership and teamwork skills. They also gave me an opportunity to put my office skills to practical use.

I am very interested in working for Richardson Insurance Agency. I will telephone your office by the end of this week to arrange for an interview with you at your convenience. If you would like to speak with me before that time, please telephone me at my home number, 901-555-3245, after 4 p.m.

Sincerely,

Patrice McCrea
2316 S. Cravens
Fort Worth, TX 76132

Enclosure

LETTER 24
Block Style

Alternate
Block Style

If you are preparing this application letter in alternate block style, type the writer's address before the date.
Do not type the address after the sender's name.

Format the following handwritten application letter in block style. Remember to include the current date and an enclosure notation. Use your name and address for the writer's name and address.

Mr. Darnell Makulski
Human Resources Department
The Rogers Group
21771 Telegraph, Suite 3000
Columbus, OH 43231

Dear Mr. Makulski:

UNIT 6

LESSONS 101-120

OBJECTIVES

- Demonstrate keyboarding speed and accuracy on straight copy with a goal of 38 words a minute for 5 minutes with 5 or fewer errors.

- Demonstrate correct use of word processing features.

- Demonstrate basic design and formatting skills on a variety of reports including flyers, invitations, stationery, certificates, and newsletters.

- Compose short reports at the keyboard.

DESKTOP PUBLISHING

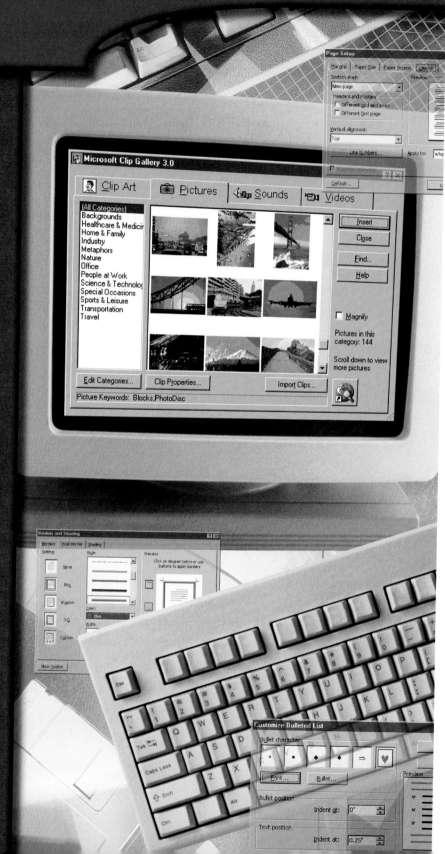

I would like to apply for the position of Administrative Assistant for your company. My high school English teacher, Ms. Lorie Gold, informed me of this position.

The experience I gained working summers as a volunteer office clerk for the American Heart Society qualifies me for the position with your company. My enclosed resume shows that most of my duties involved daily use of keyboarding, filing, and communications skills. This experience would be especially beneficial to your company.

My computer skills and my English skills are well above average, and I feel that I could perform any of the jobs I would be called upon to do with a high degree of competence.

It would be a pleasure to work for your company as an administrative assistant. Please allow me the opportunity to discuss my special qualifications with you in greater detail during an interview. You can reach me at my home number, 301-555-4774, any time after 3 p.m.

Sincerely,

PORTFOLIO
Activity

Search your local newspaper for a job you think you would be interested in applying for. Then, compose a letter of application for the position. In the letter mention that you are enclosing a resume. Format the letter correctly, and be sure to proofread carefully and correct all errors. Ask your teacher to review your letter for content. Once you are sure you have a well-written letter, print a copy and add it to your portfolio.

TABLE 42
Boxed Table

Create a 5-column, 10-row boxed table. Add 10-percent fill to the braced column headings. Sum columns B–E. Automatically adjust the column widths. Center the table vertically and horizontally.

SALES ANALYSIS Borden Manufacturing Company June 30, {year}				
	1st Quarter		2nd Quarter	
Salesperson	Units	Gross Sales ($)	Units	Gross Sales ($)
Robert Brazinski	10	427.70	29	1,240.33
Carol Dawkins	18	769.86	17	727.09
Janice Greene	20	855.40	28	1,197.56
Carlos Bieseda	17	727.09	24	1,026.48
Diane Kessler	15	641.55	25	1,069.25
Charles Young	19	812.63	32	1,368.64
TOTAL				

LESSON 60 REVIEW

OBJECTIVES:

- Review personal-business and business letters.
- Review application letters.
- Learn rules for semicolons.
- Type 33/3'/5e.

A. WARMUP

Type each line 2 times.

Speed
Accuracy
Language Link
Numbers

1 The old man paid for the yard work before he left for town.
2 Ezra jokingly vowed to question tax payments for his cabin.
3 The woman, however, was unable to provide proper childcare.
4 Send them to 6738 East 29 Street, Chicago, 60610 by May 19.

| 1 | 2 | 3 | 4 | 5 | 6 | 7 | 8 | 9 | 10 | 11 | 12

 LANGUAGE LINK

B. SEMICOLONS

Study the rule and the example that follows. Then correct any errors in punctuation in lines 5–8.

Rule 8: Use a semicolon between two independent clauses when one or both clauses have commas in them.

> *We ordered peanuts, popcorn, and candy; but only peanuts and candy were sent.*

5 We saw Jake, Pat, and Leo but Jim, Hal, and Ray were gone.
6 Lea needs a mouse, a disk, and a CD but she has a printer.
7 I took math, English, and science music and art were my electives.
8 She got cards, gifts, and a cake I took her out to dinner.

LETTER 62
Modified-Block Style

Type the following business letter in modified-block style. Use today's date.

Dr. David Rosenbloom / The Open University / Maks Rhoho Educational Center / 255 Klausner Street / Tel-Aviv 61392 / ISRAEL / Dear Dr. Rosenbloom:

¶The Board of Directors for the Atlanta International School, Atlanta, Georgia, (United States) is personally inviting you to become a member of their board. Your name was suggested at the summer meeting of the Foundation of International Schools in Geneva, Switzerland.

¶Your credentials contain most of what our personnel are seeking. We are impressed with your work as a Professor of Psychology in Tel-Aviv and notice that you have done extensive work with youth groups. Dr. Rosenbloom, we have a great need for someone with your talent and experience. We feel you could make an outstanding contribution as a member of the Board of Directors here in Atlanta.

¶Please respond as quickly as possible. You may telephone me at 404-555-1454 or send an e-mail to me at Aistalk@aol.com.

Yours truly, / Dr. Lien Vandermark, President / Atlanta International School / urs

MEMO 8
Template

Complete the following memo using the first memo template listed in your word processing software.

TO: Allison Wong / **CC:** Zachary Barkley / **FROM:** Rocio Cunningham / **DATE:** February 15, (year) / **SUBJECT:** Council Meeting

¶The office council meeting originally scheduled for Tuesday, February 23, has been changed to Thursday, February 25, upon the advice of Mr. Brown, our company's legal counsel. A revised agenda is attached.

¶There will be time for each person to voice his/her feelings on all major issues concerning changing personnel. Everyone's personal opinion will be taken into consideration before final decisions are made.

¶If you cannot attend the meeting, please send a representative who can speak for your department.

urs / Attachment /

SKILLBUILDING

C. PREVIEW PRACTICE

Type each line 2 times as a preview to the timings that follow.

Accuracy
Speed

9 type being learn classes example students keyboard accuracy
10 future choose skills that more plan good will able work big

D. 3-MINUTE TIMINGS

Take two 3-minute timings on lines 11–19. Note your speed and errors.

Goal: 33/3'/5e

11   Once you leave school, you should know that you must   11
12 acquire additional skills. On the job you will need good   22
13 work habits, teamwork skills, and technical skills. Plan to   34
14 take some courses that will help you advance in your career.   45
15   You should also realize that the skill you learn in   56
16 this class is just one example of the kind of skill you   67
17 will need on the job. Just about every job now requires   79
18 using a keyboard. Learn this skill as well as you can so   90
19 that you can succeed in your career choice.   99

| 1 | 2 | 3 | 4 | 5 | 6 | 7 | 8 | 9 | 10 | 11 | 12_{SI 1.25}

CULTURAL CONNECTIONS

The length of the workday and days of the week people work are different in various countries. Many companies, especially those in warmer climates, close their business for two to four hours during the middle of the day. In some countries, Thursday and Friday are days off with one day reserved for worship. The Korean workweek is Monday through Saturday and sometimes Sunday.

WORD PROCESSING APPLICATIONS

LETTER 25
Block Style

Compose and type a letter of application for the position in the classified ad shown on the next page. Review Lesson 59 before you begin composing. Review the format for personal-business letters and block-style letters in Lesson 48.

5 "Remember" said Sara "turn off the lights when you leave."
6 Sharon asked "Would you like to have half of my sandwich?"
7 "If you have not eaten lunch yet" said Bev "let's eat."
8 "I can hardly believe it is afternoon" said the professor.

SKILLBUILDING

C. CONCENTRATION

Type the following paragraph 1 time. Every time a number appears, replace it with a number that is two greater. For example, replace two with four and five with seven.

9   Three students wanted five notebooks, three calendars,
10 six mechanical pencils, four black markers, seven sheets of
11 poster paper, and eight ink pens for the school store. They
12 planned to market these items to students to make a profit.

WORD PROCESSING APPLICATIONS

LETTER 61

Block Style

Type the following business letter in block style. Use today's date.

Ms. Wynona Foster / Owner / Frills & Fluff Fine Fashion / 560 James Naismith Drive / Gloucester, Ontario / CANADA /K1B5N / Dear Ms. Foster:

¶Thank you for your clothing merchandise order. The New York Fashion Show was the best we have presented. We were delighted that you could attend.

¶Your purchase entitles you to a 25-percent discount on your next order. We know that our business relationship with Frills & Fluff Fine Fashion will be long-lasting. / Sincerely yours, / Yolanda McDonald / Merchandise Marketing / urs

ADMINISTRATIVE ASSISTANT

Fast-paced, downtown office seeks full-time administrative assistant. Applicants must type 40 wam, be proficient in word processing, have some desktop publishing knowledge, and be detail oriented. We offer competitive salary and benefits. Send resume to:

Human Resources Office
Suite 200
4700 Village Road
Columbus, Ohio 43235

LETTER 26
Modified-
Block Style

Type the following letter in modified-block style. Use the current date and remember to add an enclosure notation and your reference initials.

Ms. Marcia Chisholm / 15 Lynch Street / Mobile, AL 36604 / Dear Ms. Chisholm:

¶Our conference on November 3 and 4 was a great success. Your expertise helped to generate solid plans for the program, and I thank you for two positive days.

¶Enclosed are the summary of notes from our meeting, a new outline of your book, and a list of concerns about the outline. Please review these materials and let me know if you have any changes. As you recall, we did not have time to discuss everything on our agenda at the meeting.

¶As you review the outline, please check for the correct sequence and whether or not it is complete. Please provide your suggestions and concerns to me by December 4. I look forward to hearing from you.

Sincerely yours, / Diane Daniels / Editorial Advisor

LESSON 100

FORMATTING REVIEW

OBJECTIVES:

- Learn to use commas with direct quotations.
- Review formats for letters, memos, and tables.

Type each line 2 times.

Speed 1 Shaun typed by touch in order to type at his fastest speed.
Accuracy 2 Viv poured a liquid that froze quickly into the beige jars.
Language Link 3 Alana asked, "Did you record that book on a separate disk?"
Numbers/Symbols 4 By October 10 you need to order 253# of Item #46 @ $798.15.
| 1 | 2 | 3 | 4 | 5 | 6 | 7 | 8 | 9 | 10 | 11 | 12

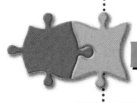

LANGUAGE LINK

B. COMMAS WITH DIRECT QUOTATIONS

Study the rules and examples below. Then edit lines 5–8 to correct any errors in punctuation.

Rule 21: Use a comma before a direct quotation.

The magician said, "Hokus pokus."

The officer replied, "The fingerprints are in the lab for analysis."

Rule 22: Use a comma after a direct quotation.

"Over here," shouted the traffic officer.

"All books are to be returned within one week," the statement read.

Rule 23: Use a comma before and after a direct quotation.

"When you go outside," said Mom, "be sure to wear a coat."

"When you drive my car," said Dad, "be very careful!"

UNIT 4

LESSONS 61–80

OBJECTIVES

- Demonstrate keyboarding speed and accuracy on straight copy with a goal of 35 words a minute for 3 minutes with 5 or fewer errors.

- Demonstrate correct use of word processing features.

- Demonstrate an understanding of proofreaders' symbols by editing copy marked for revision.

- Demonstrate basic formatting skills on a variety of tables, reports with special features, and multipage reports from a variety of copy—arranged, unarranged, rough draft, and handwritten.

- Compose sentences and short paragraphs at the keyboard.

WORD PROCESSING

¶You know that there is now an hour and a half for the lunch break. This will give employees time to work out, eat their lunches, and attend to personal matters before the afternoon shift begins.

¶Please encourage all those employees that you supervise to use this modern, new workout facility. It's free to employees during the week and open on Saturdays for employees and their families. / urs

PORTFOLIO
Activity

Choose one memo from these three to add to your portfolio. If you made any errors, correct the errors. Then print a copy and add it to your portfolio folder. Next, compose a short paragraph about why you chose this particular memo.

WORDS TO LEARN

adjusting column widths

dot leaders

endnotes

footnotes

hanging indent

header/footer

join/merge cells

left indent

margins

number columns

table create

table position

CAREER BIT

AIR TRAFFIC CONTROLLER Air traffic controllers ensure the safe operation of commercial and private aircraft. Their main responsibility is to organize the flow of aircraft in and out of the airport. Relying on radar and visual observation, they closely monitor each plane. In addition, controllers keep pilots informed about changes in weather conditions. The Federal Aviation Administration (FAA) is currently developing and implementing a new automated air traffic control system. As a result, more powerful computers will help controllers deal with the demands of increased air traffic. Some traditional air traffic controller tasks—like determining how far apart planes should be kept—will be done by computer. Improved communication between computers on airplanes and those on the ground is making the controller's job a little easier.

MEMO 6
Template

Complete this memo using the first memo template listed in your word processing software. Use today's date.

TO: Daniel Whitebuffalo / **FROM:** Ellen Herrera /
SUBJECT: Technology in Education Conference
¶The TIE conference will be held again this year in Snowmass.
¶There will be rooms available at the Aspen Lodge for all of our personnel. I've asked that the management make our stay more personal by reserving the entire west wing of the lodge for our group.
¶I've attached directions to the lodge; however, the company will provide us with a minivan. If you wish to ride in the mini-van, please contact me via e-mail. The address is: eherrera@ccsd.k12.ca.us. The minivan will pick us up in front of the school. We will leave promptly at 8 a.m. on Thursday, September 16. I hope you choose to join me in the ride to Snowmass. The fall tree colors will be beautiful at that time. I look forward to seeing you then. / urs / Attachment

MEMO 7
Template

Complete the following memo using the first memo template listed in your word processing software. Use today's date.

TO: Nina Lewis, Supervisor / **CC:** Marc Pak / **FROM:** Sam Roshdy / **SUBJECT:** Employees' Gym
¶The new gym and the Olympic swimming pool are now open for employee use. Thanks to your support of this effort, the company has equipped this gym for their personnel with most of the exercise equipment needed for a good 30-minute workout.

LESSON 61

LETTERS WITH COPY AND DELIVERY NOTATIONS

OBJECTIVES:

- Improve keyboarding skills.
- Format letters with copy and delivery notations.

A. WARMUP

Type each line 2 times.

Speed
Accuracy
Language Link
Numbers/Symbols

1 I feel sure he will be here in time to drive the boys home.
2 Six jumped from the quarry blaze, right into Lake Cragview.
3 Club dues must be paid now; however, you can pay next week.
4 Ryan saw Jack's dog's leash on Tim's brother's front porch.
| 1 | 2 | 3 | 4 | 5 | 6 | 7 | 8 | 9 | 10 | 11 | 12

SKILLBUILDING

B. 30-SECOND TIMINGS

Take two 30-second timings on lines 5–6. Then take two 30-second timings on lines 7–8. Try to increase your speed on each timing.

5   Rush to finish the drill lines before time runs out.   11
6 Keep wrists and arms quiet as your fingers strike the keys.   23

7   When the batter heard that sound of breaking glass, he   11
8 knew without looking that the home run had truly gone home.   23
| 1 | 2 | 3 | 4 | 5 | 6 | 7 | 8 | 9 | 10 | 11 | 12

C. DIAGNOSTIC PRACTICE: ALPHABET

Turn to the Diagnostic Practice: Alphabet routine on page SB-1. Type one of the Pretest/Posttest paragraphs and note your errors. Then type the corresponding drill lines 2 times for each letter on which you made 2 or more errors and 1 time for each letter on which you made only 1 error. Finally, repeat the same Pretest and compare your performance.

D. COPY NOTATIONS

When you send a copy of a memo to someone in addition to the addressee, type a copy notation on the memo. Many memo templates already have a field where you can simply insert the names of the people to whom you want to send copies of the memo. If there is no field, then type the copy notation as follows:

1. Type the copy notation on the line below the reference initials or below the enclosure or attachment notation.
2. At the left margin, type a lowercase *c* followed by a colon (*c:*)
3. Press the tab and type the name of the person receiving the copy.

E. ATTACHMENTS

When material is physically attached to a memo (either clipped or stapled), type an attachment notation below the reference initials. To type the attachment notation:

1. Press enter once after typing your reference initials.
2. Type the word *Attachment* at the left margin.

WORD PROCESSING APPLICATIONS

MEMO 5
Template

Complete this memo using the first memo template listed in your word processing software. Use today's date.

TO:/ Katrina Stevens / **CC:** / Marshall McElreath **FROM:**/ Justine O'Neal / **SUBJECT:** / Evaluation Criteria
¶Please refer to the attachment as you develop your suggestions for the evaluation criteria for the new department personnel brochure. Please give thought to developing at least five suggestions.
¶Submit your suggestions to me via e-mail by October 1. My personal e-mail address is joneal@jobs.personnel.gov.co.us. I assure you that all of your suggestions will be kept confidential in my personal mailbox. We will meet on October 5 in the Spruce Conference Oval Room to review all of your suggestions, develop a list of 25 criteria for personnel evaluation, and plan the brochure. / urs / Attachment

D. COPY NOTATIONS

When you send a copy of a letter to someone in addition to the addressee, type a **copy notation** on the letter.

1. Type the copy notation on the line below the reference initials or below the enclosure or attachment notation.
2. At the left margin, type a lowercase *c* followed by a colon *(c:)*.
3. Press the tab and type the name of the person receiving the copy. If more than one person is to receive a copy, type each name on a separate line, aligned at the tab.
4. Use a title before the name only if the first name or initial is unknown.

When you do not want the addressee to know that someone else is to receive a copy, use the notation *bc:* (blind copy). To add a blind copy notation:

1. Print one copy of the letter.
2. Type the *bc* notation 2 lines below the last item in the letter, and print another copy.

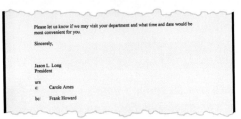

E. DELIVERY NOTATIONS

When a letter is being sent by a special method (fax, registered, certified, etc.), type the appropriate notation on the line below the reference initials. For example, a letter that is being faxed would have the notation *By fax* below the reference initials.

LESSON 99

MEMOS WITH COPY NOTATIONS AND ATTACHMENTS

OBJECTIVES:

- Improve keyboarding skill.
- Format memos with copy notations and attachments.
- Reinforce typing from script and rough draft copy.

A. WARMUP

Type each line 2 times.

Speed
Accuracy
Language Link
Numbers/Symbols

1 All of the errors have been corrected in the final project.
2 Pat quickly froze the gold mixtures in five old brown jars.
3 The old woman in the shoe said, "No more children, please."
4 Kenny & April ordered 50# of potatoes (red) @ $.45 a pound.
| 1 | 2 | 3 | 4 | 5 | 6 | 7 | 8 | 9 | 10 | 11 | 12

SKILLBUILDING

B. TECHNIQUE TIMINGS

Take two 30-second timings on lines 5–6. Then take two 30-second timings on lines 7–8. Focus on the technique at the left.

Keep your eyes on the copy.

5   We sit and toss rocks in the lake as the sun sets, but   11
6 we cannot see if they are going to skip over the big waves.   23

7   The lane that goes to the lake turns and goes to town,   11
8 but we do not know if you can use it all the way right now.   23
| 1 | 2 | 3 | 4 | 5 | 6 | 7 | 8 | 9 | 10 | 11 | 12

C. DIAGNOSTIC PRACTICE: ALPHABET

Turn to the Diagnostic Practice: Alphabet routine on page SB1. Type one of the Pretest/Posttest paragraphs and identify any errors made. Then type the corresponding drill lines 2 times for each letter on which you made 2 or more errors and 1 time for each letter on which you made only 1 error. Finally, repeat the Pretest and compare your performance.

LETTER 27
Modified-Block Style

Format this letter in modified-block style. Address a No. 10 envelope to the addressee, and append/add it to the document.

(Current Date) / Mr. Theodis Chamberlin / 17934 Roscommon Lane / Detroit, MI 48227 / Dear Mr. Chamberlin:

¶Enclosed is the TSA loan form that you requested when we talked today. Please complete the form by filling out the highlighted areas, and return the form to me in the enclosed envelope.

¶If you elect to pay via checking account, please attach a voided check. If you elect to pay by savings account, fill out the information requested about your savings account.

¶I am pleased to tell you that I have been assigned as your financial advisor as of today. Call me if you have any questions about completing the form.

Yours truly, / Tamika Murphy / urs / Enclosures / c: Karl Mendoza

LETTER 28
Block Style

Format this letter in block style. Address a No. 10 envelope and append/add it to the document.

(Current Date) / Ms. Annette Birdsong / General Manager / Fabric Palace / 3799 Tower Place / Waterbury, CT 06704-0543 / Dear Ms. Birdsong:

¶I am happy to report that we do have washed silk in a variety of colors. It can be shipped to you the same day that your order is received.

¶Simply choose the colors you want from the attached sample card; then call 1-800-555-9877 to place your order. If you prefer, you can mail the order using the form on the back of the sample card. Hopefully, you will be able to take advantage of our "quantity discounts" that will allow you to pass along the savings to your customers.

¶We look forward to receiving your order soon. / Sincerely, / Stephen Leiberman / Sales Manager/ urs / Attachment/ c: James Hollingshead / Mary Lee / bc: Richard Holiday

LETTER 60

Modified-Block Style With Indented Paragraphs

Type this business letter in modified-block style with indented paragraphs.

(Current Date) / Oksana Khizir / Elbrussky Prospekt 78-3 / Tyrnyanz, KBR 361600 / RUSSIA / Dear Ms. Khizir:

¶Careers in international marketing are everywhere, not only with firms involved directly with international business, but also with those that might be entering the global marketplace in the foreseeable future. Our firm, U.S. Industries, Inc., is one of those just entering the global market.

¶The CEO of our company met you last month when she was in Russia. She was impressed with your knowledge of politics, geography, and world history. Also, your sensitivity to the differences between cultures impressed her. You have mastered the English language, both written and spoken. These are all qualities necessary to have a successful career in international marketing.

¶We are hopeful that you will accept our offer of a position in our International Marketing Department.

Yours truly, / Joseph R. Murray / International Marketing Director / urs

PORTFOLIO Activity

Choose one of the international letters you have just completed. If necessary, correct any errors you may have made. Then, print one copy of the letter to add to your portfolio. Explore other cultural differences such as posture, gestures, facial expression, and so on, between Americans and people abroad.

LETTER 29
Modified-Block Style

Format this letter in modified-block style.

(Current Date) / Mr. Julio Sanchez / 233 Orchard Drive / Topeka, KS 66605 / Dear Mr. Sanchez:

¶Your financial planner, Craig Fulton, has shared with me your request to surrender your annuity policy with National Investors. Please consider the financial strength of our company before you make your final decision about this matter.

¶Before we process your request, we want to be sure you understand that a portion of the funds you withdraw may represent taxable income. You should contact your tax advisor to learn of the possible tax consequences of this withdrawal.

¶Please sign and return the enclosed Request for Surrender Information form indicating whether you wish to proceed with your request for surrender. If you have any questions, call our toll free number at 1-800-555-4885. / Yours truly, / Ali Faruk / Chief Executive Officer / urs / Enclosure / By fax / c: C. Fuller

PORTFOLIO
Activity

Open one of the letters you completed in this lesson and correct any errors you may have made. Then, print a copy of the letter and add it to your portfolio. Next, explain why it is important to add delivery notations to letters. List some other methods of deliveries that might be used.

Type this personal-business letter in modified-block style.

(Current Date) / Michael Renard / EuroBureau Interim / Rue de Hesperange 5 / L-1731 / LUXEMBOURG / Dear Mr. Renard:

¶Please send me an application form for your organization. I am interested in applying for a job as a temporary office assistant/computer operator in Luxembourg during the summer months of June, July, and August.

¶I will graduate from Evergreen High School in May and will be available for employment on June 1. I speak fluent German as well as French and Italian. My clerical and computer skills are excellent. My typing speed is 90 words a minute with 95 percent accuracy; I can efficiently use any computer in either a DOS or Windows environment.

¶I have spent the past three summers traveling in Europe, so I am familiar with the differences in culture, the various governments, and the transportation systems.

Sincerely, / Michele LaGare / 4810 South Longs Peak Road / Longmont, CO 80501

CULTURAL CONNECTIONS

Color should be taken into consideration if you are dressing for business abroad. In some cultures, only royalty wears certain colors, and other colors may convey grief. For example, in Malaysia, you should not wear yellow, blue, or white; in Thailand, you should not wear black or purple; in Japan, you should not wear mauve; in Greece, you should not wear black.

LESSON 62

LETTERS WITH POSTSCRIPTS

OBJECTIVES:

- Compose at the keyboard.
- Format letters with postscripts.
- Type 35/3'/5e.

A. WARMUP

Type each line 2 times.

Speed
Accuracy
Language Link
Numbers

1 It is easier to build good habits than to break bad habits.
2 Fritz quietly welcomed the five tax guides back from Japan.
3 Each student has two chances; therefore, the odds are good.
4 The 28 boys chose 29 books, 30 bags, 31 pens, and 32 disks.
| 1 | 2 | 3 | 4 | 5 | 6 | 7 | 8 | 9 | 10 | 11 | 12

LANGUAGE LINK

B. COMPOSING AT THE KEYBOARD

Answer the following questions with complete sentences.

5 How have computers changed our lives?
6 Why is appearance important when going for a job interview?
7 If you could write a book, what topic would you choose? Why?

FACT FILE

A computer virus is a program that "infects" computers. Some viruses are mild and may only cause messages to appear on screen. Other viruses are extremely destructive and can erase everything stored on a computer. Computer viruses are usually spread from machine to machine by infected disks or through Internet connections to unsafe sites.

E. INTERNATIONAL ADDRESSES

International mailing addresses are similar to domestic mailing addresses. International addresses may also include:

1. Numbers to identify the routing of the correspondence.
2. The name of the country typed in all capital letters as the final line of the address.

WORD PROCESSING APPLICATIONS

LETTER 58
Block Style

Type the following business letter in block style.

(Current Date) / Mr. George Grinderemann / Arnoldstrabe 56 / 22256 Hamburg / GERMANY / Dear Mr. Grinderemann: /

¶The VanHughes School of Fine Arts is pleased to notify you of your acceptance into our program. George, you realize that only a select few new students are accepted each year.

¶We considered your outstanding scholastic record at your school in Hamburg, Germany, and looked favorably upon your many extracurricular activities. Our Board of Directors unanimously voted you to be our foreign exchange student of the year.

¶Next month we will be sending you more information regarding the VanHughes School of Fine Arts, its housing choices, courses of study, and the many extracurricular activities we have available. You'll find that our faculty and staff are skilled, knowledgeable, and interested only in helping you succeed in a career in fine arts.

¶We look forward to hearing from you soon.

Sincerely yours, / Dr. Paula Toddsworthy / President / urs

SKILLBUILDING

C. PREVIEW PRACTICE

Type each line 2 times as a preview to the timings that follow.

8 stack enough quickly produce reference examining Organizing
9 finished leaving within pencil permit spend small time such

D. 3-MINUTE TIMINGS

Take two 3-minute timings on the paragraph. Note your speed and errors.

Goal: 35/3'/5e

10   Organizing the work space where you spend most of your 11
11 time will permit you to work more quickly and also produce 23
12 more. Check to see that all work still to be done is in one 35
13 stack and all work just finished is in another. Do you have 47
14 enough pens and sharp pencils? Are small things, such as 58
15 paper clips, staples, and tape, kept in a handy place? Are 70
16 reference books easy to reach from the work station? Time 82
17 spent examining your work space now can save time later. 93
18 Getting organized can lead to better use of time and space. 105
| 1 | 2 | 3 | 4 | 5 | 6 | 7 | 8 | 9 | 10 | 11 | 12 SI 1.25

JOURNAL ENTRY

Describe yourself in terms of how organized you are. For example, do you keep your room neat? Then, rate your-self in terms of organization.

SKILLBUILDING

C. PREVIEW PRACTICE

Type each line 2 times as a preview to the timings that follow.

Accuracy
Speed

14 who true quite traits choices realized examining individual
15 describe lifestyle identity achieve personal start will you

D. 5-MINUTE TIMINGS

Take two 5-minute timings on the paragraphs. Note your speed and errors.

Goal: 37/5'/5e

16 Most decisions about your present lifestyle have been	11
17 made for you by your parents. Your current way of life is	23
18 quite often defined by your role as a member of a family	34
19 and as a student. Your personal identity is closely related	46
20 to how you live. In fact, your lifestyle and who you are as	58
21 an individual are often linked.	64
22 As an adult, you will make almost all of the choices	75
23 that will determine your lifestyle. These decisions might	87
24 help you define your personal identity. It is never too	98
25 early to begin examining lifestyle features that you want	110
26 to have when you are older. When you can describe those	121
27 traits, you can start setting goals and selecting options	132
28 that will help you achieve the way of life you want to have	144
29 as an adult.	147
30 To live your life in a way that gives you peace and	158
31 joy, your needs must be satisfied, most of your wants must	169
32 be realized, and your style of living should be true to the	181
33 values you hold.	185

| 1 | 2 | 3 | 4 | 5 | 6 | 7 | 8 | 9 | 10 | 11 | 12SI 1.35

E. LETTERS WITH POSTSCRIPTS

A **postscript** (PS:) is an additional message in paragraph form at the end of a letter. To format a postscript:

1. Press ENTER 2 times after the last item in the letter.
2. If letter paragraphs are blocked, type the postscript at the left margin. If paragraphs are indented, indent the postscript.
3. Type *PS:* followed by 1 space; then type the message.

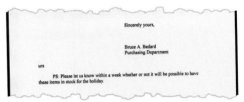

WORD PROCESSING APPLICATIONS

LETTER 30

Modified-Block Style With Indented Paragraphs

Format the following letter in modified-block style with indented paragraphs. Remember to indent the first line of the postscript.

(Current Date) / Ms. Rachael Goldstein / 65 Sparks Avenue / Portland, ME 04102 / Dear Ms. Goldstein:

¶As you know, the National High School Student Council is having its annual meeting in Denver, Colorado, next summer. As president of your school student council, you were recommended to our National Board as being an energetic, enthusiastic, and knowledgeable leader.

¶We are looking for students who are willing to spend two to three weeks during June or July to help plan the annual National High School Student Council event. You would fly to Denver and stay with one of our host families. Each weekday we will be working at my high school, Lincoln High, for four to six hours. We will be making minor revisions to a general outline from last year's national meeting.

¶I look forward to hearing from you with your acceptance to be a part of this national high school event. Your participation will certainly be well received by any college you plan to attend. / Sincerely, / Nicholas Bono, President / urs / c: Jamie Bluto / PS: Please contact me as soon as possible by phone at 303-555-1800 or by e-mail at nbono@alhs.dpsd.k12.co.us.

LETTERS WITH INTERNATIONAL ADDRESSES

OBJECTIVES:

- Compose at the keyboard.
- Type 37/5′/5e.
- Learn to type letters with international addresses.

A. WARMUP

Type each line 2 times.

Speed
Accuracy
Language Link
Numbers/Symbols

1 You can opt to leave things as they are and make no change.
2 Jacqueline was vexed by the folks who got the money prizes.
3 The vice president said, "Let's use dates we can maintain."
4 Take a 3-, 4-, and 5-minute timing on 186-C, pages 279-280.
| 1 | 2 | 3 | 4 | 5 | 6 | 7 | 8 | 9 | 10 | 11 | 12

LANGUAGE LINK

B. COMPOSING AT THE KEYBOARD

Redundancy is using several words that mean the same thing. For example, instead of using the phrase, "the same identical items," use just the word *identical*.

Type the following paragraph eliminating the redundant wording.

5   When driving to school, I take the same identical
6 route each day. I have a car that is small in size.
7 Two friends ride along with me. Each and every day we
8 get to class at about the same time. One day we tried
9 another different route and got lost. We rode around in
10 circles before we found our way. We repeatedly asked
11 many times for directions. The only other alternative
12 we had was to not repeat again the exact same route. We
13 decided we would continue using our original old route.

LETTER 31

Block Style

Format the following letter in block style.

(Current Date) / Mr. Jon Nagata / Takata Motor Company / 5800 Alder Drive S. / Tempe, AZ 85283 / Dear Mr. Nagata:

¶Surprisingly, many of us do not want to say no—to customers, sales-people, or employees—especially if they smother us with kindness and cheer. As we deal with these types of people more often, we begin to think of them as family. And, we all know how difficult it is to say no to family members.

¶That is the ploy of many salespeople worldwide. In America, we know the push of the salesperson who takes us to lunch, finds us tickets to the ball game, finds us tickets to the theater, or tells us how much he or she thinks of our spouse or children. This is all done with the pur-pose of making us feel guilty when we are ready to negotiate on price or terms.

¶Do not be afraid to set limits. The more precise your limits, the greater respect you will receive. Most of us want to be liked, but we should not let human feelings get in the way of business judgment. Saying no and saying it firmly will make you feel better—and will help your organization.

¶I hope this "hint" about our culture will help you when you visit other companies in the United States next month, Mr. Nagata. / Sincerely yours, / Nick DelVichicco / Consultant / urs / By fax / bc: Carole Schmidt / PS: Our representative, Christine Chung, will meet you on the 20th and accompany you on your visits.

LETTER 32

Modified-Block Style

Format the following letter in modified-block style. Use the current date.

Ms. Heidi Flaharty / 2039 Northrup Street, Apt. 224 / Denver, CO 80205 / Dear Ms. Flaharty:

¶Thank you for agreeing to speak to the students in my Word Processing 2 class on the topic of the office of the future. I heard your interesting presentation on this topic at the Vocational Training Association Convention. I know your ideas are going to be interesting to my students. ¶The class meets on Mondays at l0:30 a.m. in the Buhl Building of our campus in Westchester. I am hopeful that your schedule will permit you to grant this request. ¶Please contact me at 303-555-3298 to let me know what date would be convenient for you to speak. After I speak with you, I will be able to finalize my syllabus. / Yours sincerely, / Sybil Belletarre / Instructor / urs / By Next Day Express

TABLE 40

Create a boxed table with 3 columns and 9 rows in portrait orientation. Merge the first two cells in row 9. Shade the column headings with 20-percent fill. Insert a double line below the column headings and above the TOTAL line. Align the entries in columns 1 and 2 at the left; align the entries in column 3 at the right. Use the SUM feature to calculate the total salaries.

BRANCH MANAGER SALARIES January 1, {year}		
Office	**Manager**	**Salary**
Atlanta	Harrison Wilson	69,750
Boston	Audrey Pritchett	63,900
Chicago	Martin Sellers	62,800
Dallas	Leigh Martinez	68,500
Salt Lake City	William Beauchamp	64,350
Tulsa	Isabella Montgomery	68,890
TOTAL SALARIES		

TABLE 41

Open Table 39. Insert a TOTAL row after the last entry. In cell A8, type TOTAL PRICE. Delete all inside vertical lines in row 8. Format all the cells in column C (but not the column heading) with dollar signs and two decimal places. Then calculate a total for Price.

CULTURAL CONNECTIONS

Ukraine, which was once a part of the Soviet Union, became an independent republic in 1991. The rich fertile soil and plentiful rainfall in Ukraine are ideal for farming. Farmers grow a variety of grains as well as potatoes and sugar beets. Because of the abundant grain harvests, Ukraine is often called the breadbasket of Europe.

LESSON 63

REINFORCEMENT: LETTERS

OBJECTIVES:

- Learn about semicolons with independent clauses.
- Refine keyboarding skill.
- Format letters in a variety of styles.

A. WARMUP

Type each line 2 times.

Speed
Accuracy
Language Link
Numbers/Symbols

```
1  All of the fans were glad to hear news that their team won.
2  Jan very quickly froze both mixtures in the deep brown jar.
3  The legal offices will move; however, her office will stay.
4  Our Orders #207 and #208 and #209 were paid by Check #1317.
   |  1  |  2  |  3  |  4  |  5  |  6  |  7  |  8  |  9  |  10  |  11  |  12
```

LANGUAGE LINK

B. SEMICOLONS WITH INDEPENDENT CLAUSES

Study the rule and the examples that follow. Then correct any errors in punctuation in lines 5–8.

Rule 9: Use a semicolon to join two closely related independent clauses that are not connected by a conjunction (such as *and, but, or,* or *nor*).

> *Melissa wanted to climb to the top of the mountain; Harry did not.*
>
> *Harry was studying long hours; he was working days.*

```
5  Last year I invested in stocks after that I had less cash.
6  They gave an excellent presentation mine was not terrific.
7  Rene was saving his money he looked forward to his cruise.
8  Buy bananas while you are out I will get the other fruits.
```

C. PRACTICE

In the chart below, find the number of errors you made on the Pretest. Then type each of the designated drill lines 2 times.

Pretest Errors	0–1	2	3	4+
Drill Lines	12–16	11–15	10–14	9–13

Accuracy

9 useful column divide multiply formulas required spreadsheet
10 work using useful effort subtract numbers software required
11 numbs numeric division formulate subtraction multiplication
12 actions addition columnar requisite effortless requisitions

Speed

13 column meets with will used know kind for one use and of by
14 tool soft save hour form ware sheet one can use add row how
15 working rowing tools knows your full cane can you use if to
16 subs work add use the add are you how add it an if is on or

D. POSTTEST

Repeat the Pretest. Compare your Posttest results with your Pretest results.

WORD PROCESSING APPLICATIONS

TABLE 39

Create a 5-column, 7-row boxed table in landscape orientation. Shade the column headings with 20 percent fill. Insert a double line below the column headings. Align the entries in columns 1, 2, and 5 on the left; align the entries in columns 3 and 4 on the right. Adjust the column widths so that all entries fit on a single line.

DATA WORKS, INC.
Monthly Hardware Purchases
April {year}

Customer Name	Account No.	Price	Telephone No.	Item Description
Ferstad, Rhonda	F901-76-3488	535.75	505-555-8900	17" .42 mm flat screen monitor
Keller, Tenille	K854-00-3550	375.99	505-555-3409	24-bit color scanner
LaBerge, Paul	L258-04-3891	325.75	505-555-7833	Color laser printer
Persson, Andrew	P789-00-3548	98.99	505-555-6673	10X CD-ROM drive
Toring, Jan	T901-75-3487	315.95	505-555-7834	15" .28 mm flat screen monitor

SKILLBUILDING

C. 30-SECOND OK TIMINGS

Take two 30-second OK (error-free) timings on lines 9–10. Then take two 30-second OK timings on lines 11–12. Goal: no errors.

```
 9        People make decisions each day; most are just routine,   11
10  but some require exact thinking and the ability to analyze.    23

11        Maxine had five jobs requiring zest and nearly perfect   11
12  work habits; I explained that a few jobs involve hazards.      23
    | 1 | 2 | 3 | 4 | 5 | 6 | 7 | 8 | 9 | 10 | 11 | 12
```

D. DIAGNOSTIC PRACTICE: NUMBERS

Turn to the Diagnostic Practice: Numbers routine on page SB-4. Type one of the Pretest/Posttest paragraphs and identify any errors made. Then type the corresponding drill lines 2 times for each number on which you had 2 or more errors and 1 time for each number on which you made only 1 error. Finally, repeat the Pretest and compare your performance.

WORD PROCESSING APPLICATIONS

LETTER 33
Block Style

Format this letter in block style.

January 20, {year}/ Mrs. Blair Piapot / 706 Middleton Avenue / Tunica, MS 39175 / Dear Mrs. Piapot:

¶We at Dream Vacations are certainly able to assist you with your travel plans. We have years of experience helping our customers get the most for their travel dollar. One of our agents, Theresa Sullivan, will be happy to help you with ideas to make your trip to Alaska a memorable one.

¶I have enclosed several brochures giving descriptions both of cruises and airfare/hotel packages. Take some time now to look them over. Theresa will call you to work out the best time to meet as soon as you are ready.

¶If you have any questions or need additional information, please do not hesitate to call. It is a pleasure to be of service to you.

Cordially yours, / Carole Defazio / urs / Enclosures /c: Theresa Sullivan / bc: Carmella Rosito

LESSON 97

REVIEW

OBJECTIVES:

- Improve keyboarding skill.
- Review tables with sums.

A. WARMUP

Type each line 2 times.

Speed
Accuracy
Language Link
Numbers/Symbols

1 You must work very hard at this job to improve your skills.
2 Brown jars would prevent the mixture from freezing quickly.
3 The president said, "Let's give support to our leadership."
4 The L & C 10 3/4% bonds (due 2013) are at 175; bid 169 3/8.
| 1 | 2 | 3 | 4 | 5 | 6 | 7 | 8 | 9 | 10 | 11 | 12

FACT FILE

According to the Guinness Book of World Records, Shakuntala Devi completed the fastest mathematical computation in June 1980. She multiplied (in her head!) two randomly selected 13-digit numbers in just 28 seconds. A computer can accomplish this same feat in less than one second.

SKILLBUILDING

B. PRETEST

Take a 1-minute timing on the paragraph. Note your speed and errors.

5   A spreadsheet is a useful software tool if you know   11
6 how to use one. You can save hours of effort if you are   22
7 required to work with rows and columns of numbers by using   34
8 formulas to add, subtract, multiply, and divide numbers.   45
| 1 | 2 | 3 | 4 | 5 | 6 | 7 | 8 | 9 | 10 | 11 | 12

Format this personal-business letter in modified block style.

June 4, {year}/ Mr. Lyle Martin / Director, Customer Relations / Speedy Striders, Inc. / 8406 Hull Street / Henderson, NV 89015 / Dear Mr. Martin:

¶I purchased a pair of Speedy Striders, Model X7, from The Sports Store in the Dequindre Mall on April 15. Although I have always had good service from your shoes, this pair turned out to be defective.

¶I ran practice laps in the shoes during April and May with no problem. When I wore them in the Memorial Day Fun Run on May 30, I had a problem with my right shoe. The sole of the shoe ripped apart from the sides of the shoe; I was forced to drop out of the race. This was a serious problem for me because participation in the marathon was a requirement in my Health 155 class at Hillsdale College.

¶When I took the shoes back to the store, the manager refused to exchange the shoes or refund my money. This situation has been very frustrating for me. I would appreciate your help in getting a refund and clearing up this matter with the instructor of my physical education class. A copy of my sales slip is enclosed along with a photograph of the shoes.

Yours truly, / Kia Strobe / 45 East Windside Street / Thousand Oaks, CA 91360 / Enclosures / By registered mail

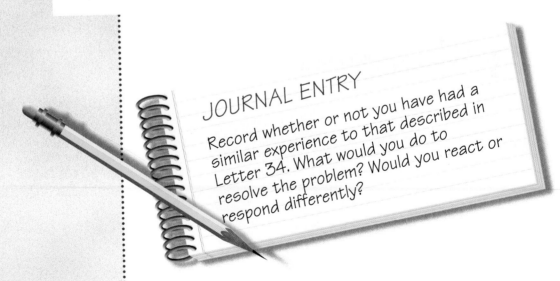

JOURNAL ENTRY

Record whether or not you have had a similar experience to that described in Letter 34. What would you do to resolve the problem? Would you react or respond differently?

TABLE 36

Create a 3-column, 8-row boxed table. Center the column headings. Center the table vertically and horizontally, and automatically adjust the columns. Total columns 2 and 3.

QUARTERLY SALES REPORT First Quarter		
Salesperson	**Quarterly Total ($)**	**Quarterly Average ($)**
Cochran, Richard	34,757	11,586
Duffy, Theodora	39,154	15,829
Frances, Parker	49,721	16,778
Hebert, Theresa	43,198	13,862
Minichiello, Pat	40,500	13,754
TOTAL		

TABLE 37

Open Table 31. Insert a TOTAL row after the last entry. Join cells A13, B13, and C13. Change the alignment in the joined cell to left. Delete the left and right borders in cell D13. In cell A13, type TOTAL EMPLOYMENT. Format cell D13 with commas and no decimal places. Then calculate a total for 1990 Employment.

TABLE 38

Open Table 29. Insert a TOTAL row after the last entry. Place a double line above the last row in the table. In cell A10, type TOTAL CALORIES. Format cells B10 and C10 with commas and no decimal places. Then calculate totals for Calories and Calories From Fat.

interNET CONNECTION

Use the Internet to search for information on calories and fats in your favorite foods. You may want to try the Website http://www.vitality.com/ to learn more about health and fitness. Write a brief summary of your findings, and share your findings with the class.

Format the following letter in modified-block style with indented paragraphs.

June 15, {year}

Ms. Juvetta Dishman
7337 Westfalia Street
Charlotte, TN 37036
Dear Ms. Dishman:

Thank you for volunteering to participate in the PLSO study. Enclosed are two consent forms, a baseline questionnaire, a baseline locator form, and a postage-paid envelope in which to return these forms.

Please read the entire consent form carefully before signing it. Keep one copy of the consent form for your records. If you have any questions about the form, please call Lynn or Vanda at 555-8706. Answer each question to the best of your ability. If there are some questions you are not able to answer, indicate that on the form, and an interviewer will telephone you for more information.

Place the completed forms (unfolded) in the envelope provided and mail them back to us. We would appreciate it if you would take time right now to fill out the forms and return them. Thank you for your assistance in this important health study of older adults.

Sincerely,

Nolan Goydos, M.D.
Principal Investigator
Enclosures
c: M. Bryant, M.D.
   R. Welsh, M.D.

C. PRACTICE

In the chart below, find the number of errors you made on the Pretest.
Then type each of the designated drill lines 2 times.

Pretest Errors	0–1	2	3	4+
Drill Lines	12–16	11–15	10–14	9–13

Accuracy

9 similar involves subjects effective expressions appropriate
10 styles effect affects writing similar sentences expressions
11 choice always involve subjective similarity appropriateness
12 style express involving difference expressive appropriately

Speed

13 writes always makes what ways your the and but may in be to
14 express subject effect affect word idea read you all the in
15 choices choice differ words word what that ways sent and is
16 press tense rents want what read sent ice sub sty off to be

D. POSTTEST

Repeat the Pretest. Compare your Posttest results with your Pretest
results.

E. DIAGNOSTIC PRACTICE: ALPHABET

Turn to the Diagnostic Practice: Alphabet routine on page SB1. Type
one of the Pretest/Posttest paragraphs and identify any errors made.
Then type the corresponding drill lines 2 times for each letter on which
you made 2 or more errors and 1 time for each letter on which you made
only 1 error. Finally, repeat the Pretest and compare your performance.

FORMATTING

F. TOTALS IN TABLES

A formula may be inserted into a table cell to perform
various calculations. To add a row or column of numbers,
you can use the SUM function.

G. SOFTWARE FEATURES

STUDENT MANUAL

Formulas

Study Lesson 96 in your student manual. Complete all the practice
activities while at your computer. Then complete the jobs that follow.

LESSON 64

LETTER REVIEW

OBJECTIVES:
- Improve keyboarding speed and accuracy.
- Review various letter formats.

A. WARMUP

Type each line 2 times.

Speed
Accuracy
Language Link
Numbers

1 They do not feel it is their duty to fix the flat for free.
2 Did she realize big yellow quilts from Jack were expensive?
3 Seven-digit codes were assigned; you should have yours now.
4 2301 3402 4503 5604 6705 7806 8907 2301 3402 4503 5604 6705
   | 1 | 2 | 3 | 4 | 5 | 6 | 7 | 8 | 9 | 10 | 11 | 12

SKILLBUILDING

B. 12-SECOND SPRINTS

Take three 12-second timings on each line. Try to increase your speed on each timing.

5 When you go to get your pen, will you also please get mine.
6 He did the job well and was paid by the maid who was there.
7 Now that we have the time to sit back and read, it is cold.
8 The red leaves fell from the maple tree when the wind blew.
   | 1 | 2 | 3 | 4 | 5 | 6 | 7 | 8 | 9 | 10 | 11 | 12

C. PRETEST

Take a 1-minute timing on the paragraph. Note your speed and errors.

9   The name high tech is given to a basic and useful type   12
10 of design that is changing our concept of modern living and   24
11 things we use daily. It has long enjoyed a quiet appeal in   36
12 places like restaurants and stores.   43
    | 1 | 2 | 3 | 4 | 5 | 6 | 7 | 8 | 9 | 10 | 11 | 12

LESSON 96   TOTALS IN TABLES

OBJECTIVES:

- Increase keyboarding skills.
- Use the SUM formula feature in tables.
- Reinforce the use of lines in tables.

A. WARMUP

Type each line 2 times.

Speed
Accuracy
Language Link
Numbers/Symbols

1 Our world is very different now from the way it used to be.
2 Six big men quickly won over Jeff despite his greater size.
3 Mom said, "Who wants cake?" to which Becky replied, "I do."
4 Invoice #23654, dated March 19, for 73 A-18 was 2/10, n/30.
| 1 | 2 | 3 | 4 | 5 | 6 | 7 | 8 | 9 | 10 | 11 | 12

FACT FILE

We live in a galaxy called the Milky Way. The Milky Way is made up of about 400 billion stars of which our Sun is one. There are many other galaxies in the universe, but one of the closest ones is the Andromeda Galaxy which is 2 million light years away.

SKILLBUILDING

B. PRETEST

Take a 1-minute timing on the paragraph. Note your speed and errors.

5   Effective writing always involves the choice of words   11
6 and expressions. Sentences may express similar ideas, but   23
7 style is what makes the words affect readers in different   35
8 ways. Your style should be appropriate to your subject.   46
| 1 | 2 | 3 | 4 | 5 | 6 | 7 | 8 | 9 | 10 | 11 | 12

In the chart below, find the number of errors you made on the Pretest. Then, type each of the designated drill lines 2 times.

Pretest Errors	0–1	2	3	4+
Drill Lines	16–20	15–19	14–18	13–17

Accuracy

13 own basic quiet stores design concept expensive restaurants
14 built style pipes range bright rubber window appeal designs
15 use and are wild tech living modern useful quietly changing
16 now but used come water things colors coming places enjoyed

Speed

17 glass daily wide sign such tire come like home with has not
18 homes given high tech name type long used they last now are
19 appeal living useful given basic things daily long type use
20 colors bright stores water pipes style glass range wind are

E. POSTTEST

Repeat the Pretest. Compare your Posttest results with your Pretest results.

WORD PROCESSING APPLICATIONS

LETTER 36
Modified-
Block Style

Format this letter in modified-block style and in the proper order.

June 18, {year}

Ms. Kia Strobe
45 E. Windside Street
Thousand Oaks, CA 93160

Dear Ms. Strobe:

You were justified in being angry. We are sorry for the problems you had with your Speedy striders, model X7, which forced you to drop out of the Memorial Day Fun Run. I have telephoned your physical education instructor and sent her a letter explaining your reason for not completing the class assignment. We are grateful to you for bringing this matter to our attention. The photo you sent was especially helpful.

TABLE 33

Open Table 25 and make the following changes:

1. Change the subtitle to 1969-1993.
2. Fill the column-heading cells with 20-percent fill.
3. Delete the rows representing years prior to 1969.

TABLE 34

Open Table 27 and make the following changes:

1. Delete the last three rows in the table.
2. Insert three new rows at the bottom of the table and add the following information:
   Row 6: April 7 / Pebblebrook High School / Home
   Row 7: April 12 / North Cobb High School / Away
   Row 8: April 15 / Dorsett Shoals High School / Home

TABLE 35

Open Table 33 and make the following changes:

1. Change the orientation to landscape.
2. Change the title to **U.S. PRESIDENTS, VICE PRESIDENTS, PARTY, AND YEARS IN OFFICE.**
3. Insert a new column after column A with the heading **Vice President**.
4. Add the following entries to the column: Gerald R. Ford, Spiro T. Agnew, Walter F. Mondale, George H. W. Bush, J. Danforth Quayle.

FACT FILE

The White House in which U.S. presidents live has 3 elevators, 5 major floors, 2 basements, 7 staircases, 12 chimneys, 32 bathrooms, 132 rooms, 160 windows, and 412 doors. Here are some other interesting facts about the White House. The first baby born in the White House was Thomas Jefferson's grandson in 1806. The first wedding at the White House was for Dolly Madison's sister in 1812. Cows grazed on the front lawn of the White House until 1913. The only president married in the White House was Grover Cleveland in 1886.

¶ After we recieved your letter, we conducted an investigation of our equipment. We discovered that the equipment used in sewing the Model 7X shoe is faulty. All of our dealers now have been informed of this situation, and the Model X7 Shoes have been removed from store shelves. Please take the damaged shoes to the Dequinder Mall store. The Store Manager, Mr. Kelly, has been contacted and instructed to refund your money in full.

Sincerely yours,

Lyle Martin
Director, Customer Relations

Enclosure
c: Paul Kelly

PS: We have enclosed a coupon entitling you to a free pair of shoes of your choice. We hope that this will restore your faith in speedy striders and that you will enjoy many more miles of successful marathon runs.

By Overnight Express

LETTER 37
Block-Style

Format this letter in block style and in the proper order. Make the corrections indicated by the proofreaders' marks.

(Current Date)

Mrs. Christine Piantidosi
824 England avenue
Kansas City, KS 66801

Dear Mrs. Piantidosi:

After our telephone conversation this morning concerning late delivery of three model 60 camcorders to your store, I found that

SKILLBUILDING

C. PRETEST

Take a 1-minute timing on the paragraph. Note your speed and errors.

```
 9      If you think you might enjoy a vacation by the sea for   11
10  relaxing or catching some fish, a trip to your local travel   23
11  agent may provide you with all kinds of information to help   35
12  you. A little advance planning could improve your trip.       46
    | 1 | 2 | 3 | 4 | 5 | 6 | 7 | 8 | 9 | 10 | 11 | 12
```

D. PRACTICE

SPEED: *If you made 2 or fewer errors on the Pretest, type lines 13–20 two times each.*

ACCURACY: *If you made more than 2 errors on the Pretest, type lines 13–16 as a group two times. Then type lines 17–20 as a group two times.*

```
13  dark each felt fate harm idea abide barns clock depth earns
14  jobs kits lawn mark nail ours filed guest hotel judge lapse
15  pile rank self take used wage maple named often pairs range
16  with girl rake hand mail tops label moron felon flair throw

17  able bake camp film know lack about baked canal drink enjoy
18  nova only pack rank sink tank knack labor scout thank valid
19  vain acre have knew save wave acute blank candy habit known
20  lawn fact yolk lump cast limp hilly rests cages lumpy blame
```

E. POSTTEST

Repeat the Pretest. Compare your Posttest results with your Pretest results.

FORMATTING

F. SOFTWARE FEATURES

Tables: Add/Delete Columns
Add/Delete Rows

Study Lesson 95 in your student manual. Complete all the practice activities while at your computer. Then complete the jobs that follow.

the camcorders were shiped in error to Kansas City, MO. Our headquaters upgraded the system computer which required many hours of re-entering invoices. Obviously, the error in your order happened at that time. Our records are now correct. Because of the inconvenience this errors has caused you the shipping and handling charges have been removed from the your bill. Your orders is being sent today by express delivery, and you should receive it in 24 hours. We value your patronage and we look forward to serving you for many years to come.

Sincerely,

Marlon Chevron
Manger
By fax
c: Darryl Adams

Modified-
Block Style
With
Indented
Paragraphs

Current Date
Mr. Taylor Coates
President, News Guild
28 West Adams Street, Suite 1308
Alamonte Springs, FL 32714
Dear Mr. Coates:

Because of the extraordinarily high number of claims, we have found it necessary to increase our rates. This increase is required under Part 5, page 3-PR, of Policy Amendment 15. Accordingly, we are increasing the life insurance rate to .80/$1,000 for active members and .94/$1,000 for retirees.

In addition, the amount of dependent life insurance will be reduced from $10,000 to $5,000 along with extending the current policy for one year. If you think it would help, I am willing to come to your next membership meeting to answer questions.

Sincerely,
Patrick Tecumseh
Account Representative
PS: A summary of all changes we are recommending is enclosed for your review.

LESSON 95

TABLES: ADD/DELETE COLUMNS AND ROWS

OBJECTIVES:

- Learn about quotation marks.
- Improve keyboarding speed and accuracy.
- Format tables in landscape format.
- Add and delete columns and rows.

A. WARMUP

Type each line 2 times.

Speed
Accuracy
Language Link
Symbols

1 Business law governs transactions in the world of business.
2 Had Jeff's size helped him to win quickly over Gene Baxter?
3 It takes two hands to flatten out the dough for pizza, too.
4 The word court can be a location. (I'll see them in court!)

| 1 | 2 | 3 | 4 | 5 | 6 | 7 | 8 | 9 | 10 | 11 | 12

LANGUAGE LINK

B. QUOTATION MARKS WITH DIRECT QUOTATIONS

Study the rule and examples below. Then edit lines 5–8 to correct any errors in the use of quotation marks.

Rule 20:

Use quotation marks to enclose a **direct quotation,** that is, the exact words of a speaker or a writer.

Robert said, "That is the highest grade on this project."

5 Mrs. Woo said, Rea is being considered for the promotion.
6 Yes, Jill, you're still in the running, replied Ms. Paul.
7 Ben cried, Someone stole the library book I need tomorrow.
8 Diane asked me, When did they come to take your computer?

LESSON 65

TABLES: CREATING

OBJECTIVES:

- Learn about subject/verb agreement.
- Improve keyboarding techniques.
- Learn to create tables.

A. WARMUP

Type each line 2 times.

Speed
Accuracy
Language Link
Numbers/Symbols

1 Heavy rain fell fast and hard on the game later in the day.
2 Jeff quickly took away five dozen more boxes of light pens.
3 The express elevator broke; I had to walk up eight flights.
4 ($95.15) ($59.26) ($60.37) ($71.48) ($82.59) ($90.60) ($$$)
  | 1 | 2 | 3 | 4 | 5 | 6 | 7 | 8 | 9 | 10 | 11 | 12

LANGUAGE LINK

B. SUBJECT/VERB AGREEMENT

Study the rule and examples that follow. Then edit lines 5–8 for subject/verb agreement.

Rule 10: Disregard any intervening words that come between the subject and verb when establishing agreement.

The lost box of books has been found.

The buses covered with green paint were moving very fast.

5 The books in the bookcase (was/were) rearranged by May last week.
6 The students working on the project (is/are) doing a very nice job.
7 One of the programmers (has/have) written and tested the program.
8 The contract, including all attachments, (is/are) due to be submitted today.

TABLE 32

Change the paper orientation to landscape. Then create a 4-column, 7-row boxed table. Center the table vertically and horizontally. Shade the column-heading row with 20 percent fill. Center all column headings. Align the first column on the left; align the remaining columns at the center. Note that the column heading in the first column is only a single line and the other column headings are 2 and 3 lines. Press ENTER 2 times before typing the first column heading and 1 time before typing the last one. Adjust the column widths so that the entries in column 1 are on a single line.

FIVE FASTEST-GROWING CAREERS FOR THE 21ST CENTURY (Requiring a College Degree)			
Career	% Increase in Positions by 2005	Average Starting Pay ($) for 1994 Grads	Recommended College Degree
Computer Scientist/ Systems Analyst	79	33,957	Computer Science
Physical Therapist	76	31,432	Health Sciences
Psychologist	64	20,270	Psychology
Marketing Manager	47	24,721	Marketing
Preschool Teacher	41	17,393	Education

PORTFOLIO
Activity

Choose a boxed table and an open table that you have completed in previous lessons. If necessary, correct any errors you may have made. Print one copy of each for your portfolio.

SKILLBUILDING

C. TECHNIQUE TIMINGS

Take two 30-second timings on each line. Focus on the technique at the left.

Press the space bar with a quick down-and-in motion.

```
 9  go to it go do so go be on us we do to on it at bet tip top
10  We want to go on and see that band at the park play for us.
11  Now it is my turn to tell them that we do not want it done.
12  How do you get it all done and stay in top form for us now?
    | 1 | 2 | 3 | 4 | 5 | 6 | 7 | 8 | 9 | 10 | 11 | 12
```

D. PACED PRACTICE

Turn to the Paced Practice routine beginning on page SB-7 Take three 2-minute timings, starting at the point where you left off the last time.

FORMATTING

E. PARTS OF A TABLE

1. Tables consist of vertical columns and horizontal rows. Where a column and row meet is called a **cell**. Information is typed in the cells.
2. Tables may be formatted with lines (a boxed table) or without lines (an open table). A boxed table is shown in the illustration.
3. When a table appears on a page by itself, it should be vertically and horizontally centered.
4. Align text columns at the left; align number columns at the right.

Accounting and Finance	Richards College of Business
Management and Business Systems	Richards College of Business
Mass Communications	College of Arts and Sciences
Physical Education and Recreation	College of Education

TABLE 31

Change the paper orientation to landscape. Then create a boxed table with 5 columns and 12 rows. Center the table vertically and horizontally. Insert a double line below the column headings and use 20-percent fill/shading for the column-heading row. Center the column headings and align text columns at the left and number columns at the right. Automatically adjust the column widths.

TOP TEN GEORGIA OCCUPATIONS
(Ranked by Growth Rate)

Rank	Occupation	Annual Growth Rate (%)	1990 Employment	Average Job Openings
1	Home Health Aides	10.0	3,310	388
2	Computer Engineers	7.6	1,410	137
3	Physical Therapists	6.4	2,000	172
4	Systems Analysts	6.2	11,160	789
5	Technical Writers	5.3	1,190	88
6	Physical Therapy Assistants	5.3	1,450	90
7	Medical Assistants	4.9	4,880	285
8	Medical Secretaries	4.8	4,970	351
9	Surgical Technicians	4.8	1,170	66
10	Respiratory Therapists	4.6	1,680	114

STUDENT MANUAL

Tables, Create

Study Lesson 65 in your student manual. Complete all the practice activities while at your computer. Then complete the following jobs.

WORD PROCESSING APPLICATIONS

TABLE 1

Create a table with 2 columns and 4 rows. Use the tab key to move from column to column as you fill in information.

Accounting and Finance	Richards College of Business
Management and Business Systems	Richards College of Business
Mass Communications	College of Arts and Sciences
Physical Education and Recreation	College of Education

TABLE 2

Create a table with 3 columns and 4 rows. Use the tab key to move from column to column as you fill in information.

The Great Barrier Reef	Australia	1,200 miles long
The Grand Canyon	United States	217 miles long
Nile River	Egypt and Sudan	4,160 miles long
Mt. Everest	Nepal and Tibet	29,000 feet high (est.)

FACT FILE

The koala is native only to Australia. Koalas are marsupials—mammals whose young grow and mature inside a pouch on the mother's belly. Koalas live in southeastern Australia in eucalyptus trees. These animals spend approximately 20 hours a day sleeping. The only food koalas eat is eucalyptus leaves, and they eat about 2.5 pounds of these leaves every day.

5 Sean (passed, past) the cycle driver (to, too, two) quickly to see who he was.

6 From (passed, past) experience, I have learned how (to, too, two) handle the job.

7 The (to, too, two) sisters were much (to, too, two) shy to go (to, too, two) the party alone.

8 Don said that he will go (to, too, two) the committee meeting tomorrow.

SKILLBUILDING

C. 30-Second OK Timings

Take two 30-second OK (error-free) timings on lines 9–10. Then take two 30-second OK timings on lines 11–12. Goal: no errors.

9 We are expecting two quite sizable contracts in June	11
10 from Houston Federal Credit Union and Yonkers Savings Bank.	23
11 They were amazed that they were able to cut expenses	11
12 so quickly by reducing their television advertising budget.	23

| 1 | 2 | 3 | 4 | 5 | 6 | 7 | 8 | 9 | 10 | 11 | 12 |

FORMATTING

D. Tables: Page Orientation

The default page orientation for 8.5- × 11-inch paper is vertical, or **portrait.** A page may also be formatted in horizontal orientation, or **landscape.**

E. Software Features

STUDENT MANUAL
Page Orientation

Study Lesson 94 in your student manual. Complete all the practice activities while at your computer. Then complete the jobs that follow.

LESSON 66

TABLES: COLUMN SIZE AND POSITION

OBJECTIVES:

- Adjust column widths.
- Center tables on a page.
- Type 35/3'/5e.

A. WARMUP

Type each line 2 times.

Speed
Accuracy
Language Link
Symbols

1 He may find time to go today if Dan will help with the car.
2 James Boxell, the banquet speaker, analyzed a few carvings.
3 Twenty boys will be five; they cannot register before then.
4 Attention: Dear Mr. Westin: Subject: Gentlemen: Ladies: Re:

| 1 | 2 | 3 | 4 | 5 | 6 | 7 | 8 | 9 | 10 | 11 | 12

*inter*NET C O N N E C T I O N

Using the Internet, search for information about carpal tunnel syndrome. Try searching by name or locate a medical information site. Learn what causes this problem and what can be done to help relieve the pain. Compose a short paragraph describing what you learned.

SKILLBUILDING

B. PREVIEW PRACTICE

Type each line 2 times as a preview to the timings that follow.

Accuracy
Speed

5 hesitate Extended computer different stretching revitalized
6 cause work give seat step desk walk neck mind your time not

LESSON 94

TABLES: PAGE ORIENTATION

OBJECTIVES:

- Improve keyboarding skill.
- Recognize confusing words.
- Format tables in landscape orientation.

A. WARMUP

Type each line 2 times.

Speed
Accuracy
Language Link
Numbers/Symbols

```
1 We have to learn to make introductions with poise and ease.
2 Mo brought back five or six dozen pieces of quaint jewelry.
3 The trip to Grandma's house was farther than they expected.
4 She will visit our top offices (#1 & #2): DALLAS & EL PASO.
  | 1 | 2 | 3 | 4 | 5 | 6 | 7 | 8 | 9 | 10 | 11 | 12
```

LANGUAGE LINK

B. CONFUSING WORDS

Study the confusing words and their meanings below. Then edit lines 5–8 by selecting the correct word.

passed (v.)   past tense of *pass;* move beyond; transfer of ownership; to be approved; surpass; to happen

past (adj.)   elapsed; former
   (adv.)   beyond
   (n.)   time before the present

to (prep.)   toward
too (adv.)   besides, also
two (adj.)   one more than one

As we passed the house, we had fond memories of the past.

He too left to shop at the two stores.

Take two 3-minute timings on the paragraph. Note your speed and errors.

Goal: 35/3'/5e

7	Workers may hesitate to take work breaks because they	11
8	feel they should not take the time. Extended sitting at a	22
9	computer can cause muscle pain. Experts say we should take	34
10	short breaks to refresh body and mind. Get out of your seat	46
11	and step around your desk. Walk to a different section of	58
12	the office. Do exercises that will relax your shoulders and	70
13	your neck. Just stretching at your desk will help to ease	81
14	stress. A quick change of pace can give your mind a chance	93
15	to shift gears. Then, you can return to work revitalized.	105

| 1 | 2 | 3 | 4 | 5 | 6 | 7 | 8 | 9 | 10 | 11 | 12 SI 1.30

FORMATTING

D. COLUMN WIDTHS AND TABLE POSITION

When you create a table, the table is horizontally centered between the margins and extends from the left margin to the right margin. All columns are the same width. If a column contains long entries or short entries, you may want to change the width of the columns to make the table more readable or more attractive.

Once you change the column widths, the table will no longer be horizontally centered. Therefore, you must reposition the table so that it is centered horizontally.

E. SOFTWARE FEATURES

STUDENT MANUAL

Table Position   Adjusting Column Width

Study Lesson 66 in your student manual. Complete all the practice activities while at your computer. Then complete the jobs that follow.

TABLE 30

Create a 3-column, 10-row boxed table. Center the table vertically and horizontally. Center the column headings and add 10 percent shading. Add a double line below the column headings. Automatically adjust the column widths.

DOUGLAS COUNTY STAR STUDENTS (Highest Grade Point Averages)		
Student	**School**	**Teacher**
Richard Milton	Lakewood High School	Katherine Godwin
Leslie Littlefield	Green Meadow Academy	Daniel L. Smithers
Marilyn Edenfield	Trapp High School	Clemmons Watson
Larry Adamson	J. W. Briggs High School	Francis Jackson
Brock Simpson	Coosa Mountain Academy	Bernadette Franklin
Marie Teakwitha	Lithia Springs High School	Alton Williamson
Wesley Kaufman	Chappel Hill High School	Anna Ford
Edward Wue	Edison High School	Rebecca Thompson

FACT FILE

Did you know that fjords are deep, narrow valleys that stretch inland from the coasts of northern Europe, Scandinavia, and South America? Fjords were carved by huge glaciers that descended from mountains. As the glaciers flowed seaward, their enormous weight carved deep valleys—some more than 300 feet deep.

TABLE 3

Create a table with 3 columns and 4 rows. Enter the information in the cells. Use the tab key to move from cell to cell. Automatically adjust the column widths. Center the table vertically and horizontally.

Your table should look like the following table when you have completed it.

Chevrolet	October	Julia Renfro
Ford	May	Mark Karen
Chrysler	June	James Hill
Toyota	August	Meridy Street

TABLE 4

Language Arts
Connections

Create a table with 3 columns and 5 rows. Automatically adjust the column widths. Center the table vertically and horizontally.

adapt	adopt	adept
lose	loose	loss
rein	rain	reign
site	sight	cite
too	to	two

TABLE 5

Create a table with 3 columns and 5 rows. Automatically adjust the column widths. Center the table vertically and horizontally.

Coca Cola	KO	NYSE
Intel Corporation	INTC	NASDAQ
Microsoft	MSFT	NASDAQ
Nike	NKE	NYSE
Walt Disney Co.	DIS	NYSE

LANGUAGE ARTS CONNECTIONS

Table 4 contains a list of confusing words. Look up the definition for each of the words in the table; then, for each word, compose a sentence in which the word is correctly used.

TABLE 28

Create a 3-column, 8-row boxed table. Shade the column-heading row and the single performance cells with 20-percent shading. Change the lines above and below the column-heading row to double lines. Center the table vertically and horizontally. Adjust the column widths so that your table looks similar to the illustration.

ALEXANDER THEATER Fall Performance Dates		
Name of Show	**Day/Date**	**Time**
Learning Rainbow	Monday–Friday	2:30 p.m.–3:00 p.m.
The Science Guru	Monday–Friday	4:00 p.m.–4:30 p.m.
Hooping It Up	November 15	10:30 a.m.–11:00 a.m.
All Against Violence	October 16	3:30 p.m.–5:00 p.m.
Rock and Roll Times	Sunday–Thursday	8:00 p.m.–10:00 p.m.
Magic Schoolroom	Sundays	10:30 a.m.–11:00 a.m.

TABLE 29

Create a 3-column, 9-row boxed table. Center the column headings. Add a double line between each of the columns. Shade the column-heading row with a 10 percent fill. Automatically adjust the column widths.

LBO'S HAMBURGER STAND Calorie Count for Selected Menu Items		
Sandwich Item	**Calories**	**Calories From Fat**
Lucy's Grilled Chicken	290	6
Barbey's Chicken Lite	276	7
Barbey's Lite Beef	294	10
Lucy's Junior Burger	270	9
O'Brien's Lean Burger	320	10
BQ Broiler Chicken	280	10
Andy's Turkey Lite	260	6

LESSON 67

TABLES: COLUMN HEADINGS

OBJECTIVES:

- Improve keyboarding speed and accuracy.
- Compose at the keyboard.
- Format tables with column headings.

A. WARMUP

Type each line 2 times.

Speed
Accuracy
Language Link
Numbers/Symbols

1 Take good care of this car, and it should last a long time.
2 Jeff's size had helped him to win quickly over Gene Baxter.
3 Lucia had a pretty silver bracelet; she wore it constantly.
4 Using the 8% increase, we bought 25# of #112 and #64 nails.
| 1 | 2 | 3 | 4 | 5 | 6 | 7 | 8 | 9 | 10 | 11 | 12

LANGUAGE LINK

B. COMPOSING AT THE KEYBOARD

Answer the following questions with complete sentences.

5 Why do we need automobile insurance?
6 What are some of your bad habits, and how can you change them?
7 What are two things that annoy you, and why do they annoy you?

FACT FILE

The Model T Ford automobile, which was built between 1908 and 1927, was nicknamed the "Tin Lizzie."

SKILLBUILDING

Type each line 2 times as a preview to the timings that follow.

Accuracy
Speed

9 who next rapid strong require training relations innovative
10 technology graduates creative economy growth swift grow for

D. 5-MINUTE TIMINGS

Take two 5-minute timings on the paragraphs. Note your speed and errors.

Goal: 37/5'/5e

11 Many factors are changing the workplace as we move	10
12 into the next century. A strong force in the economy at	22
13 this time is the rapid growth in the information industry.	33
14 The picture for employment is quickly being changed by	44
15 advances in technology. Just a few years ago, high school	56
16 graduates who were trained in most business skills could	67
17 be hired in entry jobs and grow in these same fields with	79
18 little or no more training.	85
19 This is no longer true. Most office jobs now require	95
20 workers with creative and innovative talents as well as	107
21 good human relations and computer skills. Many technical	118
22 school and college students are soon realizing that most	129
23 of the skills they have learned may be outdated in five	141
24 or six years because of these swift changes. The world of	152
25 work is being changed so fast that workers must be willing	164
26 and able to adapt. The workers who will be able to compete	176
27 are going to be those who are learners for life.	185

| 1 | 2 | 3 | 4 | 5 | 6 | 7 | 8 | 9 | 10 | 11 | 12SI 1.40

SKILLBUILDING

C. 12-SECOND SPRINTS

Take three 12-second timings on each line. Try to increase your speed on each timing.

```
 8  It is always a good idea to take time to do your best work.
 9  Take enough time to think about it and plan each step well.
10  If you rush into a job, you may just make many more errors.
11  Now is the time you should use these tips to do a good job.
    | | | | 5 | | | 10 | | | 15 | | | 20 | | | 25 | | | 30 | | | 35 | | | 40 | | | 45 | | | 50 | | | 55 | | | 60
```

D. PRETEST

Take a 1-minute timing on the paragraph. Note your speed and errors.

```
12       Cecil must know more about my past than he does about    11
13  his own. As we walked in the hazy sunshine with friends, he   23
14  spoke above the noise around us. I was pleased that he was    35
15  able to remember things we did when we were young.           45
    | 1 | 2 | 3 | 4 | 5 | 6 | 7 | 8 | 9 | 10 | 11 | 12
```

E. PRACTICE

SPEED: If you made 2 or fewer errors on the Pretest, type lines 16–23 two times each.

ACCURACY: If you made more than 2 errors on the Pretest, type lines 16–19 as a group two times. Then type lines 20–23 as a group two times.

Up Reaches
```
16  ce cell once mice rice slice cease cedar fleece niece juice
17  me lime mime meal mere melon plume metal become slime smell
18  hi high hits hive nigh thigh chime whine chirps whips hires
19  lo lost love flow loam plods solos clots slower plops loans
```

Down Reaches
```
20  ca case cast pica carp carve cards cable capers laces cabin
21  im whim slim aims time limps crimp blimp chimes limes prime
22  rm harm worm arms army perms alarm charm squirm farms warms
23  ba bask bark barb paba bards bawls balms turban samba baits
```

F. POSTTEST

Repeat the Pretest. Compare your Posttest results with your Pretest results.

LESSON 93

REINFORCEMENT: TABLES

OBJECTIVES:

- Compose at the keyboard.
- Type 37/5'/5e.
- Review table formats.

A. WARMUP

Type each line 2 times.

Speed
Accuracy
Language Link
Numbers/Symbols

1 Some people seem to have more hours in the day than others.
2 Jeff quietly moved a dozen boxes last night by power truck.
3 First we washed our hands, then it was time to enjoy lunch.
4 The invoice #740 for $189.32 is subject to a 6.5% discount.

| 1 | 2 | 3 | 4 | 5 | 6 | 7 | 8 | 9 | 10 | 11 | 12

LANGUAGE LINK

B. COMPOSING AT THE KEYBOARD

Choose one of the scenarios below and complete it. Then continue composing until you have created a short paragraph of several sentences.

5 My friend and I were walking home after class when all of a sudden we saw . . .
6 I was driving home when I hit a patch of ice on the road. Next thing I knew . . .
7 Several of us were hiking up the steep mountain path when all of a sudden . . .
8 The building started to shake. As soon as I realized it was an earthquake, I . . .

interNET CONNECTION

Use the Internet site http://wwwneic.cr.usgs.gov/ to gather information from the National Earthquake Information Center, which is located 10 miles west of Denver, Colorado. Find out when and where the last earthquake in the world occurred. Find out when the largest earthquake in the United States occurred.

FORMATTING

G. Tables: Column Headings

Column headings describe the data in each column of a table. To format column headings:

Salesperson	Territory	No. of Units
Dawson, Angelique	Midwest	1,245
Goodfellow, Robin	Southeast	1,137
Karampalas, Stephen	Northeast	1,089
Saad, Gamal	Western	1,764

1. Type the column headings in initial caps and bold.
2. Align column headings at the left over text columns, at the right over number columns, or centered over all columns.
3. If a column heading is much wider than the data in the column (See Table 6, column 2), you may want to let it wrap to the next line or break the heading into two lines by pressing ENTER at an appropriate point.

WORD PROCESSING APPLICATIONS

TABLE 6

Language Arts
Connections

Create a 3-column, 6-row table. Type the column headings in bold. Adjust the column widths; then center the table vertically and horizontally.

Present Tense	Past Tense	Past Participle
go	went	have/had gone
run	ran	have/had run
do	did	have/had done
see	saw	have/had seen
ring	rang	have/had rung

TABLE 7

FACT FILE

Emerald refers to a bright green beryl (mineral). The word emerald is derived from the word smaragdos, a name given to a number of stones having little in common except the color green.

Create a 2-column, 7-row table. Adjust the column widths; then center the table vertically and horizontally.

Month	Birthstone
January	Garnet
February	Amethyst
March	Aquamarine
April	Diamond
May	Emerald
June	Pearl

TABLE 26

Create a 3-column, 14-row boxed table. Add 20-percent shading to the column heading row. Center the table vertically and horizontally. Adjust the column widths so that all columns are equal.

AVERAGE MONTHLY TEMPERATURES Anchorage, Alaska		
Month	**High**	**Low**
January	20	6
February	27	10
March	34	16
April	44	27
May	55	36
June	63	45
July	65	49
August	64	47
September	56	40
October	43	29
November	29	16
December	20	7

TABLE 27

Create a 3-column, 8-row boxed table. Add 20-percent shading to the column-heading row. Center the table vertically and horizontally. Automatically adjust the column widths. Add a double line above and below the column headings and to the left and right of the center column.

GIRLS' TRACK SCHEDULE Spring Hills High School		
Date	**School**	**Location**
March 3	Walton City High School	Home
March 10	Peachtree Heights Academy	Away
March 16	Bentwood Day Academy	Away
March 22	Trenton Valley High School	Home
March 27	J. C. Carlton High School	Away
March 30	Addison County High School	Home

TABLE 8

Create a 3-column, 7-row table. Press ENTER to break the column headings as shown. Then adjust the column widths, and center the table vertically and horizontally.

City of Origin	City of Destination	Date of Travel
Anchorage	Vancouver	January 1
Chicago	Quebec	March 15
New York City	Montreal	May 27
Niagara Falls	Halifax	September 10
San Francisco	Toronto	October 7
Atlanta	Calgary	December 13

FACT FILE

Did you know that a praying mantis is not a religious insect? In fact, it is a cannibal. When a mantis appears to be praying, it is actually preying. The reverential-looking position of its forelegs is really an attack position. An insect that gets within reach of a mantis is quickly captured, then eaten. This happens so quickly, that it's almost impossible to see. A praying mantis eats only live insects, and will often eat another mantis.

Illustration 2

U.S. PRESIDENTS, PARTY, AND YEARS IN OFFICE
1945-1993

President	Party	Term
Harry S Truman	Democrat	1945-1953
Dwight D. Eisenhower	Republican	1953-1961
John F. Kennedy	Democrat	1961-1963
Lyndon B. Johnson	Democrat	1963-1969
Richard M. Nixon	Republican	1969-1974
Gerald R. Ford	Republican	1974-1977
James E. Carter, Jr.	Democrat	1977-1981
Ronald W. Reagan	Republican	1981-1989
George H. W. Bush	Republican	1989-1993

open table. In Illustration 1 on page 333, a different line style was used to separate the table title from the columns. In Illustration 2, column-heading cells were highlighted with 20-percent shading.

When you select a fill pattern or shading, use 20 percent or less so that any text in the cell will be easy to read.

D. SOFTWARE FEATURES

GO TO

STUDENT MANUAL

Borders and Shading/Fill

Study Lesson 92 in your student manual. Complete all the practice activities while at your computer. Then complete the jobs that follow.

WORD PROCESSING APPLICATIONS

TABLE 25

Social Studies
Connections

Create a 3-column, 11-row boxed table. Adjust the column widths so they look similar to the illustration. Center the table vertically and horizontally. Change the lines above and below the column headings to double lines. Center the column headngs.

U.S. PRESIDENTS, PARTY, AND YEARS IN OFFICE 1945–1993		
President	**Party**	**Term**
Harry S Truman	Democrat	1945–1953
Dwight D. Eisenhower	Republican	1953–1961
John F. Kennedy	Democrat	1961–1963
Lyndon B. Johnson	Democrat	1963–1969
Richard M. Nixon	Republican	1969–1974
Gerald R. Ford	Republican	1974–1977
James E. Carter, Jr.	Democrat	1977–1981
Ronald W. Reagan	Republican	1981–1989
George H. W. Bush	Republican	1989–1993

SOCIAL STUDIES CONNECTIONS

Gerald Ford, who succeeded Richard Nixon as president, was the first U.S. president who was never elected to the office of president or vice president.

LESSON 68 · TABLES: NUMBER COLUMNS

OBJECTIVES:

- Format tables with number columns.
- Type 35/3'/5e.
- Learn software features.

A. WARMUP

Type each line 2 times.

Speed
Accuracy
Language Link
Numbers

1 We took a long trip and saw many fine sights while on tour.
2 Joe Pott quickly won over six men because of his good size.
3 The teacher gave careful directions; the pupils understood.
4 5201 6202 7203 8204 9205 1206 2207 3208 4209 5210 6211 7212
  | 1 | 2 | 3 | 4 | 5 | 6 | 7 | 8 | 9 | 10 | 11 | 12

interNET CONNECTION

Use the Internet to research the effects of stress on your
health. You may want to try some of these sites:

www.lifetimetv.com/wosport/gogetfit
www.nhlbi.nih.gov/chd
www.vitality.com

SKILLBUILDING

B. PREVIEW PRACTICE

Type each line 2 times as a preview to the timings that follow.

Accuracy
Speed

5 health thoughts feelings physical positive Practice friends
6 person habit think music comes when urge say hug day the we

LESSON 92

TABLES: BORDERS/FILL

OBJECTIVES:

- Improve keyboarding skill.
- Learn word processing features.
- Format table lines and fill.

A. WARMUP

Type each line 2 times.

Speed
Accuracy
Language Link
Numbers/Symbols

1 We can all speak well if we think about what we are saying.
2 Because he was very lazy, Jake paid for six games and quit.
3 The chapter was much longer than she had expected it to be.
4 Hasn't our July Check #830 for $149.56 been mailed to them?
| 1 | 2 | 3 | 4 | 5 | 6 | 7 | 8 | 9 | 10 | 11 | 12

SKILLBUILDING

B. 12-SECOND SPRINTS

Take three 12-second timings on each line. Try to increase your speed on each timing.

5 The goal is to do the work we have to do as well as we can.
6 Type at the speed that is well within your zone of control.
7 She can save a lot of time and effort by planning the work.
8 She cannot count on luck as a means of getting ahead today.
| | | |5| | | |10| | | |15| | | |20| | | |25| | | |30| | | |35| | | |40| | | |45| | | |50| | | |55| | | |60

FORMATTING

C. BORDERS AND FILL/SHADING

Illustration 1

U.S. PRESIDENTS, PARTY, AND YEARS IN OFFICE 1945-1993		
President	Party	Term
Harry S Truman	Democrat	1945-1953
Dwight D. Eisenhower	Republican	1953-1961
John F. Kennedy	Democrat	1961-1963
Lyndon B. Johnson	Democrat	1963-1969
Richard M. Nixon	Republican	1969-1974
Gerald R. Ford	Republican	1974-1977
James E. Carter, Jr.	Democrat	1977-1981
Ronald W. Reagan	Republican	1981-1989
George H. W. Bush	Republican	1989-1993

To highlight table cells, rows, or columns, you can change borders and add fill or shading to rows or individual cells. You can also delete all of the borders to create an

Take two 3-minute timings on the paragraphs. Note your speed and errors.

Goal: 35/3'/5e

```
 7        When it comes to health, our minds matter more than    11
 8   we know. Some studies say that a person may have feelings    22
 9   and beliefs that can improve physical well being. People     34
10   might act quite differently when they realize that how       45
11   they think could affect how they feel.                       52
12        Relax more. Be positive. Enjoy each day. Get back to    63
13   nature. Listen to the music you like. Practice the habit     75
14   of a hug a day from friends or family. Take breaks and       86
15   quiet time for yourself. Smile more often. Doctors urge      97
16   us to think good thoughts so we can live better lives.      108
     | 1 | 2 | 3 | 4 | 5 | 6 | 7 | 8 | 9 | 10 | 11 | 12  SI 1.34
```

FORMATTING

D. **Tables: Number Columns**

To format numbers in table columns:

1. Align the numbers at the right.
2. Align column headings over number columns at the right, except when all column headings are centered.
3. If necessary, adjust the width of narrow number columns to balance them with the remaining columns in the table.

E. **Software Features**

STUDENT MANUAL
Number Columns

Study Lesson 68 in your student manual. Complete all the practice activities while at your computer. Then complete the jobs that follow.

TABLE 23

Create a 4-column, 7-row open table. Center the braced column headings. Center the table vertically and horizontally. Automatically adjust the column widths.

BASEBALL SCHEDULE
July 14, {year}

American League Games		National League Games	
Toronto Blue Jays	Cleveland Indians	Atlanta Braves	New York Mets
Minnesota Twins	Detroit Tigers	Florida Marlins	Montreal Expos
Seattle Mariners	Boston Red Sox	Chicago Cubs	Pittsburgh Pirates
Baltimore Orioles	Texas Rangers	Houston Astros	Cincinnati Reds
Oakland Athletics	Anaheim Angels	San Diego Padres	Colorado Rockies

TABLE 24

Create a 2-column, 8-row boxed table. Center the table vertically and horizontally. Automatically adjust the column widths.

HONOR SOCIETY OFFICERS	
Central High School	
Kathy Chou	President
LaTasha Bennett	Vice President
Marcus Wilson	Secretary
Angel Florez	Treasurer
Holly Koskoski	Reporter
Kahlid Jordan	Historian
Benjamin Hertz	Parliamentarian

interNET CONNECTION

Use the Internet to update Table 23. Determine which cities and/or teams have changed. See if you can find information about why teams have changed cities or changed names over the years.

TABLE 9

Create a 3-column, 6-row table. Align the column headings and the text columns at the left; align the column heading and the number column at the right. Automatically adjust the column widths. Center the table vertically and horizontally.

Teacher	Course	Room
B. Blackhawk	Word Processing	109
S. Maxey	Applied Economics	2570
M. Gorman	Financial Planning	110
P. Wicker	Music Appreciation	2957
B. Sykes	Beginning Japanese	315

TABLE 10

Create a 3-column, 8-row table. Center all column headings (break them as shown). Align the number columns at the right. Automatically adjust the column widths. Center the table vertically and horizontally.

Snack Items	Total Caloric Count	Percent of Calories From Fat
Cheddar Wafers	200	12
Mini Bits of Chips	290	10
Sell Well Chips	340	21
Frizzell's Snack Crackers	190	8
Bagel Bits	120	0
Snacker Crackers	150	8
Munchos	215	11

TABLE 11

3-Column Boxed

Create a 3-column, 6-row table. Align the first column heading at the left. Align the second and third column headings at the right. Align the number columns at the right. Automatically adjust the column widths. Center the table vertically and horizontally.

Name	Gross Pay ($)	Tax ($)
Boldt, David	1,246	248
Johnson, Jay	942	188
Miller, Joan	846	168
Sipowitz, Andrew	1,050	210
Vandenburg, Harlan	976	194

E. REVERSING LINES IN TABLES

As you learned in Lesson 65, tables are created either without lines (open tables) or with lines (boxed tables). In this lesson, you will reverse this feature in the tables you create.

F. SOFTWARE FEATURES

STUDENT MANUAL

Table Lines

Study Lesson 91 in your student manual. Complete all the practice activities while at your computer. Then complete the jobs that follow.

WORD PROCESSING APPLICATIONS

TABLE 22

Create a 2-column, 8-row boxed table. Automatically adjust the column widths. Center the table vertically and horizontally.

HOMONYMS	
there	their
allowed	aloud
principal	principle
it's	its
stationery	stationary
forward	foreword
patience	patients

LESSON 69

TABLES: REINFORCEMENT

OBJECTIVES:
- Learn about subject/verb agreement.
- Improve keyboarding skill.
- Reinforce table formats.

A. WARMUP

Type each line 2 times.

Speed
Accuracy
Language Link
Numbers/Symbols

1 Rita will go to town and order two pairs of shoes for them.
2 Brown jars prevented the mixture from freezing too quickly.
3 David went to the fair; he won first prize with his squash.
4 You will get (1) more for the money and (2) better quality.
    | 1 | 2 | 3 | 4 | 5 | 6 | 7 | 8 | 9 | 10 | 11 | 12

LANGUAGE LINK

B. SUBJECT/VERB AGREEMENT

Study the rule and the examples below. Then correct any errors in subject/verb agreement in lines 5–8.

Rule 11: Subjects joined by *and* take a plural verb unless the compound subject is preceded by *each, every,* or *many a (an)*.

> *Many a computer and printer was purchased during the first quarter.*
>
> *The physician and the anesthesiologist were in a patient conference.*
>
> *Every student and instructor is hoping to obtain the test results soon.*

5 Each girl and boy (have/has) a ticket to the senior play.
6 Many a skier and skater (has/have) taken a really bad fall.
7 Both Jean and Ricki (is/are) taking a trip to Europe this fall.
8 Every dog and cat (has/have) to get rabies shots to be safe.

Unit 4 Lesson 69 **247**

C. PREVIEW PRACTICE

Type each line 2 times as a preview to the timings that follow.

Accuracy
Speed

9 express respect negative yourself effectively communication
10 situations essential feelings realize beyond ideas high own

D. 5-MINUTE TIMINGS

Take two 5-minute timings on the paragraphs. Note your speed and errors.

Goal: 37/5'/5e

Language Arts
Connections

11 In high school and beyond, the communication of ideas,	11
12 needs, wants, and feelings in the right way is a skill that	23
13 must be acquired. Parents and teachers may not be around	35
14 when you need them later. It is up to you to realize the	46
15 need for learning how to get your ideas and feelings across	58
16 to others clearly and to do so in a way that shows respect	70
17 both for yourself and for others.	77
18 Think of times when you wished you had the skill to	87
19 make your point. Perhaps you needed to know how to respond	99
20 in a job interview or how to bargain for work hours. These	111
21 situations call for good communication skills. Some people	123
22 find it easy to speak up for themselves, but many others	134
23 frequently receive negative reactions for their attempts.	146
24 It is up to you to examine your own needs and learn	156
25 how to express your ideas or feelings in an effective way.	168
26 This skill is essential in all dealings with other people.	180
27 Practice this skill often.	185

| 1 | 2 | 3 | 4 | 5 | 6 | 7 | 8 | 9 | 10 | 11 | 12SI 1.37

SKILLBUILDING

C. DIAGNOSTIC PRACTICE: ALPHABET

Turn to the Diagnostic Practice: Alphabet routine on page SB-1 Type one of the Pretest/Posttest paragraphs and identify any errors made. Then type the corresponding drill lines 2 times for each letter on which you made 2 or more errors and 1 time for each letter on which you made only 1 error. Finally, repeat the Pretest and compare your performance.

D. ALPHABET REVIEW

Type each line 2 times. Repeat if time permits.

```
 9  axle aide ache away bite brag brim bowl caps come crew chip
10  duet drag down dive east etch ends exit feud fame from flat
11  gale give glow grip hope have hill help ills into iced idea

12  joke jump jail jest knit kiln keep know line late lump lost
13  maze more mist melt norm nice nail numb odor over oath open
14  paid pour prod pest quad quip quiz quay ride reap rake room

15  sing stay sort shop team task thin tray ugly upon used unit
16  vote vast vine vest wage when wire worm axis oxen exit flax
17  yell yard year yolk yawl type zinc zeal zone zero zany buzz
```

FACT FILE

An emperor penguin can hold its breath for 15 to 20 minutes and lives an average of 15-20 years. Emperor penguins cannot fly, but small flippers help it to swim very fast. The flippers are strong enough to break a person's wrist. In the Ross Sea in Antarctica, an emperor penguin once dove to a depth of 1,584 feet. This dive, which was recorded in 1990, is the deepest dive on record for any bird.

LESSON 91

TABLES: REVERSING LINES

OBJECTIVES:

- Reinforce keyboarding skill.
- Type 37/5′/5e.
- Learn software features.
- Reverse table lines.

A. WARMUP

Type each line 2 times.

Speed
Accuracy
Language Link
Numbers/Symbols

1 The temperature last night dropped below the freezing mark.
2 Jack typed four dozen requisitions for hollow moving boxes.
3 Then Coach said the prize went to whoever ran the farthest.
4 The citation for the case is 795 F.2D 1423 (9th Cir. 1996).
 | 1 | 2 | 3 | 4 | 5 | 6 | 7 | 8 | 9 | 10 | 11 | 12

SKILLBUILDING

B. TECHNIQUE CHECKPOINT

Type each line 2 times. Focus on the techniques at the left.

Lines 5–6: Space without pausing.

5 You can do much more work than you do each day of the week.
6 They will use the pay for the one day of work that she did.

Lines 7–8: Press and release the Caps Lock key without pausing.

7 Our SEVENTH ANNUAL MEETING will be held in MOBILE, ALABAMA.
8 The DAY COMPANY will sponsor our ADVISORY COUNCIL luncheon.

WORD PROCESSING APPLICATIONS

TABLE 12

Create a 3-column, 7-row table. Center the column headings. Center the table vertically and horizontally.

Name of Show	Day/Date	Time
Learning Rainbow	Monday-Friday	2:30 p.m.-3:00 p.m.
The Science Guru	Monday-Friday	4:00 p.m.-4:30 p.m.
Hooping It Up	Wed., November 15	10:30 a.m.-11:00 a.m.
All Against Violence	Wed., October 16	3:30 p.m.-5:00 p.m.
Rock and Roll Times	Sunday-Thursday	8:00 p.m.-10:00 p.m.
Magic Schoolroom	Sundays	10:30 a.m.-11:00 a.m.

TABLE 13

Create a 3-column, 8-row table, and align the column headings as follows: Align the first column heading at the left (press ENTER 1 time within the cell before you type it so that it aligns with the multiline column headings at the bottom). Align the second and third column headings at the right. Break the column headings into 2 lines as shown. Automatically adjust the column widths. Center the table vertically and horizontally.

Sandwich Items	Total Calorie Count	% of Calories From Fat
Lucy's Grilled Chicken	290	6
Barbey's Chicken Lite	276	7
Barbey's Lite Beef	294	10
Lucy's Junior Burger	270	9
O'Brien's Lean Burger	320	10
BQ Broiler Chicken	280	10
Andy's Turkey Lite	260	6

TABLE 14

Open Table 8 and make the following changes:

1. Center all of the column headings.
2. Remember to delete the hard return in each column heading.
3. Recenter the table horizontally.

MEMO 4
Template

Type the following memo. Use the first memo template in your word processing software.

TO: David J. Bacon / FROM: Wayne S. Goodin / DATE: Current / SUBJECT: Marketing Questionnaire

¶One of the questionnaires that was sent to your office at the beginning of the month should be completed by the 31st of this month. As a reminder, Section III must be completed for questions 8, 12, 18, 24, and 27. The results of the questionnaires are going to be used to compare our product sales with those of the other district offices in the eastern region. Thank you very much for your immediate response. / urs

FACT FILE

The expression "two bits" is used to indicate that you have a quarter. The origin of the word "bit" for a coin goes back to the seventeenth century when any coin in Great Britain could be called a bit. The slang migrated to the southwestern part of the United States where Mexican coins were commonly used as currency. The Mexican real (ray-AHL), which was worth about 12 and a half cents, was called a bit. When the U.S. quarter came out, it was worth about two reals, or two bits.

LESSON 70

TABLES: TITLES, SUBTITLES, AND BRACED COLUMN HEADINGS

OBJECTIVES:

- Improve keyboarding skill.
- Format tables with subtitles and braced column headings.
- Learn software features.

A. WARMUP

Type each line 2 times.

Speed
Accuracy
Language Link
Numbers

1 To reach your goal, you must learn to keep your mind on it.
2 Jars prevented the brown mixture from freezing too quickly.
3 Each pattern and bow requires at least two yards of ribbon.
4 Today's homework is to study Chapter 15, pages 136 and 137.
| 1 | 2 | 3 | 4 | 5 | 6 | 7 | 8 | 9 | 10 | 11 | 12

SKILLBUILDING

B. 30-SECOND TIMINGS

Take two 30-second timings on the first paragraph. Then take two 30-second timings on the second paragraph. Try to type with no more than 2 errors on each timing.

5   Very seldom will you be asked to type from exact copy   11
6 that has no errors. You will often have to make changes.   22

7   Most typing is done from rough-draft copy. On the job   11
8 you must be able to make a decision about correct format.   22
| 1 | 2 | 3 | 4 | 5 | 6 | 7 | 8 | 9 | 10 | 11 | 12

LETTER 57
Modified-Block Style

Type this letter in modified-block style.

(Current Date) / Alkens Industries / 750 South Filmore Street / Denver, CO 80209-5072 / Attention: Human Resources / Ladies and Gentlemen:

¶Mr. Warren Thomas was recently treated by me at Wilson Hospital. During his hospitalization, I placed him on a disability leave. I felt his condition was such that he could not return to work until his symptoms had resolved.

¶Mr. Thomas has continued in my care. He has shown good progress in recovery. On reevaluation, it is apparent that he would be able to return to work on the 15th of next month. This is sooner than I anticipated, but it reflects his positive progress.

¶If there are any other questions, please contact my office. Sincerely, / John Blackburn, M.D. / urs / c: Mr. Warren Thomas

MEMO 3
Template

Type the following memo. Use the first memo template in your word processing software.

TO: Shelby Taylor / FROM: Kenneth Anderson / DATE: July 12, {year} / SUBJECT: Company Newsletter

¶Your first issue of the *Brownfield Quarterly* was fantastic, and I want to extend my heartfelt congratulations for a job well done. Even though this was your first edition of the newsletter using our new desktop publishing software, I think the finished product was great!

¶The Projects Update on page 2 was especially informative because you let us know the major projects our employees have been working on this quarter. We certainly need to know what is going on throughout the plant. I have heard many other employees make very favorable comments about the newsletter, especially this section.

¶Keep up the good work, Shelby. / urs

Type each line 2 times.

9 They found 10 @ 56, 56 @ 47, 47 @ 38, 38 @ 29, and 29 @ 10.
10 Our new scale shows #10 at 29#, #38 at 47#, and #29 at 56#.
11 Gray,* Moletti,* Young,* Hernandez,* and Jones* won prizes.

12 Our show tickets should cost us $10, $29, $38, $47, or $56.
13 Your sales increased 10%, 29%, 38%, 47%, and 56% last year.
14 Lea & Madera, Yung & Poe, and Day & Cole are all attorneys.

15 Label the square cartons as 47-10, 56-38, 38-47, and 10-29.
16 We know that 38 + 47 = 85, 29 + 10 = 39, and 56 + 70 = 126.
17 Lund (Utah), Leon (Iowa), and Troy (Ohio) were represented.

FORMATTING

D. TABLES WITH TITLES AND SUBTITLES

VISITATION REPORT			
June 30, {year}			
First Quarter		**Second Quarter**	
Month	City	Month	City
January	New York City	April	New Orleans
February	San Francisco	May	Kansas City
March	Philadelphia	June	Jacksonville

Most tables have titles to identify what is in the table and column headings to identify what is in the columns. Tables may also have subtitles that further describe the information in the table. Titles and subtitles are typed in the first row of the table. To format a table with a title and a subtitle:

1. Join the cells in the first row of the table.
2. Center and type the title in all caps and bold.
3. Press ENTER 1 time.
4. Center and type the subtitle in initial caps (no bold).
5. Press ENTER 1 time to leave a blank line.

E. BRACED COLUMN HEADINGS

Braced column headings are headings that apply to more than one column of a table. In Table 16, *First Quarter* and *Second Quarter* are braced headings. To create a braced heading:

1. Determine which cells need to be joined.
2. Select the cells and join them.
3. Because braced headings apply to more than one column, they should always be centered.

LETTER 56
Block Style

Type the following letter in block style.

(Current Date) / Ms. Ruthe Barichello, Department Chair / English Department / Central High School / 3474 Maple Avenue / Carrollton, GA 30118 / Dear Ms. Barichello:

Subject: Effective Leadership

¶As we discussed at our meeting last week, there are certainly several traits that we should be aware of when selecting the next members of the department. Are leaders born or made? No one is really sure, but there are four specific actions that successful leaders should carry out regardless of the organization they lead. Effective leaders should:

1. Make others feel important and emphasize others' strengths and contributions, not their own. If leaders' goals are self-centered, followers will lose their enthusiasm quickly.

2. Promote a vision. Followers need a clear idea of where they are being led. A leader needs to provide that vision. Followers need to understand that vision or goal and buy into it.

3. Follow the golden rule. A leader should treat followers the way he/she likes to be treated. That means admitting mistakes.

4. Criticize others only in private. Public praise encourages others to excel.

¶Our first interview is scheduled for next Monday in the board conference room at 9 a.m. I look forward to seeing you then. / Sincerely, / Casey Javonovich / Board Chairman / urs

FACT FILE

Herbert Hoover was a mining engineer. He managed gold mines in Australia and later worked in mines in China and started a mining company. Herbert Hoover was also the thirty-first president of the United States.

F. SOFTWARE FEATURES

STUDENT MANUAL

Join Cells

Study Lesson 70 in your student manual. Complete the practice activities while at your computer. Then complete the jobs that follow.

WORD PROCESSING APPLICATIONS

TABLE 15

Create a 2-column, 9-row table. Join the cells in the first row and center and type the title and subtitle. Remember to leave a blank line after the subtitle. Center the column headings. Center the table vertically and horizontally.

NATURAL WONDERS OF THE WORLD (Listed by World Travelers and Explorers)	
Name	**Location**
Carlsbad Caverns	United States (New Mexico)
Caves and Prehistoric Paintings	France and Spain
Giant Sequoia Trees	United States (California)
Grand Canyon	United States (Colorado River)
Great Barrier Reef	Australia
Paricutin (young volcano)	Mexico
Victoria Falls	Zimbabwe

TABLE 16

Create a 4-column, 6-row table. Join the cells in the first row and center and type the title and subtitle. Join the cells in columns 1 and 2 in the second row; then join the cells in columns 3 and 4 in the second row. Center all of the column headings. Center the table vertically and horizontally.

SEMI-ANNUAL VISITATION REPORT June 30, {year}			
First Quarter		**Second Quarter**	
Month	**City**	**Month**	**City**
January	New York City	April	New Orleans
February	San Francisco	May	Kansas City
March	Philadelphia	June	Jacksonville

LESSON 90

REVIEW

OBJECTIVES:

- Reinforce keyboarding techniques.
- Improve keyboarding skill.
- Reinforce letter and memo formats.

A. WARMUP

Type each line 2 times.

Speed
Accuracy
Language Link
Numbers/Symbols

1 Elaine invited several of her friends over for the evening.
2 Why would quick brown foxes want to jump over any lazy dog?
3 Rather than go any farther, they stopped to get directions.
4 Only 4% of our current PCs are equipped with CD-ROM drives.
| 1 | 2 | 3 | 4 | 5 | 6 | 7 | 8 | 9 | 10 | 11 | 12

SKILLBUILDING

B. TECHNIQUE TIMINGS

Take two 30-second timings on lines 5–6. Then take two 30-second timings on lines 7–8. Focus on the technique at the left.

Keep your eyes on the copy.

5   Try to type each letter of the alphabet as quickly as   11
6 you can without having to stop to look where the keys are.   23

7   As you type, think about where each letter is located.   11
8 Then type with your eyes closed to see if you learned well.   23
| 1 | 2 | 3 | 4 | 5 | 6 | 7 | 8 | 9 | 10 | 11 | 12

C. PACED PRACTICE

Turn to the Paced Practice routine beginning on page SB7 Take three 2-minute timings, starting at the point where you left off the last time.

LESSON 71

TABLES: REVIEW

OBJECTIVES:

- Learn about subject/verb agreement.
- Improve keyboarding speed and accuracy.
- Review table formats.

A. WARMUP

Type each line 2 times.

Speed
Accuracy
Language Link
Numbers/Symbols

1 The goal of the girl is to work to be the best she can be.
2 Dave froze the mixtures in the deep brown jug too quickly.
3 On January 9 my insurance premium will increase by $93.95.
4 I purchased 13 dozen pens @ $11.05. (The sale ends today!)
| 1 | 2 | 3 | 4 | 5 | 6 | 7 | 8 | 9 | 10 | 11 | 12

LANGUAGE LINK

B. SUBJECT/VERB AGREEMENT

Study the rule and the examples that follow. Then correct any errors in subject/verb agreement in lines 5–8.

Rule 12: If two subjects are joined by *or, either/or, neither/nor,* or *not only/but also,* the verb should agree with the subject nearer to the verb.

> *Either the lifeguard or the swimmers have reported a shark in the water.*

> *Not only the page proofs but also the color template is ready to be returned.*

5 Either my supervisor or the vice president (has/have) to sign my expense report.
6 Neither I nor my children (was/were) watching that particular program.
7 Not only the assistants but also the managers (wants/want) to attend.
8 Either you or your classmates (is/are) able to take up a collection for that.

STUDENT MANUAL
Templates

Study Lesson 89 in your student manual. Complete all the practice activities while at your computer. Then complete the jobs that follow.

WORD PROCESSING APPLICATIONS

MEMO 1
Template

Prepare the following memo using the first memo template listed in your word processing software.

MEMO TO: Darrell Stevens / **FROM:** Jim Goodwin / **DATE:** August 12, {year} / **SUBJECT:** Executive Meeting
¶Our next Executive Meeting will be held on August 22, and I'd like to present your report from the Systems Committee Evaluation at the meeting. Since I have invited other department heads to attend, please bring a minimum of 20 copies of your report.
¶I appreciate all the hard work you've put into this project, and I look forward to presenting your report next week. / urs

MEMO 2
Template

Type this memo using the first memo template in your word processing software.

MEMO TO: Janie Lane / **FROM:** Allen T. Wilson / **DATE:** September 21, {year} / **SUBJECT:** Industry Certification
¶I would like to congratulate you and the members of your department for receiving industry certification in April. All of you have worked very hard during the last two years preparing for this process, and I am extremely proud of this accomplishment for you and for our school.
¶Being industry-certified indicates that our Business Education Department has met the standards set by business and industry for meeting the needs of our students. I truly believe that they will be better employees and better citizens after taking our business courses. The industry certification distinction will definitely help to recruit students.
¶Congratulations for a job well done from the entire staff and student body! / urs

SKILLBUILDING

C. 30-SECOND OK TIMINGS

Take two 30-second OK (error-free) timings on lines 9–10. Then take two 30-second OK timings on lines 11–12. Goal: no errors.

```
 9        I quickly explained that only a few big jobs involve    11
10  hazards, but the managers say we need more safety measures.    23

11        Peter reviewed the subject before giving Kay and Max a   11
12  quiz. Both of them like using the computer to take tests.      23
    | 1 | 2 | 3 | 4 | 5 | 6 | 7 | 8 | 9 | 10 | 11 | 12
```

D. PRETEST

Take a 1-minute timing on the paragraph. Note your speed and errors.

```
13        Can you name the five steps in the cycle of processing   11
14  information? First is input. The next step is processing.      23
15  Output is the third step. The fourth step is distribution.     35
16  The last step is storage.                                      40
    | 1 | 2 | 3 | 4 | 5 | 6 | 7 | 8 | 9 | 10 | 11 | 12
```

E. PRACTICE

In the chart below find the number of errors you made on the Pretest. Then type each of the designated drill lines 2 times.

Pretest Errors	0–1	2	3	4+
Drill Lines	20–24	19–23	18–22	17–21

Accuracy
```
17  quire words future format mailed certain involves publicize
18  saves input phase public fourth output retrieval processing
19  modes backs third others lasted storage changed information
20  next steps named saving inform getting require distribution
```

Speed
```
21  files other words done this back last all the can use on be
22  store disks forms some them five mode and has job put up to
23  first cycle right name form have been rib you out for is in
24  names which third mail that four sets may mat his her of or
```

F. POSTTEST

Repeat the Pretest. Compare your Posttest results with your Pretest results.

SKILLBUILDING

C. 30-Second OK Timings

Take two 30-second OK (error-free) timings on lines 9–10. Then take two 30-second OK timings on lines 11–12. Goal: no errors.

```
 9        I did not realize that Kevin quietly joined the army   11
10  six months before he was graduated from Paul High School.    22

11        Analyze the quality of these extra blank cartons that  11
12  they gave us with the monthly shipment mailed this June.     22
   | 1 | 2 | 3 | 4 | 5 | 6 | 7 | 8 | 9 | 10 | 11 | 12
```

D. Technique Checkpoint

Social Studies
Connections

Keep other fingers in home position while reaching to the tab.

Type each line 2 times. Tab to begin each line. Focus on the technique at the left.

```
13  Thomas Edison was born in Ohio.
14  His childhood home is now a museum.
15  He is best known for inventing the lightbulb.
16  He also invented a talking doll.
17  He was a close friend of Henry Ford.
```

FORMATTING

E. Memo Templates

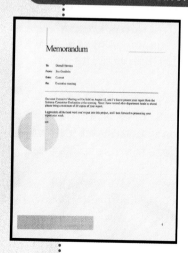

Memos are written messages sent from one person to another in the same organization or business. Memos are less formal than letters and do not have salutations or closing lines.

Most word processing programs now include memo templates. **Templates** are forms that have been designed so that you can move quickly from one data entry area to the next to fill in necessary information. Memo templates usually include the guide words *TO:, FROM:, DATE:,* and *SUBJECT:.*

TABLE 17

Create a 3-column, 8-row table. Center the column headings. Align the number column on the right. Automatically adjust the column widths. Center the table vertically and horizontally.

MAJOR U.S. RIVERS (From *U.S. Geographic Textbook*)		
River	**Length**	**Origin**
Arkansas	1,460	Colorado
Colorado	1,450	Colorado
Columbia	1,240	British Columbia
Mississippi	2,350	Minnesota
Missouri	2,320	Montana
Tennessee	900	North Carolina

TABLE 18

Create a 4-column, 10-row table. Center the column headings. Align the number columns on the right. Automatically adjust the column widths. Center the table vertically and horizontally.

PARKS HIGH SCHOOL HONOR GRADUATES (GPA From 3.50 to 4.00)			
3.75 GPA to 4.00 GPA		**3.50 GPA to 3.74 GPA**	
Student	**GPA**	**Student**	**GPA**
Bryce Bynum	4.00	Aaron Christopher	3.73
Jennifer Click	4.00	Shelley Lyons	3.70
Samuel Dornbusch	3.98	Kelley Lavender	3.65
Rose Barstow	3.97	James Crawford	3.62
Isaac Heyman	3.90	Brandon Lee	3.57
Charlotte Mendosa	3.85	Karen Brackett	3.52
Neil Pacioni	3.80	Charlotte Diaz	3.50

TABLE 19

Create a 6-column, 8-row table similar to the illustration on the next page. Center all column headings. Align the number columns on the right. Automatically adjust the column widths. Center the table vertically and horizontally.

LESSON 89

MEMO TEMPLATES

OBJECTIVES:

- Learn about confusing words.
- Learn word processing features.
- Format memos using templates.

A. WARMUP

Type each line 2 times.

Speed
Accuracy
Language Link
Numbers/Symbols

```
1 We are planning to have a cookout when we meet at the lake.
2 All four mixtures in the deep brown jug froze very quickly.
3 We usually vacation at a place that is south of the border.
4 Invoice #70-2 read: 653# "Extra" @ $4.89 per lb., less 10%.
  | 1 | 2 | 3 | 4 | 5 | 6 | 7 | 8 | 9 | 10 | 11 | 12
```

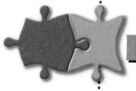

LANGUAGE LINK

B. CONFUSING WORDS

Study the confusing words and their meanings shown below. Then edit lines 5–8 by selecting the correct word.

than (conj. or prep.)   in comparison with
then (adv.)   at that time

farther (adv.)   to a greater distance
further (adv.)   in addition to

```
5 Rather (then/than) stay at home, we saw a movie and (then/than)
  had pizza
6 After studying the map (further/farther), we realized we were
  50 miles (further/farther) (then/than) we should have been.
7 First we visited Niagara Falls, (then/than) we drove
  (further/farther) into Canada to visit Toronto.
8 The board members agreed to discuss the matter
  (further/farther).
```

ANTARCTICA EXPLORATIONS (Expeditions to the South Pole)					
1772-1928			**1929-1989**		
Year	**Explorer**	**Mode of Travel**	**Year**	**Explorer**	**Mode of Travel**
1773	Cook	Ship	1929	Byrd	Airplane
1908	Shackleton	Pony sled	1935	Ellsworth	Airplane
1911	Amundsen	Dog sled	1946	Ronne	Airplane
1912	Scott	Dog sled	1958	Thiel	Tractor
1928	Wilkins	Airplane	1989	Murden & Metz	Skis

FACT FILE

The blue whale is the largest animal in the world—probably the largest that ever lived. Antarctic blue whales can be over 100 feet long and weigh more than 150 tons. A blue whale's heart alone may weigh as much as 2,000 pounds (as much as a small car).

In spite of their huge size, most blue whales are gentle, placid browsers that strain vast amounts of ocean for the krill (small shrimp) on which they feed. Blue whales are known to migrate from the South Pole to the Equator in small packs.

LETTER 55
Block Style

Type this letter in block style.

(Current Date) / Mr. Sullivan D'Amico / D'Amico & McGrawth Legal Firm / 404 West Broadway / Suite 220 / Denver, CO 80501 / Dear Mr. D'Amico:

¶Thank you for your letter asking about my new book, *Listening Is an Art.* In the book, I stress that listening is not a spectator sport. It requires active participation.

¶As a listener, you need to encourage your speaker by visibly paying close attention. Body language on your part is often a great encouragement to the speaker. Listed below are several of the topics I cover in the book:

1. Paraphrase the content. In your own words, repeat what you are hearing. Encourage the speaker by letting him/her know that you are listening.

2. Be involved in the conversation. Go beyond paraphrasing to enforce understanding by adding comments to the person's discussion.

3. Feed back feelings. Reflect the feelings you hear by expressing your opinion about the topic being discussed. If you can, ask direct questions of the speaker.

¶I hope, Mr. D'Amico, that this gives you an idea of what I'm writing about. I've mailed you an autographed copy of my book for your enjoyment.

Yours truly, / Bonnie Ryan, Author / urs

FACT FILE

Most software packages have a variety of templates available for memos and other documents. Even though these templates can save you time, determine whether or not your employer wants you to use the templates or format documents differently.

REPORTS WITH PARENTHETICAL REFERENCES AND QUOTES

OBJECTIVES:

- Review the format for an academic report.
- Learn the format for long quotes and works cited.
- Learn software features.
- Type 35/3′/5e.

A. WARMUP

Type each line 2 times.

Speed
Accuracy
Language Link
Numbers

```
1  The team has worked hard to solve the problem for the firm.
2  Six big jet planes quickly zoomed over the five old towers.
3  I visited Western High School located in western Milwaukee.
4  Our 15 girls and 25 boys ate 8 pies, 8 cakes, and 9 pizzas.
   | 1 | 2 | 3 | 4 | 5 | 6 | 7 | 8 | 9 | 10 | 11 | 12
```

SKILLBUILDING

B. PREVIEW PRACTICE

Type each line 2 times as a preview to the 3-minute timings that follow.

Accuracy
Speed

```
5  several everyone stressful management inadequate everything
6  people time gift less seem have they plan want tips item up
```

FORMATTING

F. LETTERS WITH NUMBERED LISTS

A numbered list is often included in the body of a letter. Use the automatic numbering feature to create the list. Leave a blank line before the first and after the last numbered item. Single-space the list.

WORD PROCESSING APPLICATIONS

LETTER 54
Modified-Block Style

Type the following letter in modified-block style.

(Current Date) / Dr. Jaune Sakyesva / 2042 East Bellview Parkway / Suite 109 / Denver, CO 80202-1956 / Dear Dr. Sakyesva:

¶We are happy to respond to your letter requesting information about our next seminar on current ISSUES IN SOCIETY. This series of seminars has been successful because we have addressed some of the major issues our society faces today, and we have offered helpful suggestions on how to deal with them.

1. The seminar will be held August 21 from 9 a.m. until 3 p.m. at the Inn of the Rockies, 404 West Mountain Drive. A map is enclosed with this letter.
2. Lunch will be provided by Epicurean Delight. Call 699-555-1245 to specify your luncheon choice from those items listed in our brochure.
3. There will be three speakers and a chance for questions after each talk.
4. Tapes from other seminars will be available for purchase in the lobby during the luncheon break and at the conclusion of the seminar.

¶As soon as we have confirmations from the speakers, I'll send you literature regarding each speaker and his/her qualifications. Thank you for your interest in the seminar.

Sincerely, / Maya Harris / Public Relations Director / urs / Enclosure

Take two 3-minute timings on the paragraph. Note your speed and errors.

Goal: 35/3'/5e

7	Time is a gift we all have. A day is the same length	11
8	for all of us. Some people always seem to have time for	22
9	everything and everyone. Other people just never seem to	33
10	have enough time to do all the things they want to do. This	45
11	difference may be due to people not having an adequate plan	57
12	to manage the time they do have. Experts in time management	69
13	have decided on several tips for better use of time. Make	81
14	lists of things to do and check each item as it is done.	92
15	Your day will be less stressful if you manage your time	104
16	wisely.	105

| 1 | 2 | 3 | 4 | 5 | 6 | 7 | 8 | 9 | 10 | 11 | 12 SI 1.26

FORMATTING

D. Reports With Parenthetical References

When you use facts, ideas, and information of others in a report, you must give credit to those people. One acceptable format to use is the MLA (Modern Language Association) style for **parenthetical references.** In this style, a quotation is followed by the author's or source's name in parentheses. Follow these guidelines to format parenthetical references:

1. Include the author's name and the page number(s) of the source in parentheses; for example, (Adams 157–158).
2. If the author's or source's name is used before the quote, include only the page number(s) in parentheses; for example, (157–158).
3. If there are two or three authors of the source, include all authors' names in parentheses; for example, (Jones, Cass, and Noel 199).

SKILLBUILDING

C. PRETEST

Take a 1-minute timing on the paragraph. Note your speed and errors.

```
 9        In the past decade, computers have affected almost      12
10   every job in the business office. Today, it is very common   22
11   to see computers being used that are smaller and six to ten  34
12   times quicker than they were only a few short years ago.     45
     | 1 | 2 | 3 | 4 | 5 | 6 | 7 | 8 | 9 | 10 | 11 | 12
```

D. PRACTICE

In the chart below, find the number of errors you made on the Pretest. Then type each of the designated drill lines 2 times.

Pretest Errors	0–1	2	3	4+
Drill Lines	16–20	15–19	14–18	13–17

Accuracy
```
13  just during decade faster smaller invaded business addition
14  past about coming become common powerful possible computers
15  now have would popular horizon machines business technology
16  six more find would quite become smaller possible computers
```

Speed
```
17  office being today every this task all now are the it in so
18  years their time more were used find this that not of is to
19  become makes will hard that they then much new and on be or
20  times today find such does much just work few ago use on of
```

E. POSTTEST

Repeat the Pretest. Compare your Posttest results with your Pretest results.

LANGUAGE ARTS CONNECTIONS

In 1962, Martin K. Specter invented the word *interrobang*. When someone shouts with alarm and asks a question at the same time, the sentence could end with an interrobang. The first part of the word, *interro*, is short for interrogation point, which is another name for a question mark. An interrogation is a questioning, which comes from the Latin *inter*. The ending, *bang*, was originally a printer's slang word for an exclamation point. Interrobang has now migrated into the world of computer terminology.

4. If there are four or more authors, include the first author's name followed by *et al.;* for example, (Martin et al. 215–217).

5. If there is no author, include a shortened version of the title and the page number(s) in parentheses; for example, (Critical Essays 59).

E.   QUOTATIONS IN REPORTS

Short Quotations (less than 4 lines):

1. Enclose direct quotations in quotation marks. Do not use quotation marks with indirect quotes or paraphrased remarks.

2. Type the parenthetical reference 1 space after the closing quotation mark or the last word of an indirect quote. Type the ending punctuation mark after the reference.

Example: ". . . until we receive confirmation" (Barton 96).

Long Quotations (4 or more lines):

1. Leave a blank line before and after the quote.

2. Do not use quotation marks.

3. Indent the quote 1 inch from the left margin.

4. Type the parenthetical reference 1 space after the ending punctuation mark.

Example: . . . by tomorrow at the latest. (Johnson 41)

F.   SOFTWARE FEATURES

STUDENT MANUAL

Left Indent   Right Indent   Hanging Indent

Study Lesson 72 in your student manual. Complete all the practice activities while at your computer. Then complete the jobs that follow.

*inter*NET C O N N E C T I O N

Use the Internet to search for Websites that provide information on time management. Try the site, http://www.day-timer.com. Take the time management quiz. Then, prepare a brief paragraph describing the results of the test of your time management skills.

LESSON 88

LETTERS WITH NUMBERED LISTS

OBJECTIVES:

- Learn capitalization rules for compass points.
- Improve keyboarding skills.
- Format letters with numbered lists.

A. WARMUP

Type each line 2 times.

Speed
Accuracy
Language Link
Numbers/Symbols

1 Richard can ask what size tent he should take for the trip.
2 Jena quickly seized the wax buffer and removed a big patch.
3 Publisher's Clearing House gave away three million dollars.
4 The booklets are AB-GN, catalog item XH479/162CLW @ $13.50.
| 1 | 2 | 3 | 4 | 5 | 6 | 7 | 8 | 9 | 10 | 11 | 12

LANGUAGE LINK

B. CAPITALIZATION

Study the rule and examples below. Then correct any errors in capitalization in lines 5–8.

Rule 19:

Capitalize compass points (such as *north, south,* or *northeast*) only when they designate definite regions.

The forecaster said that the cold front was moving from the west and would blanket the Midwest with snow by Thursday.

5 If you are traveling to the north today, be careful of fog.
6 Paula lived in the north until she moved south to Florida.
7 Karen sold the most homes in the southern part of the city.
8 The flooding was severe in the southeast and midwest.

Type the following report in academic style. Double-space the report.

(Your Name)
(Your Teacher's Name)
(Class Name)
(Current Date)

Employee Absenteeism

"Absence makes the heart grow fonder" (Bayly 1). This quote may apply to the absence of a loved one; however, it is not true in the case of employee absence.

Some feel that a paycheck is enough incentive to come to work. Others feel that what happens once employees arrive can increase absenteeism. Hawkens writes in his book, <u>Management by Communication</u>:

> It will help to work with employees rather than manage them and to keep open lines of communication. There is no greater obstacle to successful communications than the refusal of a manager to willingly communicate with those who are under his or her direct line of control and an unwillingness to practice this activity on a day-to-day basis. (22–23)

Employers have studied reports explaining why employees are absent. They have found that lack of good quality child care is one big factor. In response to this need, some employers have set up child care facilities at the work site (Stone and Burlingham 47).

The solution to the problem of employee absenteeism will take effort on the part of both workers and employers. Workers must understand how their job performance affects business success—and whether or not they will even have a job. Employers need to continue to try to help employees overcome factors that cause them to be absent.

If necessary, refer to formatting instructions on page 139 for academic reports.

LETTERS 51–53
Block Style

Create a data file with these field names: Title, FirstName, LastName, Address, CityStateZIP, Physician, State. *After you have created the data file with these field names, create the following three records.*

Record 1	**Record 2**	**Record 3**
Ms. Faye Hayes	Mr. Alvin Morgan	Mr. Lloyd Blairstone
450 Marshall Avenue	742 Huck Road	7500 Lada Lane
Hickory, NC 28611	Lexington, SC 29072	Thomaston, GA 30286
Dr. Millhouse	Dr. Stewart	Dr. Abernathy
North Carolina	South Carolina	Georgia

After you create the data records, type the following form letter in block style. Note that two of the data fields appear within the body of the letter. Then, merge the data records with the form letter to create Letters 51–53.

June 6, {year}

<<Title>> <<FirstName>> <<LastName>>
<<Address>>
<<CityStateZIP>>

Dear <<Title>> <<LastName>>:

¶Your physician, <<Physician>>, recommended you as a person who might benefit from participating in a research study on the problems of aging. This study is being conducted through the medical school at Wayne State University. The examinations included in the study will be at no cost to you.

¶Please read the brochure describing the study, complete the enclosed questionnaire, and return it to me by June 30. A postage-paid return envelope is also enclosed for your convenience.

¶Your participation in this study will help us reach our goal for the number of respondents we hope to include from <<State>>. If you have any questions, call me at 810-555-4575. I look forward to including you in this study.

Sincerely,

Donald L. Gaddis, M.D.
Project Director

urs
Enclosures

LESSON 73

REPORTS WITH WORKS CITED PAGE

OBJECTIVES:

- Improve keyboarding technique.
- Compose at the keyboard.
- Learn software features.
- Learn to format a Works Cited page.

A. WARMUP

Type each line 2 times.

Speed
Accuracy
Language Link
Numbers/Symbols

1 You will need to learn new ways to work and save more time.
2 The judge quickly gave back six of the prizes to the women.
3 Not only they but also I am playing golf and swimming soon.
4 Report #R102 (prepared by Rothe & Roy) shows a 2% increase.
   | 1 | 2 | 3 | 4 | 5 | 6 | 7 | 8 | 9 | 10 | 11 | 12

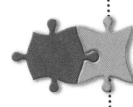

LANGUAGE LINK

B. COMPOSING AT THE KEYBOARD

Answer the following questions with complete sentences.

5 Who are three people you would most like to meet, and why would you like to meet them?
6 If you could travel with a famous person, who would that be, and why did you choose that person?
7 If you could design your dream vacation spot, what would it look like?

LETTER 50
Modified-
Block Style

Type the following letter in modified-block style with indented paragraphs.

(Current Date) / Ms. Kateri Tahoma / Administrative Assistant / Diabo Construction Company / 330 Cooper Avenue / Lincoln, NE 68506 / Dear Ms. Tahoma:

¶You are invited to attend a seminar entitled "Listening Skills—Do You Hear When You Listen?" It will be held at the Cornhusker Hotel in Lincoln on June 17 from 9 a.m. until 3 p.m.

¶The registration fee of $50 includes the seminar and a luncheon from noon until 1:30. During lunch you will be able to view fashions from DeLilli Designs. Your employer, Diabo Construction, will pay your registration fee.

¶This professional seminar will be well worth the time away from the office if you take the right approach. Here are a few suggestions that will help you turn this seminar into a valuable experience. Prepare yourself by reading the information provided by your company. List at least five specific questions you want answered. Use break time to network and talk to your peers. Bring business cards to exchange. When you receive one, make a note on the back about the person giving it to you. Collect handouts from all the speakers. Read your notes. Review and prepare a summary of what you experienced and learned. You also might listen for suggestions on how to be a better listener. The presenters will give the audience time to role-play and use specific techniques of listening.

¶If you follow these little hints, the seminar will be informative as well as enjoyable for you. We are looking forward to seeing you at the Cornhusker. / Sincerely, / Dana Olsen, Coordinator / Climbing the Ladder, Inc.

SKILLBUILDING

C. TECHNIQUE TIMINGS

Take two 30-second timings on each line. Focus on the technique at the left.

Space without pausing.

8 Now that I have my own car, I can drive to all of my games.
9 If I have to see him just now, he must come to this window.
10 My dad took a long trip and fished in the river for a week.
11 Our mom went to a spa to rest and relax while our dad read.
| 1 | 2 | 3 | 4 | 5 | 6 | 7 | 8 | 9 | 10 | 11 | 12

FORMATTING

D. WORKS CITED PAGE

Molivida 4

Works Cited

Blue, Leslie. Free College Cash. Detroit: Fact File Press, 1997.

Drake, M. L. "Your Guide to Finding College Cash." Business Week 14 September 1998:

112-113.

Kent, Dennis M. Financial Aid Opportunities for Undergrads: Step-by-Step. New York:

Visible Ink Press, 1996.

Redburn, Philana H. Secrets to Finding Maximum College Financial Aid. 9th ed. Chicago:

Student College Aid Publishing Division, 1998.

Spinner, June Ann and David R. Webster. Scholarships and Financial Aid for the Disabled

Student. Redwood City: Redwood Publishers.

In MLA-style reports, the **Works Cited page** is an alphabetical list of all the sources you have cited. To format a list of works cited:

1. Begin the Works Cited section on a new page, continuing the page numbers from the report.
2. Use the same side margins as in the report, and use double spacing.
3. Create a header with the report author's name and page number aligned at the right margin; for example, Sanders 4. Press ENTER 1 time after typing the page number.
4. Center and type the title *Works Cited* in initial caps approximately 1 inch from the top of the page.
5. Arrange the list alphabetically by authors' last names.
6. Begin each entry at the left margin, and indent carryover lines 0.5 inch (use a hanging indent).

Take two 5-minute timings on the paragraphs. Note your speed and errors.

Goal: 37/5'/5e

7   The term credit means buying now and paying later. It   11
8 is similar to borrowing cash. One reason people use credit   23
9 is because they do not have the cash to pay for something   34
10 at the time they want to buy it.   41

11   Many people now use credit cards to purchase things.   52
12 Credit cards are easy to obtain and use, and people are   63
13 quick to use them as borrowed money for extra things they   75
14 cannot afford. They build up debts they just cannot pay.   86

15   People of all ages and all income levels can easily   97
16 get into debt with credit cards. They do not realize that   108
17 using credit comes with a high price. Often, cardholders   120
18 pay finance charges or interest on unpaid bills for their   131
19 purchases.   133

20   In spite of this, most people will need to establish   144
21 a good credit record. They will need a steady job with   155
22 stable income, and they must prove that they will repay   166
23 any money they borrow. Once people have their good credit   178
24 ratings, they must maintain them.   185

| 1 | 2 | 3 | 4 | 5 | 6 | 7 | 8 | 9 | 10 | 11 | 12 SI 1.38

MATH CONNECTIONS

Check your local newspapers or use the Internet to determine the various interest rates on most credit cards. Based on your findings, determine how long it would take and how much interest you would pay if you bought something that cost $700 and paid a minimum amount of $10 every month toward your bill. Have your teacher check your math.

STUDENT MANUAL

Header/Footer

Study Lesson 73 in your student manual. Complete all the practice activities while at your computer. Then complete the jobs that follow.

WORD PROCESSING APPLICATIONS

REPORT 18

Type the following report in academic style. Type the Works Cited page as the last page of the report. Use your name, your teacher's name, your course title, and the current date in the heading. Use only your last name with the page number.

Paying College Costs

¶It is assumed that students will continue their education beyond high school. Some graduates will attend community colleges or four-year colleges and universities immediately after high school graduation. Some graduates will work part-time and take classes over an extended period of years. Redburn states that:

Some will obtain vocational skills by attending career-specific schools and training programs. No matter what path is taken, all who seek post-high-school training face the problem of paying the ever-increasing costs of higher education. Next to your home, this may be the most expensive investment you make. (2)

¶Financial aid can be the answer. It is best to begin by examining the several types of financial aid available. There are scholarships, loans, and grants that do not have to be repaid. There are work-study programs and internships, which allow students to work and earn tuition. Some scholarships are granted by extracurricular organizations and may require a formal membership or a period of active participation. It is important to start your research early so that you have enough time to locate and meet application deadlines for a variety of awards (Kent 97).

¶The U.S. Department of Education offers six main student financial aid programs: Pell Grants, Supplemental Education Opportunity Grants, College Work Study, Perkins Loans, Stafford Loans, and Plus Loans (Blue 202). Published guidelines showing the requirements needed to qualify for each of these programs are available. Everyone, no matter what his or her income level, can benefit by completing the paperwork for governmental financial aid.

LESSON 87

REVIEW

OBJECTIVES:

- Review business letter formats.
- Type 37/5'/5e.
- Use mail merge.

A. WARMUP

Type each line 2 times.

Speed
Accuracy
Language Link
Numbers/Symbols

1 You can stay in shape with a brisk walk three times a week.
2 Dr. Baxter was quick to analyze the four major food groups.
3 We now have two kittens I adopted after they were deserted.
4 Donald and Darlene paid $5.08 for 4 pamphlets @ $1.27 each.
| 1 | 2 | 3 | 4 | 5 | 6 | 7 | 8 | 9 | 10 | 11 | 12

SKILLBUILDING

B. PREVIEW PRACTICE

Type each line 2 times as a preview to the timings that follow.

Accuracy
Speed

5 jump steady difficult realize purchases extremely establish
6 credit afford result stable good time cash will job not has

FACT FILE

High temperatures and humidity can quickly lead to heat exhaustion. To ward off serious consequences, know these early signs and symptoms: headache, nausea, fatigue, dizziness or lightheadedness, actively sweating. Generally heat exhaustion is caused by loss of body fluids and important salts. If untreated, heat exhaustion can lead to heat stroke. To treat heat exhaustion, get into the shade or a cool place, increase fluids, and use cold, wet towels to cool down.

¶There are even financial aid programs earmarked for students with disabilities (Spinner and Webster 16). Each year millions of dollars are available as assistance for disabled students and their families. These programs are open to disabled applicants from high school through postdoctoral studies. Students with physical disabilities as well as learning disabilities (such as dyslexia) are eligible.

¶Probably the best place to begin the search for information on sources for college financial aid is in the counseling office of your school. Also, contact the financial aid office at the schools you are interested in attending as suggested by Drake (112). The task of locating ways to fund college costs may seem overwhelming. It is made easier if you start early and are well-organized in your search.

Works Cited

Blue, Leslie. Free College Cash. Detroit: Fact File Press, 1997.

Drake, M. L. "Your Guide to Finding College Cash." Business Week 14 September 1998: 112–113.

Kent, Dennis M. Financial Aid Opportunities for Undergrads: Step-by-Step. New York: Visible Ink Press, 1996.

Redburn, Philana H. Secrets to Finding Maximum College Financial Aid, 9th ed. Chicago: Student College Aid Publishing Division, 1998.

Spinner, June Ann and David R. Webster. Scholarships and Financial Aid for the Disabled Student. Redwood City: Redwood Publishers, 1998.

MATH CONNECTIONS

Use whatever sources are available such as the Internet, the library, or local colleges to determine what tuition rates for various schools are. Then, calculate how much you would need to earn or save every week in order to pay the tuition. Based on money you currently earn either through working or an allowance, calculate how long it would take you to save the entire amount of tuition.

Record 3
Mr.
Cameron
Wingert
8130 S. College Avenue
Tulsa
OK
74136

Record 4
Mrs.
Nichole
McCullum
948 S. Winston Avenue
Tulsa
OK
74112

October 1, {year}

<<Title>> <<FirstName>> <<LastName>>
<<Address>>
<<CityStateZIP>>

Dear <<Title>> <<LastName>>:

We appreciate your recent purchase of an appliance from our Shalimar Mall store. A coupon book is enclosed that should be used to make your monthly payments.

Please be sure that our mailing address shows in the window part of the envelopes that are also enclosed. For your convenience, payments may also be made at the store. We look forward, <<Title>> <<LastName>>, to serving your appliance needs in the coming years.

Sincerely,

Wilbert Crawford
Accounts Manager

Enclosures

LESSON 74

REPORTS REVIEW

OBJECTIVES:

- Improve keyboarding speed and accuracy.
- Review report formats.

A. WARMUP

Type each line 2 times.

Speed
Accuracy
Language Link
Numbers

1 When you go to look for a job, dress well and arrive early.
2 Jackie quietly gave most of his prize boxers to dog owners.
3 His surgery was May 4; he returned to work six weeks later.
4 You can telephone Myron at 318-555-2647 or at 318-555-2648.
| 1 | 2 | 3 | 4 | 5 | 6 | 7 | 8 | 9 | 10 | 11 | 12

SKILLBUILDING

B. PACED PRACTICE

Turn to the Paced Practice routine beginning on page SB-7 Take three 2-minute timings, starting at the point where you left off the last time.

WORD PROCESSING APPLICATIONS

REPORT 19

Agenda

Type the following agenda in the correct format.

ASIF TECHNOLOGY CONFERENCE / Meeting Agenda / August 12-15, {year}
1. Registration/Lobby
2. Demonstration: Virtual Reality/Mott Suite
3. Break/Curtise Suite
4. Computerized Accounting Software/Carriage B
5. Awards Luncheon/Chrysler A/B
6. Managing Files on a Computer/Carriage B
7. Break/Curtise Suite
8. Introduction: Interactive Communications/Mott Suite
9. Discussion and Evaluation/Chrysler B

C. PRETEST

Take a 1-minute timing on the paragraph. Note your speed and errors.

Symbol Diagnostic

```
 9        J&J Nursery numbered their plants. They sold 5 of #76,   11
10  69 of #42, and 25 of #38. I bought 20 bulbs* @ $2.49; now I    23
11  have to plant them. This is 20 + 40 = 60 that I have bought.   35
12  Red flowers @ $2.49 each show a profit of 8%. I'm thrilled!    47
   | 1 | 2 | 3 | 4 | 5 | 6 | 7 | 8 | 9 | 10 | 11 | 12
```

D. PRACTICE

Type lines 13–21 twice. Then repeat any of the lines that stress the symbol errors you noted in the Pretest.

```
@   13  Frank sold 15 @ 11, 20 @ 22, 25 @ 33, 30 @ 44, and 35 @ 55.
*   14  Earl selected *Rome, *Venice, *Paris, *Berlin, and *Madrid.
#   15  We see that #9 weighs 56#, #7 weighs 34#, and #8 weighs 2#.

$   16  The seven girls saved $9, $10, $38, $47, $56, $72, and $89.
%   17  On those days the market rose 3%, 5%, 7%, 8%, 12%, and 18%.
&   18  The leaders are Kim & Dave, Robert & Mary, and Kay & Peter.

()  19  Li chose Marco (Florida), Daisy (Georgia), and Alta (Utah).
-   20  The cartons were labeled as 29-92, 38-56, 47-10, and 59-28.
+ = 21  Eb said that 28 + 65 = 93, 47 + 15 = 62, and 10 + 99 = 109.
```

E. POSTTEST

Repeat the Pretest. Compare your Posttest results with your Pretest results.

WORD PROCESSING APPLICATIONS

LETTERS 46–49

Create a data file with the field names shown below, then create the four records. After the data records are complete, type the form letter in block style. Insert the fields where necessary. Merge the data file and form letter to create Letters 46-49.

Field Names: Title, FirstName, LastName, Address, City, State, ZIP

Record 1	**Record 2**
Mrs.	Dr.
Jasmine	Lewis
Graham	Garcia
7457 S. Hudson Avenue	3284 S. Utica Street
Tulsa	Tulsa
OK	OK
74136	74105

Managing Your Money 101

¶It is not easy to manage money, but this is a very important part of becoming an independent adult. When you start your first job (which will probably be a part-time job), you will be expected to take on some of the financial responsibilities for your own care that were previously met by your parents or guardians. Perhaps you will have to buy your own clothes. You will certainly have to pay for your own lunches and for your transportation to and from work. "You will have to learn to live within your means, which means spending no more than you earn, or not buying things for which you cannot pay" (Krammer and Petrie 154).

¶If you are to be successful in living within your means, you must have a plan for spending. People who do not plan often end up in trouble with credit accounts. College students are particularly at risk of overdoing it with credit if they use the many unsolicited credit cards that come to them in the mail almost as soon as they check into the dormitory. Jones tells parents to be sure that their college-age students leave for college with a sensible spending plan and lessons on how to use credit (29).

¶In order to have a realistic spending plan, you need to think about your plans—both long-range and short-range. If you want to purchase a house, for example, you will need to begin saving money for a down payment.

> One of the most important things you can do is to think of saving as you think of paying your bills—something you do every month without fail. In fact, you should think of savings as a bill you pay yourself. You may be one of the many people who are always planning to save but are constantly confronted with other ways of spending money earmarked for savings. Certainly, saving requires discipline. (Porter 163)

¶Single adults and families with young children should consider saving money for the future or providing for emergencies by investing in insurance (Topolnicki 45). Income-protection insurance will provide income for the single person or young family in case the breadwinner is unable to work. There is homeowner's insurance to cover unexpected losses of property. Car insurance is also a must. For many people, the purchase of insurance is a good way to save money for future expenses. There are many different kinds of insurance to be considered when putting together a spending plan.

LESSON 86

MERGE: FORM LETTERS

OBJECTIVES:

- Improve keyboarding skill on symbol keys.
- Create a form letter and a data file.
- Merge the form letter with the data file.

A. WARMUP

Type each line 2 times.

Speed
Accuracy
Language Link
Numbers/Symbols

```
1 The report cover is the first part of a report that we see.
2 Joey requested help to research weekly executive magazines.
3 Atlanta, Georgia, is the home office for many corporations.
4 You may reach Don any weekday at (404) 555-7139, Ext. 3286.
  | 1 | 2 | 3 | 4 | 5 | 6 | 7 | 8 | 9 | 10 | 11 | 12
```

SKILLBUILDING

B. 30-SECOND TIMINGS

Take two 30-second timings on lines 5–6. Then take two 30-second timings on lines 7–8. Try to increase your speed on each timing.

```
5      Making a speech is a frightening prospect for many of    11
6 us because we lack experience in making oral presentations.   23

7      Planning, preparing, and practicing are the best ways    11
8 to prepare for delivering an oral report to most audiences.   23
  | 1 | 2 | 3 | 4 | 5 | 6 | 7 | 8 | 9 | 10 | 11 | 12
```

¶There is help available for people who find themselves in need of help with money matters. General information can be obtained free of charge from government publications. Also, banks employ people who can provide you with information on savings and investments (Garner et al. 194–201). It would be worth your while to invest your time and money in a class to learn how to manage your money. Remember, no matter how much you earn, how you manage your money will determine the type of lifestyle you will be able to achieve.

Works Cited

Garner, Christopher et al. Personal Finance Guide for Working Couples. New York: John Wiley & Sons, Inc. 1995.

Jones, Gregory. "Teaching Young Children About Spending Money." Essence April 1996, 29–30.

Krammer, Gloria and Sylvia B. Petrie. Succeeding in the World of Finance. Bloomington: Wright Publishing 1998.

Porter, Harold. Managing Family Finances. San Francisco: Prentice Hall Press 1993.

Topolnicki, Dillard. "Getting in Touch With Your Finances." Money December 1997, 142–146.

JOURNAL ENTRY

Describe the lifestyle you would like to have once you finish school. What kind of job do you think you might have? Where would you like to live? What kind of a car would you want to drive?

STUDENT MANUAL

Mail Merge: Data File   Form File

Study Lesson 85 in your student manual. Complete all the practice activities while at your computer. Then complete the jobs that follow.

WORD PROCESSING APPLICATIONS

LETTERS 44–45

Create a data file with the field names shown below; then create the two records. After the data records are complete, type the form letter in block style. Merge the data file and form letter to create Letters 44-45.

Field Names	Record 1	Record 2
Title	Ms.	Mr.
FirstName	Teresa	Tom
LastName	Belle	Carlisle
Address	7168 Olympia Avenue	16687 E. Latimer Place
City	Dalton	Westlake
State	GA	OH
ZIP	30720	44145

January 19, {Year}

<<Title>> <<FirstName>> <<LastName>>
<<Address>>
<<City>>, <<State>> <<ZIP>>

Dear <<FirstName>>:

¶Congratulations! You are a winner in the Bold Journey Contest sponsored by *Outdoor Magazine.* You have won an entire week at Outdoor Adventure Camp in Big Branch, Utah—all expenses paid. We hope, <<FirstName>>, that you are looking forward to joining the other 49 high school students across the country who are also winners.

¶Next week we will send you all the details concerning your travel arrangements, needed equipment, and the type of clothing you should bring.

¶We look forward to seeing you at Big Branch.

Sincerely, / Brandon T. Dillard / Editor in Chief / urs

LESSON 75

FOOTNOTES AND ENDNOTES IN REPORTS

OBJECTIVES:

- Learn about commas with introductory expressions.
- Type 35/3'/5e.
- Format reports with footnotes and endnotes.
- Learn software features.

A. WARMUP

Type each line 2 times.

Speed
Accuracy
Language Link
Numbers/Symbols

1 We know that a good thing to do is to rest and read a book.
2 The lazy judge was very quick to pay tax money for the box.
3 Kia understands that the classroom rules apply to everyone.
4 Lee & Lou and Nate & Nat paid for 534# of #80 tape @ $1.28.
| 1 | 2 | 3 | 4 | 5 | 6 | 7 | 8 | 9 | 10 | 11 | 12

LANGUAGE LINK

B. COMMAS

Study the rule and the examples below. Then correct any errors in comma usage in lines 5–8.

Rule 13: Use a comma after an introductory expression (unless it is a short prepositional phrase).

In my opinion, the cars should be repaired immediately.

No, you may not take the ferry to the island.

After the flood, we sold our house and moved to a condominium.

SKILLBUILDING

C. PRETEST

Take a 1-minute timing on the paragraph. Note your speed and errors.

```
 9      To merge many addresses with one letter is truly quite   11
10   a job for certain people. However, this vexing task can be   23
11   completed very simply and in an amazingly little amount of   35
12   time with concentrated effort to learn the right technique.  47
     | 1 | 2 | 3 | 4 | 5 | 6 | 7 | 8 | 9 | 10 | 11 | 12
```

D. PRACTICE

SPEED: If you made 2 or fewer errors on the Pretest, type lines 13–20 two times each.

ACCURACY: If you made more than 2 errors on the Pretest, type lines 13–16 as a group two times. Then type lines 17–20 as a group two times.

Left Reaches

```
13  rer red were crow break dread cheer chore dream toast clerk
14  asa ask base lane flash saint hasty sauce spasm salty treat
15  rtr art dirt trim ports chart tract short trade sport train
16  tet jet team kite meter beets meets sweet liter miter white
```

Right Reaches

```
17  iui suit quit unit ruin build equip quiet quick guilt fruit
18  oio toil coil riot boil joins lions joist avoid doing onion
19  pop pods chop pose stop spoil sport adopt depot topic power
20  lol poll lots jolt told molds older holds soles folds holes
```

E. POSTTEST

Repeat the Pretest. Compare your Posttest results with your Pretest results.

FORMATTING

F. MERGE: DATA SOURCE/FORM FILE

Often it is necessary to send the same letter to many different people. A **form letter** is a letter that is typed only once but can be sent to many different people. To prepare a form letter:

1. Create a data file that contains the variable information within the letter (for example, the names and addresses of all the people to whom you want to send the letter).
2. Create a form letter with fields for the missing data.
3. Merge the form letter with the data.

5 As we discussed yesterday you must type this entire document
   for Larry.
6 After you see the package you may decide that it isn't what you
   really want.
7 In 1998 several explorers had to be rescued from the top of the
   mountain.
8 During this same period global warming was blamed for the
   avalanches.

SKILLBUILDING

C. PREVIEW PRACTICE

Type each line 2 times as a preview to the 3-minute timings below.

Accuracy
Speed

9 start resume realize involved business Employers activities
10 apply work deal good soon have help make will ask use so in

D. 3-MINUTE TIMINGS

Take two 3-minute timings on the paragraph. Note your speed and errors.

Goal: 35/3'/5e

11 You will soon be asked to write a resume to use when	11
12 you inquire about your first job. Employers realize that	22
13 you may not have a great deal of work experience, so they	34
14 tend to look more at school activities and interests. It	45
15 would be a good idea to get involved in the activities of	57
16 any clubs for business students. Your school is sure to	68
17 have at least one. If not, ask your teacher to help you	79
18 start one. You will apply what you have learned in your	90
19 classes, gain leadership skills, and make friends who have	102
20 like interests.	105

| 1 | 2 | 3 | 4 | 5 | 6 | 7 | 8 | 9 | 10 | 11 | 12 SI 1.36

LESSON 85

MERGE: FORM LETTERS

OBJECTIVES:

- Reinforce good keyboarding technique.
- Compose at the keyboard.
- Learn to do a mail merge.

A. WARMUP

Type each line 2 times.

Speed
Accuracy
Language Link
Numbers/Symbols

1 You can learn to type at a fast speed if you will practice.
2 Olmec, Zapotec, Mixtec, and Aztec were early civilizations.
3 The homework for math class was problems 45-49 on page 549.
4 Our company will buy 1/3 of their stock @ 22 7/8 per share.

| 1 | 2 | 3 | 4 | 5 | 6 | 7 | 8 | 9 | 10 | 11 | 12

LANGUAGE LINK

B. COMPOSING AT THE KEYBOARD

Choose one of the sentence fragments below, complete it, and continue composing until you have created a short paragraph with at least three sentences.

5 I was never a believer in UFOs until . . .
6 The road was dark and deserted. All of a sudden . . .
7 My phone never stopped ringing after I . . .
8 While sailing on a very windy day, we suddenly . . .

LANGUAGE ARTS CONNECTIONS

A *constellation* is an easily recognized group of stars that appear close together in the sky. These stars form a picture if you can imagine lines connecting them (connect the dots). Constellations are usually named after an animal, a character from mythology, or a common object. One well-known constellation is the Big Dipper.

E. FOOTNOTES AND ENDNOTES

In Lesson 72 you gave credit to sources of information in reports using parenthetical references. Two other acceptable methods for giving credit are **footnotes** and **endnotes.** Footnotes and endnotes should include the name of the author, the title of the book or article, the publisher, the place and year of publication, and the page numbers being referenced.

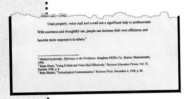

Footnotes

1. Footnotes are indicated in the body of a report by superior figures.
2. Footnotes are consecutively numbered.
3. Footnotes appear at the bottom of the page on which the reference appears.

Endnotes

1. Endnotes are indicated in the body of a report by superior figures.
2. Endnotes are numbered consecutively.
3. Endnotes appear at the end of a report, either on the last page or on a separate page.

F. SOFTWARE FEATURES

STUDENT MANUAL

Footnotes   Endnotes

Study Lesson 75 in your student manual. Complete all the practice activities while at your computer. Then complete the jobs that follow.

Thank you for evaluating our old system and for recommending such a fine new one. We are already very pleased with the new system, and I know that as we all learn to use its full capabilities, we will find it even more valuable to our operations.

Sincerely,
Jake E. Ford
President

FACT FILE

Universal time is the measure of time obtained from the rotation of Earth. This is also known as Greenwich mean time, named after the Greenwich Observatory in England. The world's time standard today is Coordinated Universal Time, which is kept by atomic clocks.

REPORT 21

Type the following business report with double spacing. Format all references as footnotes. The text for the footnotes is at the end of the report.

COMMUNICATING IN THE NEW MILLENNIUM

¶Just a few short years ago, the way we most often communicated with others was by telephone or letter. Often, using the telephone meant playing what business workers referred to as "telephone tag."[1] This name resulted from a caller's having to leave a message for someone to call back, then not being available when the call was returned. If you communicated via letters, you could never be sure exactly when the letter would be delivered.

¶With advances in technology, we now have many more options available. Among these options are voice mail and e-mail. Voice mail enables you to leave a message for someone even if you know the person is not available. It enables the person being called to answer the telephone or wait until a more convenient time to get any messages. E-mail enables you to send "written" messages to anyone at any time and have those messages delivered instantly. This is particularly useful if you must communicate with someone in a different time zone. You can send your message at a convenient time for you, and the receiver can respond at a convenient time for him or her.

¶Each of these options also has negative aspects. Many people do not like voice mail because they do not like to be greeted by a recording; others refuse to leave messages. Companies that rely on voice mail to answer and route all incoming calls risk losing the business of people who want to speak with a "real" person.[2] Have you ever been frustrated by having to listen to a long recording or a list of options before your call could be completed?

¶E-mail has provided us with a way to send instantaneous messages. However, this ease of sending messages has dramatically increased the number of unimportant messages being sent. (In other instances, using e-mail has proved to be very costly. The informality of e-mail often causes people to respond without thinking and send messages that should never be sent.) In addition, e-mail is not totally secure. Information that you don't want others to know should not be sent via e-mail.

¶ Your order for the compact disc player, model no. 34109, has been forwarded to our regional office in Dallas, Texas. We should receive it in this office by the 28th of this month. When it arrives, I will (inspect it personally) and send it to you immediately. Please let us know/if there is any other way we can be of service to you.

sincerely,

charles l. walker
sales manager

Unit 5 Lesson 84 306

LETTER 43
Modified-
Block Style
handwritten

Type the following letter in modified-block style. Use the current date and be sure to add your initials as reference initials.

DeskData Company
5339 Westhampton Court
Tempe, AZ 85284
Attention: Information Consultant

Ladies and Gentlemen:
Subject: New Desktop Publishing System

We have implemented the recommendations your company made to improve our communications at Swift Industrials. Our new desktop publishing software is providing us with printing capabilities that were not possible in the past.

We are experiencing tremendous savings in printing costs with the new system, and I know that our image has been improved because of the quality of our correspondence and reports.

¶Here are four general guidelines for using voice mail and e-mail. Whichever one you use, keep your message professional, clear, and courteous. If you are dealing with extremely sensitive information, you may want to deliver the message face-to-face or over the telephone so that there are no misunderstandings. Remember that neither voice mail nor e-mail is totally secure. If you are saying or writing something that you do not want anyone other than the recipient to know about, speak directly to him or her. Finally, be sure your messages are clear, concise, and grammatically correct.[3]

¶Used properly, voice mail and e-mail are a significant help to professionals. With courteous and thoughtful use, people can increase their own efficiency and become more responsive to others.[4]

1. Washington Korbel, *Business Procedures and Practices,* 3d ed., Chicago Innovative Publications, Chicago, Illinois, 1998.
2. Michael Kyslowsky, *Efficiency in the Workplace,* Houghton Mifflin Co., Boston, Massachusetts, 1998.
3. Susan Okula, "Using E-Mail and Voice Mail Effectively," *Business Education Forum,* Vol. 53, October 1998, p. 8.
4. Rene Shadira, "Technological Communication," *Business Week,* November 4, 1998, p. 86.

COMMUNICATION FOCUS

When you are leaving a message on voice mail, be sure to speak clearly, state the essential facts quickly, and give your name and telephone number slowly. It is also a good idea to repeat your telephone number again at the end of the message. If your message contains any unusual names, you may want to spell those names. Analyze your messages and think of ways in which you can improve them.

If you use e-mail, always remember that the person receiving your message cannot see your expression or hear the tone of your voice. Because of this, be careful what you write. Be sure that nothing you say can be taken in a way that you didn't intend. And always spell check and proofread your messages before you send them.

LETTER 41
Modified-Block Style

Type the following letter in modified-block style.

(Current Date) / Allied Automotive Corporation / 3259 Bellevue Boulevard / Novato, CA 94949 / Attention: Customer Relations Department / Ladies and Gentlemen:

¶A few weeks ago I purchased a new SouthStar from AAA Motors in Carrollton, Georgia. Since I have worked as a sales representative for an automobile dealership in the past, I know it is not too often that you receive letters that say, "Thank you." That is the reason I want to take a few minutes to tell you how pleased I am with my new SouthStar and how much I appreciate the way I was treated by your two AAA sales representatives.

¶Everything about this vehicle has measured up to my expectations. The salespeople were most courteous and helpful—there was no high-pressure sales pitch. They gave me some valuable information about the use and upkeep of the vehicle, too.

¶Congratulations! You have a fine vehicle and a super dealership in Carrollton, Georgia! / Sincerely, / David Jackson / urs

LETTER 42
Block Style

Current Date

Attention Purchasing Agent

Ladies and gentlemen:

Solar supply co.
917 west madison street
Johnson City, tn 37601

We appreciate your check in payment of order no. 16543, however, I'm returning the check to you by registered mail since the correct amount of $195.18 and your signature were omitted. Please fill in these items and return the check to us.

(handwritten edits: "the check should be" inserted; "since" struck; "were" changed to "as")

LESSON 76

REPORTS: MULTIPAGE, LEFT BOUND

OBJECTIVES:

- Improve keyboarding speed.
- Format multipage, bound reports.

A. WARMUP

Type each line 2 times.

Speed
Accuracy
Language Link
Numbers/Symbols

1 When the cat rests, it wants to lie down in the same place.
2 Jack was too lazy for the farm job; he proved quite vexing.
3 On Tuesday, it rained more than it did on Friday or Sunday.
4 We will earn 12% more on #31 & #46 if they are sold @ $200.
| 1 | 2 | 3 | 4 | 5 | 6 | 7 | 8 | 9 | 10 | 11 | 12

SKILLBUILDING

B. 12-SECOND SPRINTS

Take three 12-second timings on each line. Try to increase your speed on each timing.

5 He may not play ball if he did not yet take that math test.
6 We might have a very nice profit if the order is a big one.
7 That job might very well take much longer than you thought.
8 Justin had time to do the job because it was planned early.
| | | |5| | | |10| | | |15| | | |20| | | |25| | | |30| | | |35| | | |40| | | |45| | | |50| | | |55| | | |60

COMMUNICATION FOCUS

Follow these steps to improve your listening: Choose to listen. Listen actively. Listen for ideas and feelings. Know when to keep silent. Be flexible when taking notes. Resist distractions. Keep an open mind.

Type the following lines. As you type, change every masculine pronoun to a feminine pronoun (his to her), and change every feminine pronoun to a masculine pronoun (she to he).

```
 9  She will complete the sales report as soon as she receives it.
10  He must give her the sales figures so that she can compile it.
11  Her final copy is past-due; her boss has already asked for it.
12  Her boss will then give it to his boss, the director of sales.
```

FORMATTING

D. ATTENTION LINE

When a letter is addressed directly to a company, an **attention line** may be used to route it to a particular person or department. If you use an attention line:

1. Type the inside address, press enter 2 times, and type the attention line.
2. Spell out the word *Attention*.
3. Follow the word *Attention* with a colon and 1 space.
4. Use a salutation such as *Ladies and Gentlemen:*, *Gentlemen:*, or *Ladies:* when you use an attention line.

E. SUBJECT LINE

A **subject line** briefly identifies the main topic of a letter. To format a subject line:

1. Type the salutation, then press ENTER 2 times.
2. Type the subject line in initial caps at the left margin.
3. Follow the word *Subject* with a colon and 1 space.
4. Press ENTER 2 times and begin the body of the letter.

FORMATTING

C. LEFT-BOUND REPORTS

In a left-bound report, the left margin must be wider to allow room for the binding. To format a left-bound report, change the left margin to 1.5 inches. Do not change the default right margin.

WORD PROCESSING APPLICATIONS

REPORT 22

Type the following business report as a left-bound report. Format all the references as endnotes. Remember to add the page number to the second page of the report.

LISTENING

Everyone appreciates a good listener. Good listeners make good friends. People who are good listeners not only gain insight into other people, but they also learn about the world around them. If you want to be a good listener, you must make a conscious decision to listen. The following suggestions should help you become a better listener.

BE QUIET

Pause for several seconds before you start to talk after the one speaking to you stops. This pause allows the speaker to catch a breath and gather his or her thoughts. The speaker may want to continue. This pause also gives you time to form your response. Preparing your response while you are trying to listen often leads to missing the main point.

MAINTAIN EYE CONTACT

Look at the person who is speaking. It shows you are listening and keeps your mind from wandering. Looking directly at the speaker enables you to watch body language and behavior. Don't stare, but look into the speaker's eyes often.

LETTERS WITH ATTENTION AND SUBJECT LINES

OBJECTIVES:

- Improve keyboarding skill.
- Format letters with attention and subject lines.

A. WARMUP

Type each line 2 times.

Speed
Accuracy
Language Link
Numbers/Symbols

```
1  A strong dollar makes it easier for interest to be lowered.
2  An aqueous liquid was used externally to prevent abscesses.
3  We bought seven pies and seven dozen cookies for the party.
4  The S & P's 500 index (dividends + gains) was just over 9%.
   |  1  |  2  |  3  |  4  |  5  |  6  |  7  |  8  |  9  |  10  |  11  |  12
```

interNET CONNECTION

Use the Internet to search for information about the environment. Search specifically for things such as water pollution and air pollution. Discuss your findings with your classmates.

SKILLBUILDING

B. 12-SECOND SPRINTS

Take three 12-second timings on each line. Try to increase your speed on each timing.

```
5  Many good stocks showed slow gains even in the bull market.
6  Your credit card rate will go up if you pay late too often.
7  The people in this country save much less than they should.
8  A bank savings account is a safe way to save your earnings.
   | | | |5| | | |10| | | |15| | |20| | |25| | |30| | |35| | | |40| | | |45| | |50| | | |55| | | |60
```

DISPLAY OPENNESS

Your facial expressions and body positions convey openness. Sit or stand up straight; correct posture conveys interest. Never cross your arms or legs; such posture conveys boredom or disagreement. Do not have any physical barriers, such as a desk or a pile of books, between you and the other person.

LISTEN WITHOUT RESPONSE

Don't interrupt the speaker even if you feel that you cannot wait to express your opinions, suggestions, and comments. Marie C. Ford suggests, "Don't always have a bigger or better one of whatever the speaker is telling you about."[1] Watch your nonverbal expressions, such as shrugs and frowns. They may keep the other person from finishing the message.

SEND ACKNOWLEDGMENTS

Send acknowledgments. It is important to let the speaker know you are still listening throughout the conversation. A frequent "OK," "Yes," or nod of the head lets the speaker know that you are interested in what is being said. These signals do not imply that you agree with the speaker; they indicate only that you are hearing what is being said.[2]

Being a good listener is hard work. Sometimes it takes more effort to be a good listener than it does to be a good speaker. If you put these suggestions into practice, they will pay you big dividends.

1. Marie C. Ford and W. Ernest Ford, "The Power of Listening," *Communications Journal,* January 1998, p. 21.
2. Earl L. Belcher, *Communications for Daily Living,* Beeline Press, College Station, Texas, 1997, p. 65.

¶Before visiting a foreign country, get information about customs and cultures. Knowledge about cultural differences is vital. It will help you avoid offending someone in a foreign country. Don't be surprised if foreigners do not make eye contact. Some may make long eye contact, while others view eye contact as disrespectful. If you're confused about cultural differences, question someone who knows the culture. Most countries have days that commemorate special events. Information about social customs is very important.

¶Get to know a country's currency, and bring a translation dictionary with you so that you can refer to it for some of your basic communication needs.

¶GLOBAL TRAVEL can easily make airplane and hotel reservations for you. By making reservations in advance, you can save money and be certain you're getting the schedules you want.

¶Next week, we will be sending you a helpful booklet, *Traveling Abroad,* containing numerous helpful tips for traveling. Also included in the booklet are several detailed maps of the most popular travel destinations. These maps identify travel mileage between many cities and also highlight major scenic attractions that you may wish to visit during your trip.

¶We hope you will consider using GLOBAL TRAVEL for your travel needs. We look forward to helping you make your reservations for what we believe will be your most enjoyable travel adventure. / Sincerely, / Conrad McMurphy / Travel Agent / urs

LESSON 77

REPORTS: MULTIPAGE, LEFT BOUND

OBJECTIVES:

- Learn the rules for capitalization.
- Improve keyboarding speed.
- Format multipage, bound reports.

A. WARMUP

Type each line 2 times.

Speed
Accuracy
Language Link
Numbers/Symbols

1 You should always be honest with yourself about your goals.
2 David quickly put the frozen jars away in small gray boxes.
3 Although Bill said it wasn't, Jason thought it was farther.
4 Two items (#20 & #21) were sold for $33 each--a great loss!

| 1 | 2 | 3 | 4 | 5 | 6 | 7 | 8 | 9 | 10 | 11 | 12

B. CAPITALIZATION

Study the following rules and examples. Then correct any errors in capitalization in lines 5–8.

Rule 14: Capitalize common organizational terms (such as *advertising department* and *finance committee*) when they are the actual names of the units in your own organization and when they are preceded by the word *the*.

> *The monthly update will be presented by our Marketing Department today.*
>
> *I applied for a position as an assistant in a marketing department.*

3. For all continuation pages add a header that includes the addressee's name, the page number, and the date of the letter; align at the left margin. (See the illustration.)

4. Use widow/orphan protection to avoid single lines of a paragraph at either the top or bottom of the page.

WORD PROCESSING APPLICATIONS

LETTER 40
Modified-Block Style

Type this letter in modified-block style. Create a header for the second page.

(Current Date) / Ms. Josephine Morello / 348 Douglas Boulevard / Atlanta, GA 30303 / Dear Ms. Morello:

¶Thank you for your request for travel information.

¶You have several options for travel arrangements. You can use a travel agency, your company's travel department, or your computer (for online reservation service), or you can make all the contacts yourself. Travelers are more and more frequently using the Internet to make their airline reservations.

¶If you choose a travel agency, you will receive assistance in making airline, rental car, or hotel/motel reservations. Travel agencies use computerized databases and can find the lowest fares and most convenient flight schedules. So that you can get the exact flight and fare you want, you will need to provide the travel agent with your preferred arrival and departure dates, and cities from which you will depart. Also provide your arrival time, times of travel, and travelers' names. You may also need to provide photographs or birth certificates if you are traveling to overseas destinations.

¶Travel agencies will make hotel and rental car reservations. You can tell your travel agent exactly what you want in the way of a rental car, specify a certain hotel or motel, and ask for reservations on a specific airline. Usually, your agent will be able to fulfill the majority of your requests.

Rule 15: Capitalize names of specific course titles but not the names of subjects or areas of study.

She enrolled in Advanced Physics 201 and will also take a psychology course.

5 The editorial staff of the office technology unit worked very well together.
6 He took one class in word processing and another in database management.
7 The computer support unit works with us to keep our computers running smoothly.
8 I studied economics and took the course business communications 301.

SKILLBUILDING

C. 30-SECOND TIMINGS

Take two 30-second timings on lines 9–10. Then take two 30-second timings on lines 11–12. Try to increase your speed on each timing.

9   Driving in the country in the fall is a real treat if   11
10 you can stop and visit some local vendors along the way.   22

11   A visit to some small villages is like a trip back in   11
12 time because they work to keep things the way they were.   22

| 1 | 2 | 3 | 4 | 5 | 6 | 7 | 8 | 9 | 10 | 11 | 12

Take two 5-minute timings on the paragraphs. Note your speed and errors.

Goal: 37/5'/5e

Science Connections

7	Pollution of the earth refers to all of the ways in	11
8	which we spoil our natural surroundings. Mankind fouls	22
9	the air with gases and smoke, ruins the soil with harsh	33
10	pesticides and fertilizers, and poisons the water with	44
11	wastes. The earth can be spoiled quickly in so many ways.	55
12	We unjustifiably ruin the charm of the landscape when we	67
13	toss ugly litter on the ground and into the water. It seems	79
14	we all cause damage at one time or another.	88
15	Pollution of the air, soil, and water is one of the	98
16	gravest issues that our world faces at this time. All of	110
17	these resources are basic to the survival of all plants	121
18	and animals. Sickness and death can be caused by extreme	132
19	air pollution. Fish and other marine life are killed by	143
20	water that is badly polluted. Soil pollution reduces the	155
21	number of acres of land that can be used for food crops,	166
22	and food shortages can lead to deadly famines. Polluted	177
23	soil may also cause deadly diseases.	185

| 1 | 2 | 3 | 4 | 5 | 6 | 7 | 8 | 9 | 10 | 11 | 12 | SI 1.40

FORMATTING

D. TWO-PAGE LETTERS

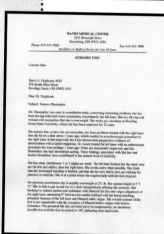

Long business letters are often continued on a second page. To format a multi-page letter:
1. Type the first page of the letter on letterhead paper; type continuing pages on plain paper of the same quality as the letterhead used for the first page.
2. Use an approximate 2-inch top margin (press ENTER 6 times) for the first page; use a 1-inch top margin for continuation pages.

REPORT 23

Type the following report as a left-bound business report. Format all references as footnotes. The text for each footnote follows the superscript number and is enclosed in brackets.

VOICE RECOGNITION: INTO THE FUTURE

¶Many newspapers, magazines, and technology demonstrations are featuring voice recognition as the wave of the future. But, is voice recognition really new?

HISTORICAL PERSPECTIVES ON VOICE RECOGNITION

¶People have been able to recognize each other's voices since language first began. You need only to watch the face of a cat or dog when its owner speaks to know that the animal has heard and recognized the voice. Call centers and other kinds of businesses have been using a type of voice (speech) recognition for years.

¶Think for a moment, though, how exciting it would be to speak to your computer and have it understand what you said. Then, it would format what you said into what you need—a letter, a report, a table, a memo, or whatever, all with your voice telling your computer what to do. Is this really possible?

SPEECH RECOGNITION IN ITS INFANCY

¶While Bell Laboratories of Lucent Technologies created the first speech recognizer in 1952, the first speech recognition capability for PCs was finally developed in the 80s. The world's first discrete speech dictation system was developed by Dragon Systems in 1990. Following that innovation was the world's first commercially available software-only dictation system.[1] [1. "Dragon Systems Leading the Industry," *Dragon Naturally Speaking Mobile Edition Product Specifications*, November 12, 1998, pp. 2-4.]

¶In 1997, Jim and Janet Baker excited the speech recognition arena with the first dictation software to handle continuous speech. The spotlight focused on *Naturally Speaking,* another Dragon Systems' product.[2] [2. "Let's Talk! Special Report," *Business Week*, February 23, 1998, p. 67.]

VOICE RECOGNITION MARCHES ON

¶The technology movement had begun in earnest. Several companies jumped into the race to capture the market and produce software capable of higher and higher feats of accuracy. Software and portable device manufacturers came out with new programs and devices. Companies such as Sony, Norcom, Olympus, Dragon Systems, Lernout & Hauspie, and IBM, to name a few, began to find this field exciting.[3] [3. Marie E. Flatley, "Voice Recognition Software," *Business Education Forum*, December 1998, p. 44.] Philips, Grover Industries, and others followed the thrill of voice recognition development with hardware and software utilities. For example, Grover Industries'

LESSON 83

TWO-PAGE LETTERS

OBJECTIVES:

- Format two-page business letters.
- Learn word processing features.
- Type 37/5'/5e.

A. WARMUP

Type each line 2 times.

Speed
Accuracy
Language Link
Numbers/Symbols

1 We must drive cautiously during the rush hours in the city.
2 Gazelles are Bovidae herbivores living from India to Egypt.
3 We need to buy 16 bars of soap. We have seven bars on hand.
4 Martin & Wills sent a check for $2,195; the bill is $3,468.
| 1 | 2 | 3 | 4 | 5 | 6 | 7 | 8 | 9 | 10 | 11 | 12

SKILLBUILDING

B. PREVIEW PRACTICE

Type each line 2 times as a preview to the timings that follow.

Accuracy
Speed

5 pollution pesticides fertilizers surroundings unjustifiably
6 litter marine water fouls ruins food used our be can all of

Web-TalkIt is an easy-to-use voice command and control utility for your default Web browser. Just say the Website you wish to visit and Web-TalkIt will go to the URL address.

USERS OF VOICE RECOGNITION

¶Large mail order and customer service companies as well as utilities, banks, airlines, stockbrokers, manufacturers, and couriers are some of the major users of voice recognition. Customers or clients can use these voice recognition systems to obtain information, service, or to order products without human contact in most instances. Adding natural language processing to speech recognition gives us an entirely new user interface, notes Michael J. Miller of *PC Magazine*.[4] [4. Michael J. Miller, "Built for Speed," *PC Magazine,* September 22, 1998, p. 4.]

¶Voice recognition programs are enabling many physically challenged persons to use their computers more efficiently and effectively. Adrian Clifton, the inspiration for Adrian's Closet, which produces a line of clothing for young people with various disabilities, is beginning to use a voice-activated computer. He cannot use his hands, but he is able to enter invoices into files with his voice-activated computer.[5] [5. Tamar Asedo Sherman, "Threads of Love," *USA Weekend*, December 4-8, 1998, pp. 18-19.]

¶Financial traders, lawyers, and physicians are using voice recognition software. Pat Higgerty, a lawyer who cannot type, firmly believes in voice recognition technology. Higgerty creates most of his own documents and enjoys preparing a document while the client is in the office, printing it, and having the client sign the document before he or she leaves the office. Higgerty emphasizes that proper training on how to use the technology is a necessity for the 98 percent accuracy that he wants to attain.[6] [6. Paul McLaughlin, "Hands-free Computing: A Voice Recognition Technology Story," *NETWORK2D Newsletter*, Spring 1997, ABA Law Practice Management Section, 1997-98, American Bar Association, pp. 8-9.]

¶Physicians are finding voice recognition ideal for dictating chart notes after patient sessions. They say they often get more accurate notes because they can say more than if they were writing charts by hand.

¶More and more applications will be developed and more people will avail themselves of voice recognition technology as it is perfected and as accuracy levels improve above the 95-98 percent level.

TAKING IT ONE STEP FURTHER INTO THE FUTURE

¶What does the future hold for voice recognition technology? Forecasters say the sky is the limit. Computers will probably arrive loaded with voice recognition software; you will be able to access the Internet quickly, and you will be able to go from link to link just by saying what topic you want to request. Innovative software and equipment will make the lives of the blind, the deaf, and others with different physical difficulties more efficient by enabling them to access their computers without using their hands.

¶Some new processors can zoom through the math used in speech recognition, making it possible to "train" the new computer to understand the user

D. POSTTEST

Repeat the Pretest. Compare your Posttest results with your Pretest results.

E. PACED PRACTICE

Turn to the Paced Practice routine beginning on page SB7. Take three 2-minute timings, starting at the point where you left off the last time.

F. TECHNIQUE CHECKPOINT

Type each line 2 times. Repeat if time permits. Focus on the technique at the left.

Press and release the shift keys without hesitating.

19 Hal traveled to the Isle of Hope to visit Kelly and Jackie.
20 Nancy traveled to London, Paris, Madrid, and Oslo in March.
21 Frances passed West Dublin on the way to East Dublin today.
22 As in the past, the Wild West Rodeo will be in Thomasville.

G. PRETEST

Take a 1-minute timing on the paragraph. Note your speed and errors.

Science
Connections

23   Recycling is the process of using goods more than one   11
24 time. Since many kinds of wastes can be reused, we must   22
25 learn just how important it is to start recycling. Glass,   34
26 cans, plastic, newspapers, and old tires can be used again.   46
   | 1 | 2 | 3 | 4 | 5 | 6 | 7 | 8 | 9 | 10 | 11 | 12

H. PRACTICE

In the chart below, find the number of errors you made on the Pretest. Then type each of the designated drill lines 2 times.

Pretest Errors	0–1	2	3	4+
Drill Lines	30–34	29–33	28–32	27–31

Accuracy

27 melted process ground turned products purposes requirements
28 paper bottles realize materials gasoline recycled newsprint
29 pulp reuse exact useful bottle highway substances important
30 such used make glass using tires clean should wastes melted

Speed

31 kinds more than time many cans into then made tires one how
32 paper ones just meet that very from must can be for new car
33 items tires then from are and for the how be if to as is it
34 goods clean down into down made time make news than old off

I. POSTTEST

Repeat the Pretest. Compare your Posttest results with your Pretest results.

in less than five minutes. Software developers that harness the power of these new processors predict that speech recognition will be a standard PC feature by the end of the year.[7] [7.Andy Reinhardt, "Computers with Sharp Ears," *Business Week*, March 8, 1999, p. 6.]

¶Is voice recognition in your future? Keep your ears sharp, watch for new developments, and you'll probably be a voice recognition technology user soon!

*inter*NET CONNECTION

Using the Internet, search for additional information on voice-recognition technology. You may want to search for products such as *Via Voice* or *Dragon Naturally Speaking*. Make a list of advantages and disadvantages of using this technology. Discuss with your classmates whether or not voice-recognition technology is appropriate for everyone.

SOCIAL STUDIES CONNECTIONS

Electronic engineers John Pierce and Harold Rosen designed the first successful communication satellites in the 1960s. Because of their developments, we are now able to enjoy cellular phones and watching far away television stations. Information is beamed up to satellites and sent back down to different places on Earth.

LESSON 82

SKILLBUILDING

OBJECTIVES:

- Improve keyboarding skill.
- Reinforce good keyboarding techniques.

A. WARMUP

Type each line 2 times.

Speed
Accuracy
Language Link
Numbers/Symbols

1 Four students from our school will run in the state finals.
2 The quadrant has been a survey device since medieval times.
3 The accountant had 100 five-column pads in his desk drawer.
4 Invoice 836-259 for $1,274.50 is subject to a 12% discount.

| 1 | 2 | 3 | 4 | 5 | 6 | 7 | 8 | 9 | 10 | 11 | 12

SKILLBUILDING

B. PRETEST

Take a 1-minute timing on the paragraph. Note your speed and errors.

5   The lady who lives at 160 North Street has 37 pairs   11
6 of shoes and 28 purses. She also has 4 sweaters, 5 skirts,   23
7 and 6 coats. She spends at least $98 each month on clothes   35
8 and $80 on pet food. She has 9 guppies, 1 bird, and 3 cats.   47

| 1 | 2 | 3 | 4 | 5 | 6 | 7 | 8 | 9 | 10 | 11 | 12

C. PRACTICE

Type each line 2 times.

1   9 We saw 11 computers, 11 boards, 11 monitors, and 11 drives.
2   10 By 2:22 p.m. on the 2d, they had 2.0 or 2.2 inches of rain.
3   11 The programs were found in seats 3, 30, 31, 32, 33, and 34.
4   12 Last night the scores were 40 to 4, 42 to 41, and 48 to 44.
5   13 The student scores on the 15th were 51, 53, 55, 57, and 59.

6   14 The spreadsheet cell listed 16, 26, 36, 46, 56, 66, and 67.
7   15 January 7, March 7, April 7, May 17, and July 17 were open.
8   16 Can Jerry add these: 1/8, 2/8, 3/8, 4/8, 5/8, 6/8, and 7/8?
9   17 They found $9.99, $9.19, $9.29, and $9.69 in the registers.
0   18 It isn't difficult to total 10, 20, 30, 40, 50, 60, and 70.

LESSON 78

REPORTS: TITLE PAGE, CONTENTS, BIBLIOGRAPHY

OBJECTIVES:

- Improve keyboarding accuracy.
- Format title, contents, and bibliography pages.

A. WARMUP

Type each line 2 times.

Speed
Accuracy
Language Link
Numbers/Symbols

1 Edward saved his files on the hard drive and on a diskette.
2 Vic quickly mixed grape juice with the frozen strawberries.
3 It is too soon for Will to know whether he passed spelling.
4 Hamilton & Jones expected a 12% increase in sales--$35,890.

| 1 | 2 | 3 | 4 | 5 | 6 | 7 | 8 | 9 | 10 | 11 | 12

SKILLBUILDING

B. 30-SECOND OK TIMINGS

Take two 30-second OK (error-free) timings on lines 5–6. Then take two 30-second OK timings on lines 7–8. Goal: no errors.

5   Peg was amazed by the fact that time management skills   11
6 are magic tools for learning very quickly how to mix tasks. 23

7   Sixty men went to a quaint village in the back country   11
8 of western New Zealand and fished for pike, jack, and gar.   23

| 1 | 2 | 3 | 4 | 5 | 6 | 7 | 8 | 9 | 10 | 11 | 12

MN	21	M may mix mad make mind month	N new nor now note next noise
OP	22	O own old oil oath ouch ought	P peg par pay prod plea purge
QR	23	Q qua qui quo quip quit quest	R rod rig rug raft ream right
ST	24	S ski six sod salt sent scale	T tag tin toy tend toil toast
UV	25	U uke urn use undo unit using	V vow van vie volt vile virus
WX	26	W why won wet wipe wrap waver	X vex fox mix lynx text waxen
YZ	27	Y yam yes yaw yoke year yards	Z zag zip zoo zinc zing zesty

E. POSTTEST

Repeat the Pretest. Compare your Posttest results with your Pretest results.

F. TECHNIQUE CHECKPOINT

Type each line 2 times. Repeat if time permits. Focus on the technique at the left.

Space between words without pausing.

28 He is the one who will pay if we go to the ball game today.
29 When all of us have gone out, you need to stay in the room.
30 You need to save as much of your pay as you can to be safe.
31 There is no one but you who knows how to lead the band now.

G. PACED PRACTICE

Turn to the Paced Practice routine beginning on page SB7. Take three 2-minute timings, starting at the point where you left off the last time.

FACT FILE

Jeffrey Hudson who was just 18 inches tall, served as a captain of the cavalry in the British Army. Hudson, who lived from 1619-1682, made his first public appearance inside a pie served at the table of the Duke of Buckingham. When Hudson was about thirty years old, he "shot up" in size, reaching a height of 3 feet, 9 inches.

C. TITLE PAGE

A **title page** is the first page of a report. It gives the title of a report, the name of the writer, the name of the person for whom the report was prepared, and the date. For academic reports, it also contains the name of the course. To format a title page:

1. Use single spacing, and center the page vertically.
2. Center all lines of text horizontally.
3. Type the report title in all caps and bold. If there is a subtitle, double-space and type the subtitle in initial caps.
4. Press ENTER 12 times and type *By* followed by your name as the writer. If there is more than one writer, single-space the names of the writers.
5. Press ENTER 12 times. Then, using single spacing, type the name of the person for whom the report was written, the name of the course (if appropriate), and the current date.

D. TABLE OF CONTENTS

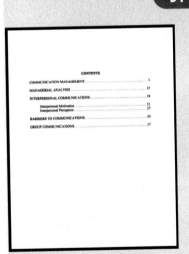

A **table of contents** may follow the title page. It is an outline of the headings in a report and the pages on which they are found. To format a table of contents:

1. Use the same margins as those used in the report.
2. Center and type the word *CONTENTS* approximately 2 inches from the top of the page (press ENTER 6 times) in all caps and bold, followed by a double space.
3. Type major headings in all caps; leave a blank line before and after them.
4. Indent subheadings and type them with initial caps and single spacing.
5. Align page numbers at the right and precede them with **dot leaders**—a series of periods that help guide the reader's eye from the headings to the page numbers.

Rule 18: Spell out the words *million* and *billion* in even amounts. Do not use decimals with even amounts. Spell out fractions.

> The multimillionaire gave almost 2 million dollars to charity.
>
> About one-half of the graduating class participated in the graduation ceremony.
>
> Each of them paid $50 for a ticket and $12.50 for parking.

5 Jan got 2 dozen pastries and a pot of coffee.
6 The agenda listed twenty-five items to be covered today.
7 779 students were there.
8 The musician recorded 7 6-track demo tapes.
9 After taxes, he was worth $4,000,000.00.
10 Only 1/3 of the students had summer jobs.

SKILLBUILDING

C. PRETEST

Take a 1-minute timing on the paragraph. Note your speed and errors.

Social Studies
Connections

11   American President Andrew Jackson was a self-made man.   11
12 He fought for and was liked by the common man. His votes   23
13 came from farmers in the South, settlers in the West, and   34
14 workers in the East.   38
    | 1 | 2 | 3 | 4 | 5 | 6 | 7 | 8 | 9 | 10 | 11 | 12

D. PRACTICE

Type each line 2 times.

A B
C D
E F
G H
I J
K L

15 A ale and ant aunt aide aisle B bid bay bud belt bulk balmy
16 C cut cat cod cove cube clerk D did dry dim dorm debt doubt
17 E ear elm end ease etch edges F fir few fly foil four front
18 G gun gag gap gaze goal grant H hit hot hue have half hitch
19 I ice imp ire into idea infer J jam jar jet jury just joker
20 K key keg kid keen kind kayak L law lad let land lamb laugh

A **bibliography** is an alphabetical listing of sources used in a report. It is very similar to a works cited page. It follows the text of the report. To format a bibliography:

1. Use the same side margins as those used in the report and use single spacing.
2. Center and type the title, *BIBLIOGRAPHY,* in all caps and bold, approximately 2 inches from the top of the page (press ENTER 6 times). Press ENTER 2 times after the title.
3. Use a hanging indent for each entry and leave a blank line between entries (press ENTER 2 times).
4. List entries in alphabetical order by authors' last names. If there is no author, alphabetize by the title of the article or book.
5. Arrange book entries as follows: author's name, title (in italics), publisher, place of publication, and year.
6. Arrange journal articles as follows: author's name, article title (in quotation marks), journal title (in italics), followed by information on the journal issue (series, volume, issue numbers; date and page numbers).

STUDENT MANUAL

Dot Leaders

Study Lesson 78 in your student manual. Complete all the practice activities while at your computer. Then complete the jobs that follow.

WORD PROCESSING APPLICATIONS

REPORT 24

Prepare a title page for Report 23. Use your name, the name of your keyboarding teacher, and the current date.

REPORT 25

Prepare a table of contents for Report 23. Use the side headings for the major entries.

REPORT 26

Prepare a bibliography for Report 23. Use the footnotes as the entries for the bibliography.

SKILLBUILDING

OBJECTIVES:

- Learn the rules for number expression.
- Reinforce good keyboarding techniques.
- Improve keyboarding skill.

A. WARMUP

Type each line 2 times.

Speed
Accuracy
Language Link
Numbers/Symbols

1 The little black puppy ran to the door to greet his master.
2 Jeff amazed the audience by quickly giving six new reports.
3 Terry is taking English Literature 215 on Tuesday mornings.
4 Can't they find Check #953 for $840, which is dated May 16?
| 1 | 2 | 3 | 4 | 5 | 6 | 7 | 8 | 9 | 10 | 11 | 12

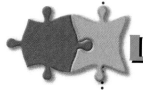

LANGUAGE LINK

B. NUMBER EXPRESSION

Study the rules and examples below. Then edit lines 5–10 to correct any errors in number usage.

Rule 16: In general, spell out numbers 1 through 10. Use figures for numbers above 10.

Only three walls have been painted.

We purchased 15 pairs of socks, 11 jackets, and 23 scarves.

Rule 17: Spell out numbers used as the first word in a sentence. Also spell out the smaller of two adjacent numbers.

Nineteen applications were processed today.

Each participant will receive three 45-minute tapes to listen to.

LESSON 79

REVIEW

OBJECTIVES:

- Reinforce report formats.
- Compose at the keyboard.
- Type 35/3'/5e.

A. WARMUP

Type each line 2 times.

Speed
Accuracy
Language Link
Numbers/Symbols

1 The grass has grown tall, and it must be mowed by Thursday.
2 Paz visited the Zagros Mountains near the Strait of Hormuz.
3 In the past, we have had our Billing Department sell candy.
4 If 33% (1/3 of total) attends #26 or #45, we will earn $90.
   | 1 | 2 | 3 | 4 | 5 | 6 | 7 | 8 | 9 | 10 | 11 | 12

LANGUAGE LINK

B. COMPOSING AT THE KEYBOARD

Answer each of the following questions with complete sentences.

5 If money were no object, what kind of a car would you like to have and why?
6 If you could live anywhere in the United States, where would you live and why?
7 If you could travel overseas, where would you like to go and why?

FACT FILE

Do not remove a disk from your computer's disk drive until the drive light is off. Removing the disk while the light is on could corrupt your disk.

WORDS TO LEARN

add/delete columns, rows	data file	landscape	reverse lines
borders/fill (shading)	form file	mail merge	templates
	formulas	page orientation	

CAREER BIT

COURT REPORTER   Court reporters take verbatim reports of speeches, conversations, legal proceedings, meetings, or other events when written accounts of spoken words are necessary for correspondence, records, or legal proof. Court reporters use stenotype machines, which enable them to record combinations of letters representing sounds, words, or phrases. The symbols are recorded on computer disks, which are then loaded into a computer that translates and displays the symbols in English. Stenotype machines that link directly to the computer are used for real-time captioning. That is, as the reporter types the symbols, the computer instantly transcribes them. This is used for closed captioning for the deaf or hearing-impaired on television, in courts, classrooms, or meetings.

SKILLBUILDING

C. PREVIEW PRACTICE

Type each line 2 times as a preview to the timings that follow.

Accuracy
Speed

8 enjoy quite pursuit difficult aptitudes analyzing happiness
9 choices future their small along must life ten way not do a

D. 3-MINUTE TIMINGS

Take two 3-minute timings on the paragraphs. Note your speed and errors.

Goal: 35/3'/5e

10 Students seldom think about their future careers in	11
11 the first six or seven years of school. They do not know	22
12 what they want to do or what skills they need to acquire	33
13 over the next few years.	38
14 It is important for students to think about and plan	49
15 for their careers. They must analyze their personal goals	61
16 and aptitudes when they choose a career. They also must set	73
17 goals throughout their lives. Any failures must not become	85
18 roadblocks in their pursuit of their goals. They should	96
19 enjoy their careers if they want to be happy.	105

| 1 | 2 | 3 | 4 | 5 | 6 | 7 | 8 | 9 | 10 | 11 | 12 SI 1.32

FACT FILE

Football appears to have its origins in rugby. In the 1800s, Princeton University students were also playing a game called ballown. Organized football games were held on the Boston Common starting in about 1860. In 1865, after the Civil War ended, colleges began to organize football games. The Princeton rules were established and the first football was patented in 1867. It is also believed that the first intercollegiate football game was between Rutgers and Princeton in 1867.

UNIT 5

LESSONS 81–100

WORD PROCESSING

OBJECTIVES

- Demonstrate keyboading speed and accuracy on straight copy with a goal of 37 words a minute for 5 minutes with 5 or fewer errors.

- Demonstrate correct use of word processing features.

- Demonstrate an understanding of proofreaders' symbols by editing copy marked for revision.

- Demonstrate advanced formatting skills on a variety of reports, letters, memos, and tables from a variety of copy—arranged, unarranged, rough draft, and handwritten.

- Compose paragraphs at the keyboard.

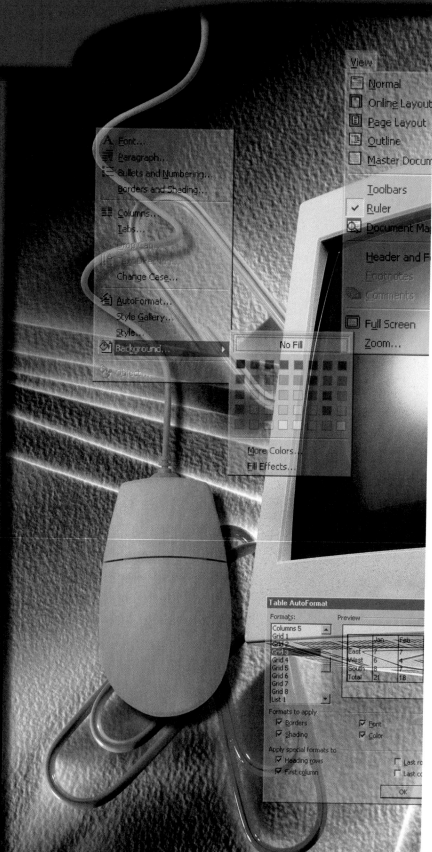

REPORT 27

Outline

REPORT 27b

Left-bound Report

Type an outline for the business report below. Use the major headings and the paragraph headings as your entries for the outline. Then type the report as a left-bound report. Add a byline below the title (press ENTER 1 time) that contains the word By followed by your name. Format the references as footnotes. The text for each footnote follows the superscript number and is enclosed in brackets.

BASKETBALL SPECIFICS

INTRODUCTION

The game of basketball is one of the most widely played and watched sports in the world. The game is played by two teams consisting of five players each. Nearly all elementary schools, high schools, and colleges in the United States have organized basketball teams.[1] [Bill Sullivan, "Basketball," *Encyclopedia Americana,* 1989 ed., pp. 106–107.]

Basketball is truly America's game since it was invented in the United States in 1891. The popularity of the game has steadily increased over the years because it is exciting to play and to watch.

DIMENSIONS

Three very important features of the official game include the specific dimensions of the basketball, the court, and the basket and backboard.

The Basketball. The ball measures about 30 inches in circumference and weighs from 20 to 22 ounces. It can be made of leather, plastic, rubber, or similar material, and it is inflated with air.

The Court. The basketball court is a hard, level surface. Most indoor courts are made of wood. Outdoor courts are made of asphalt, concrete, or any other solid material. Most high school courts measure 84 feet long by 50 feet wide. College and professional courts measure 94 feet long by 50 feet wide. The court has two sidelines, a division line, which divides the court in halves, two free-throw lanes, and two free-throw lines. Two circles, the center circle and the restraining circle, mark the middle of the court.[2] [Wiley Thomaston and Leslie Richards, *Basketball Standards and Regulations,* Daily Publishing Company, Columbia, South Carolina, 1986, pp. 234–235.]

The Basket and Backboard. A white-cord net basket attached to a backboard hangs above the middle of each end line. The net hangs down 15 to 18 inches from the ring and slows the ball as it passes through the basket. The backboard is made of glass, metal, wood, or any other hard material. It must be white or transparent and rectangular or fan-shaped. Rectangular backboards measure 72 inches wide by 48 inches high. Fan-shaped backboards are 54 inches wide by 35 inches high. The backboard must be mounted

ABSENTEEISM AND TARDINESS

The company counts on it's employees to be at work on time and on a regular basis to carry out the responsibilities of their jobs. The company expects employees to be conscientious about their attendance and punctuality. Although some absence or tardiness can be accepted, ~~poor or~~ excessive absence or tardiness will not be tolerated and will be cause for discipline, up to and including termination of employment.

Employees are not "given" a number of sick days per year. The company plan protects employees when they need it, but the plan is not a "time-off" plan. If an employee's absence record becomes ~~poor or~~ excessive, he/she may be subject to disciplinary action.

If employees must be delayed or absent, they must notify their managers of the fact and the reason for the delay or absence as far in advance of their starting time as possible.

Employees who are absent for 3 or more consecutive working days without notifying their managers may have their employment terminated.

TABLES 20–21

Prepare these tables as 2 separate documents. Center them vertically and horizontally, and automatically adjust the column widths.

ABSENCE GUIDELINES		
	Days Absent in a 6-Month Period	Days Absent in a 12-Month Period
Poor	4–5 days	7–8 days
Excessive	6 or more days	9 or more days

TARDINESS GUIDELINES		
	Times Late in a 6-Month Period	Times Late in a 12-Month Period
Poor	7–8 times	11–12 times
Excessive	9 or more times	13 or more times

4 feet inside the end line.[3] [James McLendon, "Basketball—America's Sport," *Sports Today,* December 1994, p. 23.]

Official games played in elementary school, high school, and college and by professionals use regulation basketballs, courts, baskets, and backboards. Following these standards makes the game fairer for both teams.

CLOSING

Basketball has grown in the past decade to become one of the most popular spectator sports. It is played in almost every country in the world, is popular with both young and old, and attracts both men and women players. It has been an Olympic sport for many years and will likely grow in popularity in years to come.

REPORT 28

Prepare a title page for Report 27. Use your keyboarding teacher's name, the keyboarding course in which you are enrolled, and the current date.

REPORT 29

Prepare a table of contents from the information in Report 27. Use the side headings and paragraph headings as your entries.

REPORT 30

Prepare a bibliography from the sources in Report 27. Number the bibliography as the final page in the report.

PORTFOLIO
Activity

Review the work you have done in the past ten lessons. Choose the best of each type of document. If you had any errors in any of these documents, correct the errors. Then print copies of these documents and place them in a folder as a representation of your best work. Also, print a copy of your best timing for your portfolio as an example of your speed and accuracy.

As you probably know, this event is one of our major fund-raising activities. This year our major project is Project Upgrade, which will provide training for displaced workers in our community. Thanks to the support of caring individuals such as you, Community Way will be able to provide valuable services to some of our less fortunate neighbors.

Again, thank you for your kind support.

REPORT 31

Prepare this left-bound report Correct errors in spelling, punctuation, and grammar.

FITNESS FOR WORK

The company expects all employees to be physically and mentally able to perform their jobs and otherwise meet the demands of their jobs and conditions of employment, except as required by applicable law. the company provides medical and dental benefits, which are fully described in the benefit information material, and counseling services, which are part of our employee assistance program.

This section explains the responsibility of the manager and the employee when an employee cannot report to work because of a medical condition.

~~Employee absences due to illness or injury~~

ILLNESSES AND INJURIES

The Employee's Responsibilities. An employee who is incapable of performing his/her job adequately because of a medical condition or whose presence at work might in effect other employees, should remain at home. In the case of a contagious disease, an employee should inform the manager of the extent to which he or she may have exposed co-workers.

The Manager's Responsibilities. When an employee is absent due to a medical condition for 6 or more consecutive working days, or due to a job-related injury for 1 or more days, the employee's manager must notify the human resources office by completing an absence notification form. When the employee returns to work, the manager must complete a return-to-work form and send it to the human resources office.

LESSON 80

SIMULATION

OBJECTIVES:

- Improve keyboarding speed and accuracy.
- Format and type a variety of office documents.

Type each line 2 times.

Speed
Accuracy
Language Link
Numbers/Symbols

1 Dale saw a small cabin at the end of the winding dirt road.
2 Four lawyers quickly rejected a luxury prize given to them.
3 Marge sent the project to the advertising department today.
4 Their tax was $35,489 (26% sales + 10% excise)--incredible!

*inter*NET C O N N E C T I O N

Use the Internet to search for information about wind chill factors (the topic of the Pretest). One site you may want to try is: http://www.nws.noaa.gov/er/iln/tables.htm. Learn about calculating wind chill. Search for information about the coldest temperatures and highest winds. Discuss your findings with the class.

SKILLBUILDING

B. PRETEST

Take a 1-minute timing on the paragraph. Note your speed and errors.

Science
Connections

5   The presence of wind makes it seem colder out than is   11
6 indicated by a thermometer. This can be pleasing when the   23
7 temperature is high. When temperatures are low, wind chill 34
8 becomes a threat to human beings and may cause death.   45
| 1 | 2 | 3 | 4 | 5 | 6 | 7 | 8 | 9 | 10 | 11 | 12

In the chart below, find the number of errors you made on the Pretest. Then, type each of the designated drill lines 2 times.

Pretest Errors	0–1	2	3	4+
Drill Lines	12–16	11–15	10–14	9–13

Accuracy

9 thermometer indicate presence pleasing threats humans cause
10 winter becomes highest chilling pleasure pleasant temperate
11 beings please making thermal windiest chilliest threatening
12 by colder become pleasing indicated thermometer temperature

Speed

13 a to of it is by be the out are can low than when high wind
14 a this cold make come chill cause death please threat human
15 be to on dear come when wind cloth treat threat death there
16 mom hen his ten man see low his hill that meter press three

D. POSTTEST

Repeat the Pretest. Compare your Posttest results with your Pretest results.

WORD PROCESSING APPLICATIONS

E. ORIENTATION

You will be working in the offices of the Community Way, City Center, Suite 100, 14 South Main, Akron, OH 44308. Community Way is a nonprofit, community-service organization. Today is June 6. Mrs. Alice Emerson is the director. Her assistant is Hugh Michaelson. You will help him get documents ready for Mrs. Emerson's approval. She depends on her assistant (and on you) to format the documents correctly and to catch any errors she may have missed. Mrs. Emerson prefers letters done in modified-block style with blocked paragraphs. She uses Sincerely yours, followed by her name and title on separate lines.

LETTER 39

Please send this letter today. Correct any errors.

Mr. Lester Romero / Romero Industries, Inc. / 272 Burdette Street / Akron, OH 44319 / Dear Mr. Romero:
We are indebted to you for allowing Community Way to use your facility as the site for this year's fund-raising dinner. Last Friday, 300 guests enjoyed fine dining, listening to music, and dancing. Your lovely ballroom provided the perfect setting for this exciting event.